HOLLYWOOD

MODERNISM

In the series

Culture and the Moving Image

edited by Robert Sklar

HOLLYWOOD MODERNISM

FILM AND POLITICS IN THE AGE OF THE NEW DEAL

Saverio Giovacchini

Temple University Press　PHILADELPHIA

Temple University Press, Philadelphia 19122
Copyright © 2001 by Temple University
All rights reserved
Published 2001
Printed in the United States of America

Library of Congress Cataloging-in-Publication Data
Giovacchini, Saverio, 1963–
Hollywood modernism : film and politics in the age of the New Deal / Saverio
    Giovacchini.
        p. cm. — (Culture and the moving image)
    Includes bibliographical references and index.
    ISBN 1-56639-862-2 (cloth : alk. paper) — ISBN 1-56639-863-0 (pbk. :
    alk. paper)
        1. Motion picture industry—California—Los Angeles—History. 2. Motion
pictures—Political aspects—United States. 3. Europeans—California—Los
Angeles.   I. Title.   II. Series.
PN1993.5.U65 G552 2001
791.43'658—dc21   00-053215

To Anne-Sophie

Contents

Acknowledgments

Many people contributed comments, ideas, and enthusiasm to the writing of this book. My largest debt is to Thomas Bender at New York University; he has spent many hours reading several drafts, challenging some aspects of my argument, and unfailingly encouraging me throughout the many years it took to transform a rather vague dissertation prospectus into a book.

Robert Sklar has supplied me with a model of film scholarship from the time I first read his *Movie-Made America* in its Italian translation. As a member of my dissertation committee and as the editor of this series, Bob has contributed immensely to sharpening and defining the argument of this book.

Insightful comments on different parts and incarnations of this work have been offered by Anne-Sophie Cerisola, Guido Fink, Sam B. Girgus, Anna Maria Martellone, Molly Nolan, Peter I. Rose, Kathleen Williams, and Marilyn Young. Two research grants from the Research Foundation of the City University of New York made it possible for me to visit a few more crucial archival collections and complete the revisions of the manuscript.

To all who assisted in the completion of this work goes my gratitude, and I wish I could share with them responsibility for any errors that remain. Those, however, are only mine.

Finally, a special debt of gratitude goes to my parents, Silvano Giovacchini and Lidia Allegrini; to my aunt, Graziella Giovacchini; to my brother and sister, Tommaso Giovacchini and Leah Reballos; and to my beautiful niece, Dalisay Giovacchini-Reballos.

This book is dedicated to Anne-Sophie Cerisola. Let me assure the reader that while she neither typed nor proofread it, she helped me in much more important ways. And I love her very much.

HOLLYWOOD
MODERNISM

Introduction
Taking Hollywood Seriously

The purpose of this study is to connect the historical development of Hollywood's cinematic style with the social and political history of the Hollywood community. Substantial elements
of Hollywood classical cinema are the result of a political and
esthetic negotiation engaging European anti-fascist refugees,
radical urban American intellectuals, and studio executives
from the early 1930s to the late 1940s. This negotiation was
an integral part of the intellectual and political debates of the
New Deal era, and it left a profound mark on some of the films
Hollywood made in this period.

An effort to contextualize Hollywood and its films plays a
crucial role in this work. In the 1930s and 1940s, Hollywood
was not a "Baghdad by the sea"[1] separated from the rest
of the United States. Nor were its films a simple reflection
of the commercial nature of the studio system. Rather, the
Hollywood community was animated by many of the same
debates that were the center of the political and intellectual
discourse in New York. Like their colleagues back East, in
fact, intellectuals in Hollywood were part of the leftist political
culture of the 1930s, and they discussed the democratization
of modernism, its politicization, and the formulation of a
mass-marketed progressive culture capable of dealing with the
political issues of the day.

This study identifies, chronicles, and interprets the social,
intellectual, and esthetic history of what I call Hollywood

1

democratic modernism. It examines its emergence, the transformations brought about by World War II, and its demise in the aftermath of the conflict. Hollywood democratic modernism often, though not always, took the form of social realism, and much of the present work deals with the articulation of social and political realism in the Hollywood cinema of the 1930s and 1940s. I want to give the term a broad connotation, both esthetic and political. In some sense, Hollywood films always had to communicate to their audiences a sense of "reality." The movies had to be transparent, to unravel smoothly from the beginning to the end, fostering identification with the characters on screen. Certainly, this aspect of the Hollywood norm remained central to the films produced by the studios in the 1930s. Hollywood's realism, however, deepened and expanded in the New Deal era, when the artists gathering in Southern California carried with them a concern for radical politics coupled with an interest in the reality of life in America, as well as the "documentary techniques" that could express it.[2] As the decade wore on, the "Hollywood New Yorkers"—that is, the urban American intellectuals who trekked to Southern California at the beginning of the 1930s—found ground for alliance with the "Hollywood Europeans," those European filmmakers who arrived in Hollywood from Nazi Germany and were keenly aware of the importance of films in the international struggle against Nazi fascism. The convergence in Hollywood of radical American artists, and of refugees from European fascist dictatorships, provided Southern California with a new generation of filmmakers, inclined to attune the Hollywood screen to the political reality of the day. Ultimately, Hollywood democratic modernism of the 1930s had an historical connotation as the result of a compromise between Hollywood Europeans, Hollywood New Yorkers, and studio executives within the national context of the New Deal. These forces congregated in Hollywood at the beginning of the 1930s and disbanded at the end of the 1940s, when the classicism of the Hollywood films underwent a profound redefinition and the era of "New Deal liberalism" came to an end.[3]

The fact that many Hollywood filmmakers came to embrace the slogan of realism should not, however, prevent us from appreciating the looseness of the term. Realism was a word often used with a variety of meanings. In 1939, Mordecai Gorelik, Pare Lorentz, Fritz Lang, and Ernst Lubitsch all advocated a realist cinema although, as we shall see, with different degrees of conviction and a vast array of meanings. They often disagreed on what reality and the techniques for its reproduction meant, and on the reasons for pursuing a popular audience. Loose as it was, however, cinematic realism was a concept appealing enough to gather a new generation of filmmakers, and a political slogan strong enough to give life to several organizations that radically changed the face of Hollywood politics. Yet the "middle ground" constituted by the slogan of realism was, at least in part, based on a misunderstanding. It also created an atmosphere that was fragile and contingent. Constant negotiations during the making of a film were commonplace, and, in time, the unstable compound that was the Hollywood community came apart.[4]

I am consciously situating my work within contemporary debates about 1930s art and esthetics. I contend that the dichotomy between modernism and realism, escapist and political art, the 1920s and 1930s, or avant-garde and Hollywood does not help us understand the type of culture that was forged in the 1930s, and of which the Hollywood community was an important segment.[5] Oftentimes, in fact, realism has been employed to establish a discontinuity between the intellectual practices of the 1920s that are characterized as modernist, escapist, and nonrealist, and those of the 1930s that are usually associated with the political and social realism of the Cultural Front.

To a large extent, this critical paradigm rests on a narrow definition of 1920s art and, more generally, of modernism. Chip Rhodes has recently questioned the supposed escapism of the 1920s, highlighting instead how "twenties literature draws its strength and vitality not from its flight from history, but from its complex, multi-leveled engagement with history."[6] In the late 1970s, Peter Gay also highlighted the inadequacy of contemporary definitions of modernism based on "a confluence of anti-rationalism, experimentalism, and alienation."[7] "The historian of Modernist culture," Gay suggested, "may best begin his revision of current, clearly inadequate interpretations by enlarging the territory of modernism."[8] Modernism was not only the adversarial, antirealist tradition that, sponsored by Lionel Trilling and Clement Greenberg among others, became dominant during the Cold War. As Thomas Bender suggests in his *New York Intellect* in reference to Randolph Bourne, "There are other equally legitimate versions of modernism that are moderate, positive, and affirming, even reformist."[9]

It is worth stressing, in fact, that at least in the United States, the dominant interpretation of the term "modernism" is almost entirely the result of the critical intervention of the so-called "New York Intellectuals" in the decades following World War II. Astradur Eysteinsson touches upon a crucial issue when he remarks that the real question is "what modernism has been made to signify, and how."[10] It becomes, therefore, quite relevant to note that many of today's critics continue to read modernism through the spectacles provided by Trilling, Greenberg, and the New Criticism.[11] But the seminal essays by Trilling and Greenberg were also—implicitly or not—an eminently *political* definition of modernism, aimed at constructing a "club" from which the dominant segment of the American Left of the 1930s was excluded.

The dominance of this particular interpretation of modernism is not surprising. Putting some distance between oneself and the leftist culture of the 1930s was a plausible choice for American intellectuals of the late 1940s and the 1950s. While it is not my task to explore the relative role of conviction and opportunism in motivating one's choice, it is undeniable that previous, and alternative, definitions of the relationship between the 1920s and the 1930s, as well as of the modernism/mass-culture dyad, existed and were less dramatic than those dominant from the Cold War onward—increasingly sculpted by an "anxiety of contamination" between high and low, mass culture and intellectual activities.[12]

In 1934, Malcolm Cowley presented in *The Exile's Return* a very smooth, continuous transition from the culture of the 1920s to the literary scene of the 1930s. The central chapter of the memoir, "Readings from the Lives of the Saints," dedicated to T. S. Eliot, James Joyce, Marcel Proust, and Paul Valéry, highlights how American intellectuals had long been at odds with these "saints" of the high modernist tradition. American modernists, it is important to note, were fully aware of the genius of these "icons" yet found their work incomplete. Cowley's portraits of Marcel Proust, writing alone in a room padded with cork to shut out the sounds of the street, and of James Joyce, unwilling to venture outside for fear of physical and bacteriological contamination, stand as symbols of a modernism that, like T. S. Eliot's *Waste Land,* has consciously "robbed [the present] of vitality."[13] On the contrary, Cowley and his generation are "excited by the adventure of living the present," even though they continue to acknowledge the "saints" as part of their esthetic and intellectual baggage.[14]

Michael Denning makes an eloquent case for the continuity between the culture of the 1920s and that of the "red decade" in his recent *The Cultural Front,* arguing that the "thirties" do not "fall outside those larger stories of modernism and postmodernism." On the contrary, the culture of the decade and in particular of its second half—which Denning names the "Age of the CIO"—was characterized by "a new social modernism" that "was built by the children of the modernist arts, struggling to assimilate and transcend its legacy of formalist experiment."[15] Likewise, James Bloom, in his intellectual biography of *New Masses* editor Mike Gold, has persuasively argued that Gold was not the "intellectual hack" that later critics accused him of being.[16] On the contrary, in his efforts to hybridize the "Prospero" of modernism with the "Caliban" of intelligibility and political engagement, Gold showed a "subversive mastery of the culture he challenged" and ultimately, Bloom concludes, attempted to reconcile "left politics and modernist poetics."[17]

A revised, more inclusive, version of modernism has important consequences for the history of the presence of radical intellectuals in Hollywood.[18] Gold was in close contact with many of the protagonists of my story, and he often referred to cinema as a way to clarify his own project. By 1930, he had already characterized the new literature he advocated as a "cinema in words,"[19] and in 1937 he saluted the "proletarian pioneers" who had traveled to Hollywood to make politically inspiring films.[20]

Ultimately, these contributions all point to the necessity of recasting the history of the Hollywood community and its cinema from the 1930s to the end of World War II within the cultural context of an increasingly politicized modernism. A modernism, I would add, that was concerned with the necessity to open up its message to the masses insofar as it was increasingly aware that the work of the previous generation of modernists had been hampered by the narrowness, elitism, and overall fragmentation of its audience.[21] Like Cowley, Gold, or German film theorist Siegfried Kracauer, Hollywood modernists recognized that much of the 1920s modernist culture had been unable to oppose—and even comment upon—the disastrous rise of fascist political movements.

The American and European intellectuals who "went Hollywood" in the 1930s were reacting to these experiences and to this partial failure. They attempted to mold a modernism that was both accessible to mass audiences and open to "political intention."[22] In this context, "going Hollywood" and lobbying for a more realistic cinema hardly meant abandoning the modernist project. Hollywood's cinema promised the construction of a democratic modernism, a common language, able to promote modernity while maintaining a commitment to democracy as well as the political and intellectual engagement of the masses.

In looking at the interaction between artists and producers, democratic modernism and Hollywood filmmaking style, I have deployed, somewhat loosely, what Theodor Adorno termed "forcefield." Members of the Frankfurt School, and in particular Adorno and Walter Benjamin, used the concept of the forcefield, or *Kraftfeld*, to describe a relationship between different cultural and social phenomena in a way that allows for interaction without ever arriving at any "extorted reconciliation." As applied to the history of Hollywood, the notion of forcefield allows us to grant a degree of agency to the artists working within the Hollywood studios without losing sight of the fundamental limits of this cultural negotiation.[23]

Too often we forget that living, working, and struggling inside and outside of the Hollywood studios was a thriving Hollywood community whose political development and intellectual debates had an effect on the ultimate product of the studios. According to many, Hollywood is and always has been a "commercial institution, engaged in manufacturing and selling a specific product in a capitalist market place."[24] For the agency and the politics of the actual filmmakers, there is hardly any room. To be sure, Hollywood filmmakers' agency was constrained. The dialogue between intellectuals and Hollywood cinema had to build on an esthetic norm—the Hollywood classical style—that had taken a definite, but not immutable, shape in the course of Hollywood history.[25] Nor was this a dialogue among equals, since power relations, though complex and ever shifting, dominated the terms of the negotiation. But the evidence increasingly emerging from the archives of the studios suggests that Hollywood filmmakers did not passively execute the will of the masters of the studios, with no control or personal interest in their work. Indeed, in the 1930s the tradition of Hollywood narrative was both fortified and redefined within a forcefield that incorporated a number of social and intellectual networks operating in the Hollywood community.

The concept of network is particularly useful for my project as well because it provides a way of analyzing how different groups in Hollywood participated in the production of films. These cultural workers were operating not only on an individual basis, but also as representatives of specific networks with a national—and at times even transnational—base.[26] In this perspective, it is useful to keep in mind that Fritz Lang was not just a Hollywood director; he was also a member of the refugee network. His actions were scrutinized not only in the Hollywood studios, but also in the pages of refugee magazines like *Aufbau*. As a refugee, Lang had to help fellow refugees while striving to make anti-Nazi films.

Likewise, John Howard Lawson was not merely a Hollywood New Yorker but also a member of the Communist Party apparatus, whose line he generally followed in the Hollywood studios.

Conceiving of Hollywood as "a city of networks" that extended beyond the horizon of Hollywood and Vine might suggest a new, less bounded way to address the cultural history of the community. Furthermore, each Hollywood participant was touched by more than one of these networks, and they were, therefore, responsive to the demands of various networks at the same time. From 1936 on, for instance, Fritz Lang and other anti-Nazi refugees identified with both the refugee network and that of the American Left.

As the Hollywood community matured, members attempted to reconcile their loyalty to translocal networks, with allegiances to the local, political culture that had given a new vitality to Hollywood and Los Angeles. Crises erupted whenever local and translocal loyalties were in conflict. This occurred, for instance, during the period of the Nazi-Soviet Pact when the Communist Party line conflicted with the anti-fascist culture of the Hollywood community. For someone like John Howard Lawson, loyalty to the party line was the main priority. But for other Hollywood communists and fellow travelers, the choice was not easy, straining the relationship between them and Lawson, and, more generally, between the Hollywood communists and the party's New York-based central committee.[27]

The main assumption behind this work is that we ought to take Hollywood seriously, something seldom done by American or European historians. Even acute scholars, openly intrigued by the historical relevance of American popular culture, often deal with Hollywood's history with a telling nonchalance rather than probing analysis.[28]

Historians often seem to take movies and their creators for granted. While there are many examples from which to choose, the following illustrate the point. In *Cheap Amusements*, Kathy Peiss's brilliant analysis of how immigrant working-class women interacted with commercialized leisure in turn-of-the-century New York City, the author candidly confesses that she has contented herself with the synopses of the films she discusses, even though these films are available to scholars in the Library of Congress and part of her argument relies substantially on the analysis of these films.[29] Larry Ceplair and Steven Englund openly claimed to have been "neither systematic nor subtle in our approach to the question of political content or the nature of politicization of movies" because of their disinterest in any "esthetic sophistication in the area of form and style."[30] In her path-breaking analysis of the effect of mass culture on Chicago's ethnically diverse working class, Lizabeth Cohen evokes the subjectivity of the receivers, depicting the way in which Chicago workers participated in mass culture forms while maintaining their ethnic and class-conscious identities. Cohen's work is a powerful historical revision of Critical Theory's assumptions about mass culture and its effects on ordinary Americans, yet she takes into account only one side of the question, never probing the subjectivity of the producers of mass-marketed cultural products.[31] In other words, one wonders how far the Chicago working class had to go in order to lend an oppositional meaning to the words uttered by Henry Fonda in his famous speech in John Ford's *Grapes of Wrath*, simultaneously endorsing the killing of a strike-breaker and hoping to be "wherever there is a fight so hungry people can eat . . . wherever there is a cop beating up a guy."

At the *akmè* of the Hollywood community in the late 1930s, Hollywood and its films were on their way to becoming a legitimate pursuit for American historians and intellectuals. Writing in 1939, Lewis Jacobs, a New Deal liberal and a filmmaker, meant his work to be a "scientific" analysis of the development of the American film industry. Jacobs saw movies as the art of the people *in potentia* and, as its Beardian title makes obvious, *The Rise of the American Film* was meant to situate American cinema within American civilization, or, as Martin Dworkin noted in his preface to the 1967 reprint of the volume, to show that Hollywood cinema "grow[s] out of immersion in its own time and place."[32]

But few followed Jacobs's mode. At the same time that New Critics made their rather narrow definition of modernism into the dominant one, popularizers of Critical Theory, such as David Riesman and Dwight Macdonald, more attuned with the reading of the *Dialektik* than with Walter Benjamin's more open-ended insights, saw movies as part of mass society's attack on the individual character of art, something to be treated at best with sympathetic condescension as "low brow," or with open contempt as "midcult."[33] In *Movie-Made America*, Robert Sklar balanced this approach, persuasively arguing that film is neither the people's art nor the simple epiphany of the will of the master, but instead one of the terrains where cultural negotiation takes place, and class and ethnic struggles are fought. "What is remarkable," Sklar argues in his conclusion, "is the way that American movies, through much of their span, have altered or challenged many of the values and doctrines of powerful social and cultural forces in American society, providing alternative ways of understanding the world."[34] Yet, few film scholars and cultural historians have taken up the most intriguing ideas put forward in Sklar's synthesis, in particular the possibility of linking Hollywood esthetics to American cultural history. In this regard, historians seem to have accepted one of the aspects of the popular version of Critical Theory that reduces actual films to a sort of undifferentiated "megatext," where each film is the same as the other.[35]

On the other hand, film scholars saw with increasing suspicion any attempt to establish a sense of causality between films and their social and cultural context, ultimately performing what Richard Maltby has aptly termed a "slide into the text."[36] As a result, the possibility—to use Dana Polan's words—of understanding cinematic narratives of a particular period as "a way open to a social moment to write a version of its own history and of its present"[37] has been rarely tested, though traces of a potentially productive contamination are visible in works by Lary May, Miriam Hansen, Tom Gunning, and Dana Polan.[38]

My study gives a chronological account of the history of the Hollywood community and its filmmaking style, underlining the continuities between the different periods without downplaying historical change. The first chapter describes the arrival in Hollywood of the anti-fascist European filmmakers and the radical intellectuals from New York. These two groups, "Hollywood Europeans" and "Hollywood New Yorkers," saw in the Hollywood of the early 1930s the possibility of molding a popular, audience-oriented, and more democratic version of modernism. The rebirth of the Hollywood community after the introduction of sound at the end of the 1920s coincides with a transnational migration that brought hundreds of intellectuals to the West Coast from the salons of New York and Europe. This migration was partly determined by technological changes, by economic choices, and by political events occurring far from the crossroads of Hollywood and Vine. But I argue that "going Hollywood" was also a chapter of the international history of modernism, one that meant to democratize and politicize it.

The starting point of the second chapter is Robert Sklar's definition of Hollywood in the early 1930s as the "golden age of turbulence." American cinema was marked by the diversity and contradictory nature of Hollywood's products.[39] An archipelago of "little islands"—to use the definition of refugee director Max Ophüls[40]—Hollywood had a fragmented social and intellectual life that largely remained within the confines of private salons, and Hollywood filmmaking echoed that centerlessness during those years.

The third chapter deals with Hollywood in the second half of the 1930s, when the number of refugees and anti-Nazi immigrants in Hollywood increased as a result of the European crisis. This chapter examines the strengthening of the alliance between Hollywood New Yorkers and Hollywood Europeans. Hollywood's social and intellectual life found a center in organizations such as the Hollywood Anti-Nazi League (HANL) and the Hollywood Democratic Committee. Politically, the focus of such an alliance was on anti-fascist mobilization and support for the administration of Franklin Delano Roosevelt. Esthetically, New Yorkers and Europeans agreed on a loose notion of political realism, a cinema able to tackle contemporary issues in terms accessible to the masses. This chapter examines the linkage between these debates and several trends in American cinema. In particular, I examine William Dieterle's Warner Bros. biopics (*Pasteur*, *The Life of Émile Zola*, *Juarez*) as films that celebrate the progressive Hollywood community of modern intellectuals able to use the mass media to engage the audience in the democratic struggle for change. I also examine the production of *Confessions of a Nazi Spy* (WB, 1939), the first major anti-Nazi Hollywood production. The production of *Confessions* fully involved Hollywood Europeans and Hollywood New Yorkers and served as the model for Hollywood progressive filmmaking throughout the war.

Centering on the crisis of 1939–1941, the fourth chapter shows how the Nazi-Soviet pact and the question of intervention divided the Hollywood community. The beginning of World War II and the turn of Soviet politics caused the demise of HANL, the "politicization" of ethnic identities (in particular the rise of exclusively refugee organizations such as the European Film Fund), and the "ethnicization" of political ones (e.g., Hollywood communists as a group defined by a precise notion of cultural and political difference) at the expense of the political and cultural cohesiveness of the Hollywood community. As a result of this crisis, alternative forms of democratic modernism emerged; while they retained emphasis on the politicization and democratization of modernism, they contested realism as its only possible incarnation.

The fifth chapter deals with the tight wartime collaboration between Hollywood New Yorkers and Hollywood Europeans in the context of the war effort. Hollywood's emergence as the center of the Los Angeles intelligentsia reached its apogee in the 1943 Writers' Congress at UCLA, where Hollywood writers, refugees, studio executives, and university professors congregated to discuss the democratic possibilities of American cinema. The enlistment of Hollywood cinema in the war effort enhanced its civic role as both entertainment and a means of political communication. In its relationship with the Hollywood studios, the Office of War Information—staffed with many members of the progressive Hollywood community—endorsed a film style that included many of the techniques discussed in the Hollywood salons and political organizations in the 1930s: the softening of the protagonist-driven narrative, the crossbreeding of entertainment and propaganda, and the insertion of newsreel footage into feature films.

The final two chapters examine the aftermath of World War II, the erosion of the Hollywood community as a cultural center, and the effect of this crisis on Hollywood progressive filmmaking. As these chapters will show, the causes of Hollywood's collapse were internal as well as external, esthetic as well as political. The crisis within the Hollywood community largely predates McCarthyism, and this may help explain why the investigations of the House Un-American Activities Committee (HUAC) were so successful and far-reaching in the film industry. Even before McCarthyism, organizations such as the Hollywood Writers' Mobilization had ceased to supply a cohesion to Hollywood intellectual and political life. United in support of Roosevelt's administration and against the common enemy of fascism during the war, New Yorkers and Europeans were increasingly divided about the issues ahead, such as the American domestic situation and the future of Germany. A revisionist attitude toward the war and its aims was visible in many of the films of the period, from *Crossfire* (1946) to *A Foreign Affair* (1948), and in magazines such as *The Screen Writer* and *Hollywood Quarterly*. Such revisionism informed the debates about the democratic possibilities of Hollywood film. Negotiated within the Hollywood forcefield by producers, Hollywood progressives, and government officials, the Hollywood war film had fallen short of the expectations harbored by some of the New Yorkers and Europeans. In fact, the re-emigration of Hollywood filmmakers to Europe and New York began immediately after the war, and an anti-realist and anti-Hollywood film avant-garde emerged in New York soon after the war. Both factors weakened the centripetal power of Hollywood and its political realism. Ultimately, the crisis also affected the language of film. The linkage between American cinema and the issues debated in the public arena became increasingly indirect, Aesopian, and metaphorical. Political realism in film survived at the margins, in works such as *Salt of the Earth* (Independent Productions Corporation, 1953), and even in the anticommunist films of the Cold War that—perversely enough—attempted to build on such tradition.

1

Modernism, Intellectual Immigrants, and the Rebirth of Hollywood

I don't know . . . how many writers would write if they knew that their work would never be read. . . . The same people who do not look down at the businessman for making money sneer at writers who work for money. They "have gone Hollywood," and they somehow have betrayed a sacred trust. . . . For me, until the black list came, Hollywood was a blessing.

Albert Maltz, *The Citizen Writer in Retrospect*, 1983

The first birth of Hollywood was due to the joint efforts of what would look today like unlikely partners: Christian settlers trying to escape the increasing commercialism of downtown Los Angeles and commercial entertainers seeking cheaper land for their enterprises. The Christian settlers came first—led by Daeida and Horace Wilcox who purchased the area in the 1880s—and transformed it into a "churchly utopia."[1] But films soon followed, with the Selig company producing movies in Los Angeles as early as 1907.

In the beginning, the relationship between the two groups was strained. In *Promised Land*, Cedric Belfrage, a British expatriate and later founder of *The National Guardian*, recorded the early conflicts between the movie industry and the Christian

13

Hollywood community, who considered Hollywood the moral capital of Southern California.[2] It soon became clear that the movie industry was there to stay. By 1926, some Hollywood boosters advertised the Los Angeles-based film industry as the fifth largest in the country. Though these claims were exaggerated, the prosperity was real and the value of Hollywood real estate was booming.[3] In 1920, Los Angeles had a population of 576,000. By 1930, the population had more than doubled to 1,230,000. But while the film industry brought in money and increased the value of land in Hollywood, the film community was not transforming the churchly utopia into the " 'Greenwich Village' artists' colony" that some had envisioned. Caught between the Christian settlers' anxiety about morality and show business's desire for profits, the prospects of Hollywood as a cultural center seemed limited. At the end of the 1920s, Hollywood could boast several high schools but not one park, several impressive movie studios but not a single theater.[4] Cedric Belfrage described Hollywood of the late 1920s as a cultural and social desert. The few society salons in Los Angeles at the time did not stand comparison even with those of nearby Pasadena. They were dominated by self-appointed *magistrae elegantiarum* such as the notorious Madame Glynn, and by "cast-off European royalty/nobility" who made a living out of telling sad stories of their endless flights and failing fortunes.[5]

By the beginning of the 1930s, however, the cultural life of the colony underwent a profound change. In June 1934, the *Los Angeles Times* reported on "the growing intellectual life of Los Angeles" that was "adding to the richness of California life."[6] For the first time since its founding, Los Angeles had a lively intellectual milieu, based in cafés, salons, and cultural organizations. Carey McWilliams, an attentive and passionate observer of California mores since his arrival there in 1922 from his native Colorado, noted in the Pasadena *Panorama* that the most striking feature of these salons, and in particular those based in Hollywood, was their increasing seriousness. Gone were the times, McWilliams said, when Hollywood parlors where dominated by bogus "poets from Chelsea, and Yogis from Bombay."[7] Hollywood was becoming worldly.

In his 1938 memoirs, British writer Cedric Belfrage remarked on the transformation in a fictional exchange of letters between two characters. In one of these letters, Don Lurie, the Hollywood correspondent of *Tickner's Magazine*, claims that because of its increasing commitment to social and economic justice "the new Hollywood . . . is getting to be a place a guy can almost be proud to live in."[8] In his second memoir of

Hollywood, written in the mid-1970s, Belfrage reiterated the point. In the 1930s, he wrote that "the movies had come of age as an industry, and there was an awareness in Hollywood. It was no longer the village remote from the world that it was in the 20s."[9] The main reason for this change was one of the most important intellectual migrations of the twentieth century: New Yorkers and Europeans had "gone Hollywood" en masse, and by 1932 *Fortune* magazine noted that the ranks of Metro Goldwyn Mayer (MGM) comprised "more members of the literati than it took to produce the King James Bible."[10]

There is a standard interpretation for this early 1930s migration to Hollywood of American and European intellectuals, attributing the "sea change" that brought these intellectuals to Hollywood to economics: the new inhabitants of Hollywood, so the argument goes, went West because of the generous salaries the industry offered. This explanation— based on a problematic opposition between modernism and mass culture, high culture and popular culture—contains the typical condescending attitude toward Hollywood and its films shared by even astute analysts of the American film industry.[11] Hollywood, the argument runs, was a commercial enterprise producing commercial goods for a capitalist market. Those films that stand out are the exceptions, the offspring of individual geniuses working in the "sausage factory." As a consequence of Hollywood's hopeless commercialism, the factors motivating this intellectual migration to Hollywood must be commercial, the conditions for a generational and transnational intellectual sellout. When it comes to Hollywood films, market value becomes ontology and—as films are collapsed into commodity—the same logic grinds their creators, *homines oeconomici*, living and dying in Los Angeles for Hollywood big bucks.

Scholars of different political and intellectual backgrounds have, in fact, embraced what I would call "the Ben Hecht interpretation" of Hollywood history. According to the lore, former New York drama critic Herman Mankiewicz sent a telegram to Hecht inviting him to Hollywood to share in the "Fresh Air Fund for New York Newspapermen" for a salary of $300 a week.[12] Giving up his real career as a theater man and a literary wit, Hecht went to Southern California, collected the fat salaries, and wrote or co-wrote a series of Hollywood masterpieces, which he held in contempt the rest of his life.[13]

Endorsed by many as the standard explanation for the intellectual migration to Hollywood during the 1930s, the "Hecht interpretation" ignores the relative obscurity, and rather unimpressive literary quality, of much of Hecht's work prior to his move to Hollywood. More importantly, the "Hecht interpretation" of Hollywood history is flawed in two ways: it dehistoricizes the migration of intellectual networks to Hollywood while revealing our contemporary unease in seeing art and mass culture as compatible.

"Going Hollywood" in the 1930s had as much to do with the intellectual biographies of young modernist writers and filmmakers as with the state of their bank accounts. For some of the modernists who originated the "Hecht interpretation," as well as for many of the post–World War II intellectuals who propagated it, American cinema was modernism's other insofar as Hollywood seemed to have uncritically embraced modernity and its techniques and fostered the spectator's emotional engagement rather than critical distance.[14] As applied to the entire generation of the new Hollywood community, however, this position is profoundly ahistorical in that it applies a predominantly post–World War II and Cold War mentality to a radically different period. It also ignores the fact that many did not consider "going Hollywood" as a radical breach with their modernist upbringing; rather, they viewed art and mass culture at least as compatible, if not entirely coterminous, spheres.

The intellectual migration that brought hundreds of American and European intellectuals to the West Coast from the salons of New York and Europe was also determined by economic choices—as was the case in much that occurred during the twentieth century—and certainly by political events occurring far from Hollywood. Yet coming to Hollywood was also a chapter in the history of modernism insofar as this intellectual migration was an attempt to democratize and to politicize modernism while broadening the size of its audience.

Hollywood New Yorkers

Until sound became fully a part of Hollywood cinema, the relationship between Hollywood and the New York art scene had been rather loose. Kenneth Macgowan was the associate editor of *Theatre Arts Monthly* and a contributor to the *New Yorker* and the New York *Tribune*. As an off-Broadway theater producer, he was the artistic director of the Greenwich Playhouse and had to his credit the production of groundbreaking Eugene O'Neil plays such as *The Emperor Jones* and *Desire under the Elms*. In 1928, convinced by his friend, director Irving Pichel, who was already working and teaching in Hollywood, Macgowan inquired about the possibility of working as a writer-producer there. But in the summer of 1928, the studios—engrossed in the problems of sound and still not sure of the future of the talkies—were simply not interested in New York theater talent, even someone as successful as Macgowan. Employment for Macgowan was, in the words of one Paramount executive, "absolutely out of the question unless you are a mechanic who knows how to make pictures talk."[15]

Once the technicalities of wiring theaters for sound and the problems of competing patent claims were solved, however, things changed. Macgowan himself abandoned his New York theater career to accept a job as a writer-producer at Fox in 1931. By that time, in fact, all Hollywood studios had begun an intense campaign of recruiting talent. Writing to his friend Preston Sturges in the summer of 1933, Charles Abrahmson noted, "It looks like a very late season for old Broadway. There is much talk but little action and the cry is material and people. The consensus of opinion is that it is almost impossible to cast a play as everyone who had or showed any merit at all is in Hollywood."[16]

The necessity of supplying words and dialogue for moving pictures required the presence of people who were in the business of creating those words. "When talking pictures came in, the producers turned to the stage in all its branches for talent that could talk," wrote *Variety* in 1930.[17] "The cinema had gone literary," echoed *The New York Times* in 1932, reporting on the producers' efforts to recruit New York writers "to compose lyrical sentences and coherent plots." The article concluded: "As long as [the pictures] are to speak, they might as well do it decently and in order."[18] For a short period of time, the deluge of filmed plays was such that The *New York Times* warned of "the sound pictures . . . swinging too far in the direction of aping the legitimate stage."[19]

Chicago newspaperman turned New York playwright Ben Hecht, his friend Herman Mankiewicz, Julius and Philip Epstein from the *Brooklyn Eagle*, and many others all came to Hollywood around the opening of the fourth decade of the century. From the "Yiddish Broadway" of Second Avenue came New York Jewish playwright Hy Kraft. From the New York literary circles came, among many others, novelists F. Scott Fitzgerald and Samuel Ornitz, author of the successful *Haunch, Paunch, and Jowl* (1923). Throughout the first half of the thirties, New York legitimate stage kept supplying Hollywood with a steady flux of writers able to produce credible dialogue for the talkies: Robert Benchley, John Huston, John

Wexley, Marc Connelly, Dorothy Parker, her husband Alan Campbell, and Donald Ogden Stewart. From the New Playwright and the Group Theater came Francis Faragoh, John Howard Lawson, Allen Boretz, and Clifford Odets.

It was not just the search for financial security that explained the decision of many of these people to move. Politically, the new Hollywood community consisted mostly of those who were active participants in that radicalization of the American Left which historian Richard Pells has described.[20] Overall, they did not take lightly their political commitments, and—as the McCarthy witch hunt would prove—many of them were ready to sacrifice their financial security in order to uphold their political beliefs. The intellectual migration that brought so many of the American urban intellectuals to the relatively undeveloped "Hollywood wilderness" had political and intellectual roots that complicate and enrich the standard Hecht interpretation. Referring to the American radicals who went Hollywood in the 1930s, Abraham Polonsky argues that "you can't possibly explain the Hollywood communists away by saying 'they came to Hollywood for the money.' . . . If they had come only for the money and glamour, a lot of them would have become stool pigeons—to hold their jobs, to continue making money and doing pictures. But only a small percentage of them [did so]."[21] No, money does not explain away this migration. Many Hollywood New Yorkers had reason to believe that, though intellectually risky and financially expedient, their Hollywood choice *might* have been compatible with their intellectual and political commitments.

Not all of the New Yorkers transplanted in Hollywood immediately saw the possibilities inherent in their new homeland. Upon seeing Hollywood Boulevard in 1933, New York writer Julius Epstein thought that it was the "sleaziest street" he had ever seen.[22] Many of the newcomers, however, soon developed a different, more complicated attitude toward Hollywood. "I don't think it is realized," Howard Koch reminisced in the late 1970s, "that perhaps what Greenwich Village was in the late teens . . . that same vitality was transferred in this period, the New Deal period, to Hollywood."[23] Budd Schulberg, when the memory of the McCarthy years and of his own decision to name names had much embittered his own memory of Hollywood, still remembered the 1930s as a special period for Hollywood intellectual life. "It was," he wrote, "almost as if the Algonquin Round Table had been moved cross country into the Garden and under the Palm trees."[24]

It was not that the Hollywood New Yorkers idealized either Hollywood or their film work. Their writings often betray a sense of frustration and an awareness of the compromises that they were bound to strike in order to see their work produced. Professional background was also important. Compared with actors and directors, writers were more likely to compare Hollywood unfavorably with the legitimate theater. Many of these filmmakers, however, maintained that Hollywood also offered room for negotiation. Howard Koch, for example, remembers that

> the people who made pictures that are remembered . . . didn't take that attitude, that the system was a factory turning out one picture after another. It was under the supervision of the well-known tycoons . . . and they weren't always the most intelligent of men, yet they gave quite a lot of leeway to talent. And I think if you fought hard enough to get what you wanted on the screen, . . . the conditions were quite favorable to doing pictures that had both entertainment and, let's say, social value.[25]

The American intellectuals' look toward Southern California should be viewed within the context of American intellectual history. As historian Richard T. Pells has argued, the beginning of the 1930s saw American intellectuals rediscovering their American roots after years of self-inflicted exile. "The search for personal freedom and an abstract international culture," writes Pells, "was giving way to a spirit of commitment and a willingness to write about 'America.' "[26] But for young radical artists and intellectuals of the 1930s, writing about America was only one option; filming it and offering it in an accessible package to the masses as the most popular folktale was almost as appealing. The dialogue with the American scene, in fact, often meant a new focus on mass media and especially mass-marketed films. Many of those who came to Hollywood in the 1930s and adapted did not share the contempt for mass-marketed cultural products that characterized later generations of intellectuals. While not a dream, Hollywood was still far from being a nightmare.

Intellectuals in Search of an Audience

Quite a few disgruntled New Yorkers ultimately abandoned Hollywood to return to New York, or treated Hollywood as a temporary occupation between jobs in Manhattan. Among the many things that annoyed them was Hollywood's quest for socially and culturally integrated audiences. In this vein, S. J. Perelman famously complained about Groucho Marx's request that he write for the "barber in Peru"—meaning Peru, Indiana—

and lamented that the great comedian was compelling him to write for a "cretinous specimen."[27] Likewise, Dudley Murphy, a New York director who had gone Hollywood in the early 1930s, lamented that "segregated audiences" exist in every field but cinema.[28] Hollywood has "all the advantages," wrote playwright Samson Raphelson in 1935, because "all the good actors are in Hollywood. All the good directors are in Hollywood. You get sinus trouble in New York." Yet according to Raphelson, New York was still preferable. Broadway still offered the writer the possibility of dialogue with a "limited audience" that might better appreciate one's ideas. "I am all for a limited audience," he concluded, "if you can afford it."[29]

Other New Yorkers, however, saw Hollywood as a place where the fragmentation that increasingly characterized American culture could be overcome. For them, Hollywood was the place where a national audience could be reconstituted across cultural boundaries that artificially divided audiences and styles into separate cultural spheres.[30] Those New Yorkers who were more likely to go Hollywood and adapt were mostly those who had previously begun a search for larger audiences and a hybridization between high and low, art and popular culture.

Critics often stress the experimentalism of the early plays of John Howard Lawson.[31] Lawson's 1923 play *Roger Bloomer* tells the story of a naive boy from Iowa who goes to New York to find himself. In the final scene, Roger Bloomer, after his lover's suicide, has a nightmare in which all "the conventions and proprieties surround ROGER threateningly in grotesque black." The boy is saved by the ghost of Louise, his dead lover, and he finally wakes up to maturity as a man and as an artist.[32] *Bloomer* is characterized by many of the standard nuances of expressionist theater (the dream sequence, the antinaturalism of symbolic characters such as "the Examiner" and "the Judge") together with the typical modernist contrast between the pastoral (Iowa) and the urban (New York City).[33] The play also shows a constant preoccupation with intelligibility. As John Dos Passos argued in his preface to the 1923 edition, *Bloomer* employs modernistic techniques to reflect "the unprecedented fever and inhumanness and mechanical complexity of American life," and it is concerned with the need to speak to a large American audience rather than to a literary elite. Dos Passos goes on to state that the play expresses "the commonest American theme—a boy running away from home to go to the big city," and that it will prove its mettle against a "New York Theater today [that] has no more to do with the daily existence of the average New Yorker, with his hunger and terrors, than it has with the pigtail of the living God at Lhasa." The acid test of the play's success will be its ability to reconstruct both an esthetic tradition and an audience, says Dos Passos. "Like everything else about American theater, a criterion of judgment exists if at all, only in vague conditional prophecy. Before we can have standards of comparison, we've got to have plays, an audience, a tradition." [34]

Beyond *Roger Bloomer*, Lawson's career in the 1920s was marked by his quest for an audience that would fully represent America's social complexity. While writing workers' theater for the New Playwrights, Lawson had passionately endorsed a theater that could be both esthetically progressive *and* emotionally appealing. Lawson was later to become the main party doctrinaire within the Hollywood community, a role that gained him the guarded antipathy of many of his fellow Hollywood leftists as well as a place on the blacklist. [35] But in 1927 the future leader of the Hollywood CP argued that

> we regard partisanship and dullness as capital dangers. We trust our spiritual limitations are not those of a soapbox. I can imagine being tremendously excited about a Fascist play, or a Catholic play, or an anti-Red play—if it contained the precious spark of exciting theater. Your professional agitator will unquestionably disagree with my statement, but it's not the business of a theater to be controlled by any class or theory. [36]

By singling out "dullness" as the capital crime for a theatrical piece, Lawson was hinting at the necessity for the artist to engage the audience's emotion. Furthermore, the artist's capacity to speak to a large audience was already tied for Lawson to what I call a poetics of hybridization—that is, an attempt to fuse different genres, media, and styles in order to capture an inter-class spectatorship. "The purpose of the stage is not to argue or convince," Lawson wrote in the 1927 article, "but to report, to see passionately and fully." Be it fascist, communist, or bourgeois, successful theater is based on the playwright's ability to fuse different codes, senses, and styles in order to communicate emotions. Lawson tellingly mixes the visual and the verbal ("to see" and "to report"), the realm of the physical with that of feelings ("to see passionately"). Good theater reconciles extremes and does not argue, but it communicates passionately.

Theater was not an experiment to be done only for art's sake. The quest for a larger American audience was reflected in a style apt to represent such a varied and polycentric constituency. The mixed, complex nature of America justified the necessity for a mixed, hybridized style. "I have endeavored," Lawson wrote in the preface to his 1925 *Processional*, "to create a method which shall express the American scene in native idiom, a method as far removed from the older realism as from the facile mood of expressionism." Far from any "anxiety of contamination," the young playwright wanted his play to be a veritable hybrid between what he called "vaudeville," avant-garde expressionism, and the "legitimate theater," which he deemed "in a feeble trance, totally removed from the rush and roar of things as they are, a sanctuary with doors barred against the world."[37]

Just as the envisioned audience had to bridge the people and the elite, the demarcation between media and genres also needed to be shattered to fully represent the complexity of the American scene. In the 1920s and early 1930s, this eagerness and keen interest for hybridization were often expressed in recurrent references to film and music. In 1930, Mike Gold judged the Marxist International Publishers too "stodgy," unable to "influence either the popular mind or the intellectual." The new "proletarian literature" was to explode the boundaries between arts and construct a "cinema in words."[38] At the end of Lawson's *Roger Bloomer*, Louise sacrifices herself to free Roger from bourgeois convention, to experience "the world out there." She tells him, "I've given you yourself, take it. . . . Face the music; what music, falling about you like rain; what splendor of broken chords, brass trumpets braying in the morning and whisper of harps in the dusk . . . and far off, listen, the tread of marching people singing a new song. . . . Good-bye. . . . A man's luck, Roger." In *Processional*, Lawson again employed the metaphor of music to express his holistic purpose. *Processional*'s subtitle is *A Jazz Symphony of American Life*, and the play was "to lay the foundations of some sort of native technique, to reflect to some extent the color and movement of the American processional as it streams about us. The rhythm is staccato, burlesque, carried out by formalized arrangements of jazz music."[39] By 1930, James Agee, the future Oscar-nominated screenwriter as well as movie reviewer for *Time* and *The Nation*, was thinking of combining poetry, music, and film in an "amphibious style" powerful enough to narrate events "as perfectly and evenly as the skin covers every organ, vital as well as trivial, of the human body."[40] Like Lawson and Gold, Agee employed the metaphor of music and cinema to render the idea of what he wanted to achieve. In 1927, he would write disparagingly of the legitimate theater to his friend Dwight Macdonald:

> Of course great things will undoubtedly be done with [the legitimate theater],
> but, possibly excepting music, I don't see how they can ever avoid being
> at least in part imitations. As for the movies, however, the possibilities are
> infinite—that is, insofar as the possibilities of an art CAN be so.[41]

Other future Hollywood New Yorkers pursued hybridization and hybridized media in order to achieve their ends. In one of his last works before leaving New York for California, Kenneth Macgowan envisioned a theater that fused together the stage and the screen. According to a fashion already experimented with in German expressionist theater, Macgowan envisioned the set of *The Red General* as a "blending of motion picture and real theater into one expressive mold." This work, dealing with postrevolutionary Soviet Union, was to be represented on a stage, while film images were projected on a screen behind the actors.[42]

By the late 1920s, some in the Hollywood community were already participating in this project. James Morrison has recently detailed how Murnau's *Sunrise* (1929) "gestur[es] at once toward the 'high' culture of modernism and the 'popular' culture of modernity and thereby signal[s] the crises of cultural value that beset these hierarchies in the age of 'high' modernism."[43] Considering the Hollywood careers of designer William Cameron Menzies, editor Slavko Vorkapich, and director Robert Florey, Brian Taves has shown how these artists continuously moved between the mainstream and the experimentalist margins of American film discourse. "The ideal thing," Florey wrote in 1929, "would be to combine artistic ideas, technique and treatment with the scenarios produced for the general public."[44] Florey successfully integrated avant-garde techniques into later studio productions and even remade his 1927 experimental film, *The Life and Death of 9413: A Hollywood Extra*, into a studio feature film—*Hollywood Boulevard* (1936). Indeed, Taves concludes that "in the past . . . a unique compatibility existed [between Hollywood and avant-garde]; the first popular American avant-garde films were created not by independents, but by individuals from within Hollywood who would continue working there."[45]

Hybridizationism in New York

The hybridization between popular art and high art seems to have been a fixed feature of 1930s cultural productions, especially those that had a major impact on Hollywood. New York leftist theaters, the starting

point for many Hollywood New Yorkers, were no exception. The Group
Theater's influence on Hollywood was both direct and indirect. Highly
respected by the Hollywood moguls and recognized by many contemporary scholars as one of the main influences in the development of
the Hollywood acting style, many of its actors, directors, and writers
(including Elia Kazan, Harold Clurman, Franchot Tone, John Garfield,
Roman Bohnen, John Howard Lawson, and Clifford Odets) eventually
came to participate directly in the Hollywood community.[46]

Probably since its inception in 1931, the New York Group Theater
of Lee Strasberg, Harold Clurman, and Cheryl Crawford had demonstrated the "twin desires for mainstream success and radical credibility."[47]
" 'Experimentation' is not the goal of art," Harold Clurman stated in 1931,
"and I hope we have said enough to make it plain that ours is not to be an
'experimental' theater. We simply wish to say the things we feel urged to
say, and to say those things as clearly, cogently, and aptly as possible."[48]

For Clurman and Strasberg, who were largely borrowing from Stanislavsky's ideas of "affected memory" in stage acting, the quest for the
audience extended to a sense of spiritual communion involving both sides
of the curtain. In a mixture of senses that reminds one of Lawson's 1927
article, the "guru" of the ensemble defined successful Group Theater as
one where "the audience can be led to see, and feel and understand from
the action on stage."[49] Clurman defended such quest for an audience,
and the artistic compromises it implied, in the essay he wrote for the
Daily Worker about the Group's production of *Men in White* (1934)
by Sidney Kingsley. The play, a hospital drama, was a commercial and
critical success, although a few critics opined that the Group had softened its avant-garde stance.[50] In the *Daily Worker*, Clurman responded
that the Group's success did not lie merely in employing the celebrated
Stanislavsky technique, but in its effort to make the technique accessible
to a larger audience. Stanislavsky's theories had already been employed
by other theatrical groups (notably the American Laboratory). The difference, however, was that while other groups had been relegated to the
artsy ghetto, the Group was the first collective, leftist, and intellectually
provocative theatrical ensemble that had been able to survive and "to
engage any audience." Ultimately, the success of *Men in White* was due
to the Group's ability to contaminate the "Group's collective technique,"
deriving from Russian avant-garde and Strasberg's own philosophical
ruminations, with "a play of a more popular notice."[51] Hybridization of
styles, and—implicitly—of highbrow and lowbrow audiences, again seems
to be the key to understanding this project.

For many Hollywood New Yorkers, the search for a larger audience was linked to an outright rejection of any vanguardism that would undermine the ambition to communicate. In 1934, the New York Film and Photo League (FPL) was split between hybridizationists and purists, a split that largely defined those more sensitive to Hollywood's charm and those who would stay in New York. Audience and communicability were again at the center of the debate. Among the purists, Leo Seltzer, Sam Brody, and Lester Balog argued for a revolutionary technique to represent the reality of the class struggle. "Truth is revolutionary" had been the slogan of French communist intellectual Henri Barbusse, and Seltzer and Brody strongly argued for a documentary cinema based on the phenomenological significance of the event, represented in an almost uncut form. In February 1934, Sam Brody noted that if you "associate film reality and its reconstructed counterpart into a unified structure . . . you find 'the sensation of reality' irremediably disrupted."[52] Mostly devoid of soundtrack and edited only to follow the chronology of the event, the FPL's early newsreels strove to "manifest" the reality of a strike rather than recast it into a dramatized narrative. In contrast, the hybridizationist group stressed narration to dramatize the event and thus engage the audience. "A mixed form of the synthetic document and the dramatic," Leo Hurwitz argued in May 1934, "is the next proper concern of the revolutionary film movement."[53] Hurwitz, Irving Lerner, and Ralph Steiner abandoned the FPL to found the NYKINO (New York Kino) and later, in 1937, Frontier Films.[54] Ultimately, some of the members of Frontier Films tried their hand in Hollywood, Irving Lerner working in a long series of films that he either directed or edited.

Predicated upon the hybridization of different intellectual styles and the idea of an emotional connection with a variegated political and social coalition, hybridization never established itself as an uncontested paradigm. The split and the debates between purists and hybridizationists characterized much of the cultural history of the early 1930s on both coasts. As a matter of fact, even among Hollywood New Yorkers—as we shall see—different interpretations of modernism and mass culture coexisted with the dominant one and forcefully emerged in moments of crisis.

In 1935, another of the leading New York workers' theaters, the Theater Union, planned the staging of Bertolt Brecht's *Mother Courage*, based on the novel by Maxim Gorki. The choice was not well thought out. Brecht and Piscator's epic theater was predicated upon the notion of *Verfremdung*, loosely translated as "estrangement effect," whereby the successful epic play would avoid any emotional identification between the actor and the spectator. *Verfremdung* means to spur the spectator into the realm of speculation and social critique by uncovering the "strange," oppressive nature of what we deem as "normal." All in all, Brecht's theater was constructed on the dichotomy between emotion and reason, but it was suspicious of the former as an obstacle to achieving the power of the latter. It ultimately rejected the "theater of feelings" that the hybridizationists endorsed. Brecht, whom the Theater Union had invited to New York, strongly argued against the group's staging of his play, which he considered a perversion and trivialization of his epic theater theories.[55] He even threatened to deny the Theater Union any right over *Mother Courage*, only to relent eventually and allow the opening of the play on November 14, 1935, at the Civic Repertory Theater.[56]

The bourgeois critics were unimpressed by the production. They pronounced the play boring, propagandistic, and lacking in dramatic charm. Brooks Atkinson argued that it was "an interesting experiment in stagecraft without much emotional vitality."[57] The liberal and radical Left, however, was divided into two camps. In *Theatre Arts*, John Gassner praised the experimental validity of the work.[58] In the *Daily Worker*, however, Mike Gold gave the play a negative review and accused the Theater Union of having lost its way. The Theater Union had given American audiences a taste of American reality with *Stevedore* and *Black Pit*, but *Mother* "was too German in form and spirit for an American audience."[59] *New Masses* noted that in the process of intellectual negotiation surrounding the staging of *Mother*, the hybridizationists had won. Stanley Burnshaw's review acknowledged the hybrid spirit of the production but suggested that while the production was Brechtian in spirit, it was also marked by a process of Americanization. The critic noted how different *Mother* was from the "realism" of the previous plays produced by the Theater Union, but also from Brecht's and Eisler's original. The Theater Union's version of *Mother* omitted one scene and one song while the operatic flair of Brecht's original production had been reduced to two pianos. The play was indeed a "mixture of styles," inscribing two constituencies as intended spectators: the avant-garde audience and, at least in the Theater Union's intention, a larger popular audience. "What is now playing at the Civic Repertory," concluded Burnshaw, "is an adaptation of the Brecht-Eisler play in accordance with the tastes and the needs of American audiences."[60]

In the end, neither Brecht nor the Theater Union came out of the experience satisfied. For Brecht, the notion of hybridization, at the level of both esthetics and audience, was problematic. In an interview with the *Daily Worker*, the playwright argued that the uncompromising style of the play was targeted to the only public allegedly able to understand it. "I found the workers by far the best audience for my plays. The bourgeoisie resent thinking in the theater. The workers enjoy thinking. They are a much better public."[61] Albert Maltz, a Theater Union playwright on his way to becoming a Hollywood New Yorker, strongly objected to Brecht's notion of workers' theater, which he considered too abstract and too narrow.

> I thought then (and I think now) that [epic theater] was nonsense; I think it's psychological nonsense and I think it's dramatic nonsense. . . . To think that audiences cannot learn from their feelings and that they can only learn through their mind, I think, is psychological nonsense.[62]

Maltz's resentment, which went beyond the political sympathies and the experience of political persecution that the two men shared, was to last for a lifetime. He stated that when Brecht came to Hollywood in 1941, "I disliked him so much from the experience in the Theater Union that I never saw him here although I knew he was here, and I knew people who went to see him."[63]

Hollywood Europeans

In his groundbreaking, albeit incomplete, biographical dictionary of German-speaking refugees in Hollywood, Jan-Christopher Horak has gathered the filmographies of more than eight hundred anti-Nazi refugees who went to Southern California from 1933 to 1945.[64] A definitive study of the history of the European emigration to Hollywood, comprehensive in regard to the different ethnic groups entering the film factory in the 1920s and 1930s, remains to be done, but thanks to Horak we can now trace the broader lines of the largest and most influential group of anti-Nazi European filmmakers.[65]

As a group, Hollywood Europeans defy characterizations other than very inclusive ones. While their social origins and education were typically middle class,[66] their economic situation at the time of their arrival in Hollywood varied, as many of the young filmmakers—such as Billy Wilder, Edgar G. Ulmer, and Thilde Fontis—were in much less florid circumstances than established stars of the stage or film, such as

Fritz Lang, Max Reinhardt, or Marlene Dietrich. Many of them were of Jewish descent, though some relevant members of the Hollywood German-speaking community—like William Dieterle, Bertolt Brecht, Oscar Homolka, and Hanns Eisler—were not.

It is even trickier to draw sharp political lines among the Hollywood Europeans, as many of them had not been vocal during the Weimar period. The problem is also complicated by the fact that we are dealing with identities in transition, continuously reshaped by the experience of emigration, anti-Nazism, and the interaction with the American scene. In the 1930s, Hollywood Europeans still encompassed both a right wing—"the FBI set" gathering at the home of Charles and Elsie Mendl, and including after 1940 the novelist Franz Werfel—and a left wing, including directors Berthold Viertel and William Dieterle as well as actor Peter Lorre. But in Los Angeles, the factions tended to overlap. Overall, by 1939—as Ernst Karl Winter argued at the time—the experience of emigration and the urgency to build an anti-Nazi front tended to blur "the old antagonism between Right and Left." [67] Bertolt Brecht and Werfel would both meet in the salon of progressive screenwriter Salka Viertel, perhaps during one of those afternoons when Salka's sons—Hanns, a CPUSA sympathizer, and Peter, a Trotskyite—were fighting over the Moscow trials.

Perhaps a distinction should be made between the first and second immigration waves—that is, between those middle Europeans arriving in Hollywood in the 1920s and those who came later. As a matter of fact, as early as 1933, new European immigrants were aware that they were not the first to come this far from the Universum Film Autionsgesellschaft (UFA) studios of Neue Babelsberg. Throughout the previous decade, several German and Scandinavian filmmakers had migrated to Hollywood. In the 1920s, in fact, some European films had been critical hits with fairly good box office takes in both the United States and Europe, prompting many studios to offer American contracts to a few of their makers. By 1922, comedian Will Rogers affirmed that if his film *The Ropin' Fool* failed at the box office, he would "put on a beard and say it was made in Germany, and then you'll call it art." [68]

Among the first Europeans to settle in Hollywood was Ernst Lubitsch, accompanied by many of his usual collaborators, such as screenwriter Hans Kräly and assistant directors Erich Locke and Henry Blanke. [69] Many followed. In 1925, Mauritz Stiller, Paul Leni, and Swedish director Victor Sjöström arrived in Hollywood. That same year, Danish director Benjamin Christensen left the UFA for MGM and Paul Fejos landed at

Carl Laemmle's Universal Studios. Friederich Wilhelm Murnau went to Fox in 1926.[70]

Some of these filmmakers were welcomed and paid well by the Hollywood studios, eager to lure the most prominent filmmakers from their major European competitors. "Almost all the German artists have emigrated," lamented Weimar theater critic Herbert Ihering in 1927.[71] With the conspicuous exception of Fritz Lang, who refused Hollywood offers in 1924 and 1925 and remained in Germany until Hitler's takeover, many of the Weimar industry's aces—from directors Ernst Lubitsch and Wilhelm Murnau to producer Erich Pommer and actor Emil Jannings—accepted Hollywood's offers and came to Southern California.

This first wave of emigration has been traditionally explained as determined uniquely by Hollywood's generous contracts. But this German version of the "Hecht thesis" ignores the connection of this migration to the international history of modernism. Most of the first wave of émigrés had enough status in their home country to allow them a more than comfortable existence, one that they could enjoy without the necessity of learning another language. For these filmmakers, in fact, Hollywood represented not merely money, but the very symbol of modernity, and at least theoretically the counterpart of a rigid German culture.

Mary Nolan has persuasively written that Fordism came to occupy a central place in Weimar's political, economic, and cultural debates.[72] "Hollywood" and its films were often used as tropes for Americanism and Fordism,[73] but both Fordism and Hollywood were defined in competing and contradictory ways.[74] German film industry's executives and conservative filmmakers professed admiration for the efficiency of the Hollywood film industry, but—as Thomas Saunders has extensively demonstrated—meant to use its methods without its content, eschewing American themes and American genres in order to preserve the German character of their films.[75]

For the same reason, engaged in a far-reaching critique of the concept of *Kulturnation*, or cultural nation, German liberal intellectuals and filmmakers maintained a much more positive attitude toward the effect of American mass-marketed cultural productions. Far from focusing exclusively on its "degradations," some European modernists looked with a certain interest to the United States and modernity. "Wie mich dieses Deutschland langweilt! . . . Bleibt: Amerika!" ("How deeply Germany bores me! . . . There remains: America!") commented the young Bertolt Brecht in 1920.[76] According to Martin Jay and Anton Kaes, German leftist intellectuals of the 1920s, unsatisfied by the nationalist and conservative traits of the traditional German culture, embraced the American mass culture "as a vehicle of modernization and democratization of both German culture and life."[77] American slapstick, concluded Siegfried Kracauer, stood for a medium that reflected modernity and its possibilities for human liberation.[78]

Fully participating in the experimental character of Weimar culture, many German filmmakers also appreciated America as the world capital of cinema technology. As a sort of intellectual pilgrimage that mirrored the Fordists' journey toward the fabled Henry Ford Works at Highland Park and River Rouge throughout the 1920s, German and European filmmakers came to Hollywood to study and marvel at the efficiency of American cinema.[79]

German actor Owen Gorin had been summoned to Hollywood in 1923 to perform in some American productions. Asked by *Filmland*, a short-lived Berlin film magazine, for an essay on his U.S. film experiences, Orin described a liberatingly modern Los Angeles, far from the stereotypical and antimodern German "dream-like image" of the American Southwest with its "nights of tropical forests, the gigantic storms, and the waterfalls." The "sensational California" was, instead, the image of modernity— a modernity that was also identified as racially and culturally open to hybridization. Gorin described his arrival in Los Angeles as

> . . . screams in all languages. Objects flying into the waiting automobiles. Japanese, Chinese, Negroes, Mexicans, and Whites drive their cars over the giant bridges of the Los Angeles river in which there is no water. Passing between high apartment buildings and one floor bungalows, one arrives in Hollywood.[80]

In 1927, Ernst Lubitsch, who abandoned a flourishing career in Berlin to come to Hollywood in 1923, described the "Hollywood Filmparadies" to *Lichtbildbühne*, arguing that "it is overall the art of American organization to tame the God of chaos, so that everything goes forward according to the plan, as it has been previously laid out in theory."[81] Lubitsch reiterated the point to *American Cinematographer*, explaining that "in Berlin, we were proud of the couple of spotlights we had, and we did not even think of all the possible lights you have here in America. From the *baby-spots* to the enormous fountain of light, the *giant-spots*. Here, it is always possible to find the particular one that befits your needs the best."[82]

Reading these émigrés' expressions of admiration for American technology, one wonders whether these utterances hint at a larger context, one in which embracing the Fordist efficiency of Hollywood studios really meant a very political rejection of the stiffening Wilhelmine culture. James Morrison may have a point in arguing that modernism rejected the "degradations and contaminants of social modernity."[83] Yet within the context of Weimar culture, one has the impression that embracing modernity may not automatically mean a rejection of modernism.

For some of those modernists who felt threatened by the idea of *Kulturnation* because of their racial, political, or gender identity, modernity—and Hollywood—may not have seemed such a bad idea compared with the stiffening German traditions. Therefore, it is neither surprising nor a sign of authorial discontinuity that Wilhelm Murnau's American film *Sunrise* gestures toward continuity with modernism while "celebrat[ing] modernity itself."[84] As a homosexual, Murnau was indeed more comfortable in the version of modernism and modernity provided by Berlin's UFA or Hollywood's studios than within that ingrained in the notion of *Kulturnation*.

For some middle European filmmakers, the celebration of technology and the loyalty to modernist forms of expression were amply compatible. They certainly did not prevent the creation of superior films, and Murnau—the highbrow creator of *Faust* and *Der Letzte Mann*—argued in 1928 that "to me America has offered new ways to pursue my artistic plans."[85] As a Jew, Billy Wilder might have felt likewise. In fact, he remembers a song popular among UFA filmmakers of the late 1920s: "Dolly is doing well / she sits in Hollywood / at a table with Lillian Gish / and where am I? / where am I?"[86] "I would have come to Hollywood Hitler or no Hitler," Wilder explained to Max Wilk in 1973. "We were picture people. We were in exile where we wanted to be."[87]

The recently published correspondence between Kurt Weill and Lotte Lenya reveals that the couple's decision to go to the United States—and to Hollywood—was not entirely motivated by Hitler. At first, the composer Weill took Hitler's takeover lightly. The day von Schleicher tendered his resignation, opening the way to Hitler's chancellorship, Weill wrote Lenya from Berlin to ask her about her skiing equipment and to tell her that the Vicomte de Noailles had just sent her a "very beautiful big purse" (letter no. 38, January 28, 1933). In a letter to his publishing house, Universal Edition, Weill opined that "what is going on here is so sick that it can't last longer than a few months" (cited in introduction to 1933, February 6, 1933). What clearly interested Weill about the United States was its popular culture, and in this context Hollywood cinema occupied a position not inferior to that of a Broadway musical. Weill was ecstatic when he received a letter from Marlene Dietrich hinting at the possibility of a job at Paramount to collaborate in a project with her and director Josef Sternberg. "I think one can only say yes to this, no?" he wrote Lenya. For Lenya as well, the offer was the vindication of Weill's career. "Wouldn't that be some triumph!" she answered the composer. "Imagine the faces of [Eric] Charell, [Bertolt] Brecht (who—once it's all settled will hear it from me through [Margarete] Steffin), and all those people in Berlin. A musical film with Sternberg and Marlene! It's unbelievable how great that would be" (letter no. 68, March 8, 1934). The project fell through, apparently because of Sternberg's lack of enthusiasm, though Weill was more than willing to negotiate. "Money doesn't matter so much on a first film over there with the best people available," Weill wrote to Lenya (letter no. 71, March 23, 1934).[88]

After the Nazi takeover, European filmmakers began to arrive without a contract or even a regular visa. Billy Wilder arrived in 1934 with a temporary visa and a three-month contract with Columbia Pictures. When the visa expired, Wilder had no choice but to leave the country, go to Mexicali, Mexico, and obtain an immigration visa with the help of affidavits from some friends.[89] What had been a trickle of talent became a stream. The influx of European émigrés into Hollywood so preoccupied some quarters that for three consecutive years, from 1936 to 1938, Congressman Samuel Dickstein (D-N.Y.) petitioned the House Immigration Committee for some kind of control over the influx "in an effort to prevent unfair competition with native performers and prevent foreign gigolos from grabbing American brides as well as fat paying U.S. jobs."[90]

What Dickstein alluded to was a change in the professional status of Europeans arriving in Southern California. In contrast to the stars of the 1920s, after 1933 less celebrated European performers were coming to Hollywood, with or without contracts. Although emigration from Germany was prompted by the situation in Central Europe, migration to Hollywood was not exclusively determined by Hitler, at least until 1938. Even more so than their predecessors in the 1920s, Europeans in the 1930s were taking into consideration all the existing alternatives. For instance, some of the German refugees more closely associated with the German Communist Party (KPD) in the Weimar period—such as Slatan Dudov, Bertolt Brecht, and Herbert Rappaport—postponed their emigration to Hollywood and moved to the Soviet Union (Dudov and Rappaport) or other European countries (Brecht).

In many cases, the move was less an advancement in the filmmaker's career than the logical development of an intellectual pursuit. As the director of the well-known Josefstadt Theater in Vienna, Otto Preminger was well on his way to a distinguished career in theater when he decided to accept Twentieth Century Fox's offer and moved to Hollywood in 1936.[91] Billy Wilder's move to Hollywood in 1934 set back his career from employed director to loosely employed screenwriter. Wilder had already covered a large part of the usual "cursus honorum" before coming to America. After a brief period as a reporter in Berlin in the 1920s, he had established himself as one of the most promising young German screenwriters. After his escape in 1933, his obvious choice was Paris. The crisis of the early 1930s had destroyed four of the major French studios (Gaumont, Pathé-Natan, Osso, and Jacques Haik), soon partly replaced with studios opened by at least seven German producers of Jewish descent.[92] Fluent in French and acquainted with the German-speaking producers, Wilder settled in Paris, where he soon graduated to directing his first feature, *Mauvaise Graine*. Perhaps fearful of Hitler's expansionist plan, and certainly intrigued by the possibilities in Hollywood, the director abandoned his French career and left for Hollywood on a tourist visa in 1934.[93]

Because of their interest in Hollywood and America, German filmmakers and film intellectuals stand out from the rest of the intellectual exiles from Central Europe. Generally speaking, literary critics and novelists dreaded the move and postponed it until the last possible moment. The first to migrate were generally the exiles of Jewish descent, eager to put an ocean between themselves and the Nazis.[94] Literary critic Ludwig Marcuse writes of his attitude toward the United States that "there was nothing I desired less. I would have migrated anywhere except to that world which appeared to me not only strange but frightening."[95] In the 1950s, Columbia University sociologist Donald Kent authored the first comprehensive study on the diaspora of German intellectuals during the 1930s but did not encompass refugee filmmakers, whom he did not consider intellectuals. Tellingly, his many interviewees related "a conviction of personal and cultural superiority" in regard to the United States and in many cases waited until the last moment before deciding to migrate overseas.[96]

Some German filmmakers, in contrast, viewed Hollywood as a possible option even before their chance to keep working in the European film industry had vanished. Fritz Lang decided to leave for Hollywood in 1934, though his reputation would have possibly allowed him to remain in Germany and would have certainly granted him an easy resettlement in France, where he finished *Liliom* in 1934 immediately before leaving for Hollywood.[97] Henry Koster, later the director of most of Deanna Durbin's vehicles, went through an experience similar to Billy Wilder's. When Koster decided to leave for Hollywood in 1936, he abandoned a promising career in Paris for an uncertain situation across the ocean. In an interview given immediately before his death, Koster remembers that although his personal friend Joe Pasternak recommended him to Universal producer Carl Laemmle, Laemmle was far from encouraging. "I'm up to my hips—and he didn't use the word 'hips'—with German directors," Laemmle is supposed to have said.[98] Hardly explained by a rigid economic interpretation, the German filmmakers' quest for Hollywood parallels in large part that of the Hollywood New Yorkers and reflects European filmmakers' long-lasting interest in Hollywood.

Furthermore, not unlike the Hollywood New Yorkers, Hollywood Europeans arrived in Southern California well groomed in a tradition of hybridization between high and low. For the New Yorkers, this hybridization was meant to reconnect their work with American society and its audiences. For the Europeans, hybridization and its techniques served as an implicit critique of nationalist culture, based on a nonhybridized pure notion of *Kultur*. Much of the 1920s German debate about American cinema revolved around the possibility of hybridizing genres and audiences. With a deeper sense of political urgency, but in terms not unlike those used by American intellectuals in the same years, German progressive filmmakers and intellectuals argued for the possibility, and even necessity, of hybridizing audiences and styles. Hybridization in Germany meant the possibility of reconstructing a democratic alternative to the notion of *Kulturnation* and the existence of separated cultural classes. While conservative critics such as Willy Haas claimed that it was possible to import American film technology and yet remain "German" as far as themes and style were concerned, progressive and liberal critics such as Herbert Ihering and Hungarian-born Bela Balasz argued that American success was based not only on technology but on a more inclusive notion of cultural democracy, one not shy about fusing art and popularity.[99] Roland Schacht, one of the most relevant of Weimar culture critics and one not particularly favorable to Americanization, recognized that the superior quality of American films was predicated upon "the 'democratic worldview' of America which understood culture as a consensual phenomenon rather than the preserve of an educated elite." Film production, therefore, was less a problem of technology than of social and cultural organization, and it "demand[ed] connectedness. community with the people."[100]

Indeed by the beginning of the 1930s, a large number of Central European intellectuals were coming to conclusions not so different from those of other American urban intellectuals, though via a different itinerary. Hollywood New Yorkers and Hollywood Europeans were members of an intellectual milieu that was rethinking modernism and avant-gardism in the face of rising fascism and economic crisis. "I would propose," Stanley Corkin suggests in his *Realism and the Birth of the Modern United States*, "that modernism need not to be tied with authoritarianism but that it easily can be."[101] At the end of the 1920s, some of modernism's most successful practitioners (such as T. S. Eliot and Ezra Pound) were certainly tied to elitism and, quite often, to reactionary politics. More importantly, in the late 1920s the modernist project seemed to be floundering on an increasingly fragmented audience and the "diffusion of literary life into particular locales and coteries."[102] Cinema—"the fullest expression and combination of modernity's attributes"[103]—promised the reconstruction of a modernistic, universal language able to engage modernity (Dos Passos's "the unprecedented fever and inhumanness and mechanical complexity of American life") without relinquishing democracy and audience.

The intellectual migration that so radically changed Hollywood was ultimately a movement spanning different nationalities and different political groups. A high degree of "anxiety of contamination" had marked the avant-garde modernism and the modernist cultural elitism during the second and third decades of the twentieth century. Now it appeared that artists on both sides of the Atlantic were testing the possibility of molding a popular, hybridized, audience-oriented, and ultimately more democratic version of the same modernist phenomenon. This trend manifested itself in Siegfried Kracauer's interest in the "topography of the ephemeral," in Fritz Lang's fusion of expressionist techniques and detective lore in his *Mabuse* saga, as well as in John Howard Lawson's attempt to hybridize expressionist theater with American themes and the American tradition of burlesque.

"Rubbing Your Nose in Realism"

In a famous letter to Dwight Macdonald, James Agee referred to the capacity of cinema to capture external reality. Outraged by an article in

Theatre Arts Monthly arguing that "realism is impossible in the movies," Agee asked Macdonald if "writing or drama [could] hope to rub your nose in realism as the movies do? Could *Potemkin* have been staged or described to even approximate the realism of the movie itself?"[104]

In Agee's estimation, however, American film remained isolated from American reality. The young critic wrote in the same letter that "all that's been done so far is to show that art is really possible on the screen. We've barely begun to stir the fringes of their possibilities though."[105]

For many of the intellectuals coming to Hollywood at the beginning of the 1930s, the promises of American film were hampered by Hollywood's penchant for escapism. In fact, while many favored a cultural democracy beyond the "segregated audiences" of the 1920s, they were not willing to compromise their politics or their esthetics. Realist cinema seemed to them a slogan particularly relevant for their task. If able to engage reality, cinema would have been the perfect medium for democratic modernism; it would have also become both politically effective and immediately comprehensible to the larger audiences they had in mind.

Many argued that cinema was going to speak to America only insofar as it would equip itself to speak *about* America. In this fashion, Albert Maltz, a communist sympathizer active on the New York literary scene until his move to Hollywood, argued in *New Theater* that a theater "of vigor" can be a success only if it "cater[s] to workers, intellectuals and all classes." Yet, being popular could not be achieved at the expense of realism. Escapism was to be avoided and reality pursued since "in a world where as much rebuilding is needed as is in ours, 'escape' literature ought to be put on a shelf and labeled 'poison.' "[106]

Throughout its five years of existence, *New Theater* consistently expressed the ambivalence of many Hollywood New Yorkers toward the possibilities of working in Hollywood. The magazine rapidly became one of the most articulate and interesting voices of the Cultural Front although, according to one of its founders, such freedom ultimately irritated Victor J. Jerome, the sectarian cultural commissar of the CPUSA.[107] In 1933, the former *Workers' Theatre* renamed itself *New Theater* and softened its class-based denomination, embracing a new, more hybridizationist philosophy. "Now more than ever it becomes necessary," the magazine proclaimed in its first issue under the new name, "for every group to work hard to spread the program of the revolutionary theater to the masses of workers and farmers, to the students in the colleges, and to the people now active in the bourgeois professions, and little theaters."[108]

Richard Pells argues that for many American intellectuals of the 1930s "the road was being paved for a relatively smooth journey from Union Square to Hollywood."[109] Yet American film's penchant for escapism remained a problem for many of them. Robert Gessner did argue in 1934 that "all revolutionary artists . . . must, in order to be at this time effectively heard, consider seriously the question of working through Hollywood."[110] But quite a few of the people writing in *New Theater*— even after the launching of the Popular Front—expressed ambivalence toward Hollywood and made Hollywood's capacity to engage contemporary issues the acid test of their concrete achievements. Opinions, though, varied and changed over time. After his 1934 article, Robert Gessner voiced his despair about the possibilities for a progressive artist to achieve anything in Hollywood. Progressive filmmakers, he concluded, had to fashion their own movies.[111] In the same issue in which Gessner lambasted Hollywood, however, Luis Norden extolled John Ford's *The Informer*, a bleak story of revolution and betrayal in British-occupied Ireland. The film, Norden concluded, was "a really great picture" marked by a "realistic" style embodied in the characters and the photography where Ford gave "the feeling of depth to a scene."[112]

Realism was not an easily definable term. Many people wrote about it, but the full contours of the notion were blurred. Not easy to pin down as an esthetic form, the desire to "rub the nose" of American film into reality was, however, what the new generation of American-born Hollywoodians shared.

On the surface, a quest for realist cinema seems at odds with the culture and the cinema of the Weimar Republic allegedly dominated by Expressionism. As we saw earlier, Peter Gay suggested a quarter-century ago that the territory of German modernism needed to be expanded beyond "the dominant reading" that sees modernism "as a confluence of anti-rationalism, experimentalism, and alienation."[113] As for cinema, Barry Salt has downplayed the influence of the Expressionist movement in German cinema.[114] Chronology helps as well, since Expressionism is usually associated with the early 1920s German cinema, peaking with *Das Kabinet des Dr. Caligari* by Robert Wiene (1920) and *Von Morgens bis Mitternacht* by Karl Heinz Martin (1920).[115] As a matter of fact, German scholars have recently warned about the habit of collapsing the entire Weimar cinema into easy labels such as Expressionism, or *neue Sachlichkeit*.[116] After the mid-1920s, German cinema veered toward integrating expressionist techniques with realistic themes—as Pabst did in *Die freudlose Gasse* (1926) and *Westfront, 1918* (1930)—and even with semidocumentary techniques such as in Walter Ruttmann's *Berlin: Die Symphonie einer Grossstadt* (1927) or in *Menschen am Sontag* (1929). The latter, the portrait of a weekend of white-collar Berliners, is particularly interesting insofar as it was made collectively by four future Hollywood Europeans: Billy Wilder, Fred Zinnemann, Edgar Ulmer, and Robert Siodmak.

For German intellectuals like Siegfried Kracauer, "Realismus" came increasingly to be identified with the lost opportunity of German film in the time of the Weimar republic. His masterpiece, *From Caligari to Hitler*, published in 1947 but mirroring Kracauer's research and intellectual development during the previous fifteen years, is more than a psychological analysis of the German mind in the period before the Nazi takeover. It also reads like a chronicle of a defeat, that of German film intellectuals and their inability to use the medium to foster democracy. Expressionism, and *Das Kabinet des Dr. Caligari* in particular, represents the German intellectual's "retreat into a shell," his/her inability to address the issues of the day. The film—and the positive reaction of the German Social Democratic Left, which Kracauer explicitly cites—show the flaws of both German psychology *and* the German political Left.[117]

The realist alternative was there in the explicit "social criticism," "photographic veracity," and "candid camera" style of G. W. Pabst's *Westfront, 1918* (1931) and *Kameradschaft* (1931), and of Slatan Dudov's *Kuhle Wampe* (1931).[118] But for Kracauer the failure of these films at the box office illuminated their political weakness, their refusal to identify their audience in broader terms. Nationalism and paranoia endorsed but not created by the German middle class became dominant and "penetrated all strata."[119] In contrast, the Left lost the cultural battle for the German soul because its films "overlooked the importance of the middle class as well as the ramified mental roots of the existing national aspirations."[120] As for communist films like *Kuhle Wampe*, they attacked "the petty bourgeois mentality" of Social Democratic workers, when "it would have been the better strategy to emphasize the solidarity of the worker masses instead of criticizing a large portion of them."[121] The battle for Germany was also lost in its cultural trenches.

When these intellectual groups began to gather in Hollywood in the first half of the 1930s, their personal pasts, present concerns, and cultural heritages separated them. They spoke different languages and came from different political and intellectual experiences. As the decade wore on, the

European tragedy increasingly marked the Europeans as refugees rather than intellectual migrants. Yet Hollywood New Yorkers and Hollywood Europeans shared a deep appreciation for Hollywood potential, as well as a more or less articulated demand for a more realistic cinema. Furthermore, going Hollywood was not an attempt to reject or sell out modernism. American and European intellectuals attempted the typical modernist fusion of idioms, within the modernist context of the most modern of the media and according to a political direction derived from the climate of the Great Depression and the threat of fascism. To them, ultimately, Hollywood offered the possibility to mix the ingredients of modernism and anti-fascist democratic politics in front of the world.

As Hollywood increasingly became a meeting place for intellectual traditions forged in Weimar film circles, Brechtian epic theaters, New York proletarian stages, and Los Angeles studios, film realism more and more took the form of an esthetic "middle ground," a place where different esthetic and political practices could meet and coalesce through some sort of "creative misunderstanding."[122] Loose in the first half of the 1930s, the Hollywood community's demand for "realism" was strengthened by the worsening of the situation in Europe. Many Hollywood Europeans came to see the politicization of Hollywood features as an important step in making American film a weapon in the anti-fascist struggle. Although vague, the slogan of realist cinema gradually supplied a common language to the various constituencies and political and social discourses that had congregated in Hollywood.

2

Salons, Bookstores, and Anti-Nazism

The Remaking of the Hollywood Community

The city is the center of far flung distances, without unity. It is no easy task to bring together diverse thousands who would eagerly rally the support of a united front, revolutionary theater. The material is here but it needs welding.

Richard Sheridan Ames, *New Theater*, 1935

n 1934, Carey McWilliams noted the increasing seriousness of Hollywood parlors. "Meetings are now held, at which the denizens of Hollywood foregather to discuss the most portentous problems and to hail the dawn of world Communism until about two o'clock in the morning when, their brows weary with the travail of thought, they sojourn to some nearby café and apotheosize the new God of their devotion."[1]

Hollywood was becoming serious, but this newly found commitment had not been made public yet. The *Los Angeles Times* reported "the growing intellectual life of Los Angeles" but also noted that "you never hear of it in the papers. Nothing said ever leaks out from behind closed doors."[2] At least until 1936, in fact, the radical ideas and the anti-fascist commitments that Hollywood New Yorkers and Hollywood Europeans were bringing into the community rarely assumed a public dimension or found adequate expression in Hollywood mainstream films.

McWilliams's observations perhaps reveal the beginning of a momentous turn in local and national politics and culture, one that would find its fulfillment in the creation of the anti-fascist community after 1936. It also offers evidence of the obstacles that the networks of the Europeans and the New Yorkers had to overcome in order to achieve the cohesiveness of later years.

When New Yorkers and Europeans arrived in Los Angeles, they found a cultural and political desert. Neither the religious reformers nor the previous generations of film people had done much to remedy the intellectual drought of the city and of Hollywood in particular. Devoid of theaters and cafés, Hollywood's life often took place in private salons where people met after traversing L.A.'s vast spaces. Hollywood Europeans and Hollywood New Yorkers still led separate lives, the former meeting almost exclusively in private homes and at the studios, the latter increasingly involved in local politics but rarely drawing it into their studio work.

The studios also contributed to this separation by directing the New Yorkers into the urban genres that characterized American film at the beginning of the 1930s and the Europeans into the *papier mâché* settings of Hollywood Mitteleuropa. Furthermore, different cultural and political experiences had given the two networks different visions. While the focus of the New Yorkers was a rediscovered American reality, the Europeans' past affected the way they saw America and the way they perceived some of the symbols invoked by the New Yorkers. Both groups wanted more than their salaries out of Hollywood, and neither saw their move as contrary to their ambitions of combining politics, esthetics, and cinema. However, Hollywood New Yorkers and Hollywood Europeans were far from united as to what direction the new Hollywood should take.

Hollywood 1930–1935

In October 1932, Charles Abrahmson, a close friend of playwright Preston Sturges and a Broadway impresario, wrote Sturges's companion, Bianca Gilchrist, to congratulate the couple for "having such an enjoyable experience in Hollywood."[3] Only a few months after his arrival in Hollywood, Sturges seemed well adjusted and optimistic. "I have tried to be friendly with everybody," he had written to Abrahmson in September, "and I don't think I am too unpopular." He had met British director James Whale and found him "a very intelligent fellow, witty and talented and it will be nice to work with him." To be sure, Hollywood had its shortcomings. Eph Asher, an associate producer at Universal, was pursuing Sturges to have him write an adaptation of *Torch Singer*, a novel on the Holman-Reynolds shooting. "The more I tell him it stinks the harder he comes after me shouting 'It ain't artistic but there's a lot of money in it.'" Still, Sturges wrote to Abrahmson, "I'm interested in my work and doing the very best I can."[4]

A few months later, Sturges's enthusiasm had cooled, especially after Universal did not pick up the option on his contract. Professional disappointment was reflected in the playwright's less positive view of Southern California, which he communicated to his friend. "I cannot understand the lack of romance in a country of sunshine and the galaxy of pulchritude advertised to the world." Abrahmson replied to Sturges, "Something is surely amiss, for you were always able to find that necessary ingredient in the most hopeless places." Abrahmson advised Sturges to stick it out: "[Hollywood] is territory for your forces to conquer."[5]

Something was indeed amiss in Hollywood in the early 1930s. When New Yorkers and Europeans arrived, what they found was not encouraging in regard to their prospects in the community. Arriving in Hollywood in 1930, Philip Dunne discovered that the New Yorkers banded together at Fox in what was called the "Fox writers' stable . . . a long row of tiny bungalow offices, dubbed Park Row by New Yorkers in exile."[6] In the early 1930s, Hollywood was just recovering from the scandals of the 1920s and sophisticated New York urbanites did not find much in the way of culture, entertainment, or social life. While a tradition of theater and social and intellectual life existed in Pasadena, centered in the Pasadena Community Playhouse and its director Gilmor Brown, Hollywood and Los Angeles by comparison were intellectually underdeveloped. "Various attempts to develop a flourishing New Theatre in the LA metropolitan area," noted Sheridan Ames in *New Theater*, "have encountered obstacles."[7] No theater existed in the Hollywood community, no café society, and no bookstore—with the conspicuous exception of Stanley Rose's on Hollywood Boulevard.

Hollywoodians—stars as well as technicians—worked hard and for long hours.[8] After a tiring day on the sets, few had the courage to venture out, and when they did they would often attend a screening of a friend's film. Few of them lived in Hollywood proper, and a nightly outing often meant more tedious hours in a car. Individual standing in the Hollywood hierarchy determined one's wages and relative address.[9] Social isolation, however, did not merely reflect the vast geography of the city. Before the politics of antifascism softened many of these boundaries, Hollywood Europeans and Hollywood New Yorkers lived separate lives; among the Europeans, different nationalities tended to keep to themselves, too. The English colony was famous for its aloofness. Hungarians rarely mingled with the Germans or Austrians, though many of them were fluent in German, having had a formative experience at UFA. Michael Korda, the son of director Vincent Korda, remembers that his father would eat only at a Hungarian restaurant close to Santa Monica Boulevard "where he could eat proper food and digest in peace."[10]

Income brackets also defined circles and entourages. The studios were a competitive environment, where people were as good as their last film and were paid accordingly. In his landmark study of the Hollywood community, Leo Rosten describes at least three strata of studio workers: (1) the "colony," overlapped with the totality of those drawing their income from the studios; (2) the "movie elite," composed of those who had achieved a relative measure of success; and (3) the "big money," comprised of those making more than $75,000 a year.[11] The three strata often mingled, Rosten suggested, but one was always aware of the existence of the strata and of his/her place within them.[12]

What also mattered to many of the Hollywood New Yorkers and Hollywood Europeans was Hollywood's failure to originate any café society. Beginning in the early 1930s, New York writers would often gather at the Stanley Rose Bookstore on Hollywood Boulevard. The bookstore had been founded in the 1920s by Rose, a Texan of dubious past. In the back of the store, past the rows of stacks and shelves, was a large room—used as a speakeasy before Prohibition ended in 1933, and afterwards as a watering hole for the likes of Gene Fowler, Horace McCoy, and William Faulkner. New York radical Lester Cole remembers the bookstore as an oasis in the desert as much as a business enterprise.

> Stanley's was a haven for Hollywood's screenwriters, novelists, poets, actors and journalists, employed or unemployed. He was generous, gave more than he took from those in need, relying on more prosperous clients for material benefits. He was rewarded by the admiration and gratitude he received when he could be of help to any of us. His business flourished along with his philanthropies. A rebel, a cynical radical, Stanley attracted notables—as well as unknowns like myself and Cedric Belfrage.[13]

The new Hollywoodians brought radical politics into not only Rose's bookstore but into the community itself. Hollywood New Yorkers were an important element in the early effort to unionize Hollywood, founding the Screen Writers' Guild in 1933 and the Screen Directors Guild and the Screen Actors Guild in the following months, often in the face of producers' opposition.

Some Hollywood New Yorkers also participated in the politics of California in the early 1930s. According to Leo Rosten, Upton Sinclair's 1934 campaign for governor of California "was Hollywood's first all-out plunge into the water of politics." With the exception of the Warners, all the studio heads took the side of Republican candidate Frank Merriam, manufacturing ad hoc newsreels and forcing employees to "donate" a day's wages to finance their $500,000 contribution to the state GOP. Some stars, including James Cagney, rebelled.[14] Francis Xavier Scully, a New York-born intellectual who had recently relocated to Hollywood from Nice, France, led Hollywood progressives such as Lillian Hellman, Dorothy Parker, Charlie Chaplin, Groucho Marx, and Donald Ogden Stewart into the Authors' League for Sinclair.[15]

The 1934 campaign was both a starting point and a lesson for the new Hollywoodians. It stimulated their interest in local politics but ended in failure, with Merriam, "the dull Republican horse," winning the race for governor by a landslide. To Hollywood progressives, the defeat proved the weakness of a divided front, while—to a degree—showing the Communist Party's national bureaucracy how difficult it was to control the Hollywood community. The Socialist Party of America (SPA) and the Communist Party of the United States of America (CPUSA) refused, in fact, to withdraw their candidates, but many of their members and fellow travelers—such as James Cagney and Frank Scully—worked in the Sinclair campaign.[16]

Given the illustrious precedent of media manipulation orchestrated by Theodore Roosevelt and the World War I Creel Committee, Greg Mitchell goes probably too far when he associates the California election of 1934 with "the birth of media politics." This election does, however, mark the entry of Hollywood cinema into the political sphere. Not only did the studio brass endorse Merriam, but they used film and in particular the notorious *California Election News* shorts series to discredit Sinclair. In many ways the shorts were a mockery of what the New Yorkers were to advocate in later years. They were patterned on a documentary style (doctored by the studios), were in touch with the issues of the day (and consistently presented the anti-Sinclair point of view), and explicitly referred to the notion of "people," if only to make brutal fun of it. In *California Election News No. 3*, for example, the hobos on their way to

California are identified as being "men of all classes." Interviewed by the "inquiring cameraman," some of them answer that they come from all over America: "Texas . . . Pennsylvania . . . Montana . . . New Jersey."[17]

Clearly, Hollywood was a battlefront. While events such as individual contributions to the cause of the Salinas strikers or Tom Mooney's release from prison were important, Hollywoodians had a specific field of action. Either Hollywood was to be involved in the battle for democracy, or cinema was to remain a weapon in the hands of conservatives. The gubernatorial campaign and the producers' obviously illicit practices revealed the limits of both American democracy and the techniques of modernity left in the hands of the economic elite. "After 1934," remembers liberal New Yorker Philip Dunne, "we said: 'Never Again.'"[18] After seeing $50 deducted from his check for the benefit of the GOP, Billy Wilder wondered aloud: "I left fascism for this?"[19]

But in the early 1930s, Hollywoodians met and discussed films and politics in private ways, with individual salons functioning like islands in the oceanic texture of the city. When people such as John Bright, Sam Ornitz, and Robert Tasker first came to Hollywood, private homes rather than public halls were the debating arena for politics and Hollywood films. John Bright remembers that

> I was flattered to become part of what Sam [Ornitz] called 'Monsieur De Staël salon,' his comic designation for the group which often came together at his unpretentious little Hollywood apartment. Writers in the main, including, consistently or occasionally, Guy Endore, John Wexley, Nathan Asch, Lester Cole, Vera Caspary, Bob Tasker and myself; plus Lincoln Steffens, Ella Winter and Langston Hughes when they came south from Carmel. The sessions were spirited, political and not at all doctrinaire, laced with skepticism and healthy dubiety.[20]

The organization of Hollywood Europeans before 1936 was also marked by the group's relative insularity and modest size. Most of the intellectual, and literary, anti-Nazi émigrés arrived in the United States after the *Kristallnacht*, but anti-Nazi filmmakers had begun to arrive in California before 1938. The data painstakingly assembled by Jan-Christopher Horak documents that about 15 percent of the "Film-emigranten" arrived in Hollywood between 1933 and 1937. If we are to use the professional category of anti-Nazi refugee directors as a sample, only three arrived in Hollywood in 1933, followed by five in 1934 and five more in 1935.[21] Furthermore, the number of French and British Hollywoodians remained rather low.[22]

Private homes were the main meeting places for the European refugees, who often gathered at the home of Salka Viertel. A former actress and, later, screenwriter and confidante of superstar Greta Garbo, Viertel was the estranged wife of German director Berthold Viertel. Berthold and Salka had come to Hollywood in 1928, but the director had left soon after for the East Coast. Salka remained, and by the mid-1930s her home at 165 Mabery Road was a popular salon featuring frequent guests such as Ernst Lubitsch, Fred Zinnemann, and later Thomas and Heinrich Mann. In the words of literary critic Ludwig Marcuse, one of Viertel's frequent guests, the meetings at Mabery Road were "as though a terrible earthquake had occurred and the survivors had gathered to be counted, still overwhelmed and yet already filled with new hopes."[23]

The home of director Joe May and his wife Mia was another small refugee salon, well known for the quality of food prepared by Mia. German-speaking filmmakers such as Otto Preminger, Walter Reisch, and Ernst Lubitsch often met there. At times politics defined a particular salon. While leftists met at Viertel's home, conservative refugees met at the home of the Charles and Elsie Mendl, a circle Otto Preminger called the "FBI set" because of its political views.[24]

Many Hollywood Europeans perceived that the fragmentation of L.A. life hampered their ability to help relatives and friends left behind in Europe. Relief efforts, which began around 1935, were left largely to private initiative. Until 1936 no agency existed in Los Angeles to organize the anti-fascist struggle, or to cater to the needs of the anti-Nazi refugees. The most important Jewish organization, incorporated in 1936 as the German-Jewish Club of 1933, was devoted to social activities, but until 1936 it had no structure dealing with the issue of refugees, or even Nazism.[25] Refugees in need were often unaware of the complexities of the studio hierarchy and frequently unable to get in touch with the prominent Europeans they had met in Europe. Actor Rudolf Amendt naively wrote a letter to refugee producer Henry Blanke at "Warner Bros." to inquire about a job in the production of *The Life of Émile Zola*. Precious time was lost, and when Blanke received the letter, he scribbled on the borders in German: "Unfortunately sent to the wrong address."[26]

Other times, relief efforts were haphazard, based on a first-come, first-served basis that left many unsatisfied. Ferdinand Brüchner asked his friend Fritz Lang whether it was advisable for a friend of Brüchner's, a leader of the Austrian Communist Party, to come to Hollywood "to gather funds for his group" and "to win friends to his cause and lecture about the situation."[27] Lang answered that he wanted "to help him very much" but cautioned Brüchner that Hollywood money was scarce at the moment, as "the majority of the people have given a lot to all possible causes."[28]

In 1935, Charlotte Dieterle solicited funds for the *Europäischen Hefte*, a progressive refugee newspaper edited in Prague by Willi Schlamm. "I have already organized a meeting here in February," she wrote director Fritz Lang, "and—thanks to the help of Prof. [Max] Reinhardt, Lubitsch, Joe May, [E. A.] Dupont and ourselves—I have put together 500.00 dollars as a contribution, which I have sent in due time." Yet Dieterle had not been able to reach more potential contributors. Her contacts were limited, and she had to rely on other refugee friends to spread the word across the L.A. community. "I have asked Salka Viertel, who knows you personally, to get in touch with you," she continued, "but I have not yet received any answer from you." Lang promptly replied. He had not seen Salka for a while and she had not yet spoken to him about the matter. He would be glad to contribute $100.[29]

Realism and People Narrative

The debate about the possibilities of making Hollywood film into an instrument of democracy revolved around a constellation of ideas about "realist cinema" and "people." First and foremost, Hollywood cinema was to avoid escapism. While some of the people interviewed in the first issue of *New Theater* had manifested interest for mass-marketed cinema, all of them had argued against Hollywood's escapism.[30]

The antidote to escapism was American reality, to be injected in the themes, in the characters, and in the techniques employed by Hollywood filmmakers. A good Hollywood film was to promote social engagement in its audience by tackling the issues of the day and proposing progressive solutions. It was to be "propaganda," as Philip Sterling noted in the first issue of *Films*. Never mind that much of what American cinema had produced in its first forty years was the "perpetuat[ion] of the existing order. . . . No propaganda exists without counter propaganda. If the chief function of the film today is a fond, uncritical defense of the *status quo*, we can assume that, from the invention of the Kinetoscope to the last Academy dinner, *there has also existed a tradition of protest, of the urge of social change.* Not only can this assumption be made; it can be documented and designated as the democratic tradition on the screen."[31] Unearthing this "democratic tradition," Sterling pointed to Griffith's *A Corner in Wheat* (Biograph,

1909), Lubitsch's *Broken Lullaby* (Paramount, 1932), and William Well-man's *Wild Boys of the Road* (First National, 1933) as examples.

Sterling's examples of "democratic tradition on the screen" also ges-tured toward a narrative style that built on the emotional engagement of the audience with the action on the screen. Slowly but surely, many American progressive film intellectuals were building on rather than rejecting Hollywood classical style. *New Republic*'s critic Otis Ferguson argued that *Black Fury*, for all its problems and the obvious studio-imposed softening of the anticapitalist message, was better than Wilhelm Pabst's *Kameradschaft* because its characters "are so cleverly worked into a pattern of cause and result, environment and hopes, that they were neither block symbols nor foreigners, but people you knew and hoped the best of."[32] Even revolutionary cinema, Ralph Steiner and Leo Hurwitz wrote in February 1935, "depends for its effectiveness on the emotional involvement of the audience in these situations. . . . Unless the audience response is obtained, films, however profound and socially important in subject, will be lifeless and socially ineffectual."[33]

The problem, New York critics suggested, was not emotional identifi-cation, but the way Hollywood had channeled it. On the level of narrative structure, the main issue with Hollywood cinema was its "burbankiza-tion," its inability to go beyond personal conflicts. Social issues could not be engaged often enough, because the "social" or the "historical" frame "must *never* compete with Paul Muni."[34] Hollywood movies were hope-lessly individualist and protagonist-driven. In Harry Alan Potamkin's words, American films were rarely, if at all, "social segment films." Overall, they had remained "personality films. . . . Unfortunately, the individual-istic, star-systematized cinema makes no strenuous effort to make one of the two, which is the Soviet intention."[35] Writing in *Vanity Fair* about Fritz Lang's *M*, Pare Lorentz identified the crux of the debate in a balanced way when he noted, "We get no more interesting pictures from Europe than we do from Hollywood. . . . Actually you can look at a hun-dred German pictures, and you'll find that a majority of the directors are patently imitating Hollywood." Russian and German directors, however, are able to debunk the protagonist-driven structure and replace it with what Lorentz calls "comradeship":

> There is no acting in [*M*]. Every character, from the murderer to the most insignificant extra, is beaten into subordination. You feel as though you were watching a newsreel. Never for an instant do you say, 'Ha, what an actor!' There are no camera angles, no whirling cogs, no Coney Island tricks with

faces thrown out of focus. . . . In a job such as *I Am a Fugitive from a Chain Gang*, every man and woman within a hundred yards from the camera is acting his head off, figuring that he is Clark Gable, or Garbo.[36]

For the same reason, the critic and would-be filmmaker saluted Ford's *The Informer* as a masterpiece. In the film, in fact, the director never allows the character of Gypo Logan (played by Victor McLaglen) to control the picture or its mise en scène. It is the film and its collective that work, as opposed to the Hollywood norm in which "all logic, balance and drama . . . are thrown aside in order that the one personality may be blown to the skies."[37]

The critique of the protagonist-driven film was not unusual in a period when, as Dorothy Parker stated, "there is no longer 'I' there is 'we.' "[38] At the first congress of the League of the American Writers, Kenneth Burke suggested that the symbol of "worker" was not attuned to the reality of class struggle in America and that, in its stead, the revolutionary intellectuals should use the symbol of "people," which was "more basic, more an ideal incentive." Such symbolism, he argued, had the advantage of being more in tune with American reality. Furthermore, "the symbol of the people as distinct from the proletarian symbol also has the tactical advantage of pointing more definitely in the direction of unity. . . . It contains the ideal, the ultimate classless feature which the revolution would bring about—and for this reason seems richer as a symbol of allegiance."[39]

Later in his life, Burke recalled that his proposition was not welcome at the American Writers' Congress.[40] By the time of the congress, however, several of the future Hollywood New Yorkers were already familiar with the idea of recasting their work within the symbolic mold of the people. Their favorite periodical had already lost its class-based denomination in 1933, when *Workers' Theater* had been renamed *New Theater*. The 1932 manifesto of the League of Professional Groups, *Culture and the Crisis*, already contained the idea of a progressive alliance going beyond the limits of the working class, the "muscle workers," to embrace white-collars workers and intellectuals.[41] One of the defining texts of the radical New Yorkers, Clifford Odets's *Waiting for Lefty*, featured an intern and a laboratory assistant siding with the working class against warmongers and anti-Semites.[42] Indeed, as Michael Denning has recently argued, Burke's argument "stands as another key formulation of the theory of the Cultural Front."[43]

The debates about the construction of a narrative model that would soften and broaden the protagonist-driven Hollywood narrative to incorporate and represent the "people" concept was part of a general dialogue about symbols and cultural strategies that engaged a large section of the American intelligentsia of the 1930s. In this aspect, too, the new generation of Hollywood participants showed how connected they were to the national, intellectual arena. To be sure, they also shared its limits. Recently, Michael Denning has argued that the recurrence of "people" as well as of its ancillary term "America" in the debates of the Cultural Front did not mean that the Cultural Front "ignored issues of race and ethnicity in the pursuit of a nationalist rhetoric." On the contrary, it articulated a "pan-ethnic Americanism" receptive to the diversified ethnic past and present of the United States.[44]

Denning's thinking is stimulating, yet it is important here to distinguish between inclusiveness and assertiveness. Certainly, the Cultural Front notion of "people" was as inclusive as any symbol in American history. "Am I an American?" sang Paul Robeson, reciting the words of communist balladeer Earl Robinson. "I am just an Irish, Negro, Jewish, Italian, French and English, Spanish, Russian, Chinese, Polish, Scotch, Hungarian, Litvak, Swedish, Finnish, Canadian, Greek and Turk, and Czech and double Czech American."[45] Nonetheless, it seems that this list emphasizes the idea of a shared national present (the obvious pun of the "double Czech American") over differences in ethnic and racial origin among the American public (the "men in white skin" and their brothers in black). The "people" of the Cultural Front, in fact, rarely articulated or asserted the notion of ethnic, racial, and gender difference.

The idea of the "people"—with its "relaxed inclusiveness"—allowed its champions to ally themselves with a vast array of political subjects inside and outside of Hollywood, and thus contributed to making the Hollywood community possible.[46] But it is useful to keep in mind that the people-narrative that the New Yorkers strove to effect in Hollywood was structured less as a post–World War II public sphere than as a nineteenth-century discourse about the public.[47] Its inclusiveness purported to be national, genderless, and colorless, though it was, ultimately, gendered and racialized. Indeed, as Gary Gerstle writes, the culture of the 1930s, of which the New Yorkers were part, strove to be first of all national-popular and it "could not, or did not, introduce into political debate issues of ethnic—and for that matter racial or gender—equality."[48]

New Yorkers in Hollywood

Any attempt to synthesize American cinema of the early 1930s is a daunting task and one likely to be frustrated by what Robert Sklar has called the "turbulence" of this period. For many reasons in the early 1930s, the Hollywood forcefield was in a period of radical transition. For starters, its functioning was modified by the creation of the Production Code Administration (PCA) and the strengthening of the Hollywood moral code. Less in opposition than in collaboration with the studio executives, in fact, many of the religious leaders of the nation equipped Hollywood censors with a tight instrument of self-censorship. From 1934 on, the PCA and its head, Joe Breen, had the task of seeing to it that every film distributed in the majors' theaters conformed to the dicta of the 1930 production code.[49] Furthermore, after the introduction of sound requiring a large amount of capital to wire theaters and stages, financial control of the industry shifted to the East Coast.[50] New stars emerged, a new generation of Hollywoodians came to Southern California, and new genres, with which cinema had merely experimented before, became a staple of Hollywood production.

It is hard to overestimate the effect of the introduction of sound on American film and the social and intellectual composition of the Hollywood community. According to an editorial in *New Republic*, until the late 1920s and the advent of the talkies, movies were an "entirely independent form of entertainment." Hollywoodian were mostly "people who had trekked to California, thrown in their lot with the films, and settled down permanently to work, to experiment and to express themselves" in the new medium. Talkies, however, changed it all. "It is no longer the case of writers going movie. . . . It is not alone dramatists with stage hits or actors with perfect diction who are in demand. Along with these, the talkies have imported to Hollywood songwriters, hoofers, vaudeville teams, night club entertainers, and Metropolitan Opera Stars."[51] The "metropolitan taste," commented The *New York Times*, had gone Hollywood.[52]

The new genres reflected the urban roots of filmmakers. The most representative of gangster, fallen woman, shyster, or prison films invariably bore the mark of this new generation. The "unnamed city" of *The Front Page* was adapted by Bartlett McCormack from Ben Hecht's and Charles McArthur's Broadway play; the gangsters of Hecht's *Scarface*, John Bright's *Public Enemy*, and W. R. Burnett's *Little Caesar* came out of the 1926 stage melodrama *Broadway;* the new urban stars—"city boys" such as James Cagney, John Garfield, Humphrey Bogart, Paul Muni, and Edward G. Robinson—all came out of New York theater to give faces, gestures, and personae to the urban, celluloid hoodlums.[53] James Cagney, Lincoln Kirstein noted in *Hound and Horn*, was "the first definitely metropolitan figure to become national."[54] Across the gender line, Marlene Dietrich, Jean Harlow, and Mae West changed the image of screen femininity.

The degree to which the films of the early "Golden Age of Turbulence" reflected the New Yorkers' political esthetics is the more difficult question.[55] Kirstein was certainly correct in his evaluation of Cagney. With few exceptions, however, New York intellectual circles considered Hollywood as embodying the possibility, rather than the actuality, of progressive cinema. As late as 1934, Robert Forsythe (a.k.a. Kyle Chrichton) lamented in *New Theater* the fate of the "earnest writers who have gone to Hollywood . . . to produce pictures that could be enjoyed by people who had managed to get through the 7th grade."[56] The same issue of the magazine featured an essay by Robert Gessner, arguing that "all revolutionary artists aiming at undermining the ideological structure of the middle class and consolidating the working class must, in order to be at this time effectively heard, consider seriously the question of working through Hollywood."[57] But one year later Gessner had changed his mind and seemed to side with Forsythe. Hollywood was a dead end for the progressive artist, and progressive filmmakers had to fashion their own movies.[58]

Until 1936, *New Theater* was consistently ambivalent as to the possibilities of working productively and progressively in Hollywood. In the same issue in which Gessner lambasted Hollywood, Luis Norden extolled Ford's *The Informer*, a bleak story of revolution and betrayal in occupied Ireland. The film, Norden concluded, was "a really great picture" marked by a "realistic" style embodied in the characters and the photography where Ford managed to give "the feeling of depth to a scene."[59] In *New Masses*, Harry Alan Potamkin wrote that gangster films were "part of America's celebration of her corruption."[60] As Robert Sklar points out, Lincoln Kirstein came to doubt that Cagney would have been able to survive Hollywood. Audiences had waited in vain for the actor to make a cinematic *Waiting for Lefty*, but Warner instead cast him in *Taxi!*—a movie that bowdlerized the story of the cabbies' struggle against the taxi trust. "Cagney wanted such a story," commented Potamkin in *Close Up*, and so did radical writer John Bright, but the producers rejected it.[61]

The urban settings of many of these films called for a certain degree of social realism. As a genre much visited by the new generation of Hollywoodians, however, the gangster film monitored both the urban writers' scarce radicalization and the system's capacity to withstand progressive efforts. As opposed to the environmentalist gangster films of later years, the early gangster pictures pretend to reflect society via the figure of the gangster, rather than explaining him via the reference to societal unbalances. The prologue of *Public Enemy* makes clear that the film's goal is "to depict an environment," not to explain its social consequences. If the movie gives reasons for its characters' actions, these are personal rather than social. John Bright, Kubec Glasmon, James Cagney, and veteran screenwriter Harry Thew all concurred in making *Public Enemy*'s Tommy Powers a "roughneck sissy," apparently self-sufficient and yet neurotically prone to violence and dependent on the women surrounding him.[62]

Either because of Hollywood censorial efforts, or because of Hollywood New Yorkers' ineffectiveness, the relatively sudden rise to stardom of the protagonists of these films is also explained by the leeway given stars such as Cagney, Muni, and Robinson. Whether or not we can read them as a perverse rendition of the classic Horatio Alger rag-to-riches tales, early film gangsters share with Alger's characters the desire to exercise complete control over their fate.[63] Conversionist stories, these films show their protagonists in the process of completely recreating themselves, from their profession, their economic situation, and their romantic allegiances down to their very name.

When the film industry Left attempted to sneak something into Hollywood movies, the result was so ambiguous as to be almost disappointing. On paper, *Black Fury* (WB, 1935) seemed to be a promising story for the Hollywood progressives. The film originated from a treatment about Virginia coal miners written by Pare Lorentz. The filmmaker had submitted the idea to the studio as a possible subject for Paul Muni.[64] However, *Black Fury*'s credits do not report Lorentz's contribution to the film. The temporary script still had enough elements of both the story "Jan Volkanik" by progressive Judge M. A. Musmanno and the play "Bohunk" by Harry R. Irving to deal rather effectively with the coal mining conglomerate's attempts to crush the miners' union.[65] But the finished film was a far cry from progressive cinema. Miner Joe Radek (played by Paul Muni) is driven crazy not by the inhuman conditions in the mines, but by his girlfriend's eloping with a factory guard. Deranged, Radek abandons bread-and-butter unionism and embraces all-out revolution.

Unwittingly, he becomes an instrument of the agent-provocateurs sent by the mine companies under the guise of radical unionists. Eventually, Radek sees the light, saves the mines, wins back the girl, and rejoins moderate unionism.

This "burbankization" was a direct result of the intervention of the studio and of the Breen office, afraid of an all-out attack on the mining interests. In September 1934, Joe Breen had written directly to Warner to recommend caution and to warn lest "vicious brutality [be] assigned to the Coal and Iron policemen." If not perfect, conditions in the industry had to be shown as "vastly improved and . . . getting better all the time."[66] Warner associate producer Hal Wallis had written to producer Robert Lord "that we should make all changes indicated by Breen, and, if necessary, bend over backwards to eliminate anything unfavorable to the coal mining industry."[67] After seeing the final script, Breen and *New Masses* had opposite reactions, bearing witness to the relations of power within the early 1930s Hollywood forcefield. While *New Masses* termed *Black Fury* a "fascist film" and a product of the pressures on the studio by the "Hollywood Hussars," Breen wrote Warner to commend Wallis for doing "exactly as we suggested."[68]

Progressive Hollywood New Yorkers and the Chain Gang Cycle

The chain gang cycle, a subgenre of the prison film, was developed a few years after the gangster film. The American Film Institute Catalogue lists only three films set in this category between 1932 and 1933: the low-cost production *Hell's Highway* (RKO, 1932), the major production *I Am a Fugitive from a Chain Gang* (WB, 1932), and *Laughter in Hell* (Universal, 1933) from a book by the radical New York writer Jim Tully.[69] In their differences and similarities, these films document the alternatives open to New Yorkers within the Hollywood forcefield of the early 1930s.

American liberals and radicals had long condemned the use of convict labor for the construction of roads and the production of common goods. On stage, the prisoners' plight had been a fertile territory for leftist urban playwrights. John Wexley's *The Last Mile* (1930), the story of an inmate on death row, had won popular and critical accolades during its run on Broadway and launched the Hollywood careers of its stars, Spencer Tracy and Clark Gable. In June 1932, the death of a New Jersey teenager, Arthur Maillefert, in a Florida prison "sweat box" had profoundly shocked Northern opinion. In *Harper's* magazine, Walter Wilson wondered whether the chain gang persisted in the South "because Southerners are naturally depraved."[70] John L. Spivak, a communist writer from New York, wrote a passionate attack on the institution, while *Harper's, New Republic,* and *Outlook* launched a campaign for the abolition of the chain gang.[71] As the Southern states were the only ones to permit convict labor, the campaign mixed humanitarian and anti-Southern feelings, building on a tradition of reform that was predominantly urban, Northern, and politically liberal.

The Studio Relations Committee (SRC), Hollywood's pre-PCA self-censorship board, was clamping down on the gangsters at large in the streets of Hollywood films. Once caught and convicted, however, the criminal was less threatening, and he or she could be looked upon with sympathy. In September 1931, the board of directors of the Motion Pictures Producers and Distributors Association (MPPDA) proposed stopping the production of gangster films altogether, thus denying representation to the criminal at large. Nothing was said, however, about the prison film cycle.[72] Once punished, the criminal could be readmitted, if not to society, then at least into Hollywood narrative.

As articulated by *I Am a Fugitive from a Chain Gang* and *Hell's Highway*, the chain gang film documents how an urban tradition of reform arrived in Hollywood at the beginning of 1932. A comparison between the production histories of the two films also accounts for the relative rigidity of Hollywood discourse in the early 1930s. Working outside of the big-budget productions—in low-profile projects of the major studios and in the little B and C movie production houses—demanded speed and efficient management of very scant resources. Such constraints, however—as in the production of *Hell's Highway*—afforded a degree of freedom from studio pressures, as B and C producers were often unable to supervise the details of individual productions. Bernard Vorhaus, later chased back to his native England by the blacklist, was able to direct the anti-racist *Way Down South* from the script by Langston Hughes in the context of Sol Lesser's B unit.[73] Reminiscing about his early 1940s work for producer Seymour Nebenzahl, Douglas Sirk notes that in the low-budget productions he had more control over the film. "It was better," the director told *Filmkritik.* "In some of my first movies, I had more freedom from the OK to the story to the release."[74]

Hell's Highway was directed by Rowland Brown from a script by Brown, Robert Tasker, and Sam Ornitz. "The first story to be screened in the new convict camp cycle" according to *Variety*'s review,[75] the film was a low budget affair making the most of Richard Dix's fading box office appeal. Brown had made *Quick Millions* (Fox, 1931)—in Harry Potamkin's words "the best [gangster] film of the garrulous era."[76] The writers, Robert Tasker and Samuel Ornitz, were two novelists well-known in New York literary circles. In particular, Tasker was some sort of sensation. H. L. Mencken's *American Mercury* magazine had published several of the stories Tasker had authored while doing time in San Quentin for armed robbery. Both writers were radicals. Ornitz was already a member of the Communist Party, while Tasker was a personal friend of Tom Mooney, whom he had met during his stay in San Quentin.[77]

Hell's Highway succeeded in bending the relatively new formula of the prison film into a strong progressive statement. Dix plays the role of Duke, a rather unapologetic convicted murderer in a Georgia prison. A local entrepreneur, Mr. Billing, employs the convicts to work inhuman shifts to build a state highway, ironically named Liberty Road. Criminal by chance but rebellious by nature, Duke leads the convicts' resistance until his kid brother joins the gang as a convict. To protect his brother from the sadistic guards, Duke takes a tamer attitude, but upon learning that his parole has been denied, he escapes along with several other convicts. What follows is one of the most brutal manhunts in the history of American cinema: convicts are executed on the spot, fed to hungry bulldogs, and a deaf-mute prisoner is shot when he fails to answer the guards' questions.

As envisioned by Brown and his writers, the film ended on a hopeless but defiant note with Duke being shot while making a last dash for liberty. After an L.A. preview, however, RKO revised the ending to show the ultimate triumph of reform as well as the punishment of Mr. Billing.[78] *Variety* commented that "it would take much more to lift the story out of the sloughs."[79] As it stands now, the film remains impressive for the depiction of prison injustice and the inmates' solidarity across racial lines. As became common in later chain gang films, in *Hell's Highway* the racial dimension of Southern gangs was indicated by the predominance of gospel and blues in the sound track.[80] As opposed to *Road Gang* and *Fugitive*, however, the black presence is neither marginalized to a few scenes, nor merely suggested by soundtrack blues. *Hell's Highway* constructs its plot around a racially mixed chain gang ("the preponderance of the convict labor [in the film] is Negro," commented *Variety*).[81]

Highway's "contamination" between races parallels the film's hybridization between genres. Besides supplying the customary musical commentary to the plot, black convicts work, fight, and escape alongside white prisoners. The black presence is also the element where the film becomes more *artistically* innovative. The script by Brown, Ornitz, and Tasker situated *Hell's Highway* firmly within the political avant-garde. Paralleling the hybridization between different arts that was popular in the modernism of the 1920s, *Hell's Highway* in several key scenes—all of them involving black actors—blurs the boundaries between cinema, music, and painting. When the evil prison guard, Popeye, kills his wife and blames a convict for the murder, the black convicts sing the event to the spectators, and Clarence Muse makes a drawing of the murder in front of the camera.

While *Hell's Highway* escaped the producers' censorship almost intact and remains an impressive example of both democratic modernism and the 1930s American radical tradition, the Hollywood studio system prevented such discourse from invading its center. *I Am a Fugitive from a Chain Gang*, the only major production in the chain gang genre, presented in its body the censorial working of the Hollywood forcefield. As opposed to *Hell's Highway*, *Fugitive* was realized on a major budget; by a major director, Mervyn Le Roy; and with a major star, Paul Muni. After his initial reluctance to abandon New York, where he was playing in the successful *Counselor at Law*, Muni, upon reading the script of *Fugitive*, accepted a three-picture contract from Warner.[82] Robert Elliot Burns had published the account of his experiences as a real-life fugitive in *True Detective Mysteries*, starting with the January 1932 issue. The Story Department of Warner initially recommended against buying the rights. Burns was an escaped convict and "all of the strong and vivid points in the story are certain to be eliminated by the present censorship board. . . . This book might make a picture, if we had no censorship."[83]

The film's theme also worried the SRC. In February, Jason Joy, the head of the committee, wrote Darryl Zanuck asking him to reconsider. The film might have done well in the urban centers of the Northeast, but it risked offending the rural South because of its "large Negro population."[84] Aware that the majority of the Warner theaters were located in the industrial Northeast, Darryl Zanuck was willing to take a gamble on the film.[85] For the directing job, Zanuck needed an experienced hand. Director Roy DelRuth, however, declined the assignment because of the story's "depressing nature."[86] Zanuck then offered the film to Mervyn Le Roy, a San Francisco-born director, who had been active in Hollywood since the early 1920s. As screenwriters, Zanuck chose two young playwrights—Sheridan Gibney and Brown Holmes.

Holmes was born in 1909 in California. *Fugitive* was his second film treatment, the first being his version of Dashiell Hammett's novel *The Maltese Falcon.*[87] Holmes's treatment was then given to Sheridan Gibney to adapt into a script.[88] The son of a wealthy Eastern family, Gibney was educated at Philips Exeter and Amherst after which he tried his hand in the New York theater, writing opera librettos and moderately successful plays including *The Wiser They Are* in 1931.[89] Politically progressive, Gibney was soon involved in the unionization of Hollywood screenwriters.[90]

As noted by Joseph O'Connor, the temporary script that Gibney produced for *Fugitive* lacked a precise and optimistic narrative closure. Reversing the tradition of the happy ending, the script closed on a downbeat note. Allen, the name given to the character portraying Burns, has escaped for the second time from the inhuman prison system and can no longer find gainful and lawful employment. Society has finally turned an honest man into a criminal: Allen has to steal in order to survive.

Gibney's screenplay also cast the story of Burns in the context of depression-era America at the expense of the main character's role.[91] Burns's military past, in fact quite unremarkable, was given an heroic dimension (he receives the Distinguished Service Cross), only to serve as a counterpoint for the treatment he receives from the cruel, capitalist society. Burns's enemy is the "Big American Business Man" ("with a paunch grown huge on war profit")—unnamed in the script after the manner of expressionist theater—who denies him his former job and ipso facto condemns him to hit the road. Conversely, his friends are the people: "What's a country anyway?" he tells an audience gathered around him. "It is a lot of people trying to figure out how each one can get what he needs without having to rob anybody else." Prostitutes, other convicts, the army of the American unemployed all help him along. One of them even extols the virtues of the Soviet Union, where "Everyone is working—eating—living! Why? Because the country belongs to the people, that's why."[92]

Zanuck was intrigued by the unconventional ending. The producer, however, was not willing to risk the considerable amount of energy, funds, and expectations he had sunk into the story for such a radical critique of American society. Fox reassigned Gibney's temporary script to Howard Green for a thorough rewrite. Green, born in 1893, was an old show-business hand, having worked extensively as a producer of vaudeville shows in both New York and San Francisco. Conservative in politics, he was one of the earliest opponents of the SWG's effort to unionize the

Hollywood writers and one of the founders of the Screen Playwrights, the studio-dominated company union.[93]

Gibney and Holmes had fashioned an early version of people narrative that focused on America's social plight at the expense of the protagonist's story. In Green's version, *Fugitive* was again a protagonist-driven film with Paul Muni getting the lion's share of the shots. Green's rewriting of the Gibney's script completely recast Burns's story into a more traditional, protagonist-centered plot. Allen's initial unemployment is due to his personal weakness rather than to capitalist ruthlessness. The Big American Businessman is replaced by jovial Mr. Parker, who even comes to the station along with Allen's family to welcome the hero returning from the war. Allen's restlessness, rather than capitalist greed, is the cause for his giving up a secure income to search for a better career as an engineer. While Gibney's script immersed Allen's vicissitudes in the context of depression-era America, Green's version narrowed the scope of the film. Interestingly, Allen's story becomes more the quest for familial happiness than for social justice. The film is introduced by a moving scroll attesting the authenticity of the story and signed by Burns's brother, the Reverend Vincent G. Burns. Allen's tragedy begins with his decision to sever his family ties and abandon his mother. After this initial mistake, Allen struggles to return to the happy safety of the nuclear family. Blackmailed by the evil Marie, Allen marries her. When he falls in love with Helen, however, he risks prison again in order to get a formal divorce and marry his true love. Gibney's script had Helen (in his script named Adele) as a borderline prostitute, a "cabaret ballerina," a savvy representative of the proletariat. Green transforms her into a "respectable woman." In Gibney's version, Allen's relationship to women was at the very least liberated. He had a one-night stand with a prostitute, Linda; a not entirely unpleasant relationship with Marie (a "twenty-six, dark, sexy looking" lady); and ultimately a love story with Adele, whom he meets in a club while escaping the company of his wife. If his final destination was Adele, the character was willing to take some detours. Green made everything more linear. Allen has only one true love, Helen. His hometown fiancée leaves him and disappears from the script. Marie is unfaithful. Rather than a second—or third—thought, Allen's choice to divorce Marie for Helen is now framed as the best possibility to form a family, and ideally to go back where he was at the beginning.

The film premiered on November 11, 1931, at the New York Strand to an overwhelmingly positive reaction of the mainstream press. *The New*

York Times called the film "a stirring picture" and "a vehement attack on convict camps." Rosa Pelswick noted that *Fugitive* "emerges at the Strand Theater as a powerful document, a brutally dramatic narrative of man's inhumanity to man." Bland Johaneson wrote that the film "veils none of its awful realism in conventional Hollywood prettiness."[94] The finale, with Muni muttering the famous line "I steal" while the lights go off, is still powerful and unconventionally bleak. Outdoor footage supplied by Slavko Vorkapich gave the film a documentary feeling while anchoring it firmly in the modernist tradition.

Variety noted that *Fugitive*, "tied up with the current chain gang abolition activity," captured a theme dear to liberals.[95] The liberal intellectual circles, however, gave the film a lukewarm reception. Potamkin did not review the film for *New Masses,* nor did the *Daily Worker* take notice of it. In the view of many liberal critics, *Fugitive* had been hampered by the rewriting done during production. Pare Lorentz argued that Le Roy had refused to enlarge the focus of the film beyond Muni's character, though he "could have used the man as an instrument against his background and, like the Germans and Russians at their best, manipulated people as group actors, making the prison, and not the actors, the object of the film."[96] In a penetrating, though idiosyncratic, review for the British highbrow newspaper *Close Up,* Harry Alan Potamkin wrote that *Fugitive* was the Hollywood film that had come closest to the unification of what he called "the social segment film" and the "personality film." Yet ultimately the movie revealed the "renewed concessions by the social segment film to the aggrandizement of the personage who should be the character-convergent for the happenings."[97] *The Nation* and *New Republic* were less caustic, though not exceedingly impressed. Alexander Bakshi wrote condescendingly that *Fugitive* was "a conscientious work which deals adequately, if not excitingly, with an important problem of American life."[98] *New Republic* noted the importance of the film yet argued that "the issue of the Burns case is a thousand times less important than the evil itself."[99]

Hollywood Europeans and the Making of the Hollywood Papier Mâché

Studio demands, along with language gaps and L.A.'s cultural and physical geography, contributed to the separation of Hollywood Europeans from the New Yorkers. The latter were often assigned to reshape the cinematic reality of American society and urban spaces. The former, for the most part, were confined to the Hollywood "operetta milieu," fulfilling what Guido Fink calls Hollywood's "need for Europe as a reservoir of ghosts to evoke and exorcise."[100] Between 1928 and 1935, with some exceptions, mitteleuropean actors, directors, and screenwriters worked out an operetta tradition of American cinema with its real (Vienna, Paris) and imaginary (Liliputias) destinations, characterized by glossy studio shoots, musical numbers, and a fablelike approach to the Old Continent milieu.

For some of them, this transition was consistent with their preceding careers. Ludwig Berger had made *Ein Waltzertraum* for UFA in 1925 and came to Hollywood in 1927, where Fox employed him in the making of *Playboy of Paris* (Paramount, 1930) with Maurice Chevalier. Others made the best of what they were offered. In Germany, Joe May had been among the founders of the street film genre. As soon as he arrived in Hollywood in 1934, Fox assigned him to the musical *Music in the Air.* Billy Wilder had worked in the realistic tradition in both *Menschen am Sontag* and *Mauvaise Graine*, the movie he directed in France. Though not devoid of comic relief, especially in their secondary characters, both films showed Wilder's debt to the poetics of *Neue Sächlichekeit* and focused on petty bourgeoisie; the camera indulges in long shots of the city, of its streets, parks, and inhabitants. The Paris of *Mauvaise Graine* is exhibited throughout, especially in the long sequences where the characters, a bunch of car thieves, drive around the city. In both films, Wilder made the milieu easily recognizable with an almost exclusive reliance on exterior shooting. The stories Wilder authored in the United States in the years immediately after his arrival do not follow this pattern, however. In the United States, Wilder's works became more and more mired in the operetta milieu, which his scripts superimposed to the Tyrol of *Music in the Air* (1934), the Vienna of *Champagne Waltz* (1937), and the Paris of *Lottery Lover* (1935), *Midnight* (1939), *Bluebeard's Eighth Wife* (1938), and *Ninotchka* (1939).

The American Left generally lambasted these films as the farthest thing from the "realism" they advocated. The Lubitsch touch failed to impress Potamkin, who compared it unfavorably with the "honesty and wit" of Pabst's *Dreigroschenoper*, calling it "the watch-me-as-I-apply-this" touch. These films were a little better than the Broadway musicals, but still unsatisfactory. "The Germans," the critic argued, "have been the most consistently ingenious in their renditions [of the musical film], abetted by the proof that the tradition of the Viennese Waltz is less wearying than that of the Broadway melody, however insipid its insinuations may be per se."[101]

As future developments would show, there was, if not an overlapping, at least the possibility for a dialogue. The *papier mâché* settings that the Europeans were building had more to do with politics than Potamkin perceived. Judged from the perspective of Hollywood New Yorkers, with focus on American reality, these films were bound to be deemed as failures. Contemporary reality, however, did creep into the *papier mâché*. The consciously unreal Vienna of *Champagne Waltz* and Ernst Lubitsch's *The Merry Widow;* the Paris of William Thiele's *Lottery Lover*, Mamoulian's *Love Me Tonight*, and Lubitsch's *Ninotchka* and *Angel;* the Sylvania of Lubitsch's *The Love Parade;* and the Tyrol of Joe May's *Music in the Air* all constructed the utopia of a Mitteleuropa devoid of Nazism, a "world of yesterday" (to quote the title of Stephan Zweig's autobiography) that fascism had destroyed. In the early 1930s, the international censors were more aware of the "hidden transcript" of these films than the New Yorkers. The Italian Fascist regime, for instance, considered Lubitsch's *The Merry Widow* unfit for Italian distribution because of the buoyancy with which the institution of monarchy was treated. Several scenes were to be expunged. How could the Italian people tolerate a monarch who packs his crown in his suitcase along with his other belongings?[102]

Furthermore, the operetta settings of these films drew on the European tradition of hybridization, part of the intellectual baggage that these immigrants brought to Hollywood. It also related to the eagerness to contaminate genres, audiences, and styles that characterized the New Yorkers' interest in American cinema. If the studios considered the Hollywood Europeans the best equipped to narrate Old World scenarios, it is interesting that even superstars like Ernst Lubitsch, presumably in control of his own career, chose the hybridized terrain of the Viennese "operetta" rather than more highbrow subjects.

"Das ist ka' Musik" ("This is no music"), the director of the an-der-See Theater is supposed to have told Franz Lehar upon hearing *Die lustige Witve (The Merry Widow)* for the first time. "Music" was Schubert and Brahms. Lehar's was the hybridized, popular variety composed for librettos written by Jewish playwrights. Lehar, the son of a military band leader and married to a Jewish woman, was hardly highbrow.[103] But for Lubitsch, Lehar's tunes and the libretto by Victor Leon and Leo Stein were worth his cinema. This aspect assumes a striking clarity in *Champagne*

Waltz, the story of Buzzy Bellview (played by Fred McMurray), a flashy jazz band leader who takes Vienna by storm. The film developed from an original story by Billy Wilder and Hollywood progressive Hy Kraft. In *Champagne*, not only did the genre of the operetta assume the form of a statement against cultural elitism, but it also celebrated the hybridization of the cultural traditions of the Old World with those of the New. The waltz was indeed the nineteenth-century Viennese counterpart of mass-marketed cinema, and the huge Waltz Palast of *Champagne* is a clear reminder of the huge Apollo Palast, built in 1808, and rivaling any of New York's swing ballrooms in size—thirty-six dancing arenas and room for six thousand dancers—and bad reputation.[104]

Billy Wilder played a role in the writing of the script as well. A sheet of "Data for Bulletin for Screen Achievement Records," dated September 22, 1936, lists him and Harry Ruskin as "substantial contributors," which meant that they "contributed more than 10% of the value of the completed screen play."[105] It is easy enough to recognize in Buzzy the crooner Paul Whiteman, who had been a hit in 1920s Berlin and for whom Wilder had worked as public relations man.[106] When Buzzy is down on his luck and looks for inspiration, it is the flashing neon sign advertising a Whiteman concert that the camera frames.

Champagne combines the operetta settings of the Vienna of Johannes Strauss Jr., the beer gardens, and the Prater with a tale of hybridization between genres and cultural traditions. On one level, *Champagne* is the story of the contrasted romance between Buzzy and Elsa (played by Broadway singer Gladys Swarthout), the great-grand niece of Franz Joseph Strauss and co-owner of the Vienna Waltz Palast, the temple of the waltz. After several incidents, the lovers and their music are separated. Ironically, Vienna is falling hard for the swing, while New York has discovered the waltz. The solution that the film envisions is hybridization. In the final scene, the reunion of the lovers, the hybridization between the two worlds, and the triumph of the hybrid is celebrated by a combination of camera angles and stage mechanics. The camera first frames a classical orchestra playing the "Blue Danube," then it swirls right to frame a jazz orchestra playing its own Americanized version of the same music. Suddenly, the tunes merge and the bands play together, as the stages of the two orchestras interlock and physically blend before an ecstatic New York audience.

Hollywood Europeans and "the People"

In these rather disjointed beginnings of the new Hollywood community, many elements militated against a fruitful collaboration between Hollywood New Yorkers and Hollywood Europeans. The studios demanded different things from the two networks, and the Breen office collaborated with the Hollywood brass in guarding the boundaries of the center from the rather feeble attacks of the disorganized new Hollywoodians. Yet another difficulty in their initial interactions resided in the different political languages each group spoke.

Among the intellectual baggage of the Hollywood New Yorkers was a shared notion of American people as an interclass construct that represented both the spirit of democratic America and the idealized audience. In this vision, the people was a unity that—with the exclusion of greedy capitalists—was democratically inclined and increasingly anti-fascist. In *Waiting for Lefty*, his 1935 epoch-defining one-act play, Clifford Odets (who came to Hollywood after 1936) saw the proletarization of the petty bourgeoisie as thrusting this social group into an alliance with the working class. Some of the Europeans, however, might have had a few doubts. In 1935, the anonymous editorialist of *Aufbau* wrote about the possible "Vormarsch des Antisemitismus in Amerika." As of 1935, for the commentator, anti-Semitism was not a specific feature of fascism ("Faschismus und Antisemitismus sind nicht notwendig Synonym"). Anti-Semitism was an "intellectual epidemic" ("geistige Epidemie"), one from which Fascist Italy was more immune than the United States, as Huey Long's and Father Coughlin's rhetoric and success proved.[107]

At the center of this discussion was the behavior of the middle classes in a condition of stress, such as the Weimar decade or the American Great Depression. In *Die Angestellten*, Siegfried Kracauer, the most influential cultural critic of Weimar Germany, had cautioned against the facile optimism of Weimar marxists in regard to the natural revolutionary tendencies of the displaced middle class and petty bourgeoisie. The proletarization of the more than 3.5 million members of the newly created white-collar classes was not automatically pushing them into an alliance with the working class. Made "spiritually as well as materially homeless" by the economic situation, they were actually going to be the easiest prey for any kind of demagoguery.[108] In an influential essay published in *Social Research* in 1934, Giuseppe Antonio Borgese argued that fascism had to do with the "emotionalism and pseudointellectualism" typical of petty bourgeoisie displaced by the war.[109] Karl Mannheim reiterated this point in *Man and Society in an Age of Reconstruction*, published in German in 1935 and translated into English in 1940.[110] The Weimar middle classes, subordinated by inflation, were "like an unorganized crowd which only very rarely becomes integrated." Nazi anti-Semitism was a way to ensure a sense of security for the displaced middle classes, what Mannheim called a "negative democratization. . . . The populace as a whole now becomes a privileged group in this sense and the man in the street is entitled to the privileges of being a member of a pure race, relieving him at the same time of the responsibility for individual achievement."[111]

Such interpretations fit pretty well with the immediate experience of the émigrés. Translated into the German *Volk*, "people" resonated ominously with many bad memories among the Europeans. In 1944, Franz Neumann acutely noted how a racialized notion of the "people" was at the core of the National Socialist state. Citing Disraeli, he compared it with the alternative concept of "nation" borne of the French Revolution: "The phrase 'the people' is sheer nonsense. It is not a political term. It is a phrase of natural history. A people is a species; a civilized community is a nation. Now, a nation is a work of art and a work of time."[112] At the Writers' Congress of 1935, refugee intellectual Friedrich Wolf reacted negatively to Kenneth Burke's extolling of the "people" symbol by pointing out "the similarities between this usage and Hitler's harangues of the *Volk*."[113]

It was by the German "people" that the refugees had often felt betrayed. The founding of the *Reichsverband der deutschen Lichtspielbesitzer* (March 1, 1933) and of the *Filmkammer* (July 14, 1933) did not immediately translate into the dismissal of the Jewish and anti-Nazi directors. It did, however, cause a status revolution in the German studios.[114] Many of the established Jewish filmmakers had seen themselves displaced by unknown newcomers brandishing a Nazi Party card rather than a list of film credits. Henry Koster, who was an established UFA director in 1933, was no longer welcome at his usual restaurant table after Hitler's "Unter den Linden" parade. But what was more disconcerting was that after Hitler's takeover, a failing actor whom Koster was putting up at his home left him without a word of explanation. After Hitler's electoral victory, Koster met the actor again.

> I drove my car over to the curb where he was standing, waiting for the bus. His name was Eberhardt Leithof. I said, "Eberhardt, what happened? You never

came home. Do you need anything?" He said to me, "I wish you wouldn't talk to me." I said, "I wouldn't talk to you?" He said, "I don't talk to people like you anymore," and he walked away. After I had taken care of him for months![115]

A few European intellectuals, such as Giuseppe Salvemini, were going to contribute a different interpretation of fascism, more inclined toward marxism and fitting better with the celebration of the "people's" inherent innocence. According to this point of view, fascism was the natural outlet of monopoly capitalism and the violent arm of capitalist bourgeoisie, oppressing the people through an impressive and novel police, bureaucracy, and military apparatus.[116] While such an interpretation gained some degree of consensus among Hollywood Europeans as the 1930s progressed, it might not have been completely established in the mid-1930s. Until the founding of the Hollywood Anti-Nazi League (HANL), refugees were still few in number, rarely socialized in the Hollywood Cultural Front, and—radical émigrés such as Bertolt Brecht, Oscar Homolka, Hanns Eisler, and Fritz Kortner still in Europe—lacked an organized marxist nucleus. As a matter of fact, as Brecht's failure to gather support for his "other Germany" construct a few years later will show (see Chapter 5), many Hollywood Europeans remained convinced that the "people," at least in Germany, was a consensual partner of Nazism rather than its victim.

Fritz Lang is a key example of this distrust. He knew Kracauer personally and was familiar with Mannheim's interpretation of fascism.[117] His first American film, *Fury* (MGM, 1936), represents a middle ground between his European background and his new American environment, at once reflecting his personal immersion in the milieu of the budding American cultural Left but still relating his European anxiety about the true disposition of the people. Ultimately, American progressives chose to appreciate the former and disregard the latter. Such cultural practice recognized the director's expanding circle of friends but also obscured the profound discrepancy between the filmmaker's early vision of America and that entertained by many Hollywood New Yorkers.

Arriving in Hollywood as an established European "genius," Lang seemed to walk an opposite itinerary from that of Billy Wilder, increasingly abandoning Europe and embracing cinematic realism and American reality. Before Lang came to the United States in 1934, the best known of his films fell in the category of nationalistic fantasy (*Die Nibelungen*), science fiction (*Metropolis*), or mystery (the *Mabuse* films). Goebbels picked *Die Nibelungen* as an example for the new German film industry and, according to the director, even offered Lang the opportunity to head the new Nazified German film industry.[118] Lang left Germany the day after the meeting with Goebbels, and in later years Klaus Mann credited the "monumental hollowness" of Lang's German films to Lang's Nazi first wife and collaborator, Thea von Harbou.[119]

Any interpretation of this change, however, should not underestimate the profound effect of emigration on the director's vision. His correspondence for the years between 1934 and 1936 shows an intense exchange between Lang and members of the Hollywood and New York Left intelligentsia such as Dorothy Parker, Hy Kraft, Humphrey Cobb, Vera Caspary, and Irving Lerner.[120] Such change put Lang at odds with his past and with the expectations of his new employers. David Selznick wanted him to produce something either in the vein of the *papier mâché* or futuristic adventures. The producer told his secretary Katherine Corbaley to supply the recently arrived Lang with "fantastic material of the type of Jules Verne," or "end of the world material" and "the better plays in the semi-fantastic field such as *Wings over Europe*, and the better mystery stories."[121] Corbaley complied and gave Lang synopses of many fantasy tales (among them *Lost Horizon*, later produced by Frank Capra), "the four Mu books," and Sax Rohmer's Fu Manchu stories.[122] The director, however, was not impressed. Lang wanted to depart from his past ventures. Along with the radical writer and Hollywood New Yorker P. J. Wolfson, Lang was thinking of something in the tradition of social realism, "a straight, honest document on crookedness. Similar to that done by Warner in *The Public Enemy*."[123]

Fury, the film that came out of more than two years of delays, expectations, and disappointments, was hardly an escape into the realm of science fiction or the mystery novel. The story of the attempted lynching of Joe (played by Spencer Tracy), wrongly accused of kidnapping a girl, is firmly in the tradition of social realism. It also paid tongue-in-cheek homage to a tradition of documentary filmmaking with which Fritz Lang was then quite intrigued.[124] When all evidence seems to fail, it is a newsreel that ultimately nails the presence of the lynch mob at the scene of the attempted lynching.

Walter White of the NAACP wrote MGM "to express my profound appreciation" for the film.[125] Lang's Hollywood leftist friends, such as Humphrey Cobb, praised the film for its "realism" and acknowledged that "all credit is yours for having produced it in the face of Hollywood and all that Hollywood stands for."[126] Most of the intellectual progressive magazines were impressed by *Fury*. *New Masses* praised the film but lamented the loss of the racial dimension, arguing that since the majority of the victims of lynching were African Americans, the film ultimately obscured "a complete understanding of the problem."[127] A close reading of the film, however, reveals that other elements of *Fury* kept the film from being a true model of progressive cinema, at least in terms of the criterion sketched by the contemporary American Left. *Fury* was hardly a celebration of the American people, but rather embodied a subtle distrust for the people. Under duress, in fact, ordinary Americans join not the strikers but the lynchers.

Symptomatically titled "Mob Rule," the original script for the film was tightly focused on Joe's disillusionment with the American people. In a telling scene that was shot but later edited out by producer Joseph Mankiewicz, Lang had Joe in a movie palace, listening approvingly to a speech about "the sense of *fair play* and *common sense* of the American people." When a spectator (interpreted by Ward Bond, whom the script carefully identifies as "not an alien type") objects and comments that the American people are really "sheep, palsy—sheep," Joe explodes. "I suppose it wasn't the people who made this country what it is today?"[128] By the end of the film, however, Joe has lost all trust in the "people." There is no such thing as American exceptionalism, he tells the jury; the "feeling of pride that this country of mine was different from all others" has been murdered by the lynchers. Americans are "sheep," easily turned into "a mob." "A mob doesn't think, it hasn't time to think," his fiancée Katherine tells him. This is ultimately the only reason Joe should save them from the execution. They are not even worth being granted responsibility for their actions.

In the original script, such bitterness was also emphasized by a rather open-ended conclusion, which did not feature the conventional final kiss between Joe and Katherine that was added to the film before its release.[129] Perhaps it was because of this optimistic ending that progressive American intellectuals did not pick up on the explicit equation that Lang posited between American people and an unruly mob. More likely, Lang's uncompromising condemnation of lynching fit in very well with the American progressives' campaign, and the film's endorsement of social realism helped things, too. It also helped that Lang often relied on exclusively visual effects to communicate his ideas.[130] In the lynching scene, the point of view of the mob becomes that of the spectators, visually equating them. Though contemporary film critics were, and are, generally oblivious to this, Lang thought he had been quite explicit, and explained the shot to Jimmie Vandiveer in the pre-approved text of a 1936 radio interview: "I roll the camera forward as a man would walk and thus approach the jail. *The audience becomes the mob* and together we move along up the streets and finally directly up to the sheriff himself."[131]

Lang was not alone in his pessimism as far as the American people was concerned. *Dr. Socrates* (W. B., 1935) was the twenty-second film directed by William Dieterle in the United States. From a story by W. R. Burnett, *Socrates* was, according to *Variety*, a mixture of G-men and the gangster genre "arriving at the tail ends of [both] cycle[s]."[132] For a film produced after the establishment of the PCA, *Dr. Socrates* does have a rather positive character in the gangster Red Bastian (played by Barton McLane). Violent though he is, Red lives by some kind of honor code and takes good care of his gang. The character was so positive that when McEwen received the manuscript, he wrote to Wallis that the Breen "office would take some exception to the bandit stuff which plays an important part in the story." The star of the film, Paul Muni, even entertained the idea of playing the character of Red but instead was cast as the good doctor Cardwell.[133] Cardwell was once a doctor in a big city hospital, but a fatal mistake compelled him to leave the city and move to the small provincial town of South Bend. When a member of his gang is wounded during an armed robbery, Red enlists the services of Dr. Cardwell, mockingly referred to as Dr. Socrates by the town yokels. Only at the end of the film, after the bandit kidnaps Jo (played by Anne Dvorak), the girl Cardwell has fallen in love with, does he turn against Red and actively participate in his apprehension.

The film expanded on Red's ambiguous nature as a villain, and seems to suggest that South Bend has become the real villain of the story. The local physician, Dr. Ginder, fears Cardwell's competition and tries to ostracize him. The townspeople suspect Jo of being in touch with the gangsters; when Cardwell rescues her, the people want to lynch her. This mob scene was neither in Burnett's story for *Collier's* (March 16, 1935), nor in James Cain's treatment. The extant documentation points toward Dieterle as the origin of the twist in the plot. In the script prompted by Abem Finkel and Carl Erickson at the end of May 1935, in fact, it is only Dr. Ginder, the sheriff, "and a couple of armed deputies" who come to Cardwell's house. The sheriff soon intervenes to calm the tensions between Ginder and Cardwell, saying, "There is no use getting into a scrap. We don't know for sure if the girl was in Bastian's car. Some say she was, some say she wasn't."[134] By June 13, however, the sheriff and the two deputies accompanying the hostile Dr. Ginder have metamorphosed into "a big crowd in his yard," which Dr. Cardwell refers to as a "mob." The scene was written by Mary McCall who, as was customary at the time, was secretly working as a second writer on the script. McCall's script, completed on June 8 and revised on June 11, did not yet include the mob. The reference to the mob appears after that date (on blue pages dated June 13), after McCall wrote Wallis that "I made the changes Mr. Dieterle wanted." [135] Indeed, by June 22, Hal Wallis informed Robert Lord that Dieterle (and Paul Muni) was "very pleased with the rewriting." [136]

Writing to his friend Rose Pastor Stokes in 1932, Hollywood New Yorker Samuel Ornitz complained about his recent move to Los Angeles from the East Coast. In comparison with New York, Los Angeles disappointed him both politically and esthetically. Commenting on the local political situation at the end of 1932, Ornitz concluded that Los Angeles was "the first Fascist City in America." Studio work was no paradise either, and Ornitz complained that he had one more month to go on a "miserable" studio contract. The money he earned, however, was going "to the workers' fight" and would give him "enough for a year for my book." [137] In the span of two years, however, Ornitz's attitude toward Southern California had changed. In 1934, Victor J. Jerome, in charge of cultural affairs for the CPUSA, wrote Ornitz to remind him that he had committed himself to write Rose Pastor Stokes's biography after the activist's death of cancer in March 1933. Ornitz, however, seemed distracted, and Jerome commented to him that "you have thrown yourself into the revolutionary Cultural Front in California." [138] After the chairman of the CPUSA, Earl Browder, wrote Ornitz to urge him to complete Stokes's biography, Ornitz responded that he had found "a good movie job" and that "as important as the Stokes story is, and should be, my own feeling is that the theater—as the emotional platform of propaganda—is extremely important at this time." [139]

This exchange illuminates the situation in Hollywood at the end of the first half of the 1930s. Well before the official launching of the Popular Front in 1935, Hollywood intellectuals had begun to reevaluate their prospects in Southern California and brought into the movie citadel a political engagement previously unknown on Sunset Boulevard. Rather than the stern, inaccessible style of the high modernists that was in direct opposition to Hollywood's storytelling, these artists planned to build on "an emotional platform," which, as we shall see, was akin to the Hollywood classical appeal to the spectator's emotions.

Within the sets and stages of the Hollywood forcefield, however, the studios' traditional political timidity had been institutionalized into the Breen office, which radically reshaped *Black Fury*. *Hell's Highway* was as radical as anything being produced on the New York stage, but it was still a hopelessly marginal product. By the end of 1935, the studios were not compelled to negotiate their cultural practices with a well-organized anti-fascist presence. Divided by language, studio practices, and Los Angeles geography, Hollywood New Yorkers and Hollywood Europeans rarely dined, partied, or drank together. In 1935, *New Theater* noted the paltry development made by theater in Los Angeles. "The city is the center of far flung distances, without unity. It is no easy task to bring together diverse thousands who would eagerly rally the support of a united front, revolutionary theater. The material is here but it needs welding." [140]

3

The Making of an
Anti-Fascist Community

One cannot say that American film directors have shirked the responsibility that was theirs with the great medium of the cinema at their disposal, not with such a record of achievement. These accomplishments have been cumulative, each breaks ground for the other and for new visions that will clarify the American and world scene to the millions to whom the movies are the reflection of the modern world.

Herman Weinberg, *Sight and Sound*, Winter 1938–39

n 1939, on his way back to New York after a few months' stay in Hollywood, German anti-Nazi refugee Manfred George wrote Katia Mann that he was "going back to New York" with a "heart made awfully heavy" by the idea of having left Hollywood behind ("ich schrecklich schweren Herzens zurückgefahren bin"). Looking back, the movie citadel resembled a "lost paradise" ("ein verlorenes Paradies") full of excitement, intellectual conversation, and the magic of movie making.[1] And yet George was not a provincial rube, easily impressed by the Hollywood star system and the studio glamour. Born in 1893 in Berlin as Manfred Georg,[2] he had been an editor for the prestigious publishing house Ullstein and for their trail-blazing daily, *Tempo*. His past acquaintances and collaborators had been firmly grounded in the milieu of Berlin's modernist circles. He had briefly edited an art magazine with modernist playwright Ferdinand Brüchner, and he also founded the ill-fated Republikanische Partei with *Weltbühne*'s maverick Carl von Ossietzky immediately before Hitler's election to the chancellorship. In 1938, after five years in Czechoslovakia, he moved to America. Though unable to remain in Hollywood, George's career was to flourish in the United States. Once back in New York from Hollywood in 1939, he took over the floundering organ of the Jewish Club of 1933 and transformed it into the most prominent mouthpiece of the German exiles in the United States, *Aufbau*.

Other European intellectuals shared George's enthusiasm for Hollywood. In 1937, Thomas Mann's children Erika and Klaus had visited the West Coast and met the great modernist stage director, Max Reinhardt, who told them that Hollywood was going to become "a new centre of culture" where "European and American scientists and artists will meet to prepare a home for our old culture and for the new one that is coming into being here."[3]

This chapter examines the reasons for George's enthusiasm and monitors the development of Reinhardt's prediction. Its focus is the transformation of Hollywood into an intellectual and international center, a change brought about by both European and New York emigrants to Southern California and molded by the fire of these intellectuals' anti-fascism and enthusiasm for the democratic possibilities of American film. As they changed the local, political, and intellectual scene, these migrants subtly changed themselves as well. As the 1930s went on, both groups came to perceive their move to Hollywood as less of a temporary change as they identified more and more with the local community. A novel pride and "sense of place" pervaded the struggle for unionization of Hollywood professionals as well as the activities of recently founded organizations such as the Hollywood Anti-Nazi League (HANL). As they were rooting themselves more and more in Hollywood, however, the European émigrés and New York leftist intellectuals did not cease to identify with national, and even transnational, communities.

As the worsening of the international situation brought larger numbers of European anti-fascists to the American film industry, their efforts to politicize Hollywood and its films yielded concrete results with the foundation of HANL. As a political, social, and cultural front, HANL represented a further step in overcoming the limitations of the isolated salons (described in Chapter 2), providing a focus and an organizing structure for Hollywood politics. Cinematic realism—which HANL strongly promoted in its anti-fascist version—moved from the margins of the film community to its center, informing important and increasingly ambitious Hollywood projects such as Warner's biopics and *Confessions of a Nazi Spy*.

The Founding of the Screen Writers Guild and the Hollywood Identity Crisis

Except for the occasional wild party, the moderately popular use of drugs and alcohol, and a few sex or murder scandals, early 1930s Hollywood was a rather tranquil town devoted to making motion pictures. Until the migration of the Hollywood New Yorkers, there had been no serious attempt to unionize the studios' creative labor force. In the early 1920s, the best-paid writers had formed the Los Angeles Writers' Club, located in an old mansion on Sunset Boulevard. More a social club than a union, its members enjoyed the spacious dining and billiard rooms with an atmosphere more like a country club or the New York Lambs Club.[4] In the following years, the Writers' Club was disbanded and the Screen Writers Guild (SWG) was founded (April 1933), then dismantled and replaced by the producers' pet, the Screen Playwrights Inc. (May 1936). SWG was re-admitted in 1937 via the intervention of the National Labor Relations Board (NLRB) and finally recognized as the writers' only legal representative after the June 1938 NLRB supervised elections and two more years of negotiation.[5]

By 1939, it was clear that Hollywood was no longer the company-town-with-a-touch-of-sin it had been in the early 1930s. What was also clear was that in the 1930s Hollywoodians had fought not merely about unions but also about the construction of a new Hollywood identity. The "Hollywood writers' war" demonstrates the division in Hollywood along both political and generational lines. The anti-SWG company union, the Screen Playwrights (SP), counted among its leaders such Hollywood veterans as the former president of the Hollywood Writers' Club, Rupert Hughes. A Hollywood resident since 1919, Hughes was the author of a three-volume hagiography of George Washington and owned the lavish "Arabian Nights" mansion.[6] SP stalwarts included settled Hollywoodians Patterson McNutt, William Slaven McNutt, James Kevin McGuinness, and Howard Emmett Rogers, with the addition of a young New York writer, John Lee Mahin.

In contrast, in 1933 at the first meeting of what would become the SWG, the majority of the ten people present were young urban Hollywoodians. Lester Cole, John Howard Lawson, Samson Raphelson, John Bright, Louis Weitzenkorn, Brian Marlow, Bertram Block, and Courtenay Terrett had recently arrived in Hollywood from large American metropolises. The committee in charge of drafting the working rules of the new guild included Bright, Oliver Garrett, Sam Ornitz, Robert Riskin, and S. N. Behrman, a New York wit who had trekked west in 1930. With the partial exception of Ralph Block, who was president in 1934, all the presidents of the SWG from 1933 to 1940 had come from New York: John Howard Lawson (1933–34), Ernest Pascal (1935–36), Dudley Nichols (1937–38), Charles Brackett (1938–39), and Sheridan Gibney (1939–41).[7]

In the summer of 1935, the SWG signed an agreement with the New York-based Authors League of America (ALA) and Dramatists League to form a common front in protecting the interests of creative writers across the nation. The SWG split on the issue. In favor of "amalgamation" were people such as Lawson, Ornitz, Dorothy Parker, her husband Allan Campbell, Samson Raphelson, Frances Goodrich Hackett, John Bright, and Lillian Hellman. On the other side stood the "horsemen of the apocalypse"—Patterson and William Slaven McNutt, James Kevin McGuinness, Howard Emmett Rogers, and John Lee Mahin along with veteran Hollywoodians Grover Jones and Howard Green.[8]

The fight among the Hollywood writers was as much about identity as it was about politics. In 1939, Darryl Zanuck, a veteran writer turned producer and an adamant opponent of the amalgamation, remembered the battle as a machination of the "Dramatist Guild, the ALA in New York, who hate motion pictures and hate Hollywood and make fun of it and ridicule it, and write plays lambasting it."[9] Budd Schulberg brilliantly referred to this division in his Hollywood novel, *What Makes Sammy Run*. In the novel, the main opponent of the amalgamation is writer Harold Godfrey Wilson, an "old gentleman" whose career had completely run within the confines of Hollywood. Wilson

> had come Hollywood in the early twenties working as an extra, then as a gag man, gradually fighting his way up to become one of the most important writers in the industry and now, by God, no bunch of Broadway snobs, who thought they were too good for Hollywood, was going to sit around the Algonquin and tell him what to do.[10]

And yet it was not just a matter of Hollywoodians fighting New Yorkers, or of professional screenwriters fighting writers-turned-screenwriters-for-the-money-and-the-sun, as Zanuck argued. Zanuck was actually omitting the fact that several of his opponents were increasingly identifying with Hollywood.

Some no longer considered themselves "New York writers" stranded in Hollywood, but rather were developing a professional identity that drew from both their New York *and* Hollywood activities. S. N. Behrman, who had come from New York in 1930 with a résumé that included Harvard and Columbia degrees as well as articles written for *The New Yorker*, *Smart Set*, and *The Red Book*, vented the standard anti-Hollywood view in his 1932 play *Biography*,[11] in which a brash, honest young editor tells a writer: "In the new state men like you won't have to prostitute themselves in Hollywood."[12] Yet, in 1934 in an article published in *The New Yorker*, Behrman took issue with Hollywood's New York foes such as Sidney Howard, Edmund Wilson, Moss Hart, and George S. Kaufman. Turning the tables on the New Yorkers, Behrman argued that the down-with-Hollywood spirit (as embodied in Hart's and Kaufman's play *Once in a Life Time*) was not necessarily any less commercial than Hollywood: "the satirizing of Hollywood is now firmly entrenched as one of the most thriving branches of the national literary industry." Nor was it inherently better. Hart's Hollywood work (*As Thousands Cheer*) was both "subtler and truer" than his New York work. Hollywood still produced "mob art" and New York still had the upper hand, but things could change. "Charlie Chaplin was brought to world fame by Hollywood. . . . There is no reason someone should not come along who might use this extraordinary medium with Shakespearean fullness."[13]

Behrman was not alone. New York–born Sidney Buchman, Columbia graduate and future blacklistee, had arrived in Hollywood in 1932 and joined the SWG at its inception. As the 1930s progressed, his regard for Hollywood grew. "I'm one of the few guys who think Hollywood is a training school for writers," he told the *Post*, "but that's the way it worked out for me. . . . The discipline has its value."[14] Once a writer moved to Hollywood, the world might forget that she or he was an author, concluded Norman Reilly Raine, creator of *Tugboat Annie* for the *Saturday Evening Post*, who had gone to Hollywood in 1933 and was by 1937 a stalwart supporter of the SWG. Still, Hollywood could be regenerating. Over time, said Raine, the writer "begins to feel more at home, and, curiously enough, recaptures some of that fine energy and ambition to make the grade that characterized his early efforts in fiction. It's like life backward."[15]

For some veteran Hollywoodians, screenwriting was early retirement, "a soft racket" in the words of Richard Schayer, a veteran of twenty years in Hollywood and an opponent of the SWG. But Dorothy Parker disagreed. "I have been writing for motion pictures for two years," Parker wrote. "I do not feel that I am participating in a soft racket." Screenwriting was hard work and certainly paid well, but good writing and money were not mutually exclusive. "I can look my God and my producer—whom I do not, as do many, confuse with each other—in the face and say that I have earned every cent of it."[16]

The struggle for the SWG was certainly about job solidarity and unionism. The majority of Hollywood writers were underpaid and exploited, 40 percent making less than $250 a week by 1938.[17] The SWG clearly emphasized this aspect in its negotiations with the studio executives. So did the other unions that sprang into existence, spurred by the SWG's struggle.[18] But what emerges from this period is that many Hollywoodians were beginning to refuse the conventional dichotomies between Hollywood and New York, commerce and art. If anything, they wanted to bridge them. The Hollywood screenwriter "begins to feel that his membership in the Screen Writers Guild really entitles him to be known as such," concluded Raine: a playwright for the screen, or a Hollywood New Yorker, if we are to localize this dyad of professional terms.[19]

Becoming Hollywood Europeans

Regardless of their interest for mass-marketed cinema, Hollywood Europeans often looked at their move to Southern California with a certain apprehension. Were they to Americanize, or were they to remain European? If they persisted in their identification with European culture, how would they be able to adjust to Hollywood? Conventional histories of Hollywood and of Hollywood Europeans make the exiles into one more trope for the demarcation between Europe and the United States as well as between modernism and mass culture. Authentic, modernist artists cannot be happy in Hollywood. Therefore, they are, in James Morrison's words, "a figure of pathos stripped of the originary means of expression, denied access to the native national styles that would speak his authentic identity."[20] In German, the issue of selling out disguises itself as "die Anpassung" (assimilation), a sin that distinguishes those who succeeded from those who did not. Billy Wilder, Fritz Lang, and Douglas Sirk plunged themselves into American popular culture and were successful. Max Ophüls did not, and his career was grounded.[21] As Wolfgang Gersch sees it, "Wilder, like Lang, . . . separated himself from German influences, in order to assimilate to the American Film."[22]

Matters actually were more complicated than that. Although their identities underwent profound reshaping, Hollywood Europeans rarely saw their choices in stark terms. For one thing, even the most successful— or the most assimilated—of the Hollywood Europeans identified with a solidarity network defined by the experience of exile and anti-fascism rather than by Americanization. As hundreds of Europeans arrived in Hollywood, the most visible émigrés were the ones whom the newcomer would seek for advice and help. The first rule of the refugee network required those in a position of power to help the newly arrived. In 1937, Ernst Lubitsch wrote to Hal Wallis—top producer at Warner—to ask for a contribution for the fund of the widow of Paul Grätz, a German actor who had died.[23] And Paul Weigel, another German actor stranded in Hollywood, asked Henry Blanke—"Mein lieber, guten Heinz" ("My dear, good Heinz")—whether the producer could find something for him in Blanke's film Zola.[24] Fritz Lang's correspondence during this period contains dozens of letters of refugees requesting help. Lang rarely broke the chain of refugee solidarity. In 1936, when Otto Klemperer, the director of the Los Angeles Philharmonic, recommended Frederick Kolm, a German actor, to Lang, Lang recommended Kolm to director Ernst Lubitsch and to the Hollywood refugee producers: Henry Blanke, Joseph Pasternak, and Gregor Rabinovitch.[25]

The only qualification necessary to join the network was unquestionable anti-fascism. "Everybody considers [Reinhold] Schünzel a Nazi," agent Paul Kohner wrote in 1937. Kohner, a stalwart anti-fascist himself, knew full well that the director was innocent, but his crime—to have lingered in Germany until 1937—made him unpalatable to many refugees.[26] Likewise, in 1937, Lang told his friend Charles Katz about a Mr. Fischinger who had worked in Nazi Germany before coming to Los Angeles. "I personally don't like that kind of opportunism," Lang said. "It was enough reason for me not to help him and not to pull any ropes for him. Because I think that we have enough other people who are really in distressed situations and really need a job."[27]

Successful assimilation did not mean that émigrés had to or "wanted to avoid speaking German with other immigrants."[28] Lang still used German in 1937, especially in his correspondence with literary exiles such as playwrights Ferdinand Brüchner and Manfred George, and poet Ernst Toller. Toller, who was Lang's neighbor in Santa Monica, wrote him about Kurt Grossmann's refugee group in Prague and asked him to contribute money. Lang answered affirmatively, in German.[29] Far from severing his ties with German literature, in 1935 Lang was still buying a number of German language publications from the Amsterdam-based refugee press, Querido Verlag. In particular, Lang ordered Stephen Zweig's *Erziehung von Verdun* and Wilhelm Speyer's *Der Hof der schönen Mädchen.*[30] In Santa Monica, he corresponded with Reinhard Braun, a "former editor of Querschnitt" who was able to find him several volumes by refugee authors.[31] In 1937, he was subscribing to *Volksecho* and to *PEM.*[32] As he settled down in Hollywood, Lang—like the Hollywood New Yorkers—attempted to maintain an allegiance to both local and national as well as transnational networks. Until 1936, his circle of friends largely consisted of other Europeans such as Marlene Dietrich, Peter Lorre, and Lili Latté with whom he often corresponded in German.[33] English, however, marked Lang's public and professional correspondence. But after 1936, his correspondence shows that his private world was increasingly open to an interaction with Hollywood and the American national scene.

Opposition to Nazism defined the refugee network, but it also supplied Lang with a new sense of purpose that connected him with American progressives in Hollywood. In 1936, Lang had a significant correspondence with Los Angeles progressive lawyer Charles Katz; Hollywood New Yorkers such as Dorothy Parker, Hy Kraft, and Humphrey Cobb, all active members of the Hollywood Anti-Nazi League; and with members of the New York leftist intelligentsia such as Irving Lerner and Vera Caspary.[34] By 1937, Lang contributed to many progressive and radical organizations, both American *and* European: the American League against War and Fascism, the American Committee for Anti-Nazi Literature, the Deutsch-amerikanischer Kultur-verbund, and the Associated Film Audience.[35]

As an intellectual, Lang shared with Hollywood New Yorkers an attraction to New York, but this did not conflict with his decision to work in Hollywood. During a visit to New York in January 1937, Lang wrote to his friend Hy Kraft, who had moved to Hollywood a few years earlier: "I am really in love with New York and I understand your nostalgia and your longing." In New York, Lang often went to the theater and

saw both mainstream and off-Broadway productions such as "*Stagedoor*
(lausy [*sic*] the shame of a nation), [John] Gielgud's *Hamlet* (interesting),
Dead End (excellent), and some federal theater plays (very interesting and
seditious)."[36] During that visit Lang met the radical filmmakers active in
New York Frontier Films. In particular, Lang was impressed by Irving
Lerner. Correspondence between the Hollywood director and the New
York avant-garde group member shows how in the 1930s these two worlds
were still close. By March 1937, the friendship between the two men
had become so intense that Lerner wrote Lang that his wife seemed
"to be a little suspicious of our (ahem) relationship."[37] The following
month, Lerner asked Lang to contribute a statement for Paul Strand's
upcoming book; Lang promptly complied.[38] A notoriously haughty man,
Lang sounds appreciative and friendly in his correspondence with Lerner,
who often seemed to be Lang's intellectual guide to America, advising
the director on what to see on the New York stage and which books to
buy. In April 1937, the young filmmaker asked Lang whether "you are
still interested in America. If you are, you should get hold of *Middletown*
by Robert and Helen Lynd." This book, and its companion, *Middletown
in Transition*, "are great and much better than, let us say, the Herbert
Agar book you bought."[39] By August 1937, Lerner and Frontier Films
were so in awe of Lang's work that they asked him to direct their most
financially ambitious project. Sending the script of *Pay Day*, Lerner wrote
to Lang that

> there is a purpose in sending you this script . . . *not* to ask for money! but
> something even more daring. All of us feel that the script, the story, has swell
> possibilities. This first production is a crucial one, not only for Frontier, but
> for the entire progressive and independent movie movement in America.
> And because of that, because it is so important, I am asking you if you would
> consider (providing you are free) directing it.[40]

Lang had just signed a two-year contract with MGM and could not accept
the proposal. He wrote to Lerner, however, that he hoped "that I can be
of some value."[41]

   Lang repeatedly invited Lerner to Hollywood. Lerner was eager to
come, but his wife was sick and his financial situation was difficult. If he
was to come west for some significant period of time, he needed a little
job, preferably on the set of Lang's film. Lang promptly responded that
"I will really get behind this business. . . . I too have cherished for a long
time the idea that you would come out."[42] At the beginning of 1938,
Lerner came to Hollywood and briefly worked on the set of Lang's film

You and Me. From Hollywood, he wrote an enthusiastic letter to his friend Jay Leyda, which again shows New Yorkers' fascination with Hollywood:

> I am certainly learning a great deal about commercial film production[,] and there was certainly a great deal for us to learn[,] especially in the mechanism of getting a motion picture made. I've only been on the set for three days but I have witnessed all kinds of tricky "set ups" and how they were solved.[43]

It was not a one-way relationship. By May 1936, Ralph Steiner and Elia Kazan were in the South to begin a film about "the mountain people of Tennessee."[44] At the same time Lang was tinkering with the idea of making a film about Southern sharecroppers.[45] Along with Charles Katz, a progressive L.A. lawyer, in January 1937 Lang collected articles on Southern sharecroppers and was considering possible writers for the film. Katz advised Lang to read a "tobacco auction story" in *New Masses* and suggested Paul Green, a Group Theater associate, as a writer for the film.[46] During a visit to New York in March 1937, the director met James Agee and discussed the sharecropper project. Agee offered his help and even gave Lang "the Cotton Tenant manuscript," the draft of his *Fortune* essay on the Alabama sharecroppers.[47] In April 1937, Lang began to work on *You and Me* and decided to postpone the sharecropper project, although he remained interested in it.[48] By September 1937, he was still ordering books such as Charlie May Simon's *The Share Cropper.*[49]

As the refugees settled in, many of them began to interact regularly with other Hollywoodians. Salka Viertel was a close friend of a progressive writer from New York, Sam Behrman. Behrman remembers that in 1933 Greta Garbo and Viertel would often drop by his house and, in 1965, he lovingly defined Viertel as "the greatest salonnière of modern times."[50] By 1936, Donald Ogden Stewart noted in his autobiography, Viertel salon's had outgrown its refugee-only status and turned into what he calls "a rallying point for all rebels."[51] In her autobiography, Viertel remembers how the refugees began slowly to get involved with local and national politics. By 1936 refugees were discussing the outcome of the 1936 presidential elections. By 1940, Hollywood Europeans such as Billy Wilder, Fritz Lang, and Michael Curtiz were signing appeals for Roosevelt's reelection.[52]

The Hollywood Anti-Nazi League

By the beginning of 1936, the world was becoming aware of Hitler's menace. In January 1935, the German army entered the Saar, a move made even more disturbing because of the acquiescence of the local population. In March 1936, Hitler's army invaded the Rhineland, de facto voiding the Locarno Treaty. Confronted with German aggression and the appeasement policies of the Western powers, American radicals and Hollywood Europeans found a common terrain in denouncing Hitler's regime. Leo Hurwitz stated that "radical political thinking became international. The events at home and the events of the world were clearly interrelated."[53]

Most Hollywood New Yorkers and Hollywood Europeans were anti-Nazi, but they were far from agreement on a strategy to fight the rise of fascist dictatorship. Active participants in the peace movement of the 1930s, many Hollywood New Yorkers vehemently distrusted military solutions and identified with the position of *New Theater*'s "Anti War" issue of April 1935, whose cover pictured a skeleton in a Nazi uniform wielding a camera.[54] World War I had brought curtailment of civil liberties on American soil, which should be avoided, but how to fight Hitler without engaging in war?[55]

In March 1936, twelve hundred members of the Hollywood community gathered at the Hollywood Women's Club to listen to Frederic March and his wife, actress Florence Eldridge, along with director John Cromwell reading from Irwin Shaw's *Bury the Dead* as a benefit for the Los Angeles Contemporary Theater's forthcoming production of the play. The meeting was chaired by Donald Ogden Stewart, and Hollywood New Yorkers and Hollywood Europeans—such as James Cagney and Francis Lederer—appeared as featured speakers. After the discussion, refugees and progressives discussed the possibilities of giving their political commitment a concrete, professional outlet. For refugee Francis Lederer, the antiwar theme of the play was problematic. Screenwriter Dudley Nichols argued that he was against the war but that he was no pacifist, especially given the present international situation. Actor Lionel Stander expressed the feelings of many Hollywood progressives when he declared, "I am against the war—I know it's insane—but what can I do about it?"[56] In subsequent years, Hollywood participants found a possible answer: take over the camera and use it against the Nazis. War encouraged authoritarian policies and placed the fascist marionettes behind the camera. The only way out was to confront fascism with a common front, impose political and economical sanctions on fascist and Nazi aggression, and be ready to implement any measure short of war. A democratic mass cinema could be instrumental in mobilizing public opinion and taking a strong stand against fascism.

New organizations sprang into life to join the struggle, notably in 1937 the Motion Picture Artists Committee for Loyalist Spain and in 1938 the Motion Picture Democratic Committee. But none came close to HANL for influence, membership, and capacity to radically change the Hollywood cultural and political landscape. In the 1940s, the FBI noted that the HANL "appealed to the large Jewish population in Southern California on the basis of fighting Hitlerism and drew great financial support from the producers of motion pictures on that program. . . . Its membership at the peak of its influence was approximately four thousand. Its influence spread to many times that number."[57]

The founding of HANL was spearheaded by two German refugees: Catholic anti-Nazi leader Prince Hubertus zu Löwenstein and Otto Katz. Löwenstein had come to the United States in February 1936 to gather support for the anti-Nazi cause. Willy Münzenberg, the unorthodox member of the German Communist Party (KPD) and cultural organizer, advised Löwenstein to get in touch with his friend Otto Katz, known in Hollywood as Rudolf Breda, or André Simon. Immensely likable, Katz was later the model for Lillian Hellman's Kurt Müller, the anti-Nazi character of *Watch on the Rhine*.[58] He was the perfect choice for a Hollywood fund raiser. A man of the theater, he had been an assistant of Erwin Piscator. A communist, Katz shared with his friend Paul Merker a particular sensitivity to the connection between Nazism and anti-Semitism, something unusual for the KPD, which tended to downplay the issue.[59] When Löwenstein arrived in Los Angeles, Katz "brought me immediately in touch with all the important personalities: Charles Chaplin, Fritz Lang, Clark Gable, Marlene Dietrich, David Selznick, Ernst Lubitsch, Norma Shearer, Greta Garbo, in addition to A. H. Giannini . . . [and] the archbishop of Los Angeles, John Joseph Cantwell."[60] HANL was officially launched at a banquet at the Victor Hugo restaurant in Hollywood. During the ceremony, Löwenstein gave a stirring speech and Katz demonstrated his outstanding public relations skills: a Jew and a communist, he demanded to kiss the ring of the L.A. archbishop. The next day, a confused press referred to him as Father Breda.[61]

HANL's activities soon attracted the extensive participation of German anti-Nazi refugees such as Ernst Lubitsch, one of the organization's sponsors. By May 1936, Lang was soliciting a donation for the "Löwenstein Fund" from his friend, agent Paul Kohner.[62] In April 1937, Donald Ogden Stewart, chairman of HANL, counted the director among the "the most loyal and interested friends."[63] Social networking, previously confined to private parties, now became political. In October, German screenwriter Thilde Forster wrote Lang that

> I hope that we shall renew our European acquaintance through the Hollywood anti-Nazi League, in which I am since a few weeks very actively interested. I was pleased to learn through several friends that you are working in this direction.[64]

Stewart recognized the strong participation of the Europeans in HANL. In his speech at the celebration of the organization's first anniversary, he jokingly addressed the heavily German audience as "Herren und Damen."[65]

The pages of *Hollywood Now*, the organ of HANL, frequently contained reports about the fate of anti-Nazi refugees and the situation they faced in their new homeland.[66] In one year's time HANL had become so central to the refugee community that its fame reached the East Coast, spurring Ludwig Roemer, the New York editor of the anti-Nazi *Die Clubszeitung des Deutschen Arbeiterclubs*, to send orchids to the editorial board praising *Hollywood Now*, HANL's publication, as a "splendid paper which I enjoyed very much."[67]

HANL combined the anti-fascist struggle with a practical adherence to the social rituals of the film colony. Parties and social gatherings were central to its activities. In many cases, the organization politicized the traditional hangouts of the Hollywood New Yorkers and the salons of the refugees. Anti-Nazi filmmakers often gathered for cocktails at Stanley Rose's Bookstore on Hollywood Boulevard. Salka Viertel's salon was often used for fund-raising events or for showing films such as Joris Ivens's *The Spanish Earth*. "The Popular front," Viertel recalled, "extended into my family."[68]

At HANL's first anniversary celebration, European anti-fascists such as Salka Viertel and Ernst Toller mingled with communists John Bright and Lionel Stander; Hollywood liberals Mervyn LeRoy, Chico Marx, F. Scott Fitzgerald, and Carey McWilliams; and industry notables Harry Warner, Joe Mankiewicz, and Joe Breen. After listening to chairman Stewart's speech about the European situation, American anti-Nazis and refugees danced, enjoyed the singing of Judy Garland, and—of course—talked movie business.[69] Lang, who was unable to come, contributed fifty dollars to the event.[70]

Whenever possible, HANL made sure that such activities took place in Hollywood's public spaces. Thanks to Donald Ogden Stewart's efforts, common citizens, usually not invited to Viertel's parties, could now see Ivens's *Spanish Earth* at the Roosevelt Hotel on Hollywood Boulevard.[71] By 1938, HANL had been so successful in establishing Hollywood's public life that the members' general assembly refused to change the organization's name to National Anti-Nazi League. "The name 'Hollywood' not merely describes the location of the main office of the league, but has prestige and great significance throughout the world."[72]

The purpose of HANL remained, however, to "produc[e] such creative works as will most widely spread strong sentiments against Nazism," and thus the enlistment of Hollywood in the democratic struggle remained crucial.[73] Anti-Nazi films had been produced before by small independent firms, or as low-budget B and C productions.[74] At first, HANL organized its own film production activities and, on May 30, 1937, *News Of the World* (*NOW*) announced that "a Film Project Committee" had been set up to produce a documentary film entitled "Hitler over the World."[75] But from its inception, HANL had been aware that the medium of the radical documentary, though part of the intellectual baggage of some of its members, was not likely to reach the mass constituency that the organization envisioned for the anti-Nazi struggle. As Archibald MacLeish noted in 1937, even the most powerful documentaries in the United States were "apt to begin life in a smallish radical or art theater and end in a lecture hall."[76] HANL strove to reconcile what up until that time had been considered opposites: anti-Nazi struggle and Hollywood. "If the motion picture industry could be induced to embrace the cause of anti-Nazism," wrote Löwenstein, "this would mean an important boost to our efforts."[77] Only a few months after its founding, George Oppenheimer, the chairman of HANL's membership committee, wrote that it was his intention to plan "an intense campaign to enlist studio employees to join the HANL."[78]

It was not an easy task. Hollywood's top producers were undoubtedly committed to the idea that a money-making film was a good film, regardless of its position toward Hitler. Furthermore, the notion of cinema as entertainment had been inscribed in the preamble to the 1930 code that was made compulsory by the creation of the Production Code Administration in 1934.[79] Producers were also aware that the possible loss of Germany, and German-dominated markets, would have been exceedingly painful, and they had often gone a long way to please Hitler's censors.[80] In this situation, HANL castigated those producers who were ready to negotiate with Hitler, encouraged those producers willing to make bolder pictures, and created opportunities for all the potential "players" to meet and discuss the issue. *NOW* praised Walter Wanger, the producer of the pro-Loyalist *Blockade*, for making an "emotionally stirring" movie about the Spanish Civil War, while it censured "the willingness of the industry to kiss the mat" when Fox sought Consul Gyssling's approval for *The Road Back*, when MGM muted the anti-Nazi theme in *Three Comrades*, and when the studios dropped the film version of Sinclair Lewis's *It Can't Happen Here*.[81]

HANL was also trying to make the Hollywood film more responsive to the issues of the day, while maintaining its ability to engage the masses. Thus, rather than proposing a radical change in the narrative structure of the Hollywood film, members called for an approach that allowed for the hybridization of different political and esthetic agendas. The Hollywood narrative mechanism had the advantage of reaching the millions—the value of Wanger's *Blockade* was its popularity, which was, in turn, predicated upon its staying close to the Hollywood formula. The *NOW* reviewer had some reservations about the movie: "From the standpoint of its dramatic action, [*Blockade*] has much in common with the traditional romantic spy melodrama."[82] But Hollywood narrative techniques gave the film a propaganda value "so emotionally stirring that if only a collection box could be taken, after every performance, enough money would be handed in for us to buy up Franco outright and send him as a present to Hitler."[83] What HANL advocated was for Hollywood to expand its narrow conception of film as entertainment into a broader one in which Hollywood films would become active participants in the political sphere. To do so, Hollywood had to become more and more "public," making "pictures," the reviewer of *Three Comrades* noted, "that are about things that are really happening, pictures with meaning."[84]

The Self-Figuration of the Hollywood Progressives

William Dieterle's "biopics" of European intellectuals such as Louis Pasteur, Émile Zola, Benito Juarez, and Paul Ehrlich are a prime example of how the anti-Nazi theme went from the margins to the center of American cinematic discourse. They also show the intensified collaboration between Hollywood New Yorkers and Hollywood Europeans who were finding a common terrain across the boundaries of the "metropolitan taste" and the *papier mâché* of the previous years. Dieterle's films involved many Hollywood progressives, including Sheridan Gibney, John Huston, Sig

Herzig, Edward G. Robinson, and Paul Muni, along with such Hollywood Europeans as Henry Blanke, Heinz Herald, Rudy Fehr, and Wolfgang Reinhardt.[85]

Very popular in the 1930s, these films have attracted only scant attention from scholars.[86] In a most intriguing essay, Thomas Elsaesser has built on Bertolt Brecht's definition of the films as "gallery of bourgeois figures" to argue that "the hero's struggle" in the film conceals "a figuration of Dieterle himself in his struggle with the studio system."[87] While Elsaesser's interpretation is stimulating, it does not entirely do justice to the social and political context of the contemporary Hollywood community. As the decade wore on, Dieterle's biopics became much sought-after projects for many Hollywoodians. Anti-fascist writers lined up to propose their favorite subject for the next biopic. Before leaving for New York in April 1939, Manfred George proposed to Dieterle a biopic of "Marie Tussaud," the founder of the famous wax museum in London and a refugee from the French Revolution's Terror.[88] Long after the genre had lost its steam, Max Horkheimer wrote Fritz Lang to inquire about the possibility of a biopic on Thomas More because of the man's legacy as an opposition leader.[89]

As soon as the word spread that another Dieterle's biopic was in the making, refugees and Hollywood progressives clamored to get a job on the film. When Edward G. Robinson hesitated about doing one more gangster picture, Warner producer Hal Wallis reminded him that "I also definitely recall your promises and assurances to me that if I would produce *Dr. Ehrlich* as your first picture, you would be willing to do any other property I might select as the basis of your second picture."[90]

Such enthusiasm had something to do with Dieterle's prestige, his staunch anti-Nazism, and his relentless activity in favor of destitute refugees. By the time he made *Pasteur*, Dieterle was at the core of the Hollywood intellectual community, a *trait d'union* between the Hollywood progressives and the Hollywood Europeans. Though the director was never a member of the party, a 1943 FBI report on the film colony cited the testimony of Ivan Cox, a former Communist Party member, who identified Dieterle as "a follower of the Communist Party Line."[91] By 1936, he and his wife were helping European refugees with an array of initiatives, often using Dieterle's position to promote the career of fellow Europeans. During the making of *Pasteur*, the first of his biographies, Dieterle's wife Charlotte offered Blanke some drawings by a refugee as a prop for the film.[92] During the filming of *Juarez*, studio officials complained that Dieterle had given last minute bit parts to refugee actors, and that he continuously invited students of Max Reinhardt's drama workshop onto the set.[93]

In the eyes of many Hollywoodians, the value of biopics was their esthetic and political value. As mass-marketed products dealing with cultural matters within the frame of a feature film, they well embodied that mixture of high and low that was, for many artists, Hollywood's most enticing promise.[94] The public responded to this aspect. When the story of Paul Ehrlich, the German Jewish scientist who discovered a cure for syphilis, came out, Robinson's mail included numerous letters from doctors congratulating Robinson for making science accessible to the public, some of them even suggesting that the film should be used in county hospitals for "mass public instruction."[95] Such a democratic notion of art also had political meaning. Several of Dieterle's biopics chose as their subject matter illustrious men whose lives could be easily endowed with an explicit, political sense. The ultimate hybridization,[96] these films represented women and men attempting to communicate a cultural and/or political message to highbrow and lowbrow audiences. To paraphrase Leo Lowenthal's famous definition, many of the heroes of the biopics were first and foremost "idols of cultural communication."[97] Finally, they accounted for more than the director's or, for that matter, the star's ambitions. For Hollywood participants such as Dieterle, Paul Muni, Edward G. Robinson, John Huston, or Wolfgang Reinhardt, these biopics offered the opportunity to test the limits of their dreams. The result was more "a figuration of Hollywood progressives' struggle with the studio system" than of Dieterle's personal quarrels. Rather than a person's biography, these films resembled a collective hagiography of the Hollywood progressive.

The impact of Dieterle on the script of *Pasteur* (WB, 1936) was not significant. After a series of genre films and his experience as Max Reinhardt's assistant in the shooting of *Midsummer Night's Dream* (WB, 1935), Dieterle was a respected director but no star.[98] Studio records show that Dieterle became involved with the project quite late. The shooting for *Dr. Socrates* ended on July 15, 1935, and *Pasteur*'s shooting was scheduled to begin in early August.[99] When Dieterle joined the project in mid-July, the script for the film was all but complete, though the producers allowed for some "slight changes that Dieterle and Muni might have to suggest."[100] And Dieterle wasn't the first choice. By the time he and Muni joined the company, the studio had already sounded out both

French-born director Robert Florey and Hungarian director Michael Curtiz, choosing Dieterle only because Florey had declined and Curtiz was busy with other projects.[101] The film had already been rewritten twice. Pierre Collings wrote the first version with Ed Chodorov's supervision (January 24, 1935), and Sheridan Gibney wrote the second and final version (July 22, 1935). "The slight changes" that Dieterle or Muni wanted must not have amounted to much, as the July 22 script does not reveal any major differences from the one completed on June 20, before they joined the film. Gibney had the film begin with the murder of a doctor at the hands of a husband whose wife had died of an infection after giving birth. Otherwise, the final version was close enough to the first. It depicted Pasteur's struggle against ignorance—personified by Dr. Charbonnet—and the scientist's final triumph as Pasteur was inducted into the French Academy. Both writers were given equal screenplay credit.

Begun as a side project—designed to keep Muni happy and budgeted as a cheap "A picture" for $300,000—*Pasteur* was nonetheless a success. Nominated for ten Academy Awards, the film won Oscars for best actor (Paul Muni), best script, and best original story (Sheridan Gibney and Paul Collings). Progressive magazines were also moderately impressed. Irving Lerner in *New Masses* acknowledged Dieterle's good intentions and called the film a "step forward," though Lerner recognized that the progressive message was still playing the junior role in its partnership with the Hollywood narrative mechanism. Mark Van Doren in *The Nation* appreciated the film, though he accused *Pasteur* of "romancing about science."[102]

The popular success of *Pasteur* made Dieterle a Hollywood "player" and gave him more control over his next projects. According to Marta Mierendorff, the idea for *Zola* originated in the refugee circles. Refugee writers Heinz Herald and Geza Erczeg wrote a ten-page outline for a film based on the life of the French writer and showed it to Ernst Lubitsch. Lubitsch told them to contact Henry Blanke at Warner who assigned them to write the script along with Hollywood New Yorker Norman Reilly Raine.[103] Worried by the activities of so many anti-Nazis, the German consul in Los Angeles phoned Blanke early in February to ask about the film.[104] The subject of the film was in perfect tune with Hollywood's new progressive climate. For starters, Zola was the model of many Hollywood progressives both for his role as a public intellectual and his naturalistic style. "Zola's *Germinal* was the book I admired most in those years," Elia Kazan wrote in his autobiography.[105]

Matthew Josephson had written an influential biography of the novelist, *Zola and His Times*, which was one of the sources for the script. For the German refugees, Zola was also a crucial political symbol, appropriated by the Left since the early years of the Weimar Republic because of his stance on anti-Semitism and his rejection of the siren of nationalism.[106] Soon after being assigned to the project, Heinz Herald asked the Warner research department for a copy of the famous essay by Heinrich Mann about Émile Zola."[107]

The story file for the film shows that the writers drew on a variety of sources, including Mann's essay; Josephson's novel; Henri Barbusse's *Zola*; *L'Affaire Dreyfus* by Hans J. Rehfisch and Wilhelm Herzog; and the 1930 film by refugee Richard Oswald, *Dreyfus* (Süd Film A.G.).[108] Like Oswald's *Dreyfus*, and unlike *L'Affaire Dreyfus* that focuses exclusively on the actions of the French writer, Dieterle's *Zola* features Captain Alfred Dreyfus (played by Joseph Schildkraut). Yet the director enlarged the scope of the film to more than an account of the trial. Zola's decision to write on behalf of Dreyfus remained at the center, but *Zola* encompassed the whole life of the French novelist. As a vehement attack on the arrogance of the military and the aristocracy, *Zola* worked. The film showed the French military's hatred for Zola after he published *La débâcle* and their machinations to protect the aristocratic Count Esterhazy and blame Dreyfus. *New Masses* appreciated the anti-militarism of the film and hoped it would be a trend setter. *New Republic* thought that it was "one more mature job Hollywood has turned out pretty much against the best expectations."[109]

Studio policies remained, however, a creative factor in *Zola*'s making. Pursuing assimilation into the Protestant elite, studio moguls were in fact quite timid about their ethnic origins.[110] By mid-February, Herald's and Raine's script did not veil Dreyfus's ethnicity. But on February 11, Jack Warner, a Polish-born Jew, ordered all references to Dreyfus's Jewish origin expunged from the script.[111] Dieterle and the writers made do. While Major Henry (played by Robert Warwick) reads Dreyfus's file, Dieterle has the camera skillfully panning over the file, which lists the captain as a "Jew."[112]

But *Zola* is also constructed as a vindication of the progressive Hollywoodian as a public intellectual. Perhaps the focus on Zola downplays Dreyfus, but it certainly exalts the public role of Zola, the committed writer of realistic novels. Like the progressive Hollywood camera, Zola's role is to register the truth and record it in a dramatic form for the public to see. Zola is neither an "idol of consumption" nor an "idol of production," but first and foremost an idol of cultural and political communication. Obsessively throughout the first third of the film, Zola mutters the word "truth" as he roams the streets of Paris in search of "reality." His quest acquires a visual dimension through the character of Cézanne, whom the film—contrary to historical evidence—envisions as a Dreyfusard. The relationship between the artists appears to be symbiotic, with Zola borrowing Cézanne's sketches of a young prostitute to draw upon for inspiration for his novel *Nana*.[113] *Zola* constructs a visually compelling narrative of the writer's popularity. In a powerful visualization of mass culture, huge heaps of Zola's novel *Nana* are exhibited and sold to the eager public. Dieterle's camera underlines the success of Zola's "J'accuse" by showing its capacity to reach the masses across class lines. When the author reads it aloud in the offices of Georges Clemenceau, the publisher of *L'Aurore*, the typographers stop working and listen, along with the other editors of the newspaper and Zola's friends. The camera then cuts to a linotype printing a large edition of *L'Aurore*. It is quite clear that Zola does not write for himself or for art's sake. In one of the first scenes of the film, the novelist destroys his "artsy" experiment. Like Hollywood progressive films, his works are predicated upon mass readership. They actually do not have any existence outside of the public sphere and intellectual consumption.

After *Zola*'s and *Pasteur*'s resounding success, Dieterle participated in the production of *Juarez* (WB, 1939) from the script conference stage. The film production came at a time when HANL was at the height of its influence, organizing boycotts against the visits to Hollywood studios by Vittorio Mussolini and Leni Riefenstahl.[114] Paul J. Vanderwood has analyzed how Dieterle's *Juarez* fits in with Warner Bros.' close relationship with New Deal politics. The story of Benito Juarez offered a cinematic endorsement of Roosevelt's Good Neighbor Policy by highlighting the work and dignity of a progressive Mexican statesman. Juarez, the legally elected president of the Mexican Republic, had been overthrown by Maximilian of Hapsburg with the aid of Napoleon III and had regained power by tenacity, grit, and popular support.[115]

Vanderwood, however, does not take into account the political history of Hollywood and how it marked the making of the film. Relying on John Huston's autobiography, Vanderwood downplays the conflicts between Aeneas McKenzie, the writer originally assigned to the film, and John Huston and Wolfgang Reinhardt, who, along with Abem Finkel, were assigned to rewrite the script. Reinhardt and Huston, for example, by no means "assist[ed]" McKenzie." Commenting on McKenzie's treatment, Reinhardt, the son of the great Viennese stage director, wrote—in German—to producer Henry Blanke that McKenzie had missed the point entirely. McKenzie had supplied "a historical tract but no film." The real point of the film was to highlight "the analogy between those times and the events of today in a dramatic, entertaining way." [116]

The success of the film as a democratic statement was of no small importance for Reinhardt, Dieterle, and Huston. As the international situation worsened, Hollywood Europeans and Hollywood New Yorkers were asked to "deliver the goods." Both the refugee and the American Left networks might have entertained some doubts about their capacity to bend Hollywood to anti-fascism after the incomplete successes of *Pasteur* and *Zola*. When Muni demanded more lines for himself, Reinhardt wrote to Blanke in desperation: the changes were bound to "turn this wonderful script into shit" and to confirm the "attitude in which most Europeans in New York have fallen, which comes to the sentence 'in [Hollywood] films only rubbish is to be found.'" [117] This sense of urgency is evident in many of the conversations surrounding the production of these films. Reinhardt wrote Blanke about the necessity to make the message of *Juarez* so clear that "every child must recognize that Napoleon with his Mexican intervention is no one else than Mussolini and Hitler and their adventure in Spain." [118] Dieterle asked his assistant Al Allenborn to find "some long shots of masses of people presumably listening to a speech being made by a dictator, such as shown in newsreels of Mussolini or Hitler talking." [119] As rewritten by Huston and Reinhardt, the script was both a strong anti-fascist metaphor and a modification of the Hollywood narrative, insofar as it had no defined protagonist, with the characters of Juarez, Maximilian, Carlotta, and Porfirio Diaz all competing for the spectator's attention.

With *Juarez*, what was at stake was not merely the fashioning of a strong indictment of fascism, but the vindication of those refugees and progressives who had accepted the challenge of working in Hollywood. As soon as news of Warner's plan for the production of *Juarez* spread into the community, several progressive actors mobilized to have a role in the film. Fredric March was "definitely interested in *Maximilian and Juarez* on the basis of this script"; Francis Lederer lobbied Wallis to obtain the role of Maximilian; Edward G. Robinson sounded interested; and Melvyn Douglas was "so anxious to do it" that he was willing to plead with MGM producer Eddie Mannix to be loaned to Warner Bros. for the film as "a personal favor." [120] Refugees also tried to obtain a job on the picture, appealing directly to Henry Blanke or William Dieterle. [121] Eventually, the film, from the novel *Juarez und Maximilian* by Franz Werfel, was edited by Rudy Fehr, soundtracked by Erich Korngold, produced by Henry Blanke, and interpreted by Bette Davis, John Garfield, Paul Muni, Gale Sondergaard, Walter Fenner, Walter O. Stahl, Vladimir Sokoloff, and Claude Rains.

The eighth top grossing film in 1939, and among *Film Daily*'s "Best Ten List" with a budget of $1.75 million, *Juarez* moved anti-fascism into the center of Hollywood cinematic discourse. [122] Vanderwood is correct in arguing that the film fit the New Deal discourse about the Good Neighbor Policy toward Latin America as well as Roosevelt's increasing wariness of Nazi expansionism. But the film also consistently endorsed the radical margins of such discourse. If audiences missed the parallel between Napoleon and Hitler, and between Mexico and Spain, some of the ads for the film reminded them that "it is hardly necessary to draw attention to the points of comparison in the Mexican situation . . . and the situations which have been created since 1930 in various parts of the world." [123] The film was also ahead of the contemporary American racial discourse. A first-rate Hollywood star (Paul Muni) was interpreting a Zapotec, Native-American hero. Even radical Mexican president Lazaro Cardenas is said to have enjoyed the film. The movie also won accolades from both the mainstream press and radical and intellectual journals. *New Masses* called it one of "Hollywood's grandest films"—*Juarez* had finally been able to combine the popular appeal of the Hollywood narrative with an uncompromising endorsement of the democratic and anti-Nazi struggle, a "great social use" of cinematic power. *The Nation* also recognized the movie as "an immense step forward" and "the latest offering of a new and ambitious Hollywood" in conscious opposition to "entertainment pictures." It was, Frank Hoelleinger concluded, indeed an expression of the "seriously working part of Hollywood." [124]

Confessions of a Nazi Spy

Regardless of its popular success, however, *Juarez* remained a masquerade, with Hitler behind the mask of Napoleon III. The experiment was bold but offered only a partial solution. [125] By their nature, metaphors referred to a metatextual system of innuendoes external to the plot, requiring an "intended reader" to recognize and interpret them.[126] Direct address to the general public, and outright modification of the Hollywood text, was what refugees and Hollywood New Yorkers advocated. In *Confessions of a Nazi Spy*, the denunciation of Nazism was going to be inscribed into a profound modification of the Hollywood formula.

At the beginning of 1938, HANL's intense lobbying seemed to bear some fruit. *NOW* announced that Harry Warner had declared "his intention of making important social pictures to combat Fascism."[127] The publicity that the American press gave the 1938 trials of several Nazi spies connected with the New York chapter of the German-American Bund also helped HANL's demands for an outspoken anti-Nazi film. The final result of a two-year FBI investigation, the trials exposed the activities of a relatively widespread spy ring. The mastermind of the ring was Dr. Ignatz Griebl, a prominent member of the German-American Bund, who, with the help of the Gestapo, had convinced a handful of German-American citizens to pass classified information to the German government. In the months immediately preceding the trials, FBI director J. Edgar Hoover had planned to go public on the issue and reap the windfall in public recognition, only to be preempted by one of the agents assigned to the case, Leon G. Turrou. Turrou had sold the scoop to the New York *Post* for $25,000 before the case was actually ready. Hoover dismissed the agent "with prejudice" for breaking the so-called "G-man oath" that prohibited agents from divulging the results of investigations. The state attorney in charge of the case, Lamar Hardy, enjoined the *Post* from publishing the exposé.[128] In mid-October 1938, as the trials began in the federal court in New York, the story made front-page headlines nationwide.

A film based on the trials could build on an established tradition of topical films and on the popular interest in the trials.[129] The probable sanction of a verdict issued by a federal court was going to protect the studio from Germany's attempts to stop the production of the film. In November 1938, Warner Bros. bought from Turrou the rights for a film to be made out of his installments (which the *Post* published after the end of the trial, from December 4, 1938, to January 4, 1939). The studio also hired him as technical advisor for the film.[130] No sooner had Warner announced plans for the film than members of HANL started petitioning Hal Wallis, the central producer of Warner, for parts in the movie. Edward G. Robinson, a HANL member and one of the top stars at Warner, openly hinted that his participation in the upcoming gangster film *Brother Orchid* was predicated on Wallis's willingness to let him do *Confessions*. "While on the subject of stories," he wrote to Wallis, "I want again to express a strong desire to appear in the International Spy Ring story you are going to do." Robinson was also willing to put his considerable reputation at stake in order to take part in the film. "You mentioned that the story might not be too good," he wrote Wallis, "but I see no reason why effort should not be expended to make it a knock-out of a story."[131] Similarly, Francis Lederer, a "passionately anti-German" Czech refugee, and a member of HANL on his way to relative stardom, had asked Wallis to be cast in the film.[132] Marlene Dietrich also begged Wallis for the modest and relatively unappealing role of a German hairdresser moonlighting for the Gestapo, making it clear that "money is no object."[133]

The refugee network mobilized most impressively for an opportunity to work on the picture. In 1941, Hedda Hopper remembered that "scores of actors, the great majority of them natives of Germany, clamored to have a role in the film."[134] Political consideration was mixed with economic and personal ones, since many recently arrived filmmakers were striving to get their first job in the film industry and the numerous accent roles that the film promised might indeed constitute an opportunity. For some refugees, a job in the film industry meant the possibility of using Warner's considerable leverage in Washington to rescue some family member locked in Europe by the perversely strict American immigration laws. Wolfgang Zilzer (a.k.a. Paul Andor, John Voight) asked Wallis's assistant secretary, Steven Trilling, to recommend his parents to the American consul general in Berlin so that they "may enjoy the privilege of coming into the United States under quota."[135]

Yet personal interest should not be unduly exaggerated at the expense of the evidence that points in many cases to a sincere obligation felt by refugees to participate in the project. Especially for those who still had relatives in Europe, participating in such a film was not devoid of personal risks. Steven Trilling, for instance, informed Wallis that Hedwiga Reicher, a German refugee actress scheduled to portray the wife of the leader of the Nazi front German-American organization, wanted to have her credit attributed to Mildred Embs since she "had near relatives living in Germany who [sic] she wanted to protect from Nazi retaliation."[136] According to the *California Jewish Voice*, eleven actors cast in minor roles had asked for heavy makeup and had chosen not to have their names listed in the credits.[137] The credits of *Confessions* testified to this mobilization for participation. Its stars, Robinson and Lederer, its director, the German-

Ukranian refugee Anatole Litvak, and one of its screenwriters, John Wexley, were active members of HANL, and at least twelve of the other actors listed in the film's credits were anti-Nazi refugees.[138]

Opening nationwide on May 8, 1939, *Confessions* was indeed a special film. No screen credits were given at the beginning, and immediately after the Warner logo, the movie introduced the audience to the silhouette of a radio commentator who summarized the outcome of the trials. Not revealing the names of its stars and the roles they played, *Confessions* disguised its nature as a feature film, blurring the line between fiction and authentic news.[139] Only chance prevented the masquerade from becoming complete: Litvak originally wanted Westbrook Vorhees, the voice of the *March of Time* newsreels, to deliver the opening lines, but the well-known commentator was unavailable.[140]

Many reviewers stressed the documentary effect of the film. *Variety* called *Confessions* "a frontal attack, using names and actual incidents and carrying an editorial commentator as if it were a newsreel expanded to narrative length."[141] In at least four different places, the narrative was interrupted to show documentary images of Nazi military parades, of the 1937 Congress of Germans Living Abroad, of the Anschluss, and of the German invasion of the Sudetenland. The filmmakers also modified the traditional protagonist-driven narrative of American classical cinema. Robinson, the star of the film, does not appear until halfway into the picture, when the FBI is informed by the British Secret Service that an apprehended German agent has been in contact with Kurt Schneider (played by Francis Lederer), a German-American and former U.S. soldier. Prior to Robinson's entrance on screen, the film stayed close to the facts that had emerged during the trials, as recounted by Turrou in his installments and in his book.[142]

A comparison between Turrou's accounts and the film highlights the filmmakers' manipulation of the Hollywood formula. Turrou tells the story from his point of view, introducing himself after a brief summation of the activities of Gunther Gustav Rumrich (renamed Kurt Schneider in the film) and recounting how he has become involved in the investigation. Afterward, the book becomes entirely Turrou's memoirs, describing the way he corners the spies, his thoughts, and even relationships with his family strained by the long hours Torrou devoted to the case. In placing the story in this narrative framework, Turrou was not only abiding by his own egotistic impulses, but also by the rule of the detective story and of its later subgenre, the G-man story that had become extremely popular during the 1930s, as material for both books and films.[143] G-man films and G-man true-story accounts, in fact, usually employ a similar structure that, to use Richard Gid Powers's useful analysis, includes "a villain vicious enough to be cast plausibly as a threat to the nation" and an "action hero who combined the customary savvy and strength of the traditional sleuth with a new crime-fighting style suited to the new style public enemy."[144]

The film *Confessions* hardly fits this narrative pattern, however. While the German spy ring is ominous enough to represent a sufficiently vicious villain, the figure of Renard is so downplayed both in the script (Robinson has less screen time than Francis Lederer, Paul Lukas, or George Sanders) and in Robinson's performance that it becomes strikingly different from the usual G-man "action hero." Turrou was slightly annoyed by the actor's rendition of himself. At the very least, he reportedly complained, Robinson should dress more lavishly: "I always change my clothes every day."[145] Reviewers of the film quickly picked up on this transformation of the usual G-man narrative. *Variety* noted in fact that the film "is a group's job. . . . Perhaps the smartest stint of the film director was the careful underplaying of Robinson as a G-man. This was devoid of nearly all the histrionics this actor usually employs."[146] The "underplaying of Robinson" marks the compromise that the makers of the film had been able to strike with the Hollywood classical narrative. While the film was a spy story, the unusually narrow breadth of Robinson's agent marked its debt to the tradition of radical theater and of the "Living Newspapers" and their emphasis on the collective rather than individual performance.[147]

At the same time, the makers of *Confessions* had also succeeded in making what the émigré magazine *Aufbau* termed "very strong anti-Nazi propaganda" and "America's first anti-Nazi film."[148] This achievement did not come easily. Warner's producers were quite afraid that too strong an anti-Nazi message would compromise the film's chance to receive the PCA seal of approval. In December 1938, Breen had written to Jack Warner trying to convince him to tone down the anti-German element of the script. "The material is technically within the provisions of the Production Code, but appears to be questionable from the standpoint of political censorship, both in this country and abroad." Fearing riots in their community, Breen continued, local censors were not likely "to approve a picture based on this material."[149] Hal Wallis had repeatedly complained to Robert Lord that "we are using too many pictures of Hitler in our picture. . . . Let's watch this and keep it out of sets, as I am afraid we are heaping it on too thick."[150] In particular, Wallis had told Lord to dissuade Litvak from shooting a series of fade-in/fade-outs, culminating in a swastika slowly filling the screen. The Nazi symbols, Wallis told his assistant, had to be used only "as they are necessary to the telling of the story and there is no obvious propaganda about them."[151]

The makers of *Confessions* did tone down the film's propaganda level. For instance, Litvak had planned a scene in which real footage of the Führer was projected on a backdrop while real actors appeared in the foreground.[152] This scene, however, was excised from the picture. Overall, though, refugees and Hollywood radicals held their ground against the producers' demands. The planned fade-in/fade-out made its way into the film, and images of Hitler haunt the screen from beginning to end.

As refugee and radical papers pointed out, refugees and Hollywood leftists had expanded the limits of Hollywood cinema. "Taken as pure cinema," commented *The Nation*, "*Confessions of a Nazi Spy* is first class . . . [and] is important for its theme, its style, and the advance it represents." Through them, the "strongest anti-Nazi propaganda" advocated by *Aufbau* had entered Hollywood. Some of the democratic modernist techniques of the "Living Newspapers" had transcended the Federal Theater's stages and partly informed a mass-marketed Hollywood product. The film "represent[ed] a vital technical contribution to the esthetics of the motion picture: the use of a new method of interweaving documentary and dramatic material," concluded *Film News*.[153] "The fruitful experiments of men like Joris Ivens and Herbert Kline, and neglected bands like Frontier Films, have at last reached Hollywood," noted *New Masses*. In a glowing front-page review, *NOW* also stressed that the makers of *Confessions* had "given this picture a new technique." The "newsreel effect" of *Confessions* had been enhanced as its makers "dramatized the protest of the American people" rather than celebrated individual heroism.[154]

"An Ignoble Experiment"

An outspoken anti-Nazi film, *Confessions* would have been unthinkable even a few months earlier. By 1938, Hollywood progressives and European refugees had reached some kind of "critical mass." While still employees of the studios, some of them—such as Henry Blanke, Dudley Nichols, Fredric March, Donald Ogden Stewart, Fritz Lang, William Dieterle, and Ernst Lubitsch—were in positions of power. Organizations such as HANL connected the isolated salons of the previous years, gave them a political purpose, and—more importantly—gave actors, writers, producers, Hollywood New Yorkers, and Hollywood Europeans an opportunity to meet and discuss projects and ideas. Hollywood had changed. HANL, the influx of the refugees, and the European news shaped Hollywood social life. "What was marvelous about Hollywood in the 1930s," Donald Ogden Stewart remembered, "was that the writers, and through the writers, the directors, and even some of the producers, did become politically conscious of what democracy really was. And we got it into our pictures."[155]

The development of the urban film also reflected this new sensitivity to social realism. The early urban gangsters might have been sociopaths, but the trendsetters among late 1930s gangster films—written predominantly by Hollywood New Yorkers—often situate the gangster in a harsh urban environment. "He is not at fault, it was the reformatory that ruined him," says Pat O'Brien of his childhood pal James Cagney in *Angels with Dirty Faces* (WB, 1938), a film directed by Michael Curtiz from a story by Rowland Brown, with a script by John Wexley and Warren Duff. For the spectator of the late 1930s, accustomed to making intertextual connections, the sentence struck a chord. In *Dead End* (Goldwyn, 1937) Dave (played by Joel McCrea) told the rich Griswald as much when the latter demanded that Tommy (one of the "dead end" kids) be sent to a juvenile prison. There was no craft to be learned in a reformatory: only the trade of crime that had eventually gotten Baby Face (played by Humphrey Bogart) killed. "Teach them a useful trade, does it? The man that got killed today came from this street, and from that reform school. It taught him a useful trade, all right."[156] McCrea was repeating the words of Group Theater associate Sidney Kingsley, translated for the screen by Lillian Hellman and William Wyler, via Greg Toland's camera work. And they were all repeating a concept contained in the script for *Mayor of Hell* (WB, 1933) by Hollywood New Yorker, and future blacklistee, Edward Chodorov.[157] Busby Berkeley's *They Made Me a Criminal* (WB, 1939) scripted by Sig Herzig, and *Boy Slaves* (RKO, 1939) directed by radical Hollywood New Yorker P. J. Wolfson and written by proletarian writer Albert Bein and Ben Orkow, repeated the idea: criminals are rarely born, they are often made.[158] *One Third of a Nation* was realized in the Paramount studios in Astoria for the Federal Theaters by a group of Hollywood New Yorkers that included actors Leif Erickson and Sylvia Sidney, director Dudley Murphy, and writer Oliver Garrett. In this film, the burbankization process was actually reversed.

No longer identified with an individual character, the symbol of societal inequity (the slum) became a character per se, as the talking tenement house persecutes Mary's kid brother (played by Sylvia Sidney and Sidney Lumet), taunting him into becoming an arsonist.

The theater scene, film criticism, and several of the Hollywood films that registered in the American cultural debates of the late 1930s bear the mark of gravitation toward democratic modernism and a realist paradigm as loose as it was pervasive. Orson Welles's staging of Shakespeare's *Julius Caesar*, the successful multiple-year run of *Pins and Needles* on Broadway's Labor Stage,[159] the *New York Times*, *New Masses*, and the reviews of Pare Lorentz and Otis Ferguson all recognized that art was to be both popular and realistic, that art in general and cinema in particular "is supposed to hold the mirror up to life."[160] By 1938, even Lubitsch called for "greater realism" in American film. Some films, such as *The Merry Widow* and *The Love Parade*, called for "idealization," but Lubitsch thought that, in general, cinema had the paramount responsibility to communicate "realism." Citing *Fury* as a model, he said that this film was "a realistic story which Joe Ruttenberg photographed with perfect realistic camerawork."[161] Actresses should move away from the Cinderella stereotype, concluded Bette Davis in *Screen Guild's Magazine*. The public had matured and audiences "are, unlike the silent picture days, looking for realism. They want to see human beings on the screen, not actresses."[162] By February 1939 even Will Hays, president of the Motion Pictures Producers and Distributors Association (MPPDA), concurred that America needed more "pictures treated with realism, drawn from life, of the problems of the average man and woman."[163] Margaret Thorp, an early progressive film historian, saw Hays's declaration as "the day the motion picture industry extended an official welcome to ideas."[164]

Cast against the backdrop of future developments in Hollywood films as well as against the biography of the conservative William Hays, Thorp's predictions sound rather like wishful thinking. No doubt Hays's idea of "realism" was different than, say, Lang's. But by mid-1939, the president of the MPPDA was using the same words as Hollywood Cultural Front organizations. Academic literature has largely bypassed these changes in the Hollywood community, thus underestimating the influence of Hollywood progressives and organizations such as HANL. The political "agency" of Hollywoodians is expunged from most histories of Hollywood that, curiously enough, regard American cinema as a "commercial institution" whose development was determined by the studio executives and by the iron laws of the economy.[165] Granting supreme power to either the producers or the financial offices in New York, these narratives marginalize any "struggle," agency, or resistance on the part of the employees of the film factory. Indeed, if applied to other "commercial institutions," such as the Chicago meat-packing industry in the 1930s, this kind of thinking would do away with thirty years of labor history.

If we are to integrate political and cultural history as a factor in the forcefield shaping Hollywood movies, then Hollywood New Yorkers and Hollywood Europeans must also share some responsibility for the system's limits and repressive practices. The commitment to reach larger audiences, for instance, implied an effort to make films as easily understood as the most classical of the Hollywood narratives. This in turn excluded more radical approaches. The influx of German refugees notwithstanding, Los Angeles remained quite unaffected by Bertolt Brecht's theories of representation, though he had been the most influential playwright of Weimar and an acquaintance of many Hollywood Europeans. While this was in part due to the censorial power of conservative producers, it was also a continuation of the feud between Brecht and the Theater Union, which we discussed in the first chapter.

In the case of Fritz Lang's *You and Me* (Paramount, 1938), Brechtian filmmaking ran against not only the producers' caution but also the reviews of American progressive film intelligentsia. *You and Me* was the story of two ex-convicts who struggled to do good in a hostile society. The film took a detour from the realistic paradigm to build on the Brechtian traditions of "estrangement" and "Lehrstück."[166] In several scenes, in fact, Lang interrupts the seamlessness of the narrative with songs or clearly "unrealistic" situations in order to highlight the very absurdity of the rules that regulate our life. When ex-convict Helen (played by Sylvia Sidney) decides to show a group of backsliding ex-convicts that "crime does not pay," she does it literally, drawing an elaborate equation on a blackboard. Why should she do otherwise? In the film's bleak reading of consumer society, everything is on sale; the bottom line, not morals, should determine one's behavior. This message is contained in the first song of the film—"You cannot get something for nothing"—scored by Kurt Weill and written by Sam Coslow. Following the rules of a Brechtian mise en scène, Lang took great pains to fuse the Brechtian lyrics by Coslow, the music by Weill, and his own camera movements. "It is something absolutely new," he wrote Lerner. "I mean the form of this picture, how the story is told and how the music is used as a dramatical item."[167]

In what should have been a gangster film or an example of straight realism, Lang's musical numbers and Brechtian references interrupted emotional identification and challenged the realistic paradigm. As Paramount's top producer Adolph Zukor noted, Sylvia Sidney and her blackboard were not "realistic" as a method for preventing a robbery. The problem with the film was not the benevolent portrayal of former criminals, but its very style. Zukor wrote associate William Le Baron that "I am frankly skeptical about the wisdom of the rather mystic elements that Lang has injected in the script. . . . [It] seems to me that the success of this picture is going to depend to a large extent on establishing two very real characters. . . . These mystic elements may detract seriously from this reality. . . . [And] literal-minded audiences may not relish these flights into fantasy or understand them."[168]

Protected by his producer-director contract, Lang was able to get much of his vision into the completed film. But because it undermined the paradigm of realism and emotional identification, progressive critics feared that the film's message was way over the audiences' head. The film attracted not only Zukor's ire, but also criticism from the *New York Times*, *Variety*, and James Dugan in *New Masses*. *New Masses* had not noticed Lang's problematic interpretation of the American people in *Fury*, but his infringement of the realistic paradigm in *You and Me* was unforgivable. *New Masses* concurred with Zukor that *You and Me* was "an ignoble experiment."[169]

Just as their conception of realism left little space for alternative cinematic practices, Hollywood progressives and refugees were also involved in constructing a narrative of National Socialism that was only partially able to tackle Nazi anti-Semitism, an omission conventionally blamed on the producers' desire not to "ruffle the goyim."[170] For a film so openly devoted to the anti-Nazi cause, *Confessions* is surprisingly silent on the issue of anti-Semitism. Realizing that something was missing and yet accepting the industry's rationale behind the removal, *Variety* referred to the absence of this theme as "the inevitable deletion of the Jewish question."[171] The deletion was indeed "inevitable" insofar as it was consistent both studio policies and Hollywood political culture. While they were increasingly anti-Nazi, Hollywood intellectuals by and large considered anti-Semitism a consequence rather than a constituent element of the Nazi regime. Once fascism was defeated, anti-Semitism would disappear as well. This did not mean that they were unaware or blind to the problem. *Equality*, a short-lived journal edited by, among others, Donald Ogden Stewart, Franz Boas, Hubertus zu Löwenstein, Dorothy Parker, and Albert Maltz, took an early and forceful stand against anti-Semitism and racial discrimination, at home as well as abroad. Yet as anti-Semitism was predicated on fascism, the writers and artists affiliated with the magazine understood anti-Semitism only as a superstructural expression of fascism. The former would disappear if the latter ceased to exist. Furthermore, in the essentially healthy American democracy, anti-Semitism was a temporary aberration of the system—certainly not an indigenous phenomenon. In the first issue of *Equality*, Maltz wrote that "anti-Semitism cannot triumph in the United States until democracy is conquered." If it were to be conquered, fascism would triumph and, Maltz demanded, "will it be only the Jews who suffer or will it be the whole American people, regardless of race and religion?"[172]

By 1938, many refugees may have concurred. Liberal Catholic refugee Löwenstein and communist writer Ernst Toller were also on the editorial council of *Equality*. Mary Nolan has also noted anti-Nazi exiles' "serious underestimation of the place of anti-Semitism and racism" in their interpretation of National Socialism, and Martin Jay has remarked that until the early 1940s "[Max] Horkheimer's facile dismissal of specifically Jewish problems was shared, at least in their written work, by all of his colleagues at the Frankfurt Institute of Social Research." It is difficult not to conclude that in the years and months preceding the outbreak of World War II, the increasing influence of the Hollywood Cultural Front did not translate effectively into more attention on anti-Semitism in American film.[173]

Certainly the notion of the American people, about whom many Europeans entertained some doubts as late as 1936, was more fully embraced in the context of 1939. By 1938, even the refugee magazine *Aufbau* had changed its position toward the possibility of an American version of anti-Semitism. In 1935, the paper had sounded a "Warnungsruf" (warning cry) about such a risk. Noting the anti-Semitic overtones of Father Coughlin and Huey Long's rhetoric, *Aufbau* had warned that "Fascism and anti-Semitism are not necessarily synonyms." Anti-Semitism was a "geistige Epidemie" (a spiritual epidemic). America could be infected by the latter without embracing the former.[174] But by 1939, the magazine's position had sensibly shifted. The priority was how to push the United States into safeguarding democracy and opposing Nazi expansion, not to ruffle the nation's feathers by reminding it of its domestic problems. Considering the question of "how to save America from anti-Semitism," Robert H. Jackson's editorial on the first page of *Aufbau* argued that American democracy was by nature unaffected by anti-Semitism. Ignoring much of the reality surrounding him, Jackson argued that the reason lay in "the very composition of the American people," its being "a mosaic of minorities in which no one is so dominant as to be a threat to the liberties of any. We are a nation with no permanently dominant group in religion, in nationality, in tradition, interest or in opinion." As opposed to Europe, furthermore, America was rid of want and fear because "the Administration intervenes whenever people starve."[175]

Ultimately, one must look to the celebration of the people embodied in the people-narrative for a full explanation of the "inevitable deletion" of anti-Semitism from *Confessions of a Nazi Spy*. The deletion was not, in fact, due solely to the producers' hesitations and censures. Rather, it was consistent with the introduction of the people-narrative that Hollywood progressives had advocated since the beginning of the 1930s. Any emphasis on the dangerous appeal of anti-Semitism in America would have cast a shadow of doubt on the fundamental healthiness of the American people, which Cultural Front politics was eager to celebrate. In *Confessions*, the enemy had to come from the outside; the accents of the German spies and the seedy customers of the Yorkville *Biergarten* served to isolate them from the English-speaking and healthy American body politic. The Nazi spies are the Germans who have refused to Americanize (i.e., to become "Americans of German birth") and who still love German food, music, and locales ("German food! The best in the world," declares one of the spies).

The deletion of the Jewish plight did not meet much opposition among the majority of the Hollywood New Yorkers and Hollywood Europeans involved in the film. *NOW* did not notice it. Nor, interestingly, did Manfred George in his review of the film in *Aufbau*. The deletion itself was effected by John Wexley, an active member of HANL and a communist.[176] In rewriting the film, the playwright muted all references to the anti-Semitism of the German-American Bund, while introducing several examples of loyal "Americans of German birth." The film's finale read as a celebration of both American people and American democracy. After the trial is over, Renard and the district attorney Kellogg meet in a diner. In the script, Wexley marked this locale "a truly American institution," the quintessential, nonethnic American public sphere in clear opposition to the German *Biergarten* of the German-American Bund.[177]

Renard and Kellogg overhear the conversation of a few customers at the counter, who vent their contempt for the Bundists. "The voice of the people," Kellogg comments. "And thank God for such people," Renard says in his final line. The celebration of unity of the American people is also expressed by Sol Polito's deep-focus cinematography, which in the same frame ties the bourgeoisie (Renard and Kellogg in the foreground) to the working class (the customers and the bartender in the background).

Nonetheless the deletion of anti-Semitism may not have been accept-able to everybody. Edward G. Robinson, for example, was well aware of the Nazi persecutions. In October 1938, René Cenower wrote him from Vienna that "as a Jewish woman, it is impossible for me to make a living."[178] On December 8, 1938, the actor, along with other members of the Hollywood community, signed the "Hollywood Declaration of In-dependence" from Germany, prompting Hollywood to sever its ties with the Third Reich because of—among other things—its "racial policies."[179] Producers, however, objected to the proposal, calling it impractical.[180] Some fans disagreed for their own reasons. One particularly misinformed moviegoer wrote to Robinson (who was of Jewish descent) that a "group of clever atheistic Jews . . . sit in the background and do their bossing while you godless gentiles do the fronting for them."[181] Robinson persevered. "I would give my teeth," the actor declared to *The New York Times* a few days before the shooting of *Confessions* started, "to do an American version of *Professor Mamlock*, that great story of a Jewish doctor in Nazi Germany."[182] In a memo to Wallis, Robinson emphasized this aspect as the major factor motivating him to participate in the project. Robinson stressed that he wanted to do the picture "*for my people.*"[183]

In 1940, the *New York Times'* Bosley Crowther noted that in the previous year Hollywood had shown more and more signs of the "docu-mentary influence." Manfred George, now the editor of *Aufbau*, perceived that something had changed in the Hollywood panorama. Reviewing *Confessions* in 1939, George remarked that "while until now a marked intellectual, anti-Fascist tendency showed itself only in political rallies and in the production of marginal films, . . . Hollywood is now a more important center of the intellectual struggle against the dictatorships."[184] American cinema had finally tackled the Nazis head on.

Confessions of a Nazi Spy highlights the complex mechanisms through which the democratic modernism of the new American film culture was transplanted onto the screen. Its production offers evidence of a moment when Hollywood had become a center where several intellectual and political networks were willing and allowed to participate, and where connections between different spheres of intellectual and filmic activity (radical documentary, commercial features, modernist, experimental theater) could be made. In the political and cultural negotiations surrounding the film, Hollywood progressives were not merely pawns, but rather agents actively involved in the production of a daring text.

Participation of the refugees and Hollywood leftists in *Confessions* and other films of the late 1930s brought to Hollywood traditions and techniques that were previously relegated to the radical margins of the political and cultural scene of the 1930s. The same year in which the U.S. Congress denied further funding for the Works Progress Administration (WPA) Federal Theater Project, one of the plays produced for the stage under the WPA's aegis made it to the screen. Director Dudley Murphy shot *One Third of the Nation* (1939) on location in New York streets and at the former Paramount studios in Astoria. The film was independently produced by Murphy, but the fame and strength of its cast ensured its national and commercial distribution. Written by Salka Viertel's friend Oliver Garrett from the play by Arthur Arent, the film was a "compromise." It created a "personal" angle in the love story between Mary (played Sylvia Sidney) and Peter Cortlant (played by Leif Erikson), and it softened the role of the government in the betterment of the slums. Yet it was not only a sound bite of New Deal rhetoric that made it onto the screen. Garret, Murphy, and Irving Lerner (who was recruited as first unit director) managed to maintain the condemnation of the city slums, as well as to blame those wealthy New Yorkers who rejected their social responsibilities.

Hollywood progressives did not construct their anti-fascism on what Richard Pells has called a "rebellion against Modernism." On the contrary, Hollywood anti-fascists subscribed to what Miriam Hansen has called "popular modernism," meaning that they tried to be both modernist *and* popular. The Dieterle biopics depict figures who try to make scientific (*Ehrlich* and *Pasteur*), political (*Juarez* and *Zola*), and artistic progress available to the masses.[185] Murphy—the author with Man Ray and François Leger of the avant-garde cult film *Danse Macabre*—also used expressionist camera work to give life to the tenement house of *One Third of a Nation*, which, as in the original play, "talks back" and threatens Mary's younger brother (played by Sidney Lumet).[186]

On the other hand, the realistic paradigm also contributed to fixing the boundaries of Hollywood discourse. The debates surrounding the making of some of these films show that the Hollywood community was subtly but increasingly fragmented. Filmmakers such as Lang envisioned the possibility of alternative practices of realism more in tune with Bertolt Brecht's esthetics than with John Howard Lawson's. News from Europe awoke the Jewish identity of many Hollywoodians. As this Jewish identity became increasingly mobilized by the frightening news from Germany, disagreements over the place of the Jewish question in Hollywood progressive films began to appear. Some Hollywoodians were less willing to subordinate their Jewishness to their anti-fascism. When Edward G. Robinson wrote Warner that "I want to do it *for my people*," the "people" he referred to were the Jews, not the Americans on whom the people-narrative was originally predicated. And the Nazi-Soviet pact was going to make things even more difficult.

4

Hollywood Unraveled

Community and Style, 1939–1941

That's when I became Jewish, realized that I was a Jew. I think it was in 1938.

Lionel Stander, *Tender Comrades*, 1997

n 1941, sociologist Leo Rosten noted that "before 1934, roughly, the movie colony was dismissed as a never-never land of sunny skies, Sleeping Beauties, and ivory towers. . . . In one sense, the movie makers—directors and writers as well as actors—were not considered real people at all." Politics, however, had made Hollywood tangible. "When a Joan Crawford denounced the invasion of Ethiopia, when a Fredric March pleaded for ambulances for Spain, it was like harsh voices destroying a cherished dream."[1] Hollywood involvement in progressive politics shattered this dream and reconnected the Hollywood community to Los Angeles, but it also raised suspicions among many conservative politicians. No longer a "state of mind," Hollywood's novel reality was considered threatening by some critics. And this threat, many of them argued, centered on the alliance of the Hollywood radicals and the European refugees.

Attacked from outside, the New Yorker–European alliance was also weakened by internal turmoil. The beginning of World War II and the turn of Soviet politics caused the demise of the Hollywood Anti-Nazi League (HANL), the "politicization" of ethnic identities, and the "ethnicization" of political ones at the expense of the political and cultural cohesiveness of the Hollywood community. The Nazi-Soviet Pact separated many of the Hollywood Europeans from the communist network, and the unraveling of that alliance weakened the progressives' pressure on the studios. Between April 1939 and May 1940, Hollywood did not release any overtly anti-Nazi films. When it resumed their production in the second half of 1940, it abandoned the radical narrative departure of *Confessions of a Nazi Spy.*

As the international crisis escalated during 1939–1941, intellectual and creative energies mobilized and clashed in debates over such works as Budd Schulberg's *What Makes Sammy Run?* as well as Mordecai Gorelik's *New Theaters for Old* and Lubitsch's *To Be or Not To Be.* Until that moment, the political esthetics of the Hollywood Cultural Front, centering on democratic modernism and a vaguely defined notion of realist cinema, had been loose enough to accommodate people with relatively different interpretations and agendas. The Nazi-Soviet Pact weakened such unanimity and caused some Hollywoodians to rethink the issue. Competing definitions of realism began to emerge from former members of the alliance, only to be silenced again by the new unanimity of the war.

The Hollywood Self-Portrait

There is probably no better gauge of the changes in Hollywood self-consciousness than the Hollywood self-portrait. The first of Dieterle's biopics celebrated Hollywoodians as heroes of mass communication. The films themselves and the production histories of *Zola, Pasteur,* and *Juarez* reveal a community animated by lively debate but trusting in the democratic possibilities of Hollywood modernity. Interestingly, 1939 ended with the premiere on Christmas Day of one of the most successful of Hollywood self-images, the Hollywood Theater Alliance production of *Meet the People.* Both an autobiography of the Hollywood community and an attempt to obviate one of its glaring shortcomings, *Meet the People* celebrated the results reaped by progressive Hollywood. That it was a successful theatrical production—a West Coast production profitable enough to reverse the normal East-West trajectory and travel *to* Broadway *from* Los Angeles—was not irrelevant. For many 1930s intellectuals, a thriving theater was evidence of a thriving intellectual life. In 1935, Sheridan Ames had mourned the intellectual poverty of Los Angeles, which he identified primarily with the lack of a theater tradition. Because of L.A.'s geography, he concluded, "it is no easy task to bring together the diverse thousands who would eagerly rally the support of a united front, revolutionary theater."[2] The radicalization of the New York and Berlin cultural scene had been accompanied by the reestablishment and politicization of its theaters. Besides marking New York as a lively intellectual community, the thriving workers' theaters of the early 1930s had often been active participants in the city's politics.

Small radical theaters had mushroomed in Los Angeles in the second half of the 1930s. Among them, Contemporary Theater was founded in 1934 by a coalition of Europeans and New Yorkers with the hybridizationist aim of "acquaint[ing] the general public with the most progressive thought as expressed in dramatic form."[3] After Contemporary Theater folded, Edward Gering, the brother of actress Marion Gering, founded the short-lived Modern Theater with the help of, among others, Fritz Lang, Francis Lederer, Frank Capra, and Salka Viertel.[4] In addition, refugee theater groups catered to a German-speaking clientele. In 1939, William Dieterle organized and financed the national tour of the Continental Players.[5] Run by Max Reinhardt since June 1938, the Max Reinhardt Workshop of Stage, Screen, and Radio supplied the studios with well-trained bit players and sharpened the acting skills of established stars during the productions of European and American classics.[6] The workshop's faculty well represented the alliance between Hollywood New Yorkers and Hollywood Europeans as much as it exemplified the close relationship between Hollywood and experimental cinema: William Dieterle taught "Film Directing," Henry Blanke "Film Production," Karl Freund and Rudolph Mate "Experimental Camerawork," John Huston "Screenwriting," Edward G. Robinson and Paul Muni "Acting," and Samson Raphelson "Dramaturgy."[7]

With the exception of the Reinhardt workshop, however, these radical theaters were dependent on New York for material and, in general, were not very successful. Hollywood experienced a cultural renaissance, however, with the L.A.-based Hollywood Theater Alliance, founded in early 1939 by a coalition of Hollywood New Yorkers and a few L.A. notables. The Theater Alliance was the origin of one of the most popular of the new Hollywood self-portraits. Henry Meyers, later a victim of the blacklist, remembers that its founders were "a group of theatrical people who would like to put on a show, because they missed it. They'd all been in the theater in New York, they'd been actors, stage managers, directors."[8] The Theater Alliance also had a privileged rapport with the refugees, many of whom attended its workshops to acquaint themselves with American stage techniques and used the organization's small playhouse in Hollywood to stage German-language productions.[9]

First and foremost, the Theater Alliance represented a self-conscious assessment of Hollywood's renewed intellectual life. The founders claimed that contemporary Los Angeles could now sustain a new, modern theater company since it "held a public both ready and eager to support a theater which would grow up out of the community."[10] In September 1939, the company set up production for *Meet the People* written by the Hollywood newcomer Henry Meyer and his partners, future fellow blacklistees Edward Eliscu and Jay Gorney. "The world no longer eyes Hollywood as the home of the movies and Symphonies Under the Stars," read an ad for the show.

> On the one hand, it sees the greatest concentration of literary and artistic talent, and on the other, progressive, spirited people bending their energy toward defeating bigotry and upholding the best in American tradition. Now these two groups join hands in an enterprise inevitably determined by their outlook and experience—a democratic theater. . . . A democratic theater is a community function. To permit it to be usurped for private profit and self-exploitation is to acquiesce to a commercial dictatorship.[11]

Meet the People, with its brio and its engaging tunes, pleased its critics.[12] Beginning its run on December 25, 1939, at the small Assistance League Playhouse, the show received vast popular and critical success, breaking all local box office records,[13] and then moved to the Hollywood Playhouse[14] and later to the Geary Theater.[15] By the end of the year, the Theater Alliance was planning to stage *Zero Hour* by Leslie Woolf Hedley,[16] preparing a new edition of *Meet the People* to open at the Music Box Theater,[17] and planning to become "the first community theater of Southern California."[18] In the fall of 1940, the revue opened at the Mansfield Theater on West 47th Street in New York City.[19]

Not unlike one of Dieterle's biopics, *Meet the People* was a self-portrait of the community, stressing the progress of the community while not obscuring the difficulties within the Hollywood studios. It made fun of the Hollywood producers, ("How Movies Are Made" by Milt Gross), but it opened with a skit in which Hollywood—represented as the "Sleeping Beauty"—was awakened by progressive artists and finally came in touch with the people ("The Legend of the Sleeping Beauty" by Ben and Sol Barzman). The production also recognized the privileged relationship of the Hollywood radicals with the refugees. One of the numbers, "That

Mitteleuropa of Mine," gave a benevolent portrayal of the Hollywood refugees and their plight. In the 1940s, Edwin Piscator, German progressive refugee and theater director, produced "That Mitteleuropa of Mine" at his Dramatic Workshop at the New School for Social Research in New York.[20]

The narrative strategy of the Theater Alliance's *Meet the People* reflected the cultural tradition of progressive Hollywood and celebrated the intellectual rebirth of Hollywood and its growing connection with American life. Reviewing the production, the *Hollywood Citizen News* noted how far it was from the traditional protagonist-dominated theater: "In case you haven't seen *Meet the People*, be advised that there are no stars as such." An actor could be a "principal" in one skit and a "spear carrier" in another. The skits performed at the premiere were in touch with the social and political themes of the day and revealed the breadth of the Hollywood anti-fascist milieu encompassing refugees, liberals, and Communist Party members. "Hitler is mimicked a few times," noted *Variety*, "as are Chamberlain and Stalin."[21]

The Rise of the "Refugee Problem" in Hollywood

The success of progressive Hollywood also meant greater visibility, and in the late 1930s the anti-fascist intellectual community had to confront a massive attack from conservative and isolationist quarters, spearheaded by the House Committee on Un-American Activities (HUAC) and its chairman, the conservative Texas Democrat Martin Dies. Since 1938 HUAC and Dies had manifested a profound interest in HANL for its outspoken endorsement of Roosevelt and the Loyalist side in the Spanish Civil War. In August 1938, Martin Dies accused HANL of being a communist organization. It was necessary, he concluded, that HUAC hold "hearings at which members of the film colony will be afforded an opportunity to reply to charges that they were participating in communistic activities."[22] In July 1940, John C. Leech, a repentant communist, delivered to HUAC a list of forty-two motion picture personalities whom he accused of being connected with a communist plot to overthrow the American government.[23] Among them were famous Hollywood liberals such as Humphrey Bogart, James Cagney, Philip Dunne, and Fredric March, and Hollywood Europeans such as Fritz Lang and Francis Lederer.[24]

HUAC interpreted Hollywood progressivism as the result of an alliance between foreigners from Central Europe and the American-born

Left. As far as Dies was concerned, the two networks were naturally attracted to each other. After all, Dies thought, all foreigners had a natural leaning toward radicalism. Earlier in his career, he had declared that the emigration quota acts of the 1920s were insufficient for barring radicals from entering the United States. It was high time the United States completely closed its doors to immigration and threw away the key.[25] One of the investigators of the committee, Walter Steele, had singled out *Blockade* as a " 'red front' Spanish propaganda film."[26] Steele had also attacked the activities of the refugee organizations in the United States and in particular the L.A.-based German-American Club, the German-American League for Cultural Freedom, and HANL.[27]

In a series of articles in *Liberty*, Martin Dies expressed the opinion that "communist influence" was behind the "subtle but very effective propaganda which appeared in such films as *Juarez*, *Blockade*, and *Fury*." According to Dies, Hollywood "wields the most powerful weapon of the world" and had the power to shape the public's opinion through its mastery of "the art of publicity." This power, however, needed to be controlled, since Hollywood communists had been able to forge an alliance with refugees and Jewish producers by claiming that "Russia served as a bulwark against the spread of Fascism and anti-Semitism."[28] Martin Dies's attack on Hollywood sowed seeds that were to blossom in the aftermath of World War II. In the context of 1940, though, Hollywood producers did not panic. In October 1939, a Gallup poll revealed that only 26 percent of the population thought that HUAC should investigate communist activities, holding that "illegal war propaganda" (42 percent) and "Nazi Activities" (32 percent) were more urgent.[29] While trying to soften up Secretary of Interior Harold Ickes's open contempt for Dies, President Roosevelt himself had often criticized HUAC, in 1939 defining one of its anti-communist raids as "sordid practice" and even using the FBI to try to dig up unsavory details about the congressman.[30] Y. Frank Freeman, president of the Motion Picture Producer Association, simply asked Dies to prove his accusations. "The screen industry insists that these people be either cleared or found guilty—one or the other."[31] Dies chose to retreat and dropped the charges.[32]

Dies had perceived correctly that Hollywood had moved to the Left, and he tried to counteract this shift. In the process he had put together the political language with which the Right would look at Hollywood in the following decades. The more Hollywood progressives attempted to reconnect the community with Los Angeles and the domestic situation of the United States, the more Dies attempted to make them appear un-American and disconnected from American society. The Hollywood Europeans and their alliance with the Hollywood New Yorkers made the job of Dies and his followers easier, as their un-Americanness was more concrete than vague political or esthetic definitions. The connection between refugees and Hollywood radicals became the centerpiece of subsequent attacks on Hollywood. At the beginning of 1941, an ultra-conservative radio analyst from Los Angeles argued that Hollywood "hate-inspired propaganda" was due to the alliance between American-born radicals, "the new alien refugee writers, directors, actors and actresses," and the Jewish "Imperial Families" that ran Hollywood studios. Hollywood was too un-American a place to wield so much power, and the government should break its monopoly over people's minds through legislative action such as the Neely Bill.[33]

Isolationist Senator Gerald P. Nye from North Dakota prompted the Senate Committee on Interstate Commerce to investigate "Propaganda in Motion Pictures" and the role of radicals and refugees in Hollywood warmongering. In a radio speech on August 1, 1941, he argued that in each of the Hollywood studios "there are a number of producers and directors, many of whom have come from Russia, Hungary, Germany and the Balkan Country. . . . Go to Hollywood, it is a raging volcano of war fever. The place swarms with refugees."[34] In his testimony in front of the Senate Committee, Nye repeated that "those primarily responsible for the propaganda pictures are born abroad. They came to our land and took citizenship here entertaining violent animosities toward certain causes abroad. Quite natural is their feeling and desire to aid those who are at war against the causes which so naturally antagonize them."[35]

For the refugees, Hollywood was becoming inhospitable at the very moment when they needed help the most. Between 1933 and 1939, refugee filmmakers from Central Europe had some chances of finding jobs in European film industries. After 1939, however, the collapse of the Viennese and Budapest studios, and the shaky conditions of the film industry in France, made Hollywood one of the few choices still open to the refugees.[36] In March 1941, *The New York Times* reported that between six thousand and twenty-five thousand refugees had arrived in Southern California.[37] Using refugee actors from Austria, Germany, and Hungary as a case study, Jan-Christopher Horak's useful *Fluchtpunkt Hollywood* records thirty-three arrivals between 1933 and 1936. The number increases for the following years: twenty actors arrived in 1937, thirty-four in 1938, and thirty-four in 1939.[38] In April 1939, *Variety* reported that Hollywood had to deal with a "complex problem" because of "the mounting number of refugee professionists, artists of the stage and the screen, composers and playwrights . . . appealing to all branches of the amusement field for opportunity to obtain engagements of one form or another."[39] The concern soon reached the national press. In the Hearst papers, Hedda Hopper screamed that American-born filmmakers were being replaced by refugees. "It's been a street corner joke," she wrote in October 1939, "that if you wanted a job here, you'd better say that you were a foreigner, preferably a refugee."[40]

In September 1940, G. Allison Phelps, a nationally syndicated radio broadcaster, accused Hollywood of hiring refugees in preference to American artists.[41] In response, the Motion Pictures Producers and Distributors Association (MPPDA) published the findings of a survey it had conducted showing that the Hollywood film industry employed only 18 refugees out of a total of 19,511 employees.[42] Even *The New York Times* regarded these figures as ridiculous.[43] In March 1941, D. W. Churchill wrote that the MPPDA report "may properly be given the bird." There were, Churchill declared, many more refugees in Hollywood than the MPPDA survey indicated, and they infiltrated not so much the "technical jobs . . . pretty well protected by guilds and unions" but the ranks of "producers, directors, actors, writers and composers." According to Churchill, refugees had been able to find jobs in Hollywood through the European Film Fund.[44]

Under this attack, studios seemed less and less willing to employ Hollywood Europeans. Among the thirty-eight refugee directors who arrived between 1939 and 1941, only fourteen were able to make a movie within two years of their arrival. For the remaining twenty-two, the economic readjustment occurred—if it ever did—only during World War II.[45] In 1941, the New York refugee magazine *Aufbau* published a report by Franz Bunfel concerning the job opportunities available for refugees in the L.A. area. Bunfel informed his readership that "Just in the last two years, when the emigrants' flux to the West Coast has taken a great boost, increasing difficulties presented themselves to the newcomer trying to make a living. . . . The possibility to make a living in the film industry, in the Hollywood studios, is clearly available only for exceptional, individual cases that have outstanding accomplishments."[46]

The Nazi-Soviet Pact

To make things worse, the attack against progressive Hollywood came at a time when the community was undergoing a profound crisis. At the center of the impasse was the inability of participants to maintain the system of multiple allegiances that had characterized their existence in Hollywood. Until the summer of 1939, in fact, the Hollywood front had been able to gather a diverse coalition of filmmakers around the platform of democratic modernism, anti-fascism, democracy, and a realist, politically engaged cinema. Loose definitions of fascism and democracy had kept together communists and New Deal Liberals, Europeans and New Yorkers. The *Kristallnacht* and the Nazi-Soviet Pact, however, forced Hollywoodians to choose among different priorities and to rank their multiple allegiances in diverse, and increasingly rigid, orders.

In the face of the *Kristallnacht*, the Nazi massacres in Poland, and the inaction of what *Aufbau* called the "so-called democracies" ("sogennante Demokratien"), some Hollywoodians rediscovered their Jewish origins.[47] Conflicts broke out within the Hollywood Cultural Front that had showed so much unity during the making of *Confessions*. The crisis exploded during the making of the last of Dieterle's biopics, *Dr. Ehrlich's Magic Bullet*. In this case the disagreement did not pit producers against progressives and refugees, but it did divide the Hollywood community by pitting a progressive Hollywood New Yorker against other Hollywood progressives and refugees.

Norman Burnstine, who handled the first script treatment for the film, was a radical Jewish writer from New York.[48] The idea for the film had come to him as he was driving around Los Angeles with "two of the garment-worker cast members of *Pins and Needles*." All of a sudden a car full of college students shouted anti-Semitic slogans at them. Burnstine's immediate impulse was to "ram my car into theirs, but they got away." The event, however, got him to thinking. "Continued unemployment, continued unrest, continued Nazi propaganda," he wrote to Henry Blanke, "continued Ford-financed Father Coughlin propaganda are nudging the American masses toward the pit of fascism and anti-Semitism . . . [and] in the double boiler pressure of a worse economic situation [the students'] hoots would have been clubs and bullets." In this day and age, Burnstine continued, cinema has a mission which it keeps avoiding.

In *Zola* you made a great picture but the Jewish question was handled pianissimo. You told me you wanted a story for Paul Muni. Why not the life of Ehrlich? . . . And I would hit hard the anti-Semitism that hampered Ehrlich. . . . The life of Ehrlich should be dramatized so that even the most rabid anti-Semite would say, "Admitting that all the Jews are as bad as I think they are, they must be saved if they can give us a guy like Ehrlich once in a while."[49]

Blanke assigned Burnstine to write a treatment of the film, which he delivered on October 8, 1938. The treatment mentioned Ehrlich as a "Jewish scientist" and focused on his confrontations with the anti-Semite Dr. von Wolfert. It ended with a dissolve from Ehrlich's death in 1915 to Germany 1933 as bands of marauding Nazis tear down the bust of the illustrious academic.[50]

The final script, finished at the end of October 1939 by refugee writer Heinz Herald and progressive Hollywood New Yorker John Huston, tones down the theme of anti-Semitism. Gone are the proto-Nazi Wolfert and the militantly anti-Nazi ending. In place of the Nazis, the film ends with Ehrlich dying in his bed while Hedy, his wife, plays the piano. Prior to the credits, a title reminds the audience that fifty years after Ehrlich's death many were being saved by his cure but that "because of his race the name of this life giver has been stricken from the records of his homeland, and the monuments to his honor have been torn down."[51]

Burnstine appealed to a top producer *against* refugees and Hollywood progressives. After the intervention of "the present manipulators of the Ehrlich script," Burnstine wrote Hal Wallis, the film is "emasculated." Reinhardt, Huston, and Herald have "eliminat[ed] a reference to Ehrlich's Jewishness," along with the character of Wolfert as "Teutonic believer," and they have now "attacked the ending" because "it wasn't historically true." But "the Ehrlich script without the Nazi ending remains another *Pasteur* script. . . . The thing that distinguishes Ehrlich from Pasteur is not so much that Ehrlich fought syphilis and Pastuer fought hydrophobia . . . but that Ehrlich was a Jew and Pasteur was not." Herald, Reinhardt, and Huston, however, felt differently. At issue was not anti-fascism, nor the idea that cinema should be a means of political communication, because, as we have seen, the three had been actively involved in the making of the anti-fascist biopics *Zola* and *Juarez*. At issue was the interpretation of fascism and the centrality of racial doctrine. For Burnstine, anti-Semitism was central; for Huston, Herald, and Reinhardt, capitalist greed was the core issue. John Huston, Burnstine wrote Wallis, "told me flatly that to his mind general ignorance and greed in regard to disease and health were far more important problems than anti-Semitism."[52]

In a letter to the SWG Arbitration Committee concerning the allocation of credits for the film, Reinhardt confirmed Burnstine's version. Burnstine did not deserve any credit for the screenplay, as Herald and Huston had "changed [*Ehrlich*] completely from Mr. Burnstine's theme of anti-Semitism. The subject of the picture . . . is the story of a scientific idea and the assault upon that idea by bigotry and prejudice."[53] Dieterle concurred with Huston, Herald, and Reinhardt. For the director, Ehrlich's historical importance is less about being a Jew than about being another "idol of mass communication," fighting to make scientific culture available and accessible to the multitudes. Ehrlich's story is "more than the story of a German Jewish scientist's fight for a panacea, . . . it is much greater than that. . . . Disease, as religious persecution and war, thrives in an atmosphere of ignorance and darkness. Exposed to the light, that ignorance is forced to give way to progress."[54]

As Lionel Stander stated in regard to 1938, that was the time when he "realized that I was a Jew."[55] *Ehrlich*'s production history indeed demonstrates how increasingly contested the relatively low ranking of the "Jewish question" was within the list of progressive priorities. Discussions focusing on Jewish identity and its political implications appeared in several places at the same time. Though many modern critics tend to ignore or downplay this element, much of the debate about Budd Schulberg's *What Makes Sammy Run?* focused on the Jewish issue. Written by one of the preeminent exponents of the Hollywood Cultural Front, *What Makes Sammy Run?* is a subtle portrait of the Hollywood community that reflects its struggles and contradictions through Sammy Glick's rise from the mail room of a New York newspaper to a Hollywood executive suite. Glick's story is told by Al Manheim, the alter ego of Schulberg who witnesses Sammy's "resistible" ascension from New York to Hollywood. In memoirs and cultural histories, *Sammy* is often cited as an example of the Communist Party hacks' domination of the Cultural Front because Schulberg's novel was first praised as "the Hollywood novel" and then rejected as misleading by Charles Glenn on the *Daily Worker*, possibly because of the intervention of party bureaucrats.[56]

In this vein, the story of *Sammy*'s critical reception is a melodramatic, dichotomous struggle between the young modernist writer, Budd Schulberg, and the Communist Party's hacks, and, on a larger scale, between the Cultural Front and its opponents.[57] In an effort to define the Cultural

Front as a party-dominated monolith, this version of the story ignores the fact that both those siding against the novel *and* those writing in its defense were often part of the same milieu, frequently writing on the same press. Possibly, pressures from the party leaders may have influenced Glenn's decision to change the tone of his review, but those pressures must not have been very heavy. A few days *after* Glenn's second review, the debate, in fact, was far from over, and *New Masses* published an article by Samuel Sillen claiming that Schulberg had written a "brilliant book" and "has taken the right tone. . . . His satire cuts deep; his style has unusual economy and speed."[58]

A crucial aspect of the dispute was not communism-versus-capitalism or modernism-versus-realism, but rather Schulberg's treatment of the Jewish question. The Hollywood screenwriter had in fact dealt openly with the Jewish identity of the protagonists. For Samuel Sillen, this was the correct approach; he argued in *New Masses* that the positive character of Al Manheim, who—like Glick—is Jewish, "bar[s] the way to anti-Semitic interpretations of his story." Yet Glenn's second review in the *Daily Worker* took exception to this interpretation. Furthermore, *The Clipper*, the organ of the California League of American Writers, argued that *What Makes Sammy Run?* was "a thin and not too new 'success story' "; it was too harsh on Hollywood and was borderline anti-Semitic because it argued that the Jewish Lower East Side produced only "runners" like Sammy or "rabbinical saints like [Sammy's brother] Israel."[59]

The criticism of *The Clipper* was specious and inaccurate, as the positive character of the novel, Al Manheim, is also Jewish, though neither a rabbi nor a go-getter. In the eyes of the Communist Party, however, *any* reference to Jews was problematic after August 1939 and the pact between the Soviet Union and Nazi Germany. *What Makes Sammy Run?* gave the Jewish issue center stage by focusing on several possible artic-ulations of Jewishness (Sammy's, Al's, Israel's), only one of which—Al Manheim's—is acceptable. Al Manheim followed in the tradition set up by the protagonist of Mike Gold's autobiography, *Jews without Money*. For Manheim, as for Gold's alter ego, "Jewishness, Americanness, and revo-lutionary Communism [are] compatible," as Jewish identity is associated with the poverty-stricken Lower East Side and leads to working-class consciousness.[60] Manheim, in fact, interprets Jewishness not as religion or ethnicity, ("it is not a race . . . and if it were merely a religion, all Jews like me should be excluded"[61]) but mainly as social geography, the working-class slums of the Lower East Side. It is a political and historical tradition based on solidarity ("the need of Jews to help each other in time of need"[62]) and born out of economic and social oppression. Sammy, Schulberg/Mannheim argues, is running from both his Jewish identity and his class identity as a child of the slums. Unfortunately, Schulberg's attempt to reconcile class and ethnicity floundered on the dunes of late 1939. Many voices to the contrary notwithstanding, at least on the national level, the Communist Party of the United States (CPUSA), abiding by the Molotov-Ribbentrop diplomacy that had led to the Nazi-Soviet Pact, had sacrificed the safety of the European Jewry to the security of the preeminent Socialist country and was bound to consider as too sensitive any interrogation of the political implications of Jewishness.

Just as *Sammy*'s emphasis on the "Jewish question" pitted one communist reviewer against the other, the Molotov-Ribbentrop Pact split Hollywood political life. HANL, the organization that had brought together the majority of refugees and Hollywood radicals, was smashed to pieces by the image of Stalin toasting to Hitler's health. Following a fight within the board, only communists and fellow travelers remained in the organization. In the aftermath of the Pact, remembers Bonnie Claire-Smith, the secretary of HANL, "you never saw anything like what hit the League's office. The phones didn't stop, and telegrams of withdrawal poured in."[63] Its name changed to the Hollywood League for Democratic Action, the organization continued to exist until the first months of 1940. In April, what was left of the organization published the final issue of its bulletin, acknowledging that the majority of its membership had left: "We have never abandoned the 'American way,' the democratic way," yet many former members "thought we were making a mistake. Some thought we were adopting the same policy of surrender and appeasement we had previously condemned."[64] The break-up of the largest anti-Nazi organization in Hollywood stole precious energy from the fight to enlist American film in the democratic struggle. Following the Pact, contacts between Hollywood New Yorkers and Hollywood Europeans diminished as the communists were increasingly more isolated, and many refugees retreated into more ethnically defined organizations with much narrower scope and specific focus on their immediate problems.

In 1940, the number of Americans invited to the salon of Salka Viertel decreased, and more and more refugees transferred time and money from HANL to the European Film Fund (EFF). EFF was founded in October 1938 by Hollywood agent Paul Kohner as "an organization of financial help for Europeans in dire straits, in particular refugees, and partly for artists, actors, musicians and so forth." Few refugees participated in the initial activities of the EFF, many of them preferring to work within the larger and more catholic environment of HANL. Until the end of the 1939, for example, director William Dieterle contributed only a nominal amount of his time and money to the EFF, preferring to work within HANL. By the beginning of 1940, however, the director left HANL and devoted the whole of his energy to the EFF.[65] In 1936, Ernst Lubitsch had been among the founders of HANL, but by 1939 he had abandoned it to become president of the EFF.[66] Replacing HANL after the Pact, the EFF became the center of the refugee community in Hollywood. Only after HANL collapsed was Paul Kohner able to get the majority of Hollywood refugees employed in a studio to pay the EFF a percentage from their earnings. The EFF used this money to help those émigrés who were in need of financial assistance, and it also pressured the studios to offer temporary contracts to people in Europe so that they could obtain visas. The former activity worked out better than the latter.[67] In 1940, the worst year of the refugee crisis, Paul Kohner was able to gather only twenty six-month contracts to help some refugee writers stranded in Europe.[68]

For those Hollywoodians close to the communist network, the Nazi-Soviet alliance was particularly tragic. Though understanding some of the Soviet motivations, they could not see how they applied to their local situation in the United States. "I think the Soviet Union was justified," remembers Bernard Vorhaus, a Hollywood New Yorker and future blacklistee, who was the chairman of the Hollywood Theater Alliance at the time of the Pact. But, he added, "I was also very opposed to other communist parties reducing their anti-German activities." Shortly after the Pact, Vorhaus abandoned both the party and the Theater Alliance.[69]

For many who were recently transplanted from New York, the Cultural Front had been a way to integrate themselves into the L.A. community. Paul Jarrico remembers that HANL was a way to feel part of a community, to find friends and contacts. Before the Pact,

> I never really felt that I was out of the mainstream in American politics. I felt I was on the left of American politics, but I certainly didn't feel like I was some kind of foreign agent, not just in the conventional sense of some spy from Russia, but, you know, in the sense of some man from Mars who was not really connected with what was happening and not really in tune with what was happening in his own country.[70]

The collective dimension of filmmaking made the effects of the Pact even more painful. Some Hollywood communists confessed that, though agreeing with the rationale behind it, the Pact embarrassed them in front of their friends. The Hollywood studio system made things even more difficult, since common projects compelled them to work together on a daily basis.

Proud of what they had achieved in Los Angeles, many of the Hollywood communists accused the Eastern Central Committee of the CPUSA of sabotaging a situation the complexities of which the "Eastern bosses" could not be aware. John Weber, an agent at the William Morris Agency in Hollywood, confesses that "I listened to what New York leaders had to say—and ignored it." He remembers that he and other Hollywood communists "concluded that Marxism was not some hard-line Bolshevik dedication. . . . That put us more in league with people who considered themselves not communists but progressives, and that is the area in which we had to operate in Hollywood."[71] Abraham Polonsky, a Hollywood New Yorker of Jewish extraction, calls the Eastern cadres "the fools in New York" and is overall more blunt than Weber: "We didn't give a shit [about the orders coming from the Eastern cadres]. The cultural leadership obviously didn't know what they were talking about. We ignored them out here, and we did a lot of wonderful things despite them."[72]

Budd Schulberg remembers that he thought that the Pact fit the strategy of "the real Eastern bosses, the Eddie Mannixes of the Party," to take over the Hollywood party. "By then, they felt that the Hollywood CP [Communist Party] had become quite important. . . . It became something they felt they should take over."[73] Schulberg even wrote a paper about the Pact, listing fifteen reasons why he thought it a mistake. Others, like the former chairman of HANL, Donald Ogden Stewart, reacted more subtly: his edition of the acts of the Third Congress of the League of American Writers included the speech of Vincent Sheehan, though Sheehan had recently condemned Stalin in the *New Republic*.[74] After migrating to England in 1951 as a result of the blacklist, Stewart recalled that the period of the Pact was "my first rejection of the American Communist Party's interpretation of Marxism," though he refrained from criticizing the Pact in public.[75]

In some cases the "fools in New York" were able to curb the autonomy of the rank and file in Hollywood. *Meet the People* directly satirized the Pact by showing two actors dressed like Stalin and Hitler waltzing on stage. Another skit of the revue was a hymn to FDR ("Mr. Roosevelt Won't You Please Run Again").[76] *Meet the People* preoccupied the Central Committee of the CPUSA. Danny Dare, one of the directors of the play, reported that the party intervened and had both the mockery of Stalin and the pro-Roosevelt song removed.[77] As a matter of fact, when the revue went on the road in 1940, the original format had been changed. When *Meet the People* opened in New York, neither the pro-Roosevelt song nor the anti-Stalin skit were present.[78]

Too rigid an interpretation of the effects of the Pact, however, is misleading and does not take into account how deeply the Cultural Front was embedded in the particular context of the Hollywood community. In Hollywood, the Cultural Front was less a political directive than a way of life. In the ensuing months, Hollywood communists and fellow travelers tried to balance directives coming from the national, New York-based network with a local tradition of cooperation that called for internationalism and political collaboration. Publicly, many remained within the national network, endorsing the antiwar manifestos of the League of American Writers.[79] Within the Hollywood community, however, they behaved differently, and a good number of them wrote, acted in, or directed the ten anti-Nazi pictures that Hollywood released in the second half of 1940.[80] Films directed, produced, or acted in by Communist Party members were not, indeed, films *of* the Communist Party. The twist in the party line momentarily reestablished a cleavage between the spheres of work and politics. In 1940, communist Lawson wrote the anti-Nazi *Four Sons*, Sam Ornitz scripted the anti-Nazi *Three Faces West*, and fellow traveler Howard Koch wrote the anti-Nazi parable of Elizabethan England, *The Sea Hawk*, for Hungarian director Michael Curtiz. In 1940, the star screenwriter of *Stagecoach*, Dudley Nichols, signed the antiwar manifesto of the Fourth Congress of the League.[81] The same year, however, Nichols worked with director Fritz Lang on the script of the anti-Nazi *Manhunt*. By January 1941, part of the script was almost finished and the anti-Nazi refugee Fritz Lang declared himself "in love" with Nichols's work.[82] Another of the signers of the manifesto, Lillian Hellman, wrote the anti-Nazi play *Watch on the Rhine*, a powerful piece about a member of the German underground who kills another exile to prevent him from betraying the anti-Nazi cause. Filmed by Warner Bros. during the conflict, *Watch on the Rhine* is unmistakably a call for action, "Too much talk," says one character, "by this time all of us know where we are and what we have to do."[83]

Critics from *New Masses* and *The Clipper* had to depend on linguistic gimmicks to explain how their Hollywood comrades were behaving. In *The Clipper*, Wolfe Kaufman hoped that *Four Sons*, Jack Lawson's contribution to premature anti-fascism, had been rewritten by the studio after Lawson had left Fox. Otherwise, how could one explain the film's strong interventionism? Yet the credits of *Four Sons* identify Lawson as the sole author of the film. The *New York Times* commented that "Mr. Lawson writes like a man whose heart is in what he's doing."[84] *New Masses* praised the good intentions of Hellman's play, yet argued that *Watch on the Rhine* could be "misused" since the writer did not make clear whether Kurt Müller, the hero of the play, advocated American intervention. The playwright had not expressed this clearly, and she was tangled up in a "serious political mistake."[85]

The Legacy of *Confessions*

In 1939, the alliance between refugees and Hollywood New Yorkers had centered on the possibility of Hollywood becoming a channel of democratic ideas. Realism both in subject matter and mise en scène was to be the cornerstone of a democratic Hollywood. "My faith," communist screenwriter Donald Ogden Stewart wrote in 1939 after the Third Congress of the League of American Writers, "is in the sound judgment of the people, provided they are allowed to know the facts. My hope is in the integrity of the American writers, whose duty is to see that the people know the facts."[86] Through Hollywood "realism," the American public would have been sensitized to the issues of the day. The Cultural Front had also indicated two targets for the renovated progressivism of Hollywood cameras: the America of the Great Depression and the Fascist takeover of Europe.

By the time Stewart's words were printed, however, the situation had considerably changed. While the Pact had destroyed HANL and split the Hollywood Cultural Front, weakening its ability to lobby the studios, Dies, Nye, and Phelps were attacking Hollywood as a hotbed of "red" propaganda. In place of the united front Stewart referred to, Hollywood was closer to a congeries of different voices, some of them proposing a definition of cinema and of realism quite different from what Stewart had in mind. The Hollywood coalition had lost its center.

Due to the incessant lobbying of HANL, Warner Bros. had released *Confessions of a Nazi Spy* in April 1939. Produced, directed, and scripted by members of HANL, *Confessions* constituted the embodiment of democratic modernism and Cultural Front esthetics. It was, in the words of *Aufbau*, "America's first anti-Nazi film" and evidence that "today Hollywood is a more important central point for the intellectual fight against the dictatorship."[87] With its reenactment of real events, frequent insertion of newsreels, and disposal of the classical protagonist-driven narrative, the film had given Hollywood "a new technique."[88] Renouncing any "purity of method," *Confessions* had crossbred entertainment and political education. "This sort of fictional expositions leaves you with the facts, and with the natural excitement of the facts, and provides you at the same time with an attitude toward them," noted David Wolff in *Films*. "It is a crusading picture and an immensely successful one, for the audience invariably comes out of the theatre discussing not the film as such, but its content."[89]

The general enthusiasm that accompanied the release of *Confessions of a Nazi Spy* did not last long. Studios abandoned the idea of continuing to invest in anti-Nazi themes. Originally, Warner Bros. had considered the possibility of producing a sequel to the film scripted by Leon G. Turrou.[90] A weak box office in the isolationist Midwest—so Warner executives believed—was going to be compensated for by strong revenues from the foreign markets. In August 1939, *Variety* reported that Warner Bros. was "smelling the possibility of a sequel to *Confessions of a Nazi Spy*. Foreign business is proving the hypo needed for a follow-up version."[91] This sequel never materialized. *Confessions* did poor business outside of the Northeastern seaboard, and Germany's increased military power convinced many European nations to keep away from the film. By June 1939, Great Britain had admitted *Confessions* but only after severe cuts by the censors.[92]

Unable to anticipate the future foreign policy of the Roosevelt administration, Hollywood wanted to keep away from subjects like *Confessions*. Already in May 1939, *Variety* reported that studio editors were "jittery" about treatment concerning the present international political situation, since "there is no way of telling which way the diplomatic cat will jump. Sudden declaration of war or conclusion of a peace treaty would ruin their market value."[93] At the end of October, Jack Warner announced that the politics of the studio was neutrality, "America is neutral and we are Americans. Our policy is 100% neutrality. There will be no propaganda pictures from Warner Brothers."[94]

Refugees were particularly frustrated by the situation. Their demands for anti-Nazi films had been constant in the 1930s. In 1939, Fritz Lang asked his Hollywood agent, Charles Feldman, to get him assigned to *Underground*, Warner's projected yarn on German resistance to Nazism. The director was "enthusiastic about it" and "particularly qualified" because of his experiences. Yet Feldman had been unable to accomplish that, even after Lang had agreed to cut his salary to a flat fee of $25,000 for the film.[95]

Between April 1939 and June 1940, Hollywood did not release any anti-Nazi films. After the fall of France in June 1940, a few anti-Nazi films were produced in an attempt to cater to the widespread pro-British sentiment. Yet refugees saw the limited number of Hollywood anti-Nazi films as evidence that the industry was failing to do its job. In September 1940, refugee Leo Askin wrote to freelance German writer Leo Lania and advised him not to "waste time in writing screenplays about the European problems or the war. In Hollywood, they do not want to know anything of them, or only in very particular cases."[96] In June 1940, William Dieterle argued—Will Hays's declarations notwithstanding—that Hollywood was going backward because of "reactionary elements . . . who want to undermine the production of progressive and intelligent films."[97] The following year, the director argued that Hollywood seemed "content to walk over a rainbow bridge while the world goes to pieces."[98]

Unable to address the issue directly, especially in the first months of the war, Hollywood films tackled the anti-Nazi issue as a historical metaphor. In *The Sea Hawk*, written by Hollywood radical Howard Koch and directed by Hungarian Michael Curtiz, Philip II stands by a map of the world, looking at England and planning its invasion.[99] A few months before, Curtiz and the German-born producer Henry Blanke had released *The Private Lives of Elizabeth and Essex* (WB, 1939). Considering the films in production at the time, *The New York Times* noted the rebirth of the "Elizabethan legend."[100] Napoleon was also used as a metaphor for Hitler. The British-Hungarian producer-director Alexander Korda cast British actors Laurence Olivier and Vivien Leigh in *That Hamilton Woman* (a.k.a. *Lady Hamilton*), a drama depicting the heroic struggle of Nelson's Britain against Napoleon's expansionism.[101]

The same production unit of *Confessions*, with Anatole Litvak as director and Henry Blanke as associate producer, concocted *Out of the Fog* (WB, 1940) from Irwin Shaw's *The Gentle People*, together with liberal Warner star John Garfield and radical Hollywood New Yorker Robert Rossen. In the film, Jonas and Olaf, a cook and a tailor interpreted by Thomas Mitchell and John Qualen, decide to kill a ruthless Brooklyn gangster, Harold Goff (played by John Garfield), who harasses them. Embellished by a love plot between Jonas's daughter Stella and George (played by Ida Lupino and Eddie Albert), the film turns the character of Goff into a stand-in for Nazism. In a telling scene, the gangster sneers at Olaf and Jonas, giving them the Roman salute. Later, while Olaf and Jonas are carrying him on their boat, Goff states that his philosophy is "the superior people make the inferior people work for them. What's wrong with it?" Jonas's and Olaf's struggle against Goff becomes a metaphor for anti-appeasement. "All my life I wanted peace and gentleness," Jonas tells Olaf, "but how can you convince airplanes with bombs and men with guns in their pocket? . . . If you live in the jungle and a lion kills your children, what would you do? You kill it." [102]

Originating in Blanke's unit at Warner, *The Sea Wolf* was directed by the Hungarian Michael Curtiz, scripted by Rossen from the novel by Jack London, and interpreted by Edward G. Robinson, John Garfield, and Ida Lupino. Robinson is Wolf Larsen ("a Nazi in everything but in name," notes Robinson in his autobiography), the evil captain of *The Ghost* who rules over his crew and robs other ships of their hard-earned bounties. [103] In a telling scene, the camera slowly pans over the walls of Larsen's cabin, revealing works or symbols popularly associated with Nazi ideology: Friedrich Nietzche's *The Superman* and Herbert Spencer's *The Principles of Sociology*. In the end, Larsen is defeated by the interclass alliance of Ruth (Lupino), Leach (Garfield), and the intellectual Humphrey Van Weyden (played by Alexander Knox).

The Crisis of the Realistic Paradigm

In a brilliant article published in August 1941 in the refugee magazine *Decision*, Klaus Mann argued that though its results were "muddled," *Confessions* was "an exciting promise." By contrast, other anti-Nazi films— *Mortal Storm, Four Sons*, and *I Married a Nazi*—had failed to overcome the constraints of the Hollywood genre. Nazism divided husband and wife (*I Married a Nazi*) and pitted Nazi sons against anti-Nazi brothers (*Four Sons*) and parents (*Mortal Storm*). Nazism, lamented Mann, was privatized. Abandoned was the notion of "the people" as the main protagonist of the struggle against Nazism; Nazism itself had become a family matter, almost a private vice. In these films, "what we see is the misfortune of a family, not the terrific drama of a people and a continent." [104] The privatization of the Nazi phenomenon and the loss of the people narrative as a structure left the promises of the 1930s debates unfulfilled. The Hollywood formula was not modified and, in Mann's words,

> Hollywood clings sterile and cowardly to its too familiar patterns and often-tested devices. They venture on the most appalling topic of human history

with the shabby tricks of Wild West and gangster thrillers. Don't they feel
that a new idiom is needed to communicate those tremendous experiences?[105]

Yet Mann's essay ventured further, revealing that the consensus achieved
by refugees and Hollywood New Yorkers regarding the realistic paradigm
was now being contested. Perhaps, he argued, even "the documentary
style" employed in *Confessions* was not enough to express the novelty of
Nazism. Other narrative strategies might also be used to ready American
cinema for the anti-Nazi struggle,

> for the European reality of 1941 is so utterly unbelievable, so macabre, that
> the appropriate method of mirroring it is either the direct, realistic report . . .
> or the daring transformation of this unbalanced reality into artistic images. . . .
> Surrealistic means may be sometimes more pertinent to reveal the essence of
> truth than a pedantic naturalism, which, even at its best, embraces only certain
> aspects of a complex and almost infinite drama."[106]

For Mann, democratic modernism was still the way to go. He never
questions, and actually re-endorses, the necessity of using mass media to
elevate the politics and the esthetics of the public. Realism à la "March of
Time," however, was no longer the only possible option. On the contrary,
if too simply interpreted, realism could become "pedantic naturalism." In
his article, two crucial terms of the 1930s debates—"art" and, in particular,
"surrealism"—reenter the arena.

Realism was under attack after its brief period of success. The release
of *The Grapes of Wrath*, a film that in many ways was connected with
the debates of the 1930s, did not arouse the same unanimous praise
as *Confessions*. The making of the film was a vindication of democratic
modernism and the Hollywood Cultural Front. According to Manfred
George, it was "evidence" ("Probe") of Hollywood's overcoming the
"commercial instincts" ("Geschäftsseele") of its producers and of its intent
of fulfilling its "moral and cultural possibilities of Enlightenment and
Progress."[107]

Directed by John Ford, adapted for screen by Nunnally Johnson, and
photographed by Gregg Toland, *Grapes* was more progressive than some
present-day historians are willing to recognize.[108] The film was clearly
connected with many of the debates that characterized the American
and Hollywood Left in the late 1930s, directly addressing the plight of
American farmers and employing the modernist deep-focus photography
of Gregg Toland, as well as many of the techniques of documentary films
of the period. In his column in the *Daily Worker*, Woody Guthrie called

the film "the best cussed picture I have ever seen." [109] A satisfied John Steinbeck wrote to his literary agent noting that

> Zanuck has more than kept his word. He has a hard straight picture in which the actors are submerged so completely that it looks and feels like a documentary film and certainly it has a hard, truthful ring. No punches were pulled—in fact with descriptive matter removed, it is a harsher thing than the book, by far. [110]

Nonetheless, the film was the result of a cultural forcefield and also bore the marks of the Hays office's pressures and Zanuck's caution. The harsh ending of the novel was replaced by the "we're the people" speech of Ma Joad. The script also did away with any sociological explanation for the farmers' plight, focusing its written prologue on "the weather" and erasing the chapters of the novel where Steinbeck purported to analyze the catastrophe from a point of view larger than the Joads.

The confines of "the people" did not often extend beyond those of the American family in *Grapes*. The film's concern for the family home, the sharply defined gender roles, and the images of the families each traveling on Route 66 inside separate—albeit decrepit—cars hinted at the 1950s and that decade's obsession with the nuclear family, rather than portraying the people-centered ideology of the 1930s. Instead of making the American people the protagonist, the film proposed the American family as the center of its narrative. Commenting on the new wave of Hollywood films emphasizing families such as the Joads, the Robinsons, or the O'Haras, Frank Nugent wrote that "Hollywood seems to be in a family wave, no doubt about it." [111]

Even Edwin Locke's positive review in *Films* magazine found *Grapes* lacking. Locke doubted that *Grapes* could surprise or enrage any but the most backward of its spectators. For most people, the film did not contain any new revelation, since they "already feel that something should be done about the migratory workers." Locke correctly identified the film's tension between "two endings," which were also two political metaphors, and two ideologies: "the spirit of burning revolt in Tom Joad" that did not reject violence as a political act and stood for the character's identification with the American people ("a fella ain't got a soul of his own, but only a piece of a big soul—the one big soul that belongs to everybody"), and "the final smugness of the incredible Ma." [112]

When asked to write about *Grapes*, James Agee, who had hoped Fritz Lang would use his rejected 1936 article for *Fortune* as the basis for his sharecropper project, wrote that "the things that I find objectionable [in the film] are so many, and seem to me so meaningful of so much to do with American films and general and specialized reaction to them, that there is not room within the space of any normal letter to set them down." Agee's letter did not say which aspect of the film disappointed him. It seems clear, however, that it was the entire 1930s paradigm that he meant to call into question. His soon-to-be-published *Let Us Now Praise Famous Men* was going to take issue with the realist paradigm by propelling the subjective "I" of the writer as the main filter between the reader and the Alabama sharecroppers. For *Films* magazine, Agee proposed to write about "other works of Ford's and other works of other American directors who seem to me particularly overrated: not only by the general public, but more seriously, by people whose responsibility it is to know better. I would mention, among these directors, Dieterle, Capra, and Lorentz."[113]

The most articulate and pervasive attack on the paradigm of the 1930s came from Mordecai Gorelik, a former set designer of the New York Group Theater who had gone to Hollywood to work in the RKO studio. Even more than Agee or Klaus Mann, Gorelik was an unlikely critic of Hollywood's Cultural Front rhetoric. In New York, he had staged Odets's *Golden Boy* as well as John Howard Lawson's *Loudspeaker* and *Processional*. In the acknowledgments of his book *New Theater for Old*, Gorelik referred to discussions he'd had with prominent Hollywood and New York radicals, from John Wexley to Jay Leyda. Drawing on the experience of the epic theater of Brecht and Piscator and referring throughout to Hollywood films as the counterpart of the New York stage, Gorelik argued that contemporary theater was at a crossroads between two different styles. Gorelik termed "illusory" the dominant style of production. Illusory theater was directly connected to the Naturalist school and was part of what he called "romantic realism." Illusory theater masked the conventions that made it possible and tried "to convince the spectators that the stage events which he is witnessing are not really events on the stage . . . but that they are rather a series of events unrelated to the stage and viewed by spectators in a theater as if by accident."[114] Caught in the illusion, the spectator suspended not only disbelief but also the capacity to react rationally to what he/she saw on stage. On the other hand, "conventional" mise en scène continuously manifested the presence of the narrator and reminded the spectator of the artificiality of what he/she was seeing. The audience's intellectual powers were, therefore, freed from any emotional identification with the characters, and spectators could dispassionately judge the represented action like scientists observing an experiment in a laboratory.

Though he gave some credit to *The Grapes of Wrath*, Gorelik did not conceal his contempt for what the Hollywood alliance had produced. "Naturalism," Gorelik argued, "has been perpetuated in still wider fashion by the American motion picture."[115] He then proceeded to attack all of the motion pictures that the Hollywood Cultural Front had most strongly endorsed, including *Juarez*, *Blockade*, and *The Informer*.[116] While these films showed a progress (and were even "heartening," Gorelik conceded), they were nonetheless based on an "illusory" mise en scène, pretending to be reality rather than its representation.[117]

Gorelik asked Robert Edmund Jones to write the preface for *New Theaters for Old*, but the dean of set designing eventually refused. Gorelik, Jones said, had lost track of the needs of the audiences that were going to "to stay away in very, *very*, VERY large numbers."[118] Jones professed again the ideal of the possibility to hybridize cultural audiences in order to speak to America: "I am not greatly interested in an account of what had been done of late in Russia or in Germany . . . and I feel that the American theater, expressing the American spirit if and when it comes of age, will take a form that is very different from these European forms."[119]

Given the implications of what Gorelik had stated, John Howard Lawson, the most prominent of the Hollywood communists, was given the task of responding to Gorelik in *New Masses.* According to many, Lawson was possibly the most doctrinaire of the Hollywood communists;[120] his review of *New Theaters for Old*, however, reads more as part of a conversation with an ally with whom the screenwriter respectfully, if determinedly, disagreed than as the party hack's condemnation of the infidel about to be purged. For starters, Lawson candidly admitted that the formerly united front was increasingly divided and that many shared Gorelik's concerns. Lawson conceded that the book was "one of the most important theater books of recent years" and that it spoke to the discussions occurring within the front of the Hollywood progressives, as "there are differences of opinion among progressive workers in this field." Nonetheless, he reiterated that the paradigm was still the way to go. Hollywood and Broadway should not follow the "objective reality" of the "mechanical" and "abstract" epic theater. On the contrary, they should focus more on what the ordinary men and women want. And what they want is the "stuff of life" dramatized through "tense emotional relationships." Gorelik, Lawson concluded, has forgotten that "the people want a theater as great as themselves. They enter the theater proudly, demanding their birthright: Give us the living world. Show us the wonder of men and women, so that we may laugh and look forward, knowing our strength." [121]

A month later, in April 1941, *New Masses* published Gorelik's letter in response to Lawson. In a few paragraphs, Gorelik pointed out the weakness of Lawson's argument, highlighting the looseness of the terms used by Lawson: naturalism and realism were ill-defined terms, and Lawson was the one guilty of "abstractism" since his analysis did not offer any definition of concepts such as "people" or "the stuff of life." [122] Gorelik underlined the fragility of the compromise of the 1930s. The realistic paradigm had supplied a common language, but it had not made for precision, especially in regard to the nature of reality, the possibility for cinema and stage of representing it, and the role of the audience in such a communication process. In the late 1930s, the looseness of these notions was crucial in keeping together the ample coalition that had animated Hollywood political and intellectual organizations. A counterpart of what William Stott has called the "documentary tradition" of the 1930s, the Hollywood realist paradigm comprised, in fact, radical interpretations of American reality along with celebratory, more "conservative" approaches. [123] Indeed, both attitudes had found expression in the instability of Ford's *The Grapes of Wrath*, as well as in its continuous oscillation between outrage and celebration, people and family, Tom Joad's final speech, and Ma Joad's final address. [124]

From the summer of 1939 on, however, the situation changed. Internally divided, Hollywoodians rediscovered difference and disagreement. Terms and styles that seemed to make sense only a few months before now seemed empty and in desperate need of definition. While Mann and Gorelik voiced their doubts on paper, others in the Hollywood community attacked the paradigm on film.

Citizen Kane and the Rebirth of Slapstick

Obsessed with the dichotomy between modernism and realism, high culture and mass culture, modern commentators have often and artificially separated Orson Welles's *Citizen Kane* from the Cultural Front in particular and the Hollywood Left in general. According to these critics, *Kane*, though made *in* Hollywood, is most certainly not *of* Hollywood. For historian Richard Pells, author of an influential book on the culture of the 1930s, Welles built his masterpiece on his rejection of the "pious certitudes of the Popular Front" and constructed a real and solitary example of modernist Hollywood.[125] For influential film critic Pauline Kael, the film was to be extolled for avoiding what she termed "show business Stalinism."[126] Once again, however, such interpretations rely on a narrow definition of the Cultural Front, one that sees it as a cultural milieu so monolithically anti-modernist and so single-mindedly committed to a rigidly defined version of realism that it excludes even the possibility of conversations and disagreements among its members.

The Cultural Front and democratic modernism, in fact, encompassed both partisans and opponents of Welles's film who openly vented their feelings in the press. For Cedric Belfrage writing in *The Clipper*, the organ of the League of the American Writers, the film was great just because it utilized a naturalistic version of reality to stress its subjective as much as its objective apprehension. "What other medium could show so forcefully that truth is not merely objective, but subjective also and at the same time?" Belfrage wrote enthusiastically. "The people are going to see *Citizen Kane* and not one of them will *be quite the same person after seeing it as he was before.* . . . You leave it with regret . . . feeling all your old belief in the medium restored."[127]

Indeed, Michael Denning has recently stressed that Welles's American career, from his Mercury Theater productions to *The Magnificent Ambersons*, fell almost entirely within the confines of the Cultural Front.[128] The film's direct reference to William Randolph Hearst confirmed the main axiom of cinema's realism: the necessity for cinema to engage directly political issues and real events.[129] In this regard, Gregg Toland's powerful use of deep focus cinematography was not merely a stylistic device, but an expression of the esthetic and political paradigm of the 1930s.[130] Rather than revealing the representational character of the film, in fact, Toland meant for his deep-focus shots to enhance the "realism" of the story. "Welles and I . . . felt that if it was possible, the picture should be brought to the screen in such a way that the audience would feel it was looking at reality, rather than merely at a movie."[131] Welles himself told Peter Bogdanovich that movies "still go on telling lies. . . . They pretend there's no ceiling—a big lie in order to get all those terrible lights up there. You can hardly go into a room without seeing a ceiling, and I believe the camera ought to show what the eyes see normally looking at something. That's all it was."[132]

Perhaps Welles's film was even too concerned with realism. Noting that Welles was working within a preestablished tradition, one with which he was increasingly at odds, James Agee soon questioned the

" 'originality' " of the film.[133] Agee was aware of the loose boundaries of the Hollywood paradigm, but his criticism did not rely on sharply defined boundaries between modernism and Hollywood, mass culture and avant-garde. The problem was not that Welles had chosen to work in Hollywood, nor that he wanted to bring politics and art to the masses. After all, Agee himself aspired to do so. While still writing in the perspective of democratic modernism and seeing Hollywood cinema as a vital participant in the American public sphere, Agee had nonetheless come to doubt the virtues of objective realism as an esthetic and political strategy. In search of alternative models, Agee selected Charlie Chaplin, Preston Sturges, and Ernst Lubitsch as champions of a different Hollywood modernism that was able to deal with "the issues of the day" while not relying on a realistic mise en scène.

In *The Great Dictator* Charles Chaplin surprised refugees and radical critics by using slapstick to tell the story of a Jewish barber in Nazi Germany. He transformed the SS into Keystone cops, and ghetto uprisings into pie-throwing contests. In the eyes of many critics the film's too-daring approach was rescued by its conclusion, when Chaplin abruptly had his barber address the camera about the horrors of Nazi fascism. As a narrative closure, Chaplin's speech reflected his awareness of the duty and the democratic possibilities of the medium. "My voice," he said in the film's self-conscious final address to the camera, "is reaching millions throughout the world." The anti-isolationist message of the film was ambiguous enough not to alienate completely the *Daily Worker*. Yet the "symbiosis of comedy and earnestness" seemed to Otis Ferguson to be "an unhappy state of union." In *Films*, modernist refugee critic Rudolf Arnheim remarked: "How far are Chaplin's 'realistic' pogroms from giving an idea of the horrors really happening in Germany. . . . I find it difficult to understand how after five years of Hitler terror . . . the sensitive creator of *The Gold Rush* and *Modern Times* could still have considered Fascists and Fascism as something just funny."[134]

Cries of betrayal were raised when Preston Sturges released the film he had written and directed in 1941, *Sullivan's Travels*, about the adventures of a Hollywood progressive in the midst of the Great Depression. After spending the 1930s as a screenwriter, Sturges graduated to the prestige of directing his own scripts in 1940, with *The Great McGinty* and *Christmas in July*. A personal friend of Charlie Chaplin and Lionel Stander, and of refugees Ernst Lubitsch, Max Ophuls, and Robert Siodmak, Sturges in his first films dealt with the struggles of ordinary Americans to survive in depression-era America. Specifically, *Christmas in July* (Paramount, 1940)—based on Sturges's own play, *A Cup of Coffee*, which he adapted for the screen—dealt with the adventures of an employee of a New York firm, Maxford Coffee House, who erroneously believes he has won a large cash prize. Compared with the play, the film softened the most radical lines about capitalism but maintained a strong social critique about a system in which "one half of one percent were successes and all the rest were failures."[135]

In *Sullivan's Travels*, which he wrote and directed in 1941, Sturges realized a satire of the 1930s paradigm. Writing to Bosley Crowther, he asserted that

> *Sullivan's Travels* is the result of an urge, an urge to tell my fellow filmwrights that they were getting a little deep-dish and to leave the preaching to the preachers. . . . *Sullivan's Travels* could really have been a little pamphlet sent around privately. Maybe it should have been. It starts with a discussion about movie making and during its unwinding tries a little of every form that was discussed. This makes for some horrible crimes against juxtaposition, as a result of which I have taken a few on the chin already and will take some more. One local reviewer wanted to know what the hell the tragic passages were doing in this comedy and another wanted to know what the hell the comic passages were doing in this drama. They are both right, of course.[136]

Young, *engagé*, modernist Hollywood director John Sullivan (played by Joel McCrea) proclaims his 1930s credo: he wants his "picture to be a commentary of modern conditions, stark realism . . . a document. I want it to hold up a mirror to life . . . something that would realize the potentialities of film as the sociological and artistic medium that it is." To gather firsthand experience, he hits the road and goes to see the real America. In showing Sullivan's adventures on the road, Sturges juxtaposes newsreel-like shots of bread lines and Hoovervilles with slapstick situations (pie in the face, car chases, Keystone cops, etc.). After several misadventures, Sullivan finally abandons his project. He will make Hollywood comedies that, if not politically committed, are at least able to offer some relief to a tired populace.[137] Surprised by the film, Milton Meltzer wrote in the *Daily Worker* that *Sullivan's Travels* revealed "a disturbing mixture of buffoonery and brutality." Otis Ferguson noted in *New Republic*, another champion of the realist paradigm, that "the present crude renascence of the Mack Sennett's pratfall" was incongruous with the seriousness of the situation in which Sullivan finds himself.[138]

To Be or Not to Be, directed by Ernst Lubitsch, one of HANL's founders, is a prime example of the crisis of the 1930s paradigm. By the summer of 1939, Lubitsch had left HANL but his involvement in anti-Nazi causes had continued through the EFF. He highlighted his disillusionment with communism in *Ninotchka* (MGM, 1939), a gentle satire about a Soviet commissar (played by Greta Garbo) seduced by capitalistic consumerism. Two years later, Lubitsch began the production of his first (and only) anti-Nazi film, *To Be or Not to Be*. In the film, Jack Benny and Carole Lombard are a husband-and-wife team in a theatrical company which is producing *Hamlet* during the Nazi occupation of Warsaw. By chance, rather than because of their political convictions, they become involved in the underground resistance.

A "farce" with many references to slapstick, *To Be* suggests a profound meditation about the relationship between theater, representation, and real life. In an open letter to the *New York Times*, the director admitted that "I have tried to break away from the traditional moving picture formula. I was tired of the two established recognized recipes: drama with comedy relief and comedy with dramatic relief." In opposition to the 1930s paradigm, and somewhat in tune with the "conventional" mise en scène advocated by Gorelik, Lubitsch used farce and slapstick to stress that cinema is representation rather than reality. In a war-film conspicuously devoid of newsreel footage, the bombed-out Warsaw is overtly a studio backdrop. Even Hitler walking in the streets of the city turns out to be not "the real thing," but an actor impersonating the Führer. Yet once cinema is liberated by the contingency of the "facts," Lubitsch argues, it can again push its audience to contemplate the universal. The spectators of the film are not laughing "at the expense of Poland or the Polish people. They laugh at actors . . . they laugh at something that is in no way typically Polish, but universal." Conversely, he has not "resorted to methods usually employed in pictures, novels, and plays to signify Nazi terror." His Nazis are not exceptional monsters, and the "positive characters," the adulterous Maria Tura and her husband, the "ham" Josef Tura, are no heroes. But the Nazis are men who have lost their humanity. "Brutality, flogging, and torturing have become their daily routine. They talk about it as a salesman referring to the sale of a handbag."[139]

Lubitsch had consciously violated the realist formula in one of the most heartfelt anti-Nazi films ever made. He did not openly call for the political mobilization of his audience. Rather, he dealt with Nazism but rejected any reference to realism as a way to approach the subject. Farce, in fact, seemed to have become both form and content. How could Lubitsch, many refugees and Hollywood radicals argued, have a Nazi general compare his slaughtering of Warsaw with the ham actor's slaughter of *Hamlet*? The *Daily Worker* argued that Lubitsch's treatment was "the touch of death when applied to the tragedy of our lives." Bosley Crowther, in the *New York Times*, called it "callous and macabre." Manny Farber lambasted the film in *New Republic* as a "thick skin" disaster for making "Nazi-dominated and cholera-ridden Poland a world of laughs." Hungarian-born composer Miklos Rosza, originally chosen by Lubitsch to score the film, refused to have anything to do with it. After the premiere, Lubitsch was openly criticized by long-time friends such as Billy Wilder, Alexander Korda, and Henry Blanke for what they perceived as a lack of taste on Lubitsch's part. James Agee, himself embarked on a soul-searching investigation about the relationship between cinema and truth, gave *To Be* a very positive review.[140]

Even though it was put to remarkably less polemical uses than Sturges's *Sullivan's Travels*, Lubitsch's resurrection of slapstick was more wickedly subversive than Chaplin's and had no final in-camera address as a redeeming feature. *To Be or Not to Be* criticized realism more pointedly than did *The Great Dictator* as a way to achieve meaningful political goals by calling the spectators' attention to the "conventionality" of cinema. As Donald Crafton has acutely noted, while slapstick de-centered the Hollywood classical style, it also de-centered the realistic paradigm insofar as they were both predicated upon the "realist effect," the power of cinema to communicate the illusion of truth.[141]

Gorelik, Agee, Schulberg, Lubitsch, Sturges, and Chaplin—all prominent voices—expressed a dissatisfaction with the realistic paradigm of the late 1930s. Notably, and with the possible exception of Sturges, they were all writing from the perspective of Hollywood modernism, each acknowledging the political and esthetic possibilities of good mass-marketed cinema. Their written and filmic interventions underscored the intensification of the debate within the community. The Nazi-Soviet Pact and the horrors of the war had begun to unravel the Hollywood coalition, touching off debates that only Pearl Harbor would—at least partially—muffle.

5

The "Only Respectable Clothes"

Progressive Hollywood and Democratic Realism during World War II

We suffer—we vaguely realize—a unique and constantly intensifying schizophrenia which threatens no other nation involved in this war. Geography is at the core of the disease.

James Agee, *The Nation*, 1943

n 1941, writer John Sanford seemed to have it all. In his mid-thirties and already rather successful as a novelist, Sanford had gone to Hollywood in 1936 on a contract with Paramount. In California, he met his future wife, screenwriter Marguerite Roberts. By 1941, he and Roberts co-wrote *Honky Tonk*, a comedy with Clark Gable and Lana Turner. In 1942, however, Sanford happily left it all behind to volunteer his services through the Hollywood Writers' Mobilization for the 834th Signal Service Photographic Detachment Unit headed by director Frank Capra. Once in Washington, Sanford cheerfully churned out script pages in a cubicle for twenty dollars a day.[1] At the end of six weeks, the writer had contributed two scripts: the original one for *The Battle of Russia* and another, which remained unproduced, for *Know Your Ally: Russia*. Capra liked both and asked Sanford to stay in the unit and become a commissioned officer. Sanford was ecstatic. A few days later, however, Capra asked for Sanford's resignation. Having heard rumors that Sanford was a communist, the rather conservative director did not want to risk the still uncertain status of the unit over political matters. Sanford's morale was destroyed. Although he had other options, military khakis were, as Sanford wrote to Capra, "the only clothes (aside from overalls) that the day recognizes as respectable."[2]

Sanford's story captures the ambiguity of World War II from the perspective of Hollywood progressives. It was a war they embraced wholeheartedly and yet one in which they struggled to find a legitimate role. Sanford was not the only Hollywood progressive who was dismissed because of his political views. Nor was his enthusiasm for the war exceptional. World War II was likely to be the defining event of these progressives' lives and promised to give them the opportunity to fight fascism with their real bodies or, at the very least, through their films.

For the first time, Hollywood progressives found in government agencies such as the Office of War Information (OWI) powerful allies who advocated many of the changes in Hollywood narrative that the progressive wanted to put forth. Searching for an explicitly political tradition in Hollywood films, government agencies were compelled to look for it in the intellectual circles and works of the Hollywood anti-fascists. Though semi-institutionalized as a government doctrine, the realist paradigm was also still broad enough to provide room for the coexistence of different, even contrasting, styles: from the patriotism of Frank Capra's *Why We Fight* to the democratic realism of John Huston's and William Wyler's documentaries.

After the crisis of 1939–1941, the German invasion of Soviet Russia in June 1941 had somewhat reestablished the Soviets' status as one of the leaders of the anti-fascist world struggle. After Pearl Harbor, the United States had broken free of the isolationist circles and entered the war. Indeed, for many Hollywoodians, at the beginning of 1942 the war seemed already like a victory.

The Office of War Information

Throughout the New Deal, war had been frequently used as an "analogue" of the Great Depression, but when Pearl Harbor was attacked the United States was inadequately unprepared for the fight ahead.[3] In the years prior to the war, Roosevelt had consistently frustrated the plans of those—like former World War I War Industries Board czar Bernard

Baruch—who recommended a centralized policy of mobilization. As a result, agencies with conflicting and overlapping tasks proliferated, yet Roosevelt's control over the government remained intact.[4] The same situation reigned in the field of propaganda, and especially in the film sector. Giuliana Muscio has recently documented the tight relationship between the Roosevelt White House and Hollywood during the 1930s, when the New Deal administration actively participated in the production of several documentaries endorsing its programs.[5] In 1940, however, the attempt to institutionalize this activity into a separate government agency, the U.S. Film Service, was hampered by a U.S. Congress suspicious of Roosevelt's tendency to use the agency for his immediate electoral purposes.[6] As a result, the U.S. government entered the war without any agency devoted to the production of propaganda films, and to guide and to channel the activity of the private sector of film production. Both inside and outside of the administration, many were hesitant about the creation of a specific propaganda agency, given what many considered the excesses of the Creel Committee during World War I.

These doubts were largely dispelled by America's entry into the war in December 1941. Over the next few months, the United States equipped itself with a plethora of agencies dedicated to the undermining of enemy morale and the gathering of American public consensus for the war effort. Propaganda had become another war front, and a crucial one at that. In July 1941, New York lawyer William "Wild Bill" Donovan became head of the Office of the Coordinator of Information. Appropriately enough for an agency that was later to evolve into the CIA, Donovan's task was blatant propaganda and counter-information—that is, the dissemination of false news in enemy territories. Other agencies such as Lowell Mellett's Office of Government Records (created in 1939), the 834th Signal Service Photographic Detachment Unit of the Army (1942), Nelson Rockefeller's Office of the Coordinator for Inter-American Affairs (1940), and Robert Sherwood's Foreign Information Service (1941, later Voice of America within OWI) overlapped in the common task of producing what was called either "informational" or "inspirational" propaganda, in reference to the relative measure of truth contained.[7]

Roosevelt soon decided to give a semblance of coordination to the effort in the propaganda sector through the creation of one agency that was supposedly in charge of all related chores. The Office of War Information—created with Executive Order 9182 on June 13, 1942—was headed by Elmer Davis, a nationally known and interventionist-minded radio commentator for the CBS network. OWI inherited functions and personnel from Mellett's Office of Government Records (OGR) and Robert Sherwood's Foreign Information Service. The head of OGR, Lowell Mellett, became the Washington chairman of OWI's Bureau of Motion Pictures (OWI-BMP), while Sherwood headed the overseas branch. Mellett chose Nelson Poynter as his representative in Hollywood.[8]

Roosevelt's claims notwithstanding, OWI was far from holding the monopoly on the administration of film propaganda. The army soon had its own organization, the 834th Signal Service Photographic Detachment Unit headed by Colonel Frank Capra, and Nelson Rockefeller's Coordinator for Inter-American Affairs (CIAA) continued to produce film propaganda directed at Latin America. As for the control of Hollywood films, the agency had to compete with the Office of Censorship (OOC) created on December 16, 1941, and headed by Associate Press editor Byron Price; OOC could deny exportation to liberated or allied areas of films deemed unfavorable to the image of the United States.[9] The army also constituted a further, mostly independent filter insofar as it could deny its collaboration to films whose content it deemed unsatisfactory. In addition, OWI's domestic branch came increasingly under congressional fire because of its pro-New Deal stance (like its predecessor, the Office of Government Films). In the spring of 1943, Congress cut OWI's funds by two-thirds, practically shutting down its domestic unit. Once production of domestic propaganda was curtailed, however, OWI actually increased its control over Hollywood. Ulric Bell, the energetic head of the overseas branch of the OWI-BMP, in fact devised a strategy of tight collaboration with the OOC and denied export rights to any Hollywood film that he deemed unsatisfactory.[10]

OWI's Realism

Resentful of the increasing authority of OWI, Hollywood executives often accused its representatives of incompetence. In reality, neither Poynter nor Mellett nor Bell had any experience in the making of motion pictures. However, OWI soon drew its staff from the industry itself. In 1945, the War Activities Committee calculated that seven thousand Hollywood studio employees worked for the agency at some point during the conflict.[11] This influence is evident in the first government manual to the motion picture industry issued on June 2, 1942, which was almost a verbatim version of the Hollywood paradigm of the 1930s. The war was a "people's war," both outside and inside the United States, as the manual made clear that the people of Germany, Italy, and Japan should not be confused with the enemy. Like the Hollywood progressives of the 1930s, OWI consistently employed the notion of people as a trope for its audience, refusing to distinguish among different constituencies. Like the unified, unspecified audience for Hollywood's democratic modernism of the 1930s, the intended audience for OWI's film propaganda largely overlapped with the American people. As opposed to other means of communication such as press or theater, the cinema audience was "the people," which the manual used as a synonym of intelligent (because informed) mass opinion and which overlapped with America, as a homogeneous unit going beyond the notion of class (and gender and race for that matter).

The manual also expressed faith in Hollywood cinema as a possible channel of political and factual communication, the precondition for an informed public opinion and for a democratic war. Films were to draw on the example of the past few years, such as *Confessions of a Nazi Spy*. "We believe," the manual stated, "that mass opinion is intelligent and will support an intelligent program—*if informed*." [12] Cinema, therefore, was to inform the public on a vast array of issues including the "Enemy," "The United Nations and Peoples," "Work and Production," "The Home Front," and the "Fighting Forces."

In a letter to Gardner Cowles, Jr., head of OWI's domestic branch, Hollywood producer Walter Wanger praised OWI's aims while repeating the classic Hollywood progressive conviction that cinema "was the greatest visual educational factor accepted by the masses." Radio and the press were limited in their ability to appeal to the masses, but films, "the other great American means of communication, . . . appeal to the workers, the youth, the women and those who must win the fight and the peace." The manual also repeated the caveats typical of Hollywood progressives concerning excessive narrative celebrations of individual heroism. As for the fighting forces, for example, the text noted that it was "easy to dramatize the more spectacular services of the Army. It is a more difficult but necessary job to dramatize . . . the service of Supply." [13]

Gregory Black and Clayton R. Koppes, in comparing the OWI's code with the Hollywood 1934 self-regulatory code, have pointed out how the former is as exhaustive as the latter, giving detailed instructions on how to treat any aspect of the war. [14] The differences between the two codes, however, should stand as a testament to the changes in public perception of cinema, from an institution dedicated to the accumulation of private profits to one with an increasingly public role. The 1930 Code that the Production Code Administration enforced after 1934 was based on the idea that cinema was the opposite of what OWI was telling Americans that it should be. The 1930 Code stated explicitly that its authors "regarded the function of cinema primarily as entertainment without any explicit purpose of teaching and propaganda."[15] For OWI, just like for the Hollywood progressives of the late 1930s, Hollywood had a public function of informing and educating the masses about the issues of the day. The ideals of the Hollywood community had moved from the margins to the heart of public discourse about cinema.

The overlapping of OWI's film ideology with that of the Hollywood progressives is not surprising. Hollywood New Yorkers and Europeans were in the forefront of the organization. These two groups had asked for an active anti-Nazi policy throughout the late 1930s, and America's entrance into the war presented the opportunity for them to contribute to the cause. At the outbreak of the conflict, the Hollywood community was, in fact, in the midst of a patriotic wave, and many Hollywood stars contributed to the activities of the Hollywood Canteen, founded by John Garfield and Bette Davis in the summer of 1942.[16]

Fritz Lang's contemporary correspondence contains numerous expression of this attitude. While still corresponding in German with several intellectual refugees, Lang attempted to reconcile his allegiance to local and translocal networks and communities with a deeply felt sense of American identity. The director thanked Leo Weaver, member of the Motion Picture Division Advisory Board of Flagstaff, Arizona, for appreciating his film, *Western Union*. Weaver's comments "sho[w] me that I am not a 'foreigner' anymore, but belong to America."[17]

Such enthusiasm was common among Hollywood Europeans. Charles Boyer organized the Hollywood Free France Committee in 1941.[18] British subjects such as Alexander Korda and Alfred Hitchcock had lobbied for American entry in the war since the late 1930s.[19] *Aufbau*'s Hollywood insert, "Die Westküste," proudly informed its readers of the few Hollywood Europeans who were accepted to serve in the army in some function. Alexander Esway, the Hungarian producer and director who was in France at the time of the German invasion, was reported as engaged "to teach American Army his knowledge and experience of war."[20] In February 1942, Hans Kafka appealed to all Hollywood Europeans to contribute to the war effort and invited Hollywood Europeans to enroll in the California State Guard. As noncitizens, Hollywood Europeans would not be accepted as regulars, but—Kafka announced—a few weeks earlier "permission was given [by the government] to form an auxiliary corps of 'non-citizens,' named 'Victory Legion,' with the same duties, same rights and same uniform as the main corps."[21]

Enthusiasm did not wane after the introduction of the dusk-to-dawn curfew for German, Japanese, and Italian citizens in the United States as a result of Franklin D. Roosevelt's Proclamation 2525.[22] At first, it seemed that those who enlisted in the Victory Legion were to be exempted from the curfew. A few days later, however, Kafka informed his readers that this was not the case. Hollywood Europeans, he continued, should enlist anyway "to give tangible proof of our determination to do our duty."[23] A few refugee commentators were less forgiving of the United States than Kafka was. When the curfew was announced, the refugee magazine *Aufbau* was incensed and marveled that "this has been the destiny of thousands of Hitler-haters, Jewish and Christian anti-Fascists."[24] Yet the magazine did not abandon its support of the Roosevelt administration. The measure was unfair but was justified; especially in the case of the Japanese, the magazine argued, caution was understandable.[25]

Often Hollywood Europeans claimed that they were the best equipped for fashioning the message about Germany and for speaking to the German people because of their deep knowledge of German psychology. As Fritz Lang wrote in a letter to a friend in February 1942,

> some people like Feuchtwanger, Heinrich Mann, Bert Brecht, etc., think it is aggravating to see how Anti-Axis Propaganda is handled. I do so too. This Anti-Nazi Propaganda (to me) seems to be lukewarm, without new ideas or pluck, self complecant [*sic*] and inefficient. . . . The German people will never be aroused by [it]. . . . I am reading so much in these days about what to do with the Enemy Aliens. I read about their dangerousness etc., but I don't read anything about how to use (at least part of) these Aliens for the sake of the country. I am convinced that the unused creative powers of the German immigration for example should be made useful, should be inserted into the service of the American anti-Axis-Propaganda.[26]

In March 1942, Lang applied to the War Department for a commission to make training movies for the army, only to have his services politely refused as unnecessary.[27] The reply to Lang probably hid the hard truth that many refugees were to experience: that, in the words of Senator Ralph O. Brewster of the Senate Committee on the National Defense

Program, preference was to be accorded "more seasoned" Americans over "recent citizens" whenever production of war films was concerned.[28] Robert Siodmak was prevented from taking part in the war effort because of his friendship with Charlie Chaplin.[29] Salka Viertel remembers numerous visits by FBI agents ("strong, handsome, young men, who would have served their country better in the Marines rather than harassing the refugees") asking information about her boarder, Annie von Bucovich, then employed in Washington by the Office of War Information.[30]

While noncitizens were barred from active service and subjected to limitations of their liberties, active service in the army for many native and naturalized Hollywood progressives was not possible because of their age, health, gender, or politics. Thirty-year-old Nicholas Ray tried to enlist but was given a 4-F deferral because he had lost the sight in his right eye in a car accident.[31] John Garfield applied for the army but was designated 4-F because of a congenital heart murmur.[32] John Bright was thirty-three and in good health at the time of the attack on Pearl Harbor; he immediately volunteered for active service only to be turned down because of his radical politics. Eventually Bright made it into the Coast Guard.[33] Edward Dmytryk was rejected because of his "premature antifascism,"[34] and so were the Epstein brothers, John Sanford, and Jerome Chodorov, all progressive Hollywood New Yorkers whom Frank Capra had originally chosen for his 834th Signal Service Photographic Detachment Unit, Special Service Division of the Army.[35] Philip Dunne tried to enlist in the army and was rejected on the basis of his political background. Barred from active service, Dunne worked for a while in Nelson Rockefeller's CIAA. Rumors of his political liability followed him there even after he left the CIAA, displeased with the haphazard manner in which the billionaire New Dealer was running the agency. In 1943, Dunne wrote Rockefeller asking him to dispel the rumor that he had been fired from the CIAA for being a "dangerous radical."[36] Dunne finally found a niche in the OWI, where he produced films—in particular Jean Renoir's *Salute to France*—for the liberated areas.

The networks of friendship and political commitment that had played such an important role in the Hollywood community of the 1930s were now mobilized to provide Hollywood New Yorkers and Hollywood Europeans with positions in the army or in the photographic service. Salka Viertel's son, Peter, wrote fellow Hollywood progressive John Houseman for a recommendation to the Signal Corps photographic unit headed by Fred Spacer. He was looking forward to doing "something effective and interesting" during the conflict. And the war was soon to be over—Viertel wrote in April 1942—and afterwards "we will all go back to Hollywood and make artistic movies and perhaps break the back of Paramount."[37]

A job with the OWI served for many—such as Houseman, Nicholas Ray, Dunne, Irving Lerner, and Leo Hurwitz—as an alternative to the active duty from which they were barred. Condemned by many contemporary conservative politicians as a refuge for hopeless liberal and radical intellectuals, OWI is indeed depicted as a place of masculine, martial virtues in many of the Hollywood progressives' autobiographies. OWI was "a no nonsense, no frills, no glamour" agency where the willingness to do one's part counted more than one's politics, recalls Dunne.[38] Both its radio and motion picture facilities were indeed the place where Hollywood Europeans could find some kind of job, even as "recent" citizens. In May 1943, Hans Kafka reported that "a whole regiment of European-born actors, directors, and speakers is being mobilized in Hollywood by the Overseas Bureau of the Office of War Information to turn out short features in the respective languages of their origin."[39]

While most of the Hollywood progressives characterized their experience at OWI as satisfying, they felt that it did not substitute for active service. Peter Viertel was ill-treated throughout his first eleven months in the marines because of his political views. Nonetheless, he gladly stuck it out. "Now he is assigned to the officers school," Salka wrote to a friend, "but thinks there still exists a secret file against him and the true Marine that he is, he wants to go after the invisible enemy."[40] In April 1943, while already employed at the OWI, Dunne wrote (to no avail) to Frank G. Andrew, Civil Aeronautic Administration, to ask whether he had a chance of "qualifying under [the] Navy's program" as a pilot.[41]

The Two Discourses of World War II Documentaries

The desperate tone of these letters demonstrated that for many Hollywood progressives, the anti-fascist war represented the crowning of several deeply felt political choices. It was a democratic war fought by the American people against fascism on behalf of the peoples of the world. Missing it was not so much an accident but a personal disaster—the inability to live up to one's ideals and self-image. Being there was a moment of personal glory, a moment to be endlessly represented and commemorated in writing and, as we shall see, in images.

In his autobiography, Frank Capra tellingly marked as the date of his army oath December 8, 1941—the day after the attack on Pearl Harbor—while the actual date was more than one month later, January 29, 1942.[42] In their biographies, articles, films, and letters, the Hollywood progressives who did see combat reveled in the details of their army experience and the meager existence they shared with the ordinary American boys. Going through the 1945 volume of the *Screenwriter*, the Screen Writers' Guild (SWG) magazine edited by Dalton Trumbo, one cannot escape the many "reports from a GI typewriter," memoirs written from the front by Hollywood progressives and commemorating the experience of the war.[43]

Hollywood progressives who took active part in the conflict gave visual representation to their presence on the war front. John Huston enlisted in the Signal Corps in April 1942 and was sent into the subpolar, inhospitable climate of the Aleutian Islands to shoot a documentary about American aerial attacks on the Japanese base of Kisca. In his autobiography, Huston takes pains to tell the readers that on Kisca he was one of the boys, living in a tent in the cold "along with the rest of the personnel." Huston's men were common GIs—not Hollywood professionals. Among them, Sergeant Hermann Crabtree, was

> a twin brother of Li'l Abner some six feet four inches tall and weighing over 200 pounds. I remember his enormous, ox-like eyes. I used to conjecture how much one of his eyeballs would weigh. He was strong as an Ox too. We'd load him up with the equipment . . . to take out to the planes. I could've jumped onto his back too. And I swear, he wouldn't have known the difference.[44]

The movie that came out of the experience, *Report from the Aleutians*, was—as much as Joris Ivens's *Action Stations!* (completed in February 1943 for the Royal Canadian Navy), Huston's later *The Battle of San Pietro* (1944), William Wyler's *Memphis Belle* (1944), or John Ford's *The Battle of Midway* (1942)—both a committed tribute to the common Americans living and dying in the armed forces as well as a celebration of the Hollywood progressives' presence on the scene.[45] The first reels of *Report from the Aleutians* are dedicated to identifying the soldier as a common American. The army was the successful melting pot, blending "men from Brooklyn, or from Texas" and "bookkeepers, farmers, college men" into the new common identity of "soldier," a democratic community where—as Huston's commentary notes over images of soldiers informally saluting superior officers—"there is little room for formal discipline." The rest of *Report* made sure the spectators knew that Huston and his crew were active members of this democratic community, present in the conflict and actively participating in combat. The protracted aerial assault on Kisca, shown in the last two reels of the film, constructed an esthetic of authenticity based on the "presence" of the filmmaker aboard the ship. Shot from one of the planes, the mission over Kisca situates itself within the Hollywood narrative tradition. It is what John Howard Lawson would call the "obligatory scene," the climax of the film "which the audience foresees and desires and the absence of which it may with reason resent."[46] At the same time, the realism of the scene is colored by the "presence" of the filmmaker next to the bomber's crew. When the aircraft is fired on by the enemy, the camera bounces, at times losing focus, while the commentary is replaced by frantic exchanges over the intercoms and the booming sounds of battle.

John Ford, director of *The Grapes of Wrath* and *The Informer*, was using the same technique in his *Battle of Midway*. William Wyler also used it in his Oscar-winning *Memphis Belle*. Like *Report from the Aleutians, Memphis*—which Wyler shot with William Clothier, a veteran of the Spanish Civil War[47]—emphasized the authenticity of the footage ("all scene of aerial combat film was exposed during air battles over enemy territory"), and the heroism of the men, while framing the climatic event—the Memphis Belle's last mission to bomb Wilhelmhaven, Germany—between a prologue describing the soldiers' encampment in England and an epilogue showing the plane making its return to the base. The "presence" of the director's crew on the expedition was emphasized via the bouncing of the camera on board the aircraft, which revealed the real risks run by Wyler and his crew; a cameraman, Harold Tannenbaum, was killed during the filming. Symptomatically, the whole body of Hollywood is physically exported to the battlefront via the commentary by screenwriter Lester Koenig. As the camera shows a plasma transfusion, the commentary wishfully speculates that "the blood could even be of a movie star in Hollywood."

Progressive critics took notice. Joseph Foster remarked that "by the ingenious use of the camera you become witness to every detail of such action." James Agee pointed to the "vigorous and pitiful sense of the presence, danger, skill, and hope of several human beings" and commented that "I could not guess which shots were re-enacted and which were straight records." Comparing *Memphis Belle* and *With the Marines at Tarawa* to the British *Desert Victory*, Agee wrote that they "are documentaries with which for the first time we can look the English in the eye."[48]

Through their bouncing cameras, Huston, Wyler, and Ford implicitly inserted in their films a self-portrait that represented them as soldiers, ordinary Americans fighting and risking their lives amidst ordinary male GIs. These films focused on the army as a stand-in for the American people of *Confessions of a Nazi Spy*, a predominantly male, interclass, and interethnic construct governed by internal solidarity against the enemy. Nonsoldiers and diplomats are, if present at all, ironically juxtaposed with the fighting forces, with whom the sympathy of the director lies. In *Memphis Belle*, the final reel shows the incongruous visit of the British royal family to the airbase immediately after the mission has been completed. Joris Ivens's *Action Stations!* contains a humane portrait of the crew of the U-boat sunk by the *Corvette*. Once rescued by the Canadian *Corvette*, the Germans were human again ("they were just a pack of frightened men"). The film also stressed equality between soldiers and officers: "We didn't seem officers and men at all, just human beings who were comrades." Or, in a variation of the same scene, officers and soldiers were "[h]ugging and patting on the back. Bloody thankful, no difference between officers and men.").[49]

Routinely, Huston clashed with the upper echelons of the army. Recalling his wartime experience to documentary filmmaker Midge Mackenzie, Huston recalls that *The Battle of San Pietro* was disliked by the military brass and saved only through the intercession of George C. Marshall. His 1946 documentary *Let There Be Light*, a poignant portrait of shell-shocked veterans in a Long Island hospital, was too strong for the army, deeming the film unfit for general distribution.[50] Talking to Mackenzie, Huston argued that he never saw any difference between a good feature film and a documentary.[51] As a matter of fact, these films reflected the political esthetics of 1930s Hollywood progressives, which combined newsreel and Hollywood tradition to achieve a powerful realism while emphasizing American democracy. They were, as Gary Edgerton has recently pointed out, "traditional in film form and style."[52] Wyler, Ford, Huston, and Ivens all employed the Hollywood narrative style in their war documentaries—not only in the reenactments that occupy most of the footage of John Ford's and Gregg Toland's *December 7th*, Ivens's *Action Stations!* ("Sounds like Hollywood," the Dutch filmmaker commented in a lecture he gave at USC in June 1943), or in *Memphis Belle*'s ad-libbed intercom dialogue between the bomber crewmen, but also in a narrative structure that emphasized the climax of the last-reel battle, the suspense of the return, and the eventual happy ending.[53] Their narrative style demonstrated a profound respect for the reality itself and the possibility of cinema to capture it. The long unedited sequences of Huston's and Wyler's documentaries emphasized the intrinsic value of original footage where, as Hermine Rice Isaacs put it in *Theater Arts*, "the combat photographer is forced by the circumstances of his profession to speak his piece in pictures."[54]

The surrogate presence and symbols of male bonding characteristic of progressive documentaries stands in contrast with another kind of documentary that other Hollywood participants were producing at the time. The *Why We Fight* series produced by the 834th Signal Service Photographic Detachment Unit, headed by the more conservative Frank Capra, constructed the war effort according to a different pattern. Capra was selected for the job for his mastery of cinema and his conservative political background, and he immediately purged his unit of anyone he considered too radical.[55] The series makes no effort to understand the causes of the war as anything more than an unexplained assault on the world that began with the Japanese attack on Manchuria in 1931. *Why We Fight* is also racially biased against the Japanese people. Germans were portrayed as the victims of their dictators, and Italians were hardly mentioned. (One effort in regard to the latter, *Know Your Enemy: Italy*, was never produced.) Japanese people, on the contrary, were all guilty. When progressive screenwriter Carl Foreman and Dutch director Joris Ivens singled out the Japanese elites as the real criminals in the script for *Know Your Enemy: Japan*, the army rejected their work. The final version of the script for *Japan*—drafted by Capra and Theodor S. Geisel— lumped the Japanese people together with the military and industrial elites as beastly opponents to be exterminated. "We shall never completely understand the Japanese mind," the commentary notes; "defeating this nation is as necessary as shooting down a mad dog in your neighborhood."[56]

More importantly, the seven films of the series, *Prelude to War*, *The Nazis Strike*, *Divide and Conquer*, *The Battle of Britain*, *The Battle of Russia*, *The Battle of China*, and *War Comes to America*, together with *Hitler Lives?* and *Know Your Enemy: Japan*, were strikingly different from those produced in the Army Pictorial Services units directly administered by Huston, Wyler, and Ford. Capra's series was an entirely self-referential and self-contained discourse—each film concluded by introducing the issue covered in the next installment—and represented a different approach to the war documentary than the one embodied in the films of the Hollywood progressives, stressing the power of Hollywood rather than the presence of the Hollywoodians next to ordinary male Americans in arms.

Confronted with the necessity to set up his propaganda units, Capra decided not to shoot original footage but, rather, to use footage shot by the enemy and captured by the allies.[57] Capra's choices had more than one consequence. First, the Capra-produced series, as opposed to Huston's or Wyler's films, effaced the physical presence of Hollywood in the war. Absent from Capra's films is the democratic flair of Huston's and Wyler's documentaries. In comparison with their self-portraits as democrats, Capra's documentaries inscribed the filmmaker as the "great manipulator"—not the common soldier but instead the soldier's teacher. In essence, the filmmaker is the expert who is able to reveal the truth behind the enemy's propaganda and thus is no different from the war experts—Secretary of War Henry Stimson in *Know Your Enemy: Japan* and *Prelude to War*, William Mayer in *The Battle of China*, Vice President Henry A. Wallace in *Prelude to War*, Undersecretary of State Adolf A. Berle, Roosevelt, Henry Stimson, Wendell Wilkie, General George C. Marshall, and Secretary of State Cordell Hull in *War Comes to America*, to name a few—whom Capra repeatedly cites as the authorities behind these film narratives.

Adhering to the notion of a people's war, the *Why We Fight* series (in particular *The Battle of Britain*) depicts the common man as absent or the beneficiary of the experts' information. *Prelude to War* and *War Comes to America* stress that American mistakes are due to the ordinary American, never to "experts." In both the first and last installments of the series, Coolidge's—and Roosevelt's—Secretary of War Henry Stimson is given credit for denouncing the Japanese aggression in Manchuria as early as 1931; there is no mention of Roosevelt's notorious "Good Man" telegram to Neville Chamberlain in the aftermath of Munich or of Joseph Kennedy's open sympathies with the fascists.[58] Both *Prelude to War* and *War Comes to America*, through 1939 Pathé newsreels that Capra inserted in the films, represent the statesmen as farsighted, while representing American Joes and Janes as foolhardy isolationists—ordinary people who clearly need guidance. To highlight the point that France was defeated not by Hitler but by its own "cynicism and disillusionment," *Divide and Conquer* shows working-class Parisians on strike during the invasion.

Ultimately, the war documentaries offered two discourses, at times overlapping but often diverse. In *New Masses*, Daniel Prentiss noted that the war was producing "two distinct types of documentary": one was "editorial and urgent in its approach. You feel from the outset that you are in the grip of a strong directing intelligence. Such film takes you by the hand. It shows you only what it wants you to see. The tangential and peripheral are deliberately omitted." The other type was "seemingly more casual. Its audiences appear to be left on their own. The camera becomes their eyes as they wander about town. They just happen to notice things."[59] The second type, embodied in the documentaries of Ford, Huston, Wyler, and Ivens, represented the presence of the Hollywoodian on the war front, a common man among common men, and subscribed to the ability of the filmed image to engage the pursuit of truth. The first type, on the other hand, was based on the predominance of montage and implicitly represented the Hollywoodian as the master manipulator. Any single shot was open to post-filmic manipulation, subservient to the director's dramatic/political ideal. The filmmaker wrestled with the images' power, redirected through frequent editing and an ever-present off-screen voice. In masterpieces of editing such as *Know Your Enemy: Japan*, *Prelude to War*, and *Divide and Conquer*, this manipulative technique overpowered the German and Japanese propaganda machine to scare American soldiers into action. *The Negro Soldier* (1943–44)—a project for which the military had discarded the original script by Lillian Hellman along with the original director William Wyler—manipulated American history itself. After a prologue in a black church, a breathtaking montage managed to mix the cinema of D. W. Griffith (clips from his epic on the American Revolution, *America*, 1920) with newsreel clips from Joe Louis's boxing matches and Tuskegee football games in order to recount the first two hundred years of the African American experience—all without mentioning slavery, lynching, or Jim Crow.[60]

The Fictional Body of Hollywood

Michael Paul Rogin has explored the "boundary confusion" between film and real life that allowed American studio filmmakers, such as director D. W. Griffith and actor Ronald Reagan, to erase the boundaries between film and the real world, and to imagine themselves in different—and more personally convenient—situations than those they actually lived.[61] Modern warfare, with its demand for involvement of the entire civilian population in the war effort, extends this boundary confusion even further. It is no longer solely the filmmaker's desires that may benefit from the confusion between the boundaries of his/her historical body and his/her screen persona. The state and military apparatus also profit, as Paul Virilio has argued, from the conscious blurring of the boundaries of the screen and those of the world inhabited by the masses.[62] Ordinary spectators can be marshaled into endorsing the war effort by the "authenticity" of the war films, which makes spectators "feel" the urgency of the situation.

According to James Agee, the "illusion of proximity" that the camera promised could solve the "disease of geography"[63] for the United States—a mass democracy that had never experienced the brutality of enemy invasion in the twentieth century.

> Since it is beyond our power to involve ourselves as deeply in experience as the people of Russia, England, China, Germany, Japan, we have to make up the difference as well as we can at second hand. Granting that knowledge at second hand, taken at a comfortable distance is of itself choked with new and terrible liabilities, I believe, nevertheless, that much could be done to combat and reduce those liabilities, and that second hand knowledge is at least less dangerous than no knowledge at all. And I think it is obvious that in imparting it, moving pictures can be matchlessly useful.[64]

Such "illusion of proximity," which cinema was deemed able to communicate, would prompt spectators to realize the importance of the military field and make them real participants in the war effort. During the 1898 Spanish-American War, an ad in the New York *World* stressed that war movies were "Taking New Yorkers Practically to Cuba by Photography."[65] In one of them (*U.S. Infantry Supported by Rough Riders at El Caney*, 1899), soldiers kneel down and shoot directly at the camera. This pattern of "shot in camera" extended the conflict beyond the boundaries of the screen so that the fighting involved the common spectator, the veritable doppelgänger of the common soldier.[66]

During World War II, this boundary confusion offered the anti-fascist filmmaker vicarious participation in an effort from which he/she was barred because of his/her health, gender, age, or radical politics. To the American government, it promised the strengthening of the home front and the emotional involvement of spectators in the war effort. In 1898 and even more in 1943, in films as much as in other media, American propagandists attempted to abolish the boundaries between actual combat and the American domestic scene. Actions performed in the United States mattered on the front, specifically because these boundaries were blurred. "Our outpost, your frontyard" begins Dudley Nichols's famous commentary for *The Battle of Midway*. "He talks. He dies" screamed an OWI poster. Symptomatically, the shot of *U.S. Infantry Supported by Rough Riders at El Caney* was reproduced in at least two of the most famous combat films of the war, *Bataan* (MGM, directed by Tay Garnett and written by Robert Andrews) and *Wake Island* (Paramount, directed by John Farrow and written by W. R. Burnett and Frank Butler). In *Bataan*— "our idea of a wonderfully useful picture" according to OWI's Nelson Poynter, and "the seminal film" of the combat genre according to film critic Jeanine Basinger—Robert Taylor, the last survivor of the American battalion stranded in the Guadalcanal peninsula, points his machine gun to the camera and shoots at the Japanese enemy, the trajectory of the bullets grazing the heads of the spectators in the theater.[67] *Wake Island*, a film that OWI praised profusely, tells the story of a platoon of marines wiped out by the Japanese.[68] The last scene—a Japanese grenade exploding just in front of the camera, missing the audience by a few degrees—is meant to startle the spectators.

Predicated upon both the Hollywoodians' desire and the state's necessity for communicating at least authentic-looking "second-hand knowledge," semidocumentary realism became the paradigmatic alternative for Hollywood. Many Hollywood progressives refashioned their screen personae in tune with their ideals. In many cases, their figuration on the screen projected more of their political and cultural identity than had been the case in previous years. Progressive actors, in particular, had often kept their two "bodies"—the real one and the image on the screen—separate, in part due to the relative implausibility of Hollywood films and, for some actors, because of the limited roles they were allowed to play. There had been instances when the two bodies had almost coincided, as in the case of *Confessions of a Nazi Spy*, in which many of the filmmakers had acted out their real political and social beliefs. After *Confessions*, however, its anti-Nazi star Edward G. Robinson had gone back to playing a gangster in *Brother Orchid*. But the war represented for the Hollywood progressives and the European anti-fascists an opportunity to reunite screen personae with their anti-fascist selves. Often unwilling to enlist their real bodies, in fact, the government was willing to make military use of their celluloid personae. On the screen, if not in real life, Hollywood progressives and refugees could get the anti-fascist job done. In 1943, agent Paul Kohner noted that Hollywood was pursuing "a European atmosphere" and could not do without European screenwriters, actors, directors, or producers. Actors with an accent were in high demand, and some top refugee directors and writers were earning "an average" ("durchschnittlich") of $1,500 per week.[69] "We were God those days," screenwriter Froeschel remembered.[70]

Like soldiers, the body of the actors had to be trimmed according to military needs. Veronica Lake abandoned her peekaboo hairstyle to sport a more martial haircut. Paradoxes abounded. German refugees had to invert their political biographies and portray members of the Nazi establishment, the American screen offering few opportunities to portray a German anti-Nazi. Some refused. Francis Lederer, the Czech star of *Confessions*, withdrew from Paramount's *Hostages* so as not to play a Czech Quisling.[71] But most complied and fought the screen war in disguise, enlisting en masse in the "Hollywood Hitler Gangs" to give bodies and voices to cruel screen Nazis and legitimate Hollywood's quest for authenticity. Economically, the war years were a blessing for the Europeans. "Suddenly," Frederick Kohner remembers, "the industry needed Prussian generals, bullnecked SS officers, Führers, Stuka fliers, Austrian zither players, Jewish scientists, U-boat captains, revolutionaries, spies and counterspies. Paul [Kohner] supplied them all."[72] For some of the screen gangsters, the war meant an opportunity to reshape their screen personae in a fashion more in line with their beliefs. Few gangster films were made during the war, as OWI disliked gangster films and called *Mr. Lucky*'s portrayal of a professional gambler an "unfavorable presentation of America."[73] Such a change was welcomed by some of the 1930s practitioners of the genre, such as Edward G. Robinson, who had grown weary of gangster roles.[74]

Both OWI and Hollywood progressives applauded the semidocumentary realism of some American war films. *Wake Island*, released in September 1942, was probably the first of the semidocumentaries, its credits listing half a dozen military advisors and informing the public that it was drawn entirely "from the records of the U.S. Marine Corps." In the *New Republic*, Manny Farber announced that "finally—and it's about time—Hollywood has gone to war" and hoped these films "mark[ed] the start of a new attitude."[75] *Guadalcanal Diary*, from the real-life diary of marine Richard Tregaskis, won almost as much consensus. The audience at the Roxy, wrote Crowther in the *Times*, "was visibly stirred and . . . no doubt had the impression that it was witnessing the battle of Guadalcanal."[76] In *New Masses*, Daniel Prentiss called the film "a memorable exposition of the character of American fighting men."[77]

In the films that OWI considered successful examples of Hollywood's contribution to the war effort, narrative choices endorsed the strategy of documentary realism. Howard Hawks's *Air Force*—the story of B-17 bomber *Mary Anne*'s missions from Pearl Harbor to the Battle of Coral Sea—was approved by nearly everyone, particularly the military who sent Jack Warner several letters of congratulations.[78] The reason was its realism. Low-level employees of OWI denounced the racism of *Air Force*, which in one scene charged the Japanese in Hawaii with sabotage.[79] However, both Ulric Bell, the director of OWI's overseas branch, and Nelson Poynter, OWI's representative in Hollywood, ignored the blatant anti-Japanese racism of the film, lauding it as an example of "a most wonderful contribution [to the war effort]." Poynter wrote Warner in February 1943 that "several members of our staff saw *Air Force* this week and are as enthusiastic about it as I am." Bell agreed, recommending *Air Force* for "its use overseas" and calling the film "a fine contribution to the war effort."[80] The film, concluded the *Daily Mirror*, was a "screen document" of the war, exactly communicating its experience. Therefore, "women should see such things, [as] they can't live them."[81]

Much like with real soldiers during war, *Air Force* transformed the screen personae of its interpreters by their participation in the screen war. Upon enlisting, American soldiers were given a new identity based on rank. Likewise, the credits of the film—recalling the example set in 1939 by the credits of *Confessions*—listed the actors according to the military rank of their characters, rather than according to their relative star power.[82] The film's pursuit of realism further chastised Hollywood star personae. The story of *Air Force* has neither romance nor a clear-cut protagonist. Furthermore, beginning with his initial treatment of the film, Dudley Nichols replaced Hollywood glamour with wartime rigor. The first scenes were to be only "faces, instruments, making us feel the excitement of this difficult work. We don't tell what it is about. The men have oxygen tubes protruding from their masks. We can cut in on the 'intercom' . . . and get the 'feel' of what it is like to be on a bombing mission.[83] In the finished film, a production note from Warner remarked, "Only 20 percent of the footage of *Air Force* has dialogue; ordinarily there is twice that much conversation . . . [and] the average of close-ups per foot of film has been reduced by 90 percent, thus heightening the speed and tempo tremendously."[84] James Agee, who was not very sympathetic to the Hollywood war effort and the kind of realism it was pursuing, noted in *The Nation* the "gladdening effort to get away from the movie faces and to give the men diverse and authentic speech."[85]

War directives, filmmakers' desires, and war-film narrative conventions ultimately complemented each other. *Air Force* was directed by Hawks, scripted by Dudley Nichols, and interpreted by a mixture of professional and semiprofessional actors led by John Garfield. It was a success in the eyes of both the OWI and the Hollywood progressives—a "remarkably good movie," according to the *Daily Worker*.[86]

For the moment, Hollywood progressives and progressive critics were essentially willing to make a trade-off, overlooking the obvious anti-Japanese racism of the film in exchange for an emphasis on realism and people's narrative embodied in the heterosocial, collective protagonist—the crew—fighting together with "teamwork," in the words of *The People's World*.[87] For Joris Ivens, the film was evidence of the positive changes the war was producing in Hollywood. In his cycle of lectures at the University of Southern California, the Dutch director singled out *Air Force* and *Wake Island* as the latest evidence of Hollywood's "good" side, its documentary tradition, along with *The Grapes of Wrath, Dead End, Fury, They Won't Forget, Our Daily Bread*, and *I Am a Fugitive from a Chain Gang*.[88]

That Garfield and others involved in making *Air Force* were willing to give up their star status is not surprising, as the creators of the film were engrossed in playing out their war fantasies on sound stages. Since the beginning, the military exercised a profound influence on the set of *Air Force*, offering help in the form of two technical advisors—Captain P. Triffy and Captain Theron Coulter—dispatched to the set, but making its cooperation dependent on the studio's willingness to militarize itself. The film was to be subject "to review by the war department prior to any showing (sneak preview, press or sales screenings) or public release."[89] And the studio—producers and progressives alike—merrily collaborated in the semitransformation of a studio set into a faux military camp. After Pearl Harbor, Jack Warner affixed placards all over the Burbank sound stages to inform his employees of a "ban on conversing in any foreign language."[90] Howard Hawks had Herman Lissauer put together an extensive bible "of the bombing of Pearl Harbor, especially Hickam Field, Wake Island and Manila."[91] Director Hawks and ten others, including principals in the cast, were required to take an oath, administered by government agents, that they would maintain the secrecy of official military information necessary for the filming.[92] "Christ," Hawks later commented, "he [General Henry H. 'Hap' Arnold] even made me a general for a week."[93]

Style became a weapon, the medium through which one would play out his/her passions at an imaginary level, because access to the "real thing" was unavailable. James Wong Howe, the Chinese-born director of photography and a noted Hollywood progressive, devised for *Air Force* what he called "the 'cruel system' of lighting for the Chinese playing the Japs. The principal feature of the technique is head-on lighting without any relieving, or softening spotlights, giving the subject a harsh straight black-and-white contrast."[94]

Denied American citizenship by the Chinese Exclusion Act, Howe had not been able to enlist or even serve in John Ford's unit, though Ford had invited him and pleaded Howe's case with the army and the State Department. The only path open to Howe for gaining a commission was to enlist in Chiang Kai-shek's army and then to be "loaned" to Ford's crew. The photographer refused the plan as insulting; moreover, he was not at all a supporter of Chiang Kai-shek.[95] Unable to serve in the real war, Howe translated its violence through cinematic style, using his camera to blur the boundaries between Hollywood studio films and war documentaries. In *Air Force*, Howe connected the film to the democratic realism of Huston's, Wyler's and Ford's documentaries. Like the camera of *Report from the Aleutians*, Howe's photography—as he later explained at the 1943 Congress of the Hollywood Writers Mobilization—was meant to convey an impression of presence and authenticity. For *Air Force*, Howe devised a particular technique based on the use of the Eyemo 16 mm camera, which was usually used on the front by the war photographers. In "the most spectacular explosion shots, say, the bombed ships at sea, I directed an operator to shake his camera as if from concussion, let the actors blur out of focus, and tip the camera sharply as the decks dipped high into the air. This gave the audience a sense of real participation—an effect difficult, even impossible to achieve with a big camera."[96]

One People Gone Astray

Two documentary styles had developed out of the Hollywood progressives' involvement in the war. Two images of Germany also began to emerge out of the debates and the discourse within the Hollywood community. This time, however, the debates pitted the two main protagonists of the Hollywood anti-fascist community against each other.

The Hollywood community was increasingly divided over the role of the wartime German people and the fate of Germany. In his paper entitled "On the Character of the Germans and the Nazis" presented at the 1943 Hollywood Writers' Congress at UCLA, socialist refugee Lion

Feuchtwanger argued for the difference between Nazis and Germans and warned that "under no circumstances . . . [are] the German people as such to be punished or re-educated." The guilt for Nazism and its destruction rested on the German elite, and "once the Junkers, generals and business leaders are done away with then it will soon be obvious that the Nazi coloration . . . was nothing but grease paint."[97] Thomas Mann argued along similar lines at the congress, but with an important difference. Nazis and Germans were distinguishable, the Nobel prize-winner stated, as in Germany there was " 'an inner emigration' of millions . . . awaiting the end just as we." Distinctions were difficult to make, however, on a cultural level: Nazism was indistinguishable from Germanness, as "this monstrous German attempt at world domination . . . is nothing but a distorted and unfortunate expression of that universalism in the German character."[98]

The issue of the "other Germany" and the degree of its wartime complicity with the crimes of National Socialism has been dealt with extensively by other scholars. Here it suffices to stress that Mann's position, later fully expressed in his 1945 lecture "Germany and the Germans" at the Library of Congress was one more attack on the notion of the people's basic innocence to which American liberals and radicals held fast.[99] Such positions, endorsed by some refugees and American conservatives, gathered little steam among American liberals and radicals until the late spring of 1945 when the first visual documentation on the German death camps arrived in America. Until then, in fact, the editors of the *New Republic*, *New Masses*, and *The Nation* overall blamed the German elite for the Nazi war, endorsed the necessity and the possibility of a German democratic popular movement, and repeated in some fashion that Germans "have been the victims of the world environment rather than the architects of its disaster."[100] In a 1945 speech, Hollywood progressive Edward G. Robinson stated this attitude clearly, although ironically his address was intended to introduce Thomas Mann to a Hollywood audience: "It is a dangerous aspect of our time that in many minds entire nations are confused and mixed up with their so called representatives." As for Germany, the actor continued, little "resemblance does the German people bear to the distorted mask that for the past six years has filled the world with disgust. . . . No, —no ranters, agitators, dictators represent a nation."[101]

Such a position was accepted by Hollywood New Yorkers. As an expression of the center-left coalition, the June 1942 OWI manual expressed their position clearly by saying that the enemy is larger than Hitler, Hirohito, or Mussolini but by no means does it overlap with the German, Japanese, and Italian peoples, as "it is dangerous to try and picture that all Germans, all Italians, and all Japanese are bestial barbarians. The people know that this is not true."[102] At the 1943 Hollywood Writers' Congress, the anti-Nazi film most often and most widely praised was *Hitler's Children* (RKO, 1943), directed by a future member of the Hollywood Ten, Edward Dmytryk, and written by SWG president Emmet Lavery from Gregor Ziemer's book *Education to Death*. Against the essentialism of Mann's thesis, the film upheld the idea that Nazism was the result of nurture rather than nature. The two main characters exemplify this in didactic terms: Hanna is a German-born, United States-educated young anti-Nazi, while Karl is American by birth, but Nazi by education. Yet in Lavery's and Dmytryk's optimistic view, there is hope for Karl, too. Witnessing Hanna being tortured, Karl turns the table on the Nazis and rebels, his example and martyrdom prompting several ordinary Germans to engage in small actions of sabotage. The UCLA congress applauded the film as "one of the most comprehensive pictures of the enemy," one that "vividly revealed in semi-factual form, the inside sociological deterioration" of Nazi Germany.[103] The refugee magazine *Aufbau* disagreed. Upon news that RKO was developing a film from Ziemer's book, Hans Kafka commented that the film was going to be "an impressive and solemn indictment of the New (dis)Order."[104] After seeing the final product, however, *Aufbau* remarked that *Hitler's Children* was "important and loaded [with suspense] up to the point of explosion" ("wichtig und oft bis zu Explosion geladen"). Yet the idea of Nazi Karl's coming to his senses was as "questionable" ("fraglich") as the film's unproblematic endorsement of the existence of "the other Germany" and its cursory treatment of the persecution of the Jews.[105]

The issue opened a bitter debate among Hollywood Europeans. On August 1, 1943, several Southern California exiles gathered at the home of Salka Viertel to produce a manifesto about the future of the war. The document—inspired by the Moscow Free Germany manifesto—called for the distinction "between the Hitler regime and the classes linked to it on the one hand, and the German people on the other." Only the former—Nazi officials, Junkers, and industrialists—deserved punishment and/or social and political demotion so as to open the way for real democracy.[106] In April 1944, Brecht wrote to theologian Paul Tillich that their movement had the endorsement of some Europeans, such as Heinrich Mann; actors Fritz Kortner, Lion Feuchtwanger, and Elisabeth Bergner; and directors Paul Czinner, Leopold Jessner, and

Berthold Viertel. On May 2, 1944, the Council for a Democratic Germany was officially launched with Tillich as chairman and Herman Budislawszki and Elisabeth Hauptmann as secretaries.[107] Any unity among the refugees, however, was absent. The day after the August meeting, Thomas Mann, who had initially signed the document, withdrew his name claiming— according to Brecht—that the refugees had no authority to determine the Allies' policy toward Germany. Furthermore, the key leaders of the Hollywood Europeans had conspicuously kept themselves at a distance. Not surprisingly, Brecht did not ask the conservative leaders of the community, such as agent Paul Kohner or director Ernst Lubitsch, to join. The progressive Hollywood Europeans did not join. Fritz Lang, who had been instrumental in finding Brecht a visa for the United States and had worked closely with him on the making of *Hangmen Also Die*, told his secretary not to answer Brecht when the playwright asked for Lang's name to be included in the organization.[108] By March 1944, Brecht wrote Tillich that Fritz Lang still "asked for more discussion," Dieterle was "busy with a film," and Salka Viertel, in whose house the initial meeting had taken place, had not joined.[109]

Historian John M. Spalek has recently written that the study of the anti-Nazi diaspora still misses "a study of the German political emigration as a whole" and in particular a "thorough analysis of the debate among the émigrés about the future of Germany."[110] To fill this gap is beyond the scope of this volume, but for our purposes it is fair to say that while the Brecht faction remained a minority within the community, debate about the fate of the German people also divided the community at its core; Hollywood New Yorkers seemed more in agreement with Brecht than with his fellow Germans. Transferring their interpretation of American people onto the Germans, Hollywood New Yorkers vocally advocated an optimistic solution for Germany via the reeducation of her people. The Hollywood Writers' Mobilization sponsored the L.A. premiere of *Tomorrow the World* on January 30, 1945. The film—produced by Lester Cowan, directed by Leslie Fenton, and written by Hollywood radicals Ring Lardner, Jr., and Leopold Atlas—was one in which, as Lavery wrote Cowan, "the idea content and the entertainment content are so well blended that the result is something the whole world wants to see."[111] It also endorsed the Hollywood New Yorkers' perspective that it was possible to nurture Germans back into civil society. Young Nazi Skippy Hommeier (played by Emil Bruckner) is so brainwashed as to forgive Hitlerites for the murder of his anti-fascist father, but American democratic education administered by Uncle Mike Frame (played by Frederic March) does the trick and puts him back on progressive tracks. The premiere took place at the beautiful Fox theater in Westwood, close to the refugee community of Santa Monica and to UCLA faculty housing, and attracted a large audience, including many Hollywood Europeans. During the debate following the showing of the film, part of the audience vocally objected to its general thesis. Ring Lardner, Jr., who covered the event for *Screenwriter*, took issue with a "part of the audience" who had argued that the Germans should be given an "eye for an eye" treatment.[112]

Caught between their new Hollywood alliances and their painful German past, Hollywood Europeans chose not to speak about the issue of German resistance, or German future. None of the anti-Nazi films made by German refugees, which Jan-Christopher Horak has extensively analyzed, deals expressly with the internal resistance to Nazism. This fact is striking considering those Hollywood Europeans who could have a say in the choice of their subject matter. Billy Wilder, Otto Preminger, and many others made films about the war, but—unlike their postwar work—stayed away from the German people. After *To Be or Not To Be*, Ernst Lubitsch's wartime films did not venture into contemporary themes. His *Heaven Can Wait* (Fox, 1945), in fact, dealt with turn-of-the-century New York. Judging from the fiercely anti-German *Hitler Lives?*, in the production of which Lubitsch was briefly involved, his view of "the other Germany" was hardly positive.[113] Fritz Lang's *Hangmen Also Die* (Angelus Pictures, 1943) dealt with anti-Nazi resistance but relocated it to Czechoslovakia, and—to make his point of view clearer—Lang adamantly refused Brecht's suggestion to have the Czech resisters interpreted by German actors. The result was that all freedom fighters spoke with an American accent and the German inflection consistently characterized the oppressors—most of the latter interpreted by German-born refugees.[114]

The war left Hollywood progressives in an uneasy, uncertain state. The democratic cinema that they had envisioned, and in some cases realized in the late 1930s, was akin to the democratic propaganda of World War II. Like the war's propaganda, Hollywoods' democratic modernism had called for the use of cinema and other means of modernity to educate and inform an allegedly national, multiclass audience about the political and cultural issues of the day. "Every picture is propaganda for or against something," scribbled Edward G. Robinson in his notes for a wartime interview. The key was to make it serve the cause of democracy, social equity, and civilization. With the outbreak of the conflict, the government had asked Hollywood to do just that, "pressing the studios to combine entertainment and propaganda." The task now was to continue on this road and not "toss this great educational force aside because of old fears."[115]

By 1943, the situation had become more complicated. Given their experiences, Hollywood Europeans had always considered the nature of the "people" with different eyes than did the American progressives, and the two groups were also divided on the issue of the "German people." American progressives were quite at ease displacing onto ordinary Germans many of the same democratic qualities that—at least *in potentia*—they attributed to American workers, farmers, and the middle class. But German exiles were more cautious.

Divisions among Hollywood Europeans and Hollywood New Yorkers were rising, but what about those divergent interpretations of democratic modernism that had been agitated in Hollywood before World War II? Dormant during the conflict, were they going to pop up again in the aftermath of the war? And what about the actual results of the collaboration with the U.S. government? In some sense, World War II had provided Hollywood progressives with an opportunity to test the limits of democratic modernism. Hollywood had been prompted by the government to embrace realism and the political education of the American people, but had the government-endorsed American war film lived up to those expectations? And had the collaboration with the U.S. government really been beneficial to the growth of Hollywood's intellectual and political stature? Certainly the rejection and dismissal of many Hollywoodians because of their political views was troubling. And the war did not erase the social problems that had irked so many Hollywood progressives at the end of the 1930s. At the end of World War II, as we shall see in the next two chapters, many Hollywoodians would add all these issues, balance them up, and evaluate the result of their decade-long commitment to Hollywood modernism.

6

Audiences, "People," and the Avant-Garde

The Collapse of the Hollywood Community

The unity of war years has vanished. The abstract principles of right and wrong, of justice, of humanitarian feeling to which we subscribed during the war . . . have become blurred and inapplicable to domestic situations and strains, concerning which not so long ago we were perfectly clear.

Irving Pichel, *Hollywood Quarterly*, 1947–48

The rapid collapse of democratic Hollywood in the period after the May 1947 House Un-American Committee (HUAC) hearings is surprising. In the previous decade, the community had weathered other conservative attacks as well as serious internal crises. This time, however, progressive Hollywood quickly folded. While the changes in the larger historical and national contexts are important in explaining the rapidity of the collapse, the causes of the Hollywood crisis were internal as well as external, esthetic as well as political. United in support of the Roosevelt administration and against the common enemy of fascism during the war, at the end of the conflict Hollywood New Yorkers and Europeans were increasingly divided and unable to present a united front against HUAC investigations. Tension within the Hollywood community and

164

doubts about Hollywood modernism were at first obscured by the industry's plump profits in 1945 and 1946 as well as by some of the successes that Hollywood modernism and the realist paradigm continued to score in the months following the end of World War II. Although the crisis of the Hollywood community resists a linear, diachronic chronology, it does provide the essential background in explaining the collapse of progressive Hollywood.

Many of the disagreements were related to the evaluation of the war effort. The collaboration between liberal and radical filmmakers and the American government had fallen short of the expectations harbored by some of the New Yorkers and Europeans. Oftentimes, the kind of war stories many Hollywoodians brought back to the studios had less to do with heroism on the battlefront than with censored films, rejected scripts, and politically motivated dismissals. These film-related frustrations mirrored broader ones that focused on American society's ostensible inability to deal with many of its internal problems, first and foremost its racial dilemma. Furthermore, as many of the OWI-produced and OWI-endorsed films had fallen short of the hybridizationist ideals Hollywoodians had entertained at the beginning of the conflict, the very notion of the "one, big audience" was being questioned. Sociologists such as Paul Lazarsfeld and Robert K. Merton used empirical research to refute the idea that Hollywood films appealed to a generalized, interclass audience and revealed the ways in which cultural and social factors determined a different reception in different segments of society. By 1945, the interclass, unifying symbol of the American people was increasingly replaced by a congeries of cultural classes, each associated with a particular form of cultural production—avant-garde art, folk art, mass media. In this context, and much earlier than the arrival of the HUAC's hounds, many Hollywoodians began to question their past ideas, choices, and convictions. The emergence of an anti-realist and anti-Hollywood film avant-garde (centered in New York) showed the weakening of the centripetal force of Hollywood and its political realism.

At the end of the war, doubts and uncertainties also gripped the top echelons of the studios hierarchies. Box office records notwithstanding, in the months following the end of World War II the studios received a series of bad news in the form of import quotas set up by European countries. In addition, as foreign governments threatened to curtail the importation of American films, strikers and picket lines appeared at many of the studio gates, and the White House seemed ready to reopen the anti-trust suit against the majors studios' monopoly over production, distribution, and exhibition venues.[1]

Hollywood 1943–45 and the "One Big Audience"

Even before professional media experts jumped into the fray, doubts about the existence of an interclass audience as well as the relative merits of films designed to reach it had long existed among Hollywoodians, as the case of Preston Sturges reveals. After his controversial *Sullivan's Travels*, Sturges had remained firmly connected with the Hollywood political and intellectual scene: he had been a contributor to the interventionist organization Bundles for Britain and allowed his Sunset Boulevard restaurant, The Players, to become the regular meeting hall for Charles Boyer's Free France organization.[2] His wartime comedies, however, commented harshly on both wartime political necessities and Hollywood realism, now associated with the new rhetoric of the war effort. In Sturges's *Hail the Conquering Hero* (Paramount, 1943), Woodrow Lafayette Pershing Truesmith (played by Eddie Bracken) is the son of a World War I hero who is unable to join the Marine Corps because of his numerous allergies. A group of marines on a furlough fabricate a tale of Woodrow's wartime heroism in order not to disappoint his widowed mother. The plan is so successful that the town selects Eddie as its mayor, and only then does Eddie confess the truth. Regardless, the town still wants him as a mayor.

The film was not merely a look at the emptiness of the war rhetoric; it was also a mockery of Hollywood realism placed at the service of the war effort. In the first draft of *Hail*, Sturges envisioned the credits as a reproduction of Hollywood democratic realism.

> During the main titles we have seen some heroic stuff of fighting marines, preferably jungle fighting, if available some official War [*sic*] footage. To a great screaming of sirens, we see the Newsreel stuff of the debarkation of the Guadalcanal Marines. The last shot is a walking INSERT of the blue diamond bearing the big one with GUADALCANAL written on it, surrounded by the Constellation of the Southern Cross.[3]

In 1944, when Mrs. George F. Kaufman accused the director of making films that were "destructive of moral standards," Sturges reaffirmed a notion of cinema that was alternative to the Cultural Front cinema of the 1930s and its dream of a unified, interclass audience. For Kaufman, Sturges had failed to appreciate that the range of his medium was not limited to the educated elite and had thus eschewed his responsibilities as a filmmaker. Sturges responded that the notion of a limitless, national audience inscribed in the medium of cinema did not open any democratic vista, but in fact limited the esthetic development of the medium. This notion also ignored the fact that the supposedly national and unified audience was actually divided and fragmented along educational lines. The moment had come, Sturges wrote Kaufman, to stop

> confusing the theater with an ice cream parlor. . . . It is this very habit which has caused so much unnecessary misunderstanding between well-meaning people like yourself and well-meaning people like me. Efforts to make all motion picture plays suitable to all ages from the cradle to the grave have so emasculated, Comstocked, and bowdlerized this wonderful form of theater that many adults have been driven away from it entirely.[4]

Sturges was not refuting Kaufman's accusations. He essentially accepted her description of his work. His films were not for "analphabetes," because *Hail* and his previous film, *Miracle at Morgan's Creek* (Paramount, 1942),[5] spoke to a world of moral complexities resisting the simplification of war rhetoric. Sturges was arguing for the abandonment of Hollywood's presumption to speak always to an abstraction called "the people." Film was not different from theater; it was actually a "wonderful form of theater." As such, it was up to the director to be either a vaudevillian or an "Ibsen, Shakespeare, Moliere, yes even Sophocles, Aristophanes and others who did not write for children in a chain of adult theaters or at least theaters with adult hours."[6]

What is relevant about this exchange and these films is that Sturges was clearly sketching an alternative to both wartime realism *and* Hollywood modernism. In 1940–41, this director, along with Charlie Chaplin and Ernst Lubitsch, had aroused the ire of the democratic modernists by rejecting the realist paradigm as a way to communicate politics. Yet Chaplin and Lubitsch clearly believed in the possibility of using cinema's modernist language to foster democracy and anti-fascism among the American people, and the very last shot of Sturges's *Sullivan's Travels* gestured toward the necessity for Sullivan's comedies to reach a socially varied range of audiences by superimposing fade-ins/fade-outs of laughing children, convicts, nurses, etc., over the dreamy face of Joel McCrea. But in the letter to Ms. Kaufman, Sturges argued for the abandonment of the masses and the creation, or re-creation, of segregated audiences and separate filmmaking spheres—that is, the abandonment not just of social realism, but of Hollywood modernism itself.

The war increasingly pushed other Hollywoodians toward Sturges's side. Interestingly, positions not dissimilar from his were expressed at the October 1943 Hollywood Writers' Mobilization (HWM) Congress at UCLA. This would have seemed an unlikely place to find allies for Sturges, as the HWM had been an attempt to reconstitute the pre-Pact ecumenism of the Hollywood Anti-Nazi League (HANL). The HWM Congress's advisory committee included members of different political creeds, from moderates such as Jack Warner, to liberals such as Dore Schary, Walter Wanger, and Kenneth Macgowan, to radicals such as Sidney Buchman and Dudley Nichols.[7] At the symposium, the avant-garde was represented by Leo Hurwitz, chairman of the seminar on documentary filmmaking, and by Joris Ivens, who also sat on the seminar committee.[8] The HWM Congress also seemed to begin a new era of collaboration between progressive Hollywood and progressive faculty at UCLA. Ralph Freud, UCLA theater professor, was co-chairman of the HWM Congress along with writer Mark Connelly. Psychology professor Franklin Fearing and German professor Gustave Arlt participated, while UCLA president Robert G. Sproul along with NAACP's Walter White, the director of OWI's Pacific Operations in San Francisco, Owen Lattimore, and Lieut. Col. Evans Carlson of the Marine Corps welcomed the HWM Congress.[9] The HWM Congress acknowledged the tight connection between Hollywood Europeans and Hollywood progressives. Exiles Thomas Mann, Lion Feuchtwanger, Bruno Frank, and Hanns Eisler all spoke, and some of them appeared on the roster as honorary guests. A special seminar, "Writers in Exile," focused exclusively on their experiences and problems.

Apparently, then, the HWM Congress offered the same image of unity encouraged by the war and by the nature of the Hollywood Cultural Front rhetoric as had HANL. Like HANL's formulas, the HWM Congress reiterated its faith in the hybridization between feature film and documentary. James Wong Howe, director of photography for *Air Force*, spoke of the technological changes that the war was bringing to Hollywood, including the use of the 16 mm camera and "documentary style."[10] The HWM Congress also attacked "the artificial distinction between film with social content and films designed for entertainment."[11] People narrative was also extolled by Virginia Wright and David Hanna, two screenwriters working for OWI, who noted how "deleterious" were "the melodramatic action films in which the hero, single-handedly, outwits the enemy through sheer brawn and native American ingenuity."[12] Under the surface of unanimity, however, existed a certain degree of disillusionment. In two areas, some of the papers presented at the 1943 HWM Congress vented perplexities about the 1930s paradigm. First, the war experience was increasingly teaching these people that the Hollywood narrative was not completely open to hybridization when it came to documentary techniques and war reality. And second, American and refugee sociologists questioned the empirical existence of the national "people" audience, taken for granted by the Hollywood community in the 1930s.

Both the left and right wings of the Hollywood Cultural Front questioned the possibility of hybridizing Hollywood narrative and political messages. In a lecture director Joris Ivens had given a few months earlier at the University of Southern California while he was still working on the draft of *Know Your Enemy: Japan* in the Capra unit, Ivens held out the possibility of hybridizing Hollywood and documentary. Aware that this was also a matter of personnel, the director argued that "we had to involve people working in the fiction field. This influx of professional people— if they could learn the documentary approach from the people in other countries who've done it for years—will be a tremendous help." At the HWM Congress, however, Ivens, who had recently been fired by Frank Capra from his unit in the War Department, was more pessimistic. "Pure fiction films methods have not proved well suited to the documentary field," he noted, though acknowledging the contribution of the "many Hollywood directors, writers, cameramen, editors, technicians" to the field.[13] In a nutshell, Ivens advocated the resurrection of a political and esthetic avant-garde with separate styles and audiences—a challenge to the realist paradigm, which alleged the ability of progressive filmmaking to reach across social and cultural boundaries to a unified audience that encompassed the "people."

Just as Ivens doubted that the message of the political vanguard could survive the marriage with the Hollywood narrative, other members of the Hollywood Cultural Front opposed any move to increase the ratio of political education to be injected into Hollywood films. At the 1943 HWM Congress, Arthur Mayer, the progressive, intellectually alert manager of the New York Rialto, offered a few remarks that revised important aspects of the old interpretation. The fact that Mayer was an exhibitor should not be underestimated. After two years of war and with the domestic economy in full recovery, Americans seemed to dislike entertainment laced with references to the reality of war, and Hollywood films that were closer to the semidocumentary model were not doing well at the box office. Exhibitors were understandably more concerned with this problem. Troubled by the findings of trade papers such as *Film Daily* and the *Motion Picture Herald*, many exhibitors were asking the studios to produce lighter fare.[14]

Mayer, an active participant of the 1930s' movement to make Hollywood more political, did not contest directly the essence of the paradigm.[15] In his paper, the classic 1930s films such as *Confessions of a Nazi Spy, I Am a Fugitive from a Chain Gang*, and *The Grapes of Wrath* were again extolled as models of a cinema able to tackle public issues. After analyzing the problems the paradigm was encountering at the box office, however, Mayer proposed altering the mixture of entertainment and politics by increasing the ratio of the former. *Confessions*, for example, did "a great job" insofar as it was a *"fictional* fil[m] of topical themes." Mayer argued that the film did not ignore "the fundamentals of showmanship." On the other hand, New York avant-garde groups such as Frontier Films were "idealistic young men and women . . . devoted in the highest degree to the improvement of human society." Their techniques, however, were not viable for show business because they "disregarded the fundamentals of dramatic technique" and appealed to "a limited clientele of intellectuals and reformers rather than to the great body of moviegoers."[16] While still paying lip service to the possibility of hybridizing politics and entertainment, Mayer's paper implicitly questioned the possibility of effecting it. Mayer tellingly revised the history of the Hollywood Cultural Front as well. In 1939, when *Confessions* hit the theaters, *New Masses* read the film as a continuation of the work of the New York hybridizationists and announced that "the fruitful experiments of men like Joris Ivens and Herbert Kline, and neglected bands like Frontier Films, have at last reached Hollywood."[17] But in 1943, Mayer denied the continuity between the film and the New York avant-garde. Ultimately, Mayer and Ivens were no longer sure that Hollywood and Frontier Films were entirely compatible, and, more importantly, they in fact negated the necessity for hybridization between Hollywood and the documentary avant-garde.

The belief by both Hollywoodians and the OWI in the possibility of constructing a unified audience overlapping with the American people was challenged most convincingly by Paul Lazarsfeld, a Viennese-born mathematician and sociologist, and Robert K. Merton; both were employed by the Columbia University Office of Radio Research. As a member of the Austrian Socialist Party in Vienna, Lazarsfeld had been concerned "with why Socialist propaganda was unsuccessful and wanted to conduct psychological experiments to explain this." In the early 1940s, he set out to do the same with American war propaganda.[18] Like his European research,

Lazarsfeld's American work drew from both a commitment to quantitative analysis and a deep intellectual dialogue with marxist theories from which Lazarsfeld derived his emphasis on "social stratification" as an important element in determining different reactions to the same phenomenon.[19] Lazarsfeld's and Merton's paper at the 1943 HWM Congress, later reprinted by the New York Academy of Science, commented that the notion of propaganda as interpreted by OWI and HWM was in need of vast modification. Propaganda had failed, according to the scholars, because Hollywood and OWI had taken for granted the existence of a unified audience. Empirical research had proven the existence of a multiplicity of audiences within the American people, an aspect that war propaganda had to acknowledge if it was to be successful. Response analysis proved that audiences reacted differently according to their individual agendas, social origins, and cultural backgrounds. What was relevant for "the highly articulated" was not interesting for the "inarticulate." The idea, then, was to construct the message according to the "peripheral interests of the audiences" and ask "how will [the message] be interpreted by different types of audiences."[20]

Hollywood in the Aftermath of World War II

After World War II, Hollywood had some reasons to rejoice. During the conflict, Hollywood had strengthened its ties with the L.A. intellectual community, something that was made clear when, in 1945, Kenneth Macgowan, a former Provincetown Players producer working in Hollywood since the early 1930s, was chosen to chair the new Department of Theater Arts at UCLA. In the mid-1930s, Macgowan had passionately endorsed a "drama festival at UCLA" because it would strengthen the ties between the motion picture industry and the university. The festival would offer students the opportunity for training, while allowing Hollywood producers to check out local talent firsthand.[21] Macgowan had immersed himself in democratic cultural organizations during the war. After working for a few months in the Office of the Coordinator of Inter-American Affairs, he went back to Hollywood and worked in the HWM, and—after 1945— with the radical People's Education Center.[22] By 1945, Macgowan was thinking about going into academia and was seeking advice from his friend William F. Ogburn of the University of Chicago.[23] In 1946, UCLA offered Macgowan a full professorship in the theater department, and the producer promptly accepted. The money ($4,120 for the first year)

was considerably less than a Hollywood salary, but he was confident
that he would be able to work in the industry on a freelance basis. In
addition, UCLA granted Macgowan ample responsibility by giving him
the chairmanship of the department.[24] When Macgowan accepted, the
Los Angeles *Daily News* commented: "It is good to see a university frankly
relating a portion of its activities to the culture and the economy of the
community it serves."[25] Such cooperation, according to the university
press release, was to be enhanced by UCLA's commitment to "cooperate
with the Academy of Motion Picture Arts and Science, the four major
radio broadcasting networks, and the associated Committee on Television
in developing the curriculum of the new Department" that Macgowan
was to chair.[26] "Hollywood is becoming Los Angeles," Macgowan wrote
in 1945.[27]

That same year, the Actors' Lab—the creation of Hollywood progressives such as Max Gorelik, Morris Carnovski, Roman Bohnen, Phoebe
Brandt, Jessica Tandy, and Frank Tuttle, and Hollywood Europeans
such as Henry Koster and Leo Mittler—was also continuing the work
initiated by the Hollywood Theater Alliance. By the end of 1945, the Lab
was making plans to help finance new progressive theater companies in
Austria and was prosperous enough to take out a paid ad in the *Hollywood
Reporter* celebrating its fifth anniversary as "Hollywood's contribution to
the field of institutionalized theater in America." The Lab argued for
the advantages of being based in Hollywood rather than in New York,
because "so far the economic pressure has been virtually nonexistent.
The Lab people are privately subsidized by their own earning power in
the motion picture industry."[28] Actor Roman Bohnen, writing to Cheryl
Crawford in 1945, was optimistic about the future of the theater in Los
Angeles. Rejecting Crawford's invitation to come back to the East Coast,
Bohnen reiterated that

> I too have the compulsion, indeed the pressing necessity, to build, or help
> build, something *durable*. I already have a 5 year stake in the good groundwork
> we have set down for the Actors' Lab here in Hollywood. I think my function
> should be to continue to develop the Lab idea. It is clearly workable. It
> is prospering. There will be a fine plant within two more years. From the
> personnel we have been training in a "point of view" there is emerging a
> huge body of talents that are much stronger than the original Group nucleus
> of talent.[29]

Hollywoodians were also increasingly involved in the politics of Los
Angeles. In 1944, Helen Mary Gahagan Douglas, former Broadway star

singer/actress, decided to run for U.S. Congress in L.A.'s 14th District at the urging of both her husband, Melvyn Douglas—founder of the Hollywood Democratic Committee—and President Roosevelt. By 1946 when Douglas ran again (and was again elected), she had company.[30] That year, the Hollywood coalition contributed several members to the ballots for the Democratic Party. Hollywood progressive Frank Scully ran for the state legislature, endorsed by a coalition featuring both Hollywood New Yorkers and Hollywood Europeans.[31] Liberal Emmet Lavery ran for U.S. Congress in L.A.'s 16th District.[32]

Hollywood Quarterly, founded in April 1945 and published by the University of California Press, also institutionalized the unity between the Hollywood community and L.A. intellectuals. On its editorial board sat three UCLA faculty members and two Hollywood writers.[33] In 1963, during his eulogy for *Quarterly* co-founder Kenneth Macgowan, English department professor Franklin P. Rolfe called the journal "one of UCLA's first attempt to bridge the gap between the University and the community which surrounds us."[34] In 1955, John Houseman wrote that "Hollywood seemed the proper place for [the *Hollywood Quarterly*]—with its unique opportunity for specialists in the communication fields to work closely with scholars and sociologists from the University of California at Los Angeles."[35]

Realism—long the slogan of progressive Hollywood—also seemed to rule the center of American film discourse. Among the films released in 1946, the feature that swept the Academy Awards, William Wyler's *The Best Years of Our Lives,* employed many of the techniques advocated by the 1930s' coalition. *Best Years* did not have a single protagonist, was shot on location in Los Angeles, dealt with social problems, and was photographed by Gregg Toland with a deep-focus cinematography that conveyed what Jim Windolf has recently termed "uncluttered realism."[36] According to Hermine Rice Isaacs of *Theater Arts,* American cinema revealed with *Best Years* a newfound maturity that placed it ahead of the other six arts.[37] Many also noted that *Best Years* was a film technically and emotionally born of both Wyler's and scriptwriter Robert Sherwood's firsthand wartime experiences. Furthermore, *Best Years* tackled the issue of the war without eschewing its darker sides and the dangers of its unfulfilled promises. Wyler's decision to depart from Mackinlay Cantor's novel and substitute the original spastic character with the amputee veteran gave the film what many Hollywoodians considered authenticity. Harold Russell, a real-life veteran, played himself and made film history.[38]

All these were tangible changes for the better. Hollywood progressives, however, were uneasy. In the opinion of some, it was far from certain that postwar Hollywood production would continue to explore its public role and the "issues of the day." In 1943, Billy Wilder told *Aufbau* that he had no idea about the direction of Hollywood films after the conflict. The war cycle was going to end—American audiences were showing signs of being tired of the "issues of the day." The direction in which producers would choose to go was anyone's guess.[39] Two months after the war, Albert Maltz, considering present and future Hollywood production, noted that the situation in both Hollywood and the United States did not lend itself to simplistic interpretations. It was, on the contrary, "uneasy with contrasts," all reflected in Hollywood's "anarchy of production" at the time.[40] A few months later, *Theater Arts* noted that "the unnatural peace that rushed into the vacuum left by the war has caught our poets and prophets unaware."[41] Peacetime cinema and post–World War II America resisted linear development from the ideals of the democratic war.

Furthermore, America resisted reform. After a war against fascism and racism and the bloody L.A. and New York City race riots of 1943, Jim Crow still ruled the South and racial relations remained the American dilemma. The 1943 HWM Congress had been lenient with Roosevelt and his administration, but at the risk of endangering wartime's alleged unanimity, it had also made clear that the solution to racism should not wait for the strategic necessities of FDR's "Dr. Win the War." Dalton Trumbo, though acknowledging the efforts of Howard Koch in John Huston's film *In This Our Life*, which featured a young African-American man as a law student, thundered against Hollywood's almost complete opposition to a realistic and dignified representation of African Americans.[42] If the racial situation remained unsolved in the United States as well as internationally, Harry Hoijier reminded the 1943 HWM Congress, the Allies' "victory will avail us nothing."[43]

Anti-communism was also featured among the worries of progressive Hollywood. In February 1944 director Sam Woods and other Hollywood anti-communists founded the Motion Picture Alliance for the Preservation of American Ideals (MPAPAI). The aims of the organization were made clear in a letter the MPAPAI sent to Senator Robert R. Reynolds (D-N.C.) calling him the "Nostradamus of the twentieth century." MPAPAI called for a congressional investigation of Hollywood since communists and "aliens of un-American ideology have infiltrated into the United States" with the help of the "motion picture industrial-ists."[44] One year later Senator John Rankin succeeded in getting Congress to make HUAC a permanent committee, delivering an accusatory speech on the floor of Congress: "These alien-minded Communistic enemies of Christianity, and their stooges are trying to take over the motion picture and howl to high heaven when our Committee on Un-American Activities proposes to investigate them."[45]

Anti-communist accusations had been leveled at Hollywood before. Between 1938 and 1945, Hollywood progressives had weathered the sometimes combined attacks of the Tenney Committee, the Nye Com-mittee, and the early HUAC of Martin Dies. In *Variety*, "Sid" denounced the action of the MPAPAI and challenged the organization to name the names or hit the road—the same tactics the community had successfully employed against Dies in 1940.[46] In the years prior to America's entry into World War II, government caution and popular suspicions had also not prevented Hollywood progressives from pushing the anti-fascist agenda. After 1945, however, some pivotal aspects of Hollywood's cultural and political landscape had changed.

Before 1947, Hollywood was a local community but also part of a na-tional and international network of intellectuals. Academics from UCLA participated in the Hollywood Writers' Mobilization and Hollywood intellectuals published essays in literary magazines all over the nation. But when HUAC hit Hollywood, the progressives who were still there found themselves isolated. "We sent a telegram asking for the most famous members of the literary community—Carl Sandburg, John Steinbeck, William Faulkner, Ernest Hemingway, and others," remembers Paul Jarrico, one of the Hollywood 19. "We didn't receive a single reply." Fear and personal politics certainly played a role, but perhaps in an age of separate cultural spheres, the Hollywood dream was no longer worth fighting for.

Between 1945 and 1947, Hollywood was suspended in the midst of the Old and the New. World War II had demonstrated the potential of film as an active participant in both American politics and the shaping of a democratic society, attracting to Hollywood the attention of scholars from several disciplines. The politicization of Hollywood had also brought academics into the studios and Hollywoodians into academe. Together they were on their way to creating an intellectual class in Los Angeles that was both local—that is, tied to local circumstances—and translocal, insofar as it was animated by debates about the national role of cinema in a democratic society. The collapse of the Hollywood community would soon undermine these developments. By 1950, Hollywood and Los Angeles intelligentsia would be as far apart as they were at the beginning of the 1930s.

Postwar American Intellectuals and Hollywood Modernism

The Political Crisis

Changes in Hollywood's political scene helped decenter the informal alliance between radicals and liberals that had long been one of the pivots of the Hollywood community. In the general restructuring of labor-management relationships following World War II, Hollywood was engrossed in two long strikes (March 1945—October 1945 and September 1946—April 1947) that opposed the Local 1421 of the Conference of Studio Unions (CSU), headed by aggressive unionist Herb Sorrell, against the producers and the more conservative, more docile—and more corrupt—International Association of Theatrical and Stage Employees (IATSE). During most of the 1945 confrontation, communists, faithfully abiding by the wartime no-strike pledge, did not back Sorrell and the CSU, annoying many of the noncommunist Hollywood leftists. The second strike, endorsed by the communists, alienated the liberals for its protracted and intransigent character. So divisive was the issue that Carey McWilliams interpreted the strike as a producers' plot to weaken the budding SWG.[47]

As Larry Ceplair and Steven Englund have argued in their *Inquisition in Hollywood*, changes in the strategy of the Communist Party, one of the protagonists of the Hollywood Cultural Front, also weakened the alliance between communists and liberals within the Hollywood community.[48] In 1945, the Communist Party restructured itself after Earl Browder's 1944 attempt to further the experience of the Popular Front by dismantling the party and creating the Communist Political Association (CPA). French communist leader Jacques Duclos openly criticized the American organization in April 1945, and the CPA was rapidly dismantled, the party reconstituted, and the recalcitrant Browder expelled.[49] Whatever Browder's intent, the CPA would have fit Hollywood politics like the proverbial glove. It was a loose organization that allowed its members to partake in the communist network while participating in others. Duclos's manifesto, on the contrary, narrowed the opportunity for alliance and compromise within the Hollywood community. Once again, many Hollywoodians found themselves at odds with the party. Screenwriter Leonardo Bercovici still bristles at the memory of the CPA's demise and the "speed with which everybody turned around after Browder was repudiated."[50] Upon learning of the demise of the CPA, Abraham Polonsky was flabbergasted. Sensing the turmoil, the party sent Hollywood its point man in cultural matters, William Z. Foster, to try to calm the waters. Polonsky saw the new policy as an imposition from the eastern headquarters of the party: "The people who weren't part of the Hollywood community didn't understand that they were helping to destroy an important part of the human relations." At the meeting with Foster, Polonsky—a future blacklistee—"got up and told the head of the group it was absurd, and somebody jumped up and said I should be expelled."[51] In 1952, screenwriter Bernard C. Schoenfeld attributed his resignation from the Community Party to the party's decision to terminate the CPA experience.[52] Comrade and colleague Lydia Richards concurred.[53]

Slowly but surely the attitude of *New Masses* and the *Daily Worker* toward Hollywood changed. After 1945, Mike Gold closed ranks with Dwight Macdonald as far as their judgment of Hollywood was concerned. Increasingly, the Communist Party's attitude toward Hollywood became hostile. Rebuking Albert Maltz in the *Daily Worker*, Mike Gold wondered whether he had "let the luxury and phony atmosphere of Hollywood at last poison him."[54] In 1946, after Kenneth Macgowan had expressed optimism about the possibility for a better Hollywood to educate "its audience from the bottom up," Gold—who had praised the producer's decision to move to Hollywood in 1932 along with the other "proletarian pioneers" (Macgowan had produced Gold's *Fiesta* in 1926)—wrote to Macgowan that his optimism was misplaced and that fifteen years in Hollywood should have taught him better.[55] John Howard Lawson still had some kind words for Hollywood in his 1949 *Theory and Techniques of Playwriting and Screenwriting*, but pressed by party ideologue Victor J. Jerome, by 1953 he reedited the book and argued that the motion picture "is neither creative nor in the hands of the artist. It is destructive and in the hands of the monopolists."[56]

Still, Hollywood progressive politics was less dependent on the structure and the political line of the CPUSA than on the viability of the ideal of a democratic and politicized modernism. In previous years, Hollywood communists and fellow travelers had been able to combine their loyalty to the communist national network with their experience in the

Hollywood community, even when the two were not entirely compatible. Other issues, however, contributed to weakening their commitment to Hollywood.

The Esthetic Crisis

By the middle of the 1940s, Clement Greenberg had clearly stressed that the public dimension of art was not as important as its ability to express complexities. In his 1939 essay, "Avant-Garde and Kitsch," the critic stressed the superiority of the former to the latter, which he identified with mass culture. Speaking about Stalinist Russia, capitalist America, and Nazi Germany, Greenberg remarked that the "peasants who settled in the cities as proletariats" would always choose the realism of Repin and Norman Rockwell over the complex, abstract art of Picasso. In Russia, Germany, or the United States, the masses lacked the time for the cultural "conditioning" that one needed to understand Picasso. This conditioning would be granted only when "the problems of production have . . . been solved in a socialist sense," uncontaminated by Stalinism. In the meantime, however, the masses should by and large stay out of the business of art, as the good artist should "imitate God by creating something that is valid solely on its own terms." The search for a mass audience and for hybridization between mass culture and avant-garde were indeed the problem rather than the solution.[57] Attempting to revitalize an avant-garde that was in direct opposition to mass culture, Greenberg was not much interested in the role the masses should play in the cultural itinerary toward socialism. His concerns were more with the elite ("the rich and the cultivated") on which avant-gardism depends.[58]

For Lionel Trilling as well, good literature should not be too preoccupied with the size of its audience. If anything, Trilling wanted to limit his audience to the educated middle classes. "My own literary interest," he wrote in 1939, "is in the tradition of humanistic middle thought and in the intellectual middle class which believes that it continues this tradition."[59] In 1946, he wrote that "the writer must define his audience by its abilities, by its perfections, so far as he is gifted to conceive them. . . . The word coterie should not frighten us too much. Neither should it charm us too much; writing for a small group does not insure integrity any more than writing for the many."[60]

For both Trilling and Greenberg, the entire hybridizationist project was problematic. Fusing avant-garde and mass culture was not the right way, as the problem of American democracy was the dwindling of a well-defined intellectual and artistic vanguard. Revitalizing the avant-garde, however, meant reconstituting its audience, which was not the masses but rather the cognoscenti. In a memoir about the late 1930s, Greenberg remembered that the artists whom he liked the most were those who "appeared rather indifferent to what went locally outside their immediate circle . . . worldly success seemed so remote as to be beside the point, and you did not even secretly envy those who had it."[61] It is not surprising that both critics viewed with suspicion the intellectual climate of the 1930s. In their opinion, the issue of a national audience and its political education were not of particular relevance. The artist was first and foremost to produce good art.

Far from being confined to the art and literary fields, ideas similar to Greenberg's and Trilling's are also found in the Hollywood context, testifying to the national and political context of the intellectual debates of the 1930s and 1940s. For many of the former Hollywood New Yorkers, the ideal of a democratic Hollywood had been a strong influence throughout the 1930s. It had allowed a reconciliation between one's politics and esthetics, and between the public and the private dimension of one's artistic enterprises. These hopes gave Hollywood centripetal power, and this in turn allowed a porous relationship between Hollywood filmmaking and film avant-garde. By the end of the war, however, film discourse was fragmenting, calling for separation between different spheres of filmmaking and between artists and the masses.

Albert Maltz's famous essay "What Shall We Ask of Writers," which appeared in *New Masses* in 1946, showed how Trilling's and Greenberg's concerns had expanded not only geographically, from the East Coast to Hollywood, but also politically, affecting important elements of the Hollywood communist intelligentsia. In California since 1941, Maltz was a successful writer on both coasts and a card-carrying member of the CPUSA. Maltz took a strong stand against what he considered the "vulgarization of the theory of art which lies behind left wing thinking: namely, 'art as a weapon.'" For Maltz, the Left had too often dismissed works of art on the criteria of their present political expediency. Although Maltz had a long list from which to choose an example, he chose *New Masses*'s critical review of Lillian Hellman's 1940 anti-Nazi play, *Watch on the Rhine*. He argued that the magazine had considered the play not "as to its real quality—its deep interpretation of life, character, and the social scene—but primarily as to whether or not it was the proper 'leaflet' for the moment." Ironically, when the play was released—unaltered—as a film in

1942, *New Masses* had lavishly praised it; this was not to be the magazine's last critical blunder. Maltz noted in his 1946 essay that the magazine was pouring unjustified criticism on writers such as Richard Wright and James T. Farrell because they had distanced themselves from the Communist Party. What Maltz argued for was a revision of the progressive paradigm. Rather than seeing the "good" Hollywood film as an expression of "good" politics, he advised separating the artistic output of one writer from his or her politics. "Writers must be judged by their work, and not by the committees they join in."[62]

Maltz was attacked by many.[63] The party finally put an official gag on the controversy by compelling Maltz to choose between retraction or expulsion. Historians have generally emphasized the authoritarian response, but there is more to be said.[64] For a few months, in fact, *New Masses* became a public forum in which the relation between progressive art and public life was discussed at length, and with a certain degree of openness. While the magazine did host several interventions virulently critical of Maltz, it also gave space to people such as Hollywood screenwriter Sanora Babb, who argued that she "liked Maltz's piece because it puts forward some very real criticism which must be—not answered—but explored."[65] In its "Readers' Forum" *New Masses* also published several letters in open support of the screenwriter.[66] Notably, most of the people who took part in the debate—with the exception of William Z. Foster and Howard Fast—were Hollywood screenwriters, which hints at the fact that by 1946 Hollywoodians were hotly debating and, like Maltz and his supporters, openly questioning the merits of the realist paradigm. Maltz's notion that the artist should be judged for the merits of her/his work, and not for her/his politics, in fact reestablished the schizophrenia that progressive Hollywood was meant to bypass. If good art did not need to be a vehicle for sound politics and political education, why should we expect this of Hollywood films? A good film was not necessarily a politically enlightened one. As Joseph North noted in his rebuttal to Maltz, the essay "cleave[d] the writer in two—seeing him as 'citizen' and as 'artist.'"[67] Gone was the possibility for the artists to use art and cinema—in the case of Maltz—as a means of political communication, and looming at the horizon was the possibility to rid art of any explicit link to politics as well as of any commitment to accessibility.

On the other hand, the party affirmed a narrow definition of communist art and of its intended audience. The party's strictness in defining a "politically correct art," as much as its rejection of Browderism, closed the path to that looseness of slogans and meanings on which the 1930s experience had founded itself. Gone was the possibility of an alliance with the liberals and radicals (as most of Fast's and Foster's essays were occupied by attacks on political opponents on the Left such as liberals, Trotskyites, and the *New Leader*), but gone too was the idea of the national audience overlapping with the American people.

In the profound reconfiguration of American culture following the war, intellectuals of various political and intellectual extractions seemed ready to ally themselves with a particular class at the expense of the size of their intended audience. While Lionel Trilling wanted the *Partisan Review* to speak to the "educated classes," the Communist Party meant to prod its artists to speak to a select working-class audience.[68]

The Sociologists

As artists began to distance themselves from Hollywood, European and American sociologists continued debunking the idea of a national audience. Immediately after the war, Robert K. Merton and Paul Lazarsfeld further developed the themes of the paper they presented at the 1943 HWM Congress. In *The Social Psychology of a War Bond Drive* (1946), Merton examined the effect of a radio marathon in 1943, conducted by radio personality Kate Smith, and called for a "differential analysis" of audience response to understand "why . . . certain types of listeners [were] moved to action whereas others remained unmoved."[69] In 1946, Paul Lazarsfeld published his landmark study *The People Look at Radio* on radio listening. Lazarsfeld's book was largely dependent on the 1930s debates about popular media. Like Hollywood New Yorkers and Europeans ten years earlier, the sociologist was aware—and convinced—of the great democratic potential of the media for cultural communication. Lazarsfeld was persuaded, in fact, that if the radio was used correctly, "the habits of the listeners could be elevated."[70] But for Lazarsfeld the problem was how to combine this lofty ideal with the reality of a constituency of listeners increasingly fragmented along class and cultural lines. Taste in music, for example, was "mainly a function of environmental factors," and it varied according to class, place, and education. Urban college graduates consistently demanded more sophisticated programming than the rural population, or those who had not gone past grammar school.[71] Though still maintaining the necessity of finding a middle ground, Lazarsfeld did not see "how the requirements of the intellectual avant-garde [can] be reconciled with those of the vast majority of the less demanding members of the community."[72]

What had been uncritically accepted by the democratic migration to Hollywood in the 1930s had now become an unsolved problem. Lazarsfeld thought that the media scientists should engage this aspect of modern media in order to find a solution. For the new avant-garde, the abandonment of the masses to their "midcult," lowbrow destiny was a necessary condition for the expression of the self. Dwight Macdonald agreed and cited as positive news the "recent discovery—since 1945—that there is not One Big Audience but rather a number of smaller more specialized audiences."[73]

An Audience of "A Few, Serious, Responsible Friends"

The erosion of the 1930s paradigm and the growing schism between Hollywood and "serious filmmaking" fueled interest for a New York-based avant-garde. Even before HUAC began its hearings in Los Angeles in May 1947, the paradigm was losing ground among Hollywood intellectuals. In 1946, Kenneth Macgowan maintained that Hollywood had to be responsible for the "improvement of the public taste through nothing more and nothing less than repeated experience in movie going." He was now fully aware, however, of the existence of a possible alternative, namely "the creation of a chain of small movie houses like the few scattered 'art theaters' that now show European and English films."[74]

That so many New Yorkers and Europeans continued to work in Hollywood film is evidence of the resilience of the Hollywood Cultural Front center, and of how loose were the relations between Hollywood communists and fellow travelers on one side and the New York Central Committee of the CPUSA on the other. Precious energies, however, were lost to the emerging esthetic and political avant-garde—two movements often, but not always, overlapping.

Consider the case of Alexander Hammid, formerly known as Alexander Hackenschmied. A German refugee, Hackenschmied had worked in Czechoslovakia during the 1930s and gone Hollywood in 1938, after collaborating on two anti-Nazi documentaries—*Crisis* (1938, directed by Herbert Kline and written by Hammid and Sidney Kingsley) and *Lights Out in Europe* (directed by Herbert Kline, 1939). In 1941, Hammid was working as assistant director and technical advisor for MGM and Paramount, before joining the overseas branch of OWI's Bureau of

Motion Pictures (for which he directed *The Forgotten Village*). In May 1946, Hammid published an essay in the organ of the SWG in which he openly reformulated the idea and possibility of avant-garde as well as separate cultural classes. Hammid acknowledged that for a long time progressives had perceived film as the essential "medium of mass communication." In 1946, however, the director felt that this had narrowed rather than increased the space for art in film. After looking at the limits of wartime production, he said, it is high time we consider it "a unique and largely unexplored means of creative expression." From his 1946 perspective, experimentation could no longer be part of Hollywood. On the contrary, it pertained to a separate sphere, one that was not part of the industry and did not share its audience, though the director was not yet willing to exclude possible contaminations. Rather than compatible, Hollywood and art films were inhabitants of parallel spheres. As such, Hammid concluded, they should be in the same relationship as "poetry and fine prose are to popular commercial publications or what fine arts are to commercial applied arts."[75]

A separation of spheres of filmmaking was increasingly apparent in the months and years following the war. In 1943, Hammid and his partner, Maya Deren, shot and interpreted *Meshes in the Afternoon* in Los Angeles. A milestone of American experimental cinema, *Meshes* represents the dreams (or the suicide) of a young woman in her apartment. Set ironically in "Hollywood 1943," the film established the dominance of the subconscious over reality. In 1944 Hammid made his way back from Hollywood to New York, where in 1945 he released the experimental *A Better Tomorrow*.

Joris Ivens, the Dutch progressive filmmaker, followed a similar itinerary. In contrast to Hammid, Hollywood had disappointed Ivens politically even more than esthetically. In 1941 Ivens had told his friend Jay Leyda that he saw in the jungle of Hollywood "some real game, and I would like to hunt for it."[76] In February 1943, his Hollywood agent Charles K. Feldman was still actively trying to find him employment in a Hollywood studio.[77] At the end of the war he had changed his mind. After a failed attempt to collaborate with Frank Capra on *Know Your Enemy: Japan* and another failed attempt to write a film with Vladimir Pozner for Greta Garbo (*A Woman in the Sea*), Ivens left for New York. Shortly after, he relocated to East Asia where he briefly became film commissioner for the Netherlands East Indian Government, before siding with the Indonesian rebels against Dutch colonial rule and completing the anti-imperialist documentary *Indonesia Calling* (1946). He would never work in the United States again.[78]

Ivens and Hammid are good examples of how the political and esthetic avant-garde were rapidly withdrawing from Hollywood. Those New Yorkers who remained in Southern California were again ruled by a separation of their studio work from their other, "serious" work. Milton Krims, an old hand of Hollywood progressivism, recognized this separation and proposed an "SWG short play award" that would offer writers an outlet for their artistic ambitions (which he assumed their Hollywood work was unable to fulfill) while helping them to cast aside their "inferiority complex."[79] By 1947, even the *Hollywood Quarterly* began to take into account alternatives to Hollywood. Reviewing the career of Joseph von Sternberg—whose anti-realism Lewis Jacobs had termed "a cinematic ivory tower" in 1939—avant-garde filmmaker Curtis Harrington appreciated the reasons for the director to move from Hollywood to New York and deemed his approach to cinema "of unparalleled historical importance."[80] By 1947, Jacobs—author of the Beardian classic of American film studies, *The Rise of American Film* (1939)—was himself writing an essay on "experimental cinema."[81]

With the centripetal power of Hollywood losing force, film avant-garde was again gathering momentum in New York—out of Hollywood, and out of the reach of the general public. In October 1947, Amos Vogel, a Viennese-born refugee, leased the Provincetown Theater in Greenwich Village for the first program of Cinema 16, an enterprise dedicated to noncommercial filmmaking.[82] In *Theater Arts*, German refugee and film theorist Siegfried Kracauer argued that "there seems to be a new avant-garde movement in the making. In all likelihood, it owes something to the widespread discontent with the current Hollywood product." New York, Kracauer continued, was again an avant-garde center, well represented by the new films by Hammid, Maya Deren, and Hans Richter.[83] Vogel indeed advocated a rigid demarcation of the cinematic spheres, pitting avant-garde against the "empty tinsel of Hollywood."[84] The polemical target of Vogel was not the most blatantly commercial Hollywood cinema, but rather the *good* Hollywood cinema. He extolled the films of Maya Deren insofar as they showed "something there, that to me was far more important than the so-called best Hollywood films."[85] A refugee and a socialist, Vogel called for the return of schizophrenia and separated the politics of a film from its artistic or cultural value. Cinema 16, for instance, programmed the Nazi film *The Eternal Jew* (1940) in the face of the protests of New York leftists and refugees.[86]

The polemic with Hollywood was evident in *Dreams That Money Can Buy* by Hans Richter, a leftist German refugee who was a favorite of Vogel and his circle.[87] Framed in a parodic, noirish narrative about "Joe" (played by Jack Bittner)—an unemployed veteran who begins his activity as a seller of dreams—*Dreams* "mixes dreams with reality" in its six episodes, each of them designed by a nonrealist artist.[88] The third episode—"Ruth, Roses, and Revolvers," from an idea by Man Ray— explicitly targeted the Hollywood narrative. At a picture show spectators are asked to behave exactly as the character on screen, which they sheepishly do. Taking its distance from Hollywood and its mass audience, Richter's film was playing out a crucial aspect of the new avant-garde cinema. Rejecting mass culture as corrupting, these vanguardists were hardly concerned with the mass audience. Rejecting Aristotelian mimesis and realism, they stressed the subconscious over the conscious appreciation of reality. Maya Deren's films—and *Meshes in the Afternoon* in particular—explicitly questioned whether vision and reason grant access to the structure of reality. In her films, it is the dream and the subconscious that occupy the screen, relegating the conscious life to the margins of the films.

For James Agee, the point of these films was that " 'reality,' in its conventional camera sense, cannot be turned into a work of art without being turned into a fantasia of the unconscious."[89] On his way to Hollywood ten years after the main wave of migration, Agee disagreed both with the anti-realism of the new avant-garde and with its anti-Hollywood attitude. Agee had been the most critical among the 1930s partisans of Hollywood, yet he saw Richter's and Deren's films as lacking in originality—a simple repetition of the 1920s elitist modernism. As for Hollywood, it certainly had limits but the new avant-garde had a clear liability: the "self-deceit in the direction of arrogance and artiness—the loss of, and contempt for, audience, which can be just as corrupting as its nominal opposite."[90]

From West to East

The collapse of the Hollywood community was certainly accelerated by the arrival of Parnell Thomas and the HUAC in 1947. After conducting preliminary hearings in May 1947, HUAC subpoenaed several witnesses to Washington, D.C., for a series of hearings that culminated in the confrontations between the "unfriendly ten" and HUAC and that were followed by the Waldorf Astoria statement, which officially, if obliquely, launched the anti-communist blacklist in Hollywood.

By 1950, Hollywood Europeans and Hollywood New Yorkers were leaving en masse, either chased out of Hollywood by McCarthyists and/or because they had become disillusioned about the possibilities of Hollywood. In progressive screenwriter Clancy Sigal's semimemoir *Going Away*, the protagonist inverts the cultural itinerary of the Left and treks back to New York from Los Angeles.[91] In 1948 Clifford Odets, well before his notorious performance in front of the HUAC, announced his move back to New York from the pages of the *New York Times*. "I went to Hollywood and found much of interest there. Hollywood, after all, is a piece of America, intense and emergent, crowded with a varied typical life. The cinema medium itself . . . is a very great one. Why not explore its possibilities?" The disillusionment following his forays into directing *None but the Lonely Heart* had, however, convinced Odets that Hollywood was just a "celluloid dragon scorching to death every human fact in his path."[92] Odets and many of the former Hollywood Europeans were returning not only to the former geography of the East, but also to a pre-Hollywood—and largely pre-1930s—esthetics.

Manley Halliday and Shep Stearns, the protagonists of Budd Schulberg's 1951 novel *The Disenchanted*, embody the 1920s and 1930s. Manley, possibly but certainly not solely a stand-in for F. Scott Fitzgerald, is the Pulitzer Prize-winning, fading star of the 1920s. Stearns is a twenty-three-year-old graduate of Northeastern Webster College (though, like Schulberg, a Hollywood native) who has gone back to Hollywood "with the conviction that movies, as the great new folk art, needed young men with his combination of talent and ideals."[93] Set in the late 1930s, *The Disenchanted* pits the 1920s against the 1930s, with the former routinely overcoming the latter. Manley tells Stearns that

> from an artistic point of view, I can't help thinking we had a little the better of it. . . . In this decade of yours Odets yells STRIKE and everybody puts him up with Chekov and Ibsen. . . . But just think of what we had: *The Waste Land* and Pound and Cummings—your poets are midgets compared to them—and our novelists. . . . I even think our movie stars were better, Valentino was so much more what he was than any of yours today, and Doug had more energy and Pickford and Gish were more wistful, and Barbara La Marr and Swanson were more stunning.[94]

Odets at least was still calling for realism ("the search for the reality of the age"), but his notion of audience had changed and become similar to that expressed by Preston Sturges in his exchange with Mrs. George Kaufman. Hollywood's pursuit of a national audience was no longer a possibility but a "burden." It meant making art "as accessible as chewing gum." In contrast to the public dimension of the Hollywood film, the playwright exalted a privatized dimension of art—"the inner life"—and audience—"a few, serious, responsible friends," a limited "audience that finds more enjoyment in the personally felt and written play than in Miss Grable's legs." [95]

By the end of 1947, McCarthyism had struck some of Kenneth Macgowan's friends, and, a few years later, Macgowan would be actively involved in the battle to keep UCLA free of the anti-communist Loyalty Oath. [96] By 1951, with few exceptions, UCLA professors had signed the oath. [97] The same year, *Hollywood Quarterly* had been thoroughly purged of Hollywood progressives and academics. In the case of Macgowan, his progressive past had excluded him from the editorial board. When in 1953 he proposed refugee progressive screenwriter Karl Tunberg for the board of the *Quarterly*, his recommendation worked against Tunberg. The Office of the Chancellor noted that "the mere fact that [Tunberg] was recommended by Macgowan should be enough to cause the administration to see if it couldn't find somebody in the motion picture business who possessed two very common and desirable qualifications: no subversive contacts or taints." [98]

The university administrative echelons were still quite interested in collaboration with Hollywood. In August 1947, UCLA provost Clarence Dykstra was still asking Harry Warner for his input on the theater department, feeling sure that "you might have some ideas which would be good for us to consider." [99] In this climate, however, Macgowan had doubts about the expediency of having the studios investing too much money in the department, something that raised Dykstra's "concern over the present program's being too ambitious." [100] Within UCLA, in fact, Macgowan was reproducing the example set up by his friends who had returned to the New York avant-garde. In the face of HUAC purges and the flight of the Hollywood intellectuals, Macgowan seemed animated by "an anxiety of contamination" in regard to Hollywood. Macgowan's doubts about any possible collaboration with the film industry are even more noteworthy because of his initial efforts to hybridize Hollywood and UCLA. The retreat from Hollywood became the core of Macgowan's plans. His plan for the 1948 departmental curriculum called for "a single Theater Arts Department based on the natural evolution of film and radio out of theater. Therefore, particularly the first two years of the curriculum are based on (a) a sound liberal education, and (b) basic theater." As for Hollywood, the former producer saw being in Hollywood more as a danger than an advantage. UCLA was not to become a "craft school" for the industry, nor should it attract "young men and women seeking fame and fortune, with no other concern."[101]

Characteristically, Macgowan emphasized an anti-hybridizationist stance in the Motion Picture Division of the theater department. The chairman was now concerned "more with documentary film than with the fictional film."[102] By the early 1950s, the Motion Picture Division was still underdeveloped, so much so that a young disgruntled faculty member wrote Macgowan complaining about the excessive emphasis given to theater courses and arguing that the "motion picture curriculum should be kept as far as possible from the theater."[103] Certainly for an old-school progressive like Macgowan, Hollywood was losing much of its charm. As New Yorkers trekked back East, Europeans were also leaving. Sociologist Donald Kent reported that only 1.3 percent of the "refugee intellectuals" went back to Europe at the end of the war.[104] But this figure clearly does not mirror the experience of the Hollywood Europeans. Refugee actress Valerie von Märtens remembers that in the early 1940s many Hollywood Europeans—professing their love of the United States—chastised her husband, actor-director Curt Goetz, for his eagerness to go back to Germany.[105] Among the German-speaking directors catalogued by Jan-Christopher Horak in his *Fluchtpunkt Hollywood*, however, nineteen out of sixty-nine—or 27 percent—left for Europe, though in some cases they returned to California to work in particular productions.[106] The list of returnees also includes Hollywood success stories such as Anatole Litvak, who settled in France after 1949; Fritz Lang, who went back to Germany in 1956; and, at the end of the 1950s, Douglas Sirk.

Those who remained were often discomforted. "Hollywood is bankrupt," wrote William Dieterle to fellow refugee director Ludwig Berger in 1948. "It is possible to produce films as mass products. But nobody, not even the Americans, will see them, because they are empty."[107] The physical locales of progressive Hollywood were often sold or abandoned, though often remembered with keen nostalgia. "Dear, dear, Helli, it would be so nice to have a chat in peace once again . . . as we used to do on 26th street and Mabery Road," wrote Salka Viertel to Helly Weigel,

Bertolt Brecht's wife, in 1957, referring to the couple's and her own Santa Monica residences.[108] But the Brechts had left, chased away by HUAC in 1947, and in the early 1950s Salka Viertel sold her house on Mabery Road. Her salon had thrived with refugees and American leftists in the last half of the 1930s, but now it was empty; too many had left, and the house was too big for the screenwriter who, graylisted and unemployed, needed the money from its sale. Salka made sure, however, that another progressive, producer John Houseman, would buy it. "It would be wonderful," she wrote Houseman in 1953, "to know that 165 Mabery Road, which has seen so much life and love, struggle and happiness, and which was the 'port of entry' for so many stranded souls, is a happy home for you and your family."[109]

1

"Weary Standard-Bearers of Progress"

Hollywood Progressive Cinema and the Crisis of the Hollywood Community

. . . there is a strange inconsistency in all these progressive films. Upon closer inspection one cannot help noticing that they reveal the profound weakness of the very cause for which they try to enlist sympathy. No doubt they champion social progress within the dimension of plot and dialogue, but in the less obvious dimensions they manage to suggest that liberal thought is receding rather than advancing.

Siegfried Kracauer, *Harper's Magazine*, 1948

n June 1948, Siegfried Kracauer analyzed the postwar output of progressive Hollywood films. According to the German refugee theorist, traces of the activity of the Hollywood progressives were still visible in the crop of films released after the war. Hollywood progressives had attempted to deal with the "issues of the day"—the veteran situation, anti-Semitism in the United States, and so forth—by fashioning what the German critic called "movies with a message." Compared with the films of the 1930s, however, progressive Hollywood's postwar output was hardly effective as a "standard bearer of progress" and enlightenment. Possibly, this difference was not conscious to the makers of these films but lay, to use Kracauer's

190

language, "under the surface." Under a veneer of assertiveness and enthusiasm, in fact, these films lacked the confidence of prewar progressive
Hollywood and finally proved that liberalism, rather than thriving, "is on
the defense" in Hollywood as well as in the United States.[1]

Kracauer's analysis warrants a reexamination in light of the crisis
of the Hollywood community described in Chapter 6. The emergence
of the avant-garde alternative, increasing doubts about the existence of
"One Big Audience," and reservations about America's possibilities for
democracy contributed to weakening the "narrative power" of the 1930s
paradigm. Rather than narrative control over the reality they represented,
the films by the Hollywood progressives expressed their authors' increasing uncertainties about a "narrative" that had been both an esthetic and
a political blueprint. In turn, these films' plots gestured toward an avant-
garde that, in direct opposition to the Hollywood paradigm, emphasized
the subconscious over the reality of the social environment. In some sense,
the Hollywood progressives who still remained active in the studios in the
aftermath of the war attempted to have it both ways: to be in Hollywood
and yet to be responsive to the new esthetic. This was not a new cultural
response for them. After all, in the 1930s they had seen Hollywood and
the avant-garde as at least partially coterminous filmmaking spheres. But
the post-1945 avant-garde, as opposed to the one represented, say, by the
Group Theater in the 1930s, was no longer reconcilable to Hollywood;
the avant-garde of the latter 1940s actually grew out of a dissatisfaction
with mass-marketed cultural production.

As the lure of the New York avant-garde and the erosion of the
1930s paradigm weakened the Hollywood community from the inside
and McCarthyism attacked democratic Hollywood from the outside,
what happened to social realism? Was it pushed completely out of the
center of the Hollywood style? Did it survive in other areas of American
filmmaking?

The Double Self-Portrait of the Hollywood Progressives

Progressive Hollywood produced two types of self-portraits after the war:
one virtually identical to Dieterle's biopics of the late 1930s, and the
other—which the character of George Steele in *Crack Up* exemplifies—
revealing what Dana Polan has referred to as "paranoia," the "fear of
narrative, and the particular social representation it works to uphold,
against all that threatens the unity of its logical framework."[2] In the latter

type of portrait, a sense of solitude and defeat had crept into the formerly confident self-imaging of Hollywood progressives.

Costume biopics continued to bear the mark of Hollywood progressivism. *A Song to Remember* (on Frederic Chopin) and *Rhapsody in Blue* (on George Gershwin) depicted great artists as doppelgänger of Hollywood progressives—that is, as progressive intellectuals dedicated to the communication of culture to the masses. Chopin and Gershwin were—like Émile Zola—men of the people, hybridizing audiences and styles via their medium. Reviewing Charles Vidor's biopic of Chopin, music critic Lawrence Morton reiterated the idea of a national audience, praising the film because "Jose Iturbi has played Chopin for an audience probably as numerous as the combined audiences of such famous Chopin interpreters as Liszt, De Pächman, and Paderewski." Record sales of Chopin's music from the film score showed that "if the cynic despairs, the optimist (one might say the realist) has plenty of ground for encouragement."[3] Hollywood seemed to work.

Rhapsody in Blue, scripted by Howard Koch and Elliot Paul, defined George Gershwin (played by Robert Alda) as the artist who is able to bring diverse genres and audiences together. Throughout the film, great art is defined by its pervasive power, its making itself available to popular appropriation. Schubert was great insofar as he was also a "songwriter," Gershwin's mentor, as Professor Frank (played by Albert Bassermann), reminds George. And great, too, was Shakespeare, whose verses (from *Romeo and Juliet*) George's unschooled father mutters, unaware of their highbrow origins. In Gershwin's own terms, he is successful because he "makes opera entertaining," as his agent Max Dreyfuss (played by Charles Coburn) tells him. He continuously attempts to negotiate a median between high and low, concerti and operettas, and to give "America a voice"—not by singling out an aspect or an audience, but by encompassing all its stratifications and complexities. Like the shot of the audiences in *Zola*, the great camera work by Sol Polito emphasized both the size of Gershwin's audiences and his music's uncanny ability to connect with them. The last shot of the film features "An American in Paris," performed at the old auditorium of City College on the occasion of Gershwin's death. Slowly, the camera rises over the head of the pianist to encompass the enormous crowd that is listening to the music and, beyond that, the whole city of New York. The acid test of great art—*Rhapsody* repeats again and again—is its success in communicating its message to the people.

Hollywood progressives were also producing self-portraits in less optimistic poses. *Crack Up* (RKO, 1946) was directed by Irving Reis from a script by progressive Hollywood New Yorker John Paxton.[4] The film is a thriller set in the "Manhattan Museum of Art." George Steele (played by Pat O'Brien) is a part-time curator and full-time guide to the museum's collections. At the beginning of the film, O'Brien is lecturing an audience of ordinary visitors about Jean François Millet and his work. His tone is rambunctious: "Do not be afraid to like what you like," he vaguely tells the museum visitors, and—first and foremost—"do not be pretentious." Millet was great, just because he was able to engage the attention of ordinary people. No intellectual snob, Millet was "successful in communicating what he felt was a beautiful moment." So were Dürer and Gainsborough, whose paintings George plans to show to his audience in the coming week. George then unveils another canvas, a nonrepresentational one, openly alluding to surrealism and abstract expressionism. He laughs at it along with his public. "This is nonsense. If you like it—fine. I don't." A diminutive mustached man—looking like a combination between Hitler and Salvador Dali—vocally objects. The public is with George and physically ejects the deviant. "Surrealists will be searched for weapons at the door," George concludes.[5]

George Steele is a creature of the 1930s, brandishing an abbreviated version of Hollywood's 1930s democratic modernism. He holds in high esteem the artist's ability to communicate to a large audience and also engages in a continuous struggle with the upper echelons of the museum, who consider him a "rabble rouser" and a "people's defender" because he reminds the gutless director of the art museum that it is a "public institution," not "an exclusive tea party." A reading of this film, however, shows a new element in Hollywood modernism. As opposed to the public-minded artists and anti-Nazi activists of the late 1930s as well as to the citizen soldiers of World War II, progressive characters are increasingly alone and besieged by doubts. Solitude rather than solidarity, in fact, pervades *Crack Up*.

What George Steele shares with the heroes of the 1930s Hollywood progressives' self-portraits is indeed less interesting than what makes him so different from them. As a hero of the Cultural Front, he is curiously morose and noncharismatic. Regardless of what he tells his audience, he seems to be the one who has a problem communicating with the world. Hardly a hero of mass communication, George struggles to make sense of the world around him. Memory more than anything else seems to fail him.

George's lecture itself is ambiguous, framed as it is within a protracted flashback in which he attempts to recall how he ended up intoxicated and fighting a cop inside the museum. The flashback illuminates how tenuous George's connection with reality is—no longer direct and linear, but oblique and blurred. "There's no telling," *The New York Times* noted in its review of the film, "what a man temporarily deprived of his sense might have imagined to have experienced."[6] In the end, his predicament is solved. A deranged, wildly elitist collector—who tells George that "museums have the habit of wasting great art on dullards who can't differentiate between art and trash"—has stolen two masterpieces from the museum and wants to discredit art's progressive watchdog. Intoxicated again, George is saved by the police but remains a lonely figure. Among his saviors, he remains the oddball, convinced that in a world increasingly crazy, he is the only sane person.

In a comparison with the 1930s heroes of progressive melodramas, George does not measure up. While the others were successful artists, he seems to have a problem giving his ideas a productive, creative spin. The heroes of the 1930s biopics can take care of business, of themselves, and of their dear ones; George needs his girlfriend and the police not only to save his life, but to defend the democratic calling of the art museum.

The Veteran, the Noir, and the Progressive Paradigm

As George Steele's friends try to make sense of what has happened to him, they hint that his combat experiences might be the cause of his mental confusion. The democratic war against fascism should have given the progressive cultural worker a new center and purpose, but *Crack Up* suggests that war saps strength and unbalances the mind. The ambiguities surrounding the troubled veteran in *Crack Up* aptly represents the progressive circle's unease regarding World War II, its legacy, and its now-useless warriors—all 12.1 million of them as of August 1945.[7] Films produced during the war had extolled GIs as citizen soldiers and representatives of the American people, and postwar films like William Wyler's sympathetic portrait of returning servicemen in *The Best Years of Our Lives* had been lionized by the progressive press.[8] Soon after the war, however, Hollywood progressives began to question the democratic spirit of the armed forces, 51 percent of whom, according to a poll taken in September 1945 among the American troops still in Germany, thought that Hitler had done Germany "a lot of good."[9]

In 1946, *Screenwriter* published a memoir by Leonard Spigelgass about his war experiences. Spigelgass was what many of the Hollywood progressives had wanted to be: he had actively participated in the war effort, both in the Signal Corps in the Aleutians in late spring 1943 and later in John Ford's unit. His article, however, supplied a complete counternarrative of the war. At Kisca—the army base celebrated by John Huston in *Report from the Aleutians*—Spigelgass had not come across the democratic utopia described in that film. Soldiers were anti-Semitic. "It is the Jews who are forcing us to fight Germany," an officer had told the flabbergasted Spigelgass. When the screenwriter challenged him, the soldier refused to apologize. These men were hardly the "partners to the job" of rebuilding a new, better world. By the end of his diary, Spigelgass was hoping to be sent home as soon as possible.[10]

In the first issue of *Hollywood Quarterly*, UCLA social psychologist and Hollywood Writers' Mobilization (HWM) member Franklin Fearing synthesized the ambiguity of the issue. The country owed the veterans, and yet they were undoubtedly a danger—the symbol of a warring America that progressives would have been only too glad to forego. The "warrior's return" and its solution was going to be the first great issue of the postwar years, one that the "great mass media" would have an important role in solving by educating the public and the veterans themselves.[11] Several postwar films, including many of the film noir genre, dealt with the legacy of the war and in particular with the veterans. In noting the recurrence of the veteran theme in film noir, Nicholas Christopher has recently argued that "postwar years returning veterans are often portrayed in a negative light."[12] This, however, seems too simplistic. Progressive filmmakers, in particular, cast the veteran as a rather positive—if embattled—character. This is evident in the "veteran noir," whose convoluted plot and visually deceptive atmosphere were particularly effective for rendering the contrasting commitments of the progressive Hollywoodians in regard to the former servicemen.

Crossfire (RKO, 1946) is a good example of the themes characteristic of the "veteran noir." The film was produced, scripted, and directed by an all-star team of Hollywood progressives: producer Adrian Scott, director Edward Dmytryk, and screenwriter John Paxton. Apparently the film was shot in twenty days with a relatively modest budget of $500,000 so as to beat Elia Kazan's and Darryl Zanuck's *Gentleman's Agreement*, which—like *Crossfire*—dealt with anti-Semitism.[13] However, the anti-Semitism theme seems an afterthought in *Crossfire*. Its source, Richard

Brooks's novel *The Brick Foxhole*, focused on gay-bashing in the military rather than religious or racial intolerance. According to the inclusive, but not assertive, notion of "people" shared by Cultural Fronters Scott and Dmytryk, gender, ethnic, and racial differences were "interchangeable." "In the book [the soldier] murders a fairy," Scott wrote to RKO producers William Dozier and Charles Kormer. "He could have murdered a Negro, a foreigner, or a Jew. It would have been the same thing."[14] Remaining substantially faithful to their 1930s notion of "people," Scott, Dmytryk, and Paxton focused on a definition that was inclusive, rather than one that articulated gender, sexual, or ethnic difference. Of larger relevance to the film was the issue of redeployment of the armed forces and the debate over the meaning of World War II. Many of those involved in the production of *Crossfire* must have had some ideas about veterans' issues. Dmytryk's previous film, *Till the End of Time* (RKO, 1946), was unmistakably pro-veteran—the story of a discharged serviceman struggling to readjust in postwar Los Angeles.[15] Robert Ryan had served in the marines with author Richard Brooks and had promised Brooks that if the film was ever made, he would play the villain.[16]

Crossfire tells the story of the murder of a Jewish man at the hands of a platoon of soldiers waiting in Washington, D.C., to be discharged from the army. At first the wrong man, Private Arthur Mitchell (played by George Cooper), is suspected of the crime because he cannot provide the police with a credible alibi. After a long investigation, however, Captain Finlay (played by Robert Young) discovers the truth: the man has been murdered by Monty Montgomery (played by Robert Ryan), a violent, anti-Semitic paranoid. In a final shootout in the night streets of Washington, Captain Finlay kills the psychopathic soldier.

The film is in the tradition of the 1930s, down to the portrait of Franklin Delano Roosevelt prominently exhibited in Captain Finlay's office a full year after the president's death. Following that model, *Crossfire* deals with two of the most disturbing issues of the day—the permanence of racial prejudice and the redeployment of the former warriors—advocating tolerance and social justice while remaining substantially faithful to a strong Hollywood narrative. Remembering the film in the 1990s, director Dmytryk noted that the "murder story was the sugar around the message." *Crossfire* was a success, receiving five Academy nominations and netting $1,275,000 at the box office.[17]

Enthusiastically received by progressive circles everywhere, *Crossfire* was lionized by John Houseman in the *Hollywood Quarterly*.[18] Its producer,

Adrian Scott, later a member of the Hollywood Ten, described his film as a model for postwar Hollywood grounded in the tradition established in the late 1930s. Citing *The Life of Louis Pasteur*, *The Grapes of Wrath*, *Confessions of a Nazi Spy*, and *Mission to Moscow* as his models, Scott envisioned the film as conducive to the political education of American society, specifically about the issue of anti-Semitism.[19] For once sociologists seemed to agree. Exit polls established that *Crossfire* was effective, and Scott proposed an alliance between Hollywood and "social workers and psychologists" to produce short films in an effort to solve "minority problems." Provided that many people in the industry would volunteer their time, these films could be free and available to everybody.[20]

Crossfire, however, clearly marked a change from the 1930s. Thematically, the film presented a revision of the World War II rhetoric, its dense scenario reversing all the symbols of the standard war film. The interethnic platoon of ordinary Americans in arms is riddled with hatred, and loyalty among soldiers is no longer a virtue but a rejection of the rules of citizenship. In a civil society, soldiers are a bomb waiting to explode. "Soldiers have nowhere to go unless you tell them where to go," Sergeant Keeley (played by Robert Mitchum) tells Finlay. "So they go crawling. Or they go crazy." As for the positive symbols, such as Captain Finlay, there is a strange aura of tiredness and melancholy about him ("Nothing interests me anymore. It used to, but not anymore."). "Instead of showing the strength of liberalism [he] testif[ies] to its extreme fragility," Siegfried Kracauer noted in his penetrating analysis of the film. "He seems . . . to be overwhelmed by a mood of resignation, as though he had discovered that the struggle for enlightenment is a Sisyphean task."[21] Finlay's final victory over the evil Monty is ultimately far from cathartic, as he first baits Monty into a trap, and then shoots him in the back as he escapes.

In terms of narrative style, *Crossfire* marked a departure from the progressive paradigm of the 1930s and the "uncluttered realism" of films such as *Best Years*. Remembering *Crossfire* in the 1990s, Dmytryk noted that the shadows that accompany the characters throughout the film were due to budget limitations.[22] This may be true, but the narrative structure of the film also is cluttered and nonlinear. At the beginning of the film, Montgomery recalls the moment when he has first met the victim in a bar. But his recollection is incorrect, as he is the killer and is trying to frame a fellow serviceman. Later on, Private Mitchell offers his own flashback of the event, but his memory is faulty because he was intoxicated. Significantly, in *Crossfire* as well as in *Crack Up*, flashbacks do not recuperate time gone by but rather almost always signify the protagonist's faulty grasp of reality. It is one's inability to view the past realistically that fosters confusion in the present. What these characters fail to remember, more often than not, is related to the war and its real sense. Even in *Crossfire*, the bar scene that is the focus of both attempted flashbacks refers to a discussion about the interpretation of the war. In a sense, Monty and his victim, Joseph Samuels (played by Sam Levine), vie for young Private Mitchell's soul via a discussion of the war and its results. For Monty the war is not over because of his aggressive resentment of "the stinking civilians," "the Jewboys," and "the Hillbillies." For Samuels the war is, or should be, over; he hopes that "one of these days we'll stop hating and start liking things again." The film succeeds in communicating an ultimately anguished outlook by leaving the results of that discussion unresolved. Even as we are told that the flashbacks of Monty's and Samuel's tirades are both vitiated by the faulty or prejudiced memory of those who experience them, we are left wondering who has really won. After all, Monty and Samuels end up the same way—killed by another American in the streets of the nation's capital.

John Belton, in his overview of American cinema and society, suggests that "perhaps the most existential of all noir heroes is the amnesiac."[23] In June 1946, Bosley Crowther noted that "the number of films in which amnesia is the key dramatic device is almost as large as the number in which the telephone is used as a prop."[24] The film he was specifically referring to, Joseph Mankiewicz's *Somewhere in the Night*—scripted by Mankiewicz, Howard Dimsdale, and Lee Strasberg—deals with George Taylor (played by John Hodiak), a former marine who has lost his memory in a war-related incident. The amnesiac veteran was a staple of several noir films scripted or directed by Hollywood progressives. In *Deadline at Dawn*—directed by Harold Clurman, scripted by Odets, and produced by John Houseman and Adrian Scott for RKO in 1946—a sailor stranded in New York on his way to boot camp risks being charged with the murder of a woman. His problem is loss of memory, as he cannot remember his whereabouts at the time of the killing. In Lester Cole's and Sydney Boehm's script for refugee Curtis Bernhardt's film, *High Wall* (MGM, 1947), Steven Kenet (played by Robert Taylor) is a former army pilot who is accused of murdering his wife. His condition is made worse by headaches and memory blackouts due to his war wounds. Modern medicine and hypnosis finally enable him to remember correctly and save his own life. Memory loss and veterans also figure prominently in Arthur

Ripley's *The Chase* (1946, Nero Seymour Nebenzahl) from a script by Philip Yordan. Chuck Scott (played by Robert Cummings) is a veteran down on his luck who falls for Lorna (played by Michelle Morgan), the wife of gangster Eddie Roman (played by Steve Cochran). When Chuck and Lorna decide to run away to Cuba, Chuck falls sick and can no longer distinguish between fantasy and reality. In *The Clay Pigeon* (RKO, 1948) scripted by Carl Foreman from his own original story, seaman Jim Fletcher (played by Bill Williams) wakes up from a year-long coma remembering only his name. He will need to recover his memory to save himself from being court-martialed for betraying his friend in a Japanese concentration camp. In John Cromwell's *Dead Reckoning* (Columbia, 1947), written by Oliver P. Garrett and Steven Fisher and interpreted by Humphrey Bogart, Lizabeth Scott, and Morris Carnovsky, nobody suffers from amnesia, but the past, or its correct recollection, is still at stake as Bogart, a decorated soldier, tries to uncover the shady past of his buddy who vanished just before receiving a major decoration at the end of the war.

These films suggest a curious intertwining of veterans, war, and memory (or its loss). In 1948, Siegfried Kracauer expressly linked the crisis of liberal Hollywood with the two recurrent "types" of the "ex-GI in a state of complete bewilderment" and of the tired, jaded, liberal character, the "weary standard-bearer of progress." "No doubt [these films] champion social progress within the dimensions of plot and dialogue, but in the less obvious dimensions they manage to suggest that liberal thought is receding rather than advancing. . . . Compared to those of the mid-thirties, [these films] suggest a waning of spiritual substance."[25]

Up to its conclusion, the war effort not only unified the Hollywood community after the "troubles" of 1939–41, it also supplied a narrative that overlapped with the 1930s realist paradigm. The enemy had served as a clear-cut target for the gun as much as for the camera.[26] In some sense, Hollywood movies knew what to say, when to say it, and to whom. But confronted with the widespread sense that the war had not achieved what it had set out to accomplish, or even that it had not yet ended, Hollywood progressives generated increasingly disturbed visions of the war, often relying on characters with faulty hindsight or incomplete memories. In this framework, it is not surprising that the cinematic discourse generated by Hollywood progressives—unconsciously or not—promoted the idea that the way to recover health, vision, and a sense of civic purpose was to place the war in its correct context and perspective—that is, to "remember correctly." One had to regain a sense of what he had fought and suffered for in order to be able to resume his life and build a democratic America. In cinematic terms, the path from confusion to clarity was marked by progress toward the language of realism.

In *Pride of the Marines*, the real-life story of a Philadelphia blue-collar worker who earned a Navy Cross while losing his eyesight fighting at Guadalcanal, Al Schmid (played by John Garfield) is unable to make sense of the war and to put his personal misfortunes in the perspective of building a better world. Director Delmer Daves, along with communist screenwriter Albert Maltz,[27] charted Schmid's inability to cope with his reality via a dream sequence of previous scenes from his life, which the spectators have already seen shot in realistic style (the mano a mano struggle at Guadalcanal, Schmid saying goodbye to his fiancée at the Philadelphia train station on his way to boot camp) are now shot in low angles, as negative images replace the positive. Slowly, however, Schmid gives a sense to the war as an interethnic and interracial struggle for a world and "a country where nobody gets booted around for any reason." As he makes sense of the war and of his sacrifice, his eyesight miraculously improves. The last scene has him able to distinguish the color of a Philadelphia cab—a healing, if not a healed, man.

The documentary *Let There Be Light*—John Huston's film about shell-shocked veterans in a Long Island hospital—also marks the path through which former servicemen recuperate both their memory and their place in society under the aegis of the progressive-minded Veterans Administration. The soldiers are cured by hypnosis that allows them to remember the event their mind is trying to erase. As they regain their capacity to remember, they are slowly but surely healed and can return to society.[28]

Crossfire and the other "veteran noirs" of the end of the war effectively expressed the changed situation of Hollywood progressives. They were, after all, films of social content, dealing with one of the most pressing problems in postwar America. The way they tackled this "issue of the day," however, had inexorably changed. True to the 1930s ideals, these films purported to be message films, addressing the plight of the veterans in peacetime America. The ideological confidence of the 1930s, however, had found its visual counterpart in the paradigm's realism and the sure progress toward a last-reel solution that, while often limited to the protagonists' predicament, gestured toward a more general answer to societal problems. In these postwar films, on the other hand, the unease and ambiguities of postwar America found their visual correlative in the erosion of realism and the struggle, only partially successful, to recuperate reality from dreams, nightmares, and physical blindness.

In dealing with the lure of dreams, the fright of nightmares, and the loss of eyesight, the "veteran noir" showed a propensity to engage some of the themes typical of postwar experimental cinema. Like the films of Maya Deren or Hanns Richter, the "veteran noir" was preoccupied with subconscious—often using the flashback to highlight the subjective way in which the protagonist approached the reality surrounding him or her. The recurring themes of dreams and corrupted memory inverted the relationship between avant-garde and Hollywood, paralleling *Hollywood Quarterly*'s renewed interest in cinematic avant-garde. In the 1930s, progressive New York vanguardists often went to Hollywood to learn. But in 1947, the learning process had reversed. Vanguardist Hans Richter's *Dreams That Money Can Buy* (1947) starts out as a film noir, with an off-screen voice identifying Joe as an unemployed veteran in a seedy New York apartment. But *Dreams* soon reveals itself as a parody of Hollywood. It was the Hollywood progressives who were taking avant-garde seriously, trying to integrate some of its visual lessons in their films even though they were often at odds with their intentions.

Robert Corber has demonstrated how the 1950s films of British director Alfred Hitchcock and

> cold war liberals argued that reality did not exist independently of the individual but was experienced subjectively. Privileging modes of representation that stressed the highly mediated relation between the individual and the material world, they claimed that the Cultural Front critique of American society was crudely positivistic because it focuses on the capitalist relations of productions at the expense of the construction of subjectivity.[29]

Corber's analysis of the Cold War consensus helps us understand the "veteran noir" as a transitional stage in the cinematic discourse of the American Left. As opposed to Hitchcock's Cold War films, "veteran noirs" never question the ontological realism of external reality; instead, the subconscious is usually evoked only to be explained away, or exorcised via external, objective causes: drugs, alcohol, or foul play (*Crack Up* and *Crossfire*); malaria (*The Chase*); and war wounds (*Pride of the Marines, Let There Be Light, The Clay Pigeon*, and *High Wall*).[30] And yet it would be risky to underestimate the role of the subconscious in these films. Hollywood progressives' ultimate trust in the role of objective circumstances in shaping their characters' situations functions almost as a Jamesonian "strategy of containment," working feverishly to exclude all alternative explanations that nonetheless appear only too plausible. Reading these films backward from their conclusions, one cannot escape the sense that these characters are in transition. They, as well as their creators, still believe in realism as well as in the Hollywood paradigm, but other, contrasting alternatives are looming on the horizon.[31]

The Different Faces of "the People"

During the war, fascism had supplied a real and clearly visible enemy at which Hollywood progressives could aim their cameras. In addition, anti-Nazism had kept the Hollywood front united before and during the war. Realistic Hollywood films that engaged the political issues of the day has seemed the way to go to many people of different cultural and political backgrounds. Progressive films were to celebrate the American people as the crucial and unfaltering protagonist in the struggle against Hitler. Although some Hollywoodians expressed doubt about the ability of the Hollywood film to accomplish these goals, overall the community had coalesced around the program of realist cinema and the cult of ordinary Americans. In the aftermath of the war, however, this changed. Sociologists increasingly undermined the idea that "the people" was a unified entity, and realism became less and less viable for expressing the mixed feelings that Hollywood progressives entertained about the U.S. domestic situation. Finally, the third panel of the 1930s triptych—the unanimous appreciation of the virtues of the people—began to crumble.

In a declaration from Moscow on November 1, 1943, the Allies had declared their intention to pursue perpetrators of the Holocaust "to the uttermost ends of earth."[32] The atmosphere changed, however, after the war was over and the European situation rapidly evolved into a confrontation between East and West. Following the Allies' victory, the American government rapidly discarded any policy resembling the plan proposed by Secretary of Treasury Henry Morgenthau about the radical deindustrialization of the German economy. Instead the U.S. government embraced a more benign attitude toward the vanquished enemy. As a matter of fact, in the attempt to avoid the errors of Versailles and to stabilize an anti-Soviet sector in Central Europe, the Western allies embraced the Brechtian notion of the "Other Germany," minus the idea of the persecution of German social, military, and economic leadership. As historian Enzo Collotti has shown, the Allies were aware that a thorough process of denazification would weaken the German economy along with the anti-communist and conservative parties they favored. In January 1946, the Allied Control Council issued Order No. 24, designed to prevent persons who had had more than a nominal role in the Nazi Reich from holding any position in the new German state. The directive, however, also contained a clause exempting all those persons deemed essential to German economic recovery. In April 1947, this was further softened during the meeting of the four secretaries of state in Moscow, when it was decided that denazification was partly to be run by the new German Justice Department. Eventually, a relatively large number of former Nazis ended up working for the new administration. The Democratic Republic of Germany (DDR) denounced the fact that one of the main authors of the Nuremberg Laws, Hans Globke, was now undersecretary of state. The data of the Justice Department of the Federal Republic of Germany (BRD) concerning the time span between 1945 and 1965 reveal that out of eighty thousand sentences issued against Nazi criminals, BRD issued only six thousand while the Soviet Union issued twenty-three thousand, DDR issued twelve thousand, and Poland and Czechoslovakia issued sixteen thousand.[33] Historian Richard T. Pells writes that in the U.S. controlled zone, "American policy-makers, interested now in West Germany as a potential ally in the Cold War, aborted the de-nazification crusade before it accomplished its mission."[34]

Hollywood cinema usually followed the development of American foreign policy, switching from the "beastly German" of World War II films to the ill-advised German of the postwar years. The last of the films produced by the Frank Capra unit, *Hitler Lives?*, espoused quite a vindictive attitude toward Germany. Through all twenty minutes of the film, American troops going overseas were treated to images of the innumerable deaths caused by Germany from the 1870 battle at Sedan during the Franco-Prussian War, to the trenches of Verdun during World War I, to the Nazi concentration camps at Dachau during World War II. The commentary noted that in the aftermath of each defeat the Germans had pledged repentance, only to revive aggressive tactics and stir up conflict again a few years later. Militarism was a German vice, not necessarily a Nazi one. National Socialism and the historical absence of any democratic tradition made Germany into a perverse example of mass society. The problem, the film argued, was how to sort out past and future Nazis from the anonymous masses of present-day Germans, as they all looked and sounded the same.

Six years after World War II, the problem was not so daunting. Even Nazi generals displayed courage and grace. *The Desert Fox* (TCF, 1951)— scripted and produced by *Grapes of Wrath* screenwriter Nunnally Johnson, directed and photographed by Henry Hathaway and Norman Brodine of the famous semidocumentary unit of Fox—revised Billy Wilder's and Erich von Stroheim's interpretation of the Nazi general from the 1942 *Five Graves to Cairo* and made Rommel into a romanticized victim of circumstances.[35] The turn in American foreign policy was a lesser jump for Hollywood liberals and radicals than for Hollywood Europeans. Though strongly in favor of a purge of the German elites, the HWM had championed films such as *Tomorrow the World* and *Hitler's Children*, which strongly rejected an "eye for an eye" retribution for German war crimes. Though not unanimous, this sentiment prevailed in the liberal press. In 1945, the *Nation* published an account of German POWs, arguing that German Wehrmacht soldiers, once rid of their officers, were not unlike ordinary Americans.[36] Reinhold Niebuhr authoritatively wrote that "no nation, even one so deeply corrupted as Germany was, is without its residual sources of health and sanity." Liberals should then refrain from "regard[ing] Germans from the standpoint of an inverted racial theory."[37]

For many of the American progressives, liberal leniency translated into a voracious inclusiveness, one that transposed onto the Germans the virtues of the American people. In films by Hollywood progressives such as screenwriter John Wexley (*Cornered*) and director Edward Dmytryk (*Cornered, The Young Lions*), fascism was still a present danger but ordinary Germans were either an oppressed people or simply deluded.[38] Doc, a German immigrant from the years before the war, is one of the lackluster heroes of *Asphalt Jungle* (1950), written and directed by Hollywood progressives Ben Maddow and John Huston. The film does not state Doc's motives for leaving Germany. In a temporary version of the script, Doc meets a German cab driver as he attempts to leave the unnamed city after a robbery gone awry. Doc and the cabby speak amiably in German before deciding that their moving to the United States was good "the way things turned out." "All countries are alike," Doc concludes. "People live, people die—the same everywhere."[39]

Slowly but surely, the celluloid image of Nazi Germany was changing —the vanquished prompted into redemption by the twist in American foreign policy and the Hollywood progressives' interpretation of Germany.[40] In 1958, Edward Dmytryk directed *The Young Lions*, scripted by Edward Anhalt from the novel by Irwin Shaw. The political development of the director (who had gone to jail as one of the Hollywood Ten, and then decided to name names) did not affect his interpretation of Nazism.[41] Like Karl Brunner of Dmytryk's 1943 *Hitler's Children*, the Wehrmacht soldier of *Young Lions*, Christian (played by Marlon Brando), is a "nice guy" caught up in the tragedy of history. "There is really no noticeable moral difference," Bosley Crowther wrote, "between the one German and the two Americans."[42]

Hollywood Europeans, on the other hand, saw Germany through different eyes. The refugee magazine *Aufbau* fit Niebuhr's description of the righteous liberal. Hans Kafka, the magazine reporter from the Hollywood studios, suspected that the only thing "liberated" Germans really wanted to see on their screens was Nazi heroes.[43] The magazine agreed with journalist Paul Nize, who argued that "simple justice requires that millions of Nazis be punished."[44] Hollywood Europeans' autobiographies and interviews often mention their unease in confronting postwar Germany. Billy Wilder—in Germany from May to September 1945 as an officer of the U.S. Office of Psychological Warfare—suggested that former Nazi star Anton Lang, playing Christ in a postwar passion play, be crucified with real nails.[45] Upon arriving in Frankfurt, Fritz Lang was confronted by a rude customs officer. "Are we back in Nazi times?" he immediately shot back.[46] Hollywood Europeans found that the Germans accused them of having chosen the easy way out, fleeing Germany for the plush life of Hollywood. Douglas Sirk, who had gone to Hollywood in 1940 and grown alfalfa for three years before succeeding in making his first American film, remembers that after visiting Germany in 1947, "I came back to the States feeling very demoralized. You know the Germans were blaming you for leaving when the Nazis were in power."[47]

More than anything, Hollywood refugees saw former Nazis behind every German. Coming back from the shooting of *A Foreign Affair*, Billy Wilder told *Aufbau* that Germany had not changed at all. It was a "society without any sense of shame" ("Eine schamlose Gesellschaft"), entirely run by former Nazis.[48] Douglas Sirk went to see Carl Zuckmayer's *Der Teufels General*, which featured the character of a Nazi general. The director could not stop thinking that the audience applauded the play, but "they were really applauding the Nazis."[49] "Leaving America," said Salka Viertel, referring to her former husband's return to Germany, "seemed to Berthold like a second emigration, or like a return to somebody once very dear but now disfigured and scarred by a horrible disease."[50]

Some European filmmakers—many of whom had enough clout to pick and choose their projects or to work within the independent production companies set up by Hollywood stars after the war—avoided postwar Germany altogether and went back to the *papier mâché* settings of the mid-1930s.[51] Even Fritz Lang, after the social and political realism of *Fury, You Only Live Once,* and *Manhunt,* was planning to film "Scandal in Vienna," an original story (which was never produced) that combined Emperor Franz Joseph and Buffalo Bill in a Viennese setting.[52]

When these filmmakers dealt with postwar Germany, a convoluted approach to reality and a continuous reference to masks, masquerade, and mistaken identity characterize their films. When representing Germany, the vision of the Hollywood Europeans loses confidence and becomes cluttered. Like the faltering memory of the veterans, the cinematic sight of German reality conceals more than it reveals. Even *The Search*, Fred Zinnemann's contribution to the genre and the closest to the realist paradigm of the films directed by Europeans, features a case of mistaken identity—a German orphan assumes a Jewish child's name in order to obtain better food and lodging for himself. In *Berlin Express*—directed by French-born Jacques Tourneur from a script by Harold Medford and based on an original story by refugee writer Curt Siodmak—nobody is who she/he seems to be. The film tells the story of an international coalition of American, French, Russian, and British characters who attempt to save the life of Dr. Bernard (played by Paul Lukas), a German anti-fascist leader kidnapped by the Nazi underground. At the beginning of the film, a bomb on a Berlin-bound train seemingly kills Dr. Bernard while he is on his way to address the United Nations about his plan to keep Germany united. The victim, however, turns out to be an agent of the Occupation Military Government serving as a decoy. A man initially presented as a German spy is revealed as an agent of the American War Department; an old friend of Dr. Bernard turns out to be at the Nazis' beck and call; an American GI turns out to be a Nazi; the Nazi master spy disguises himself as a former member of the French underground. Even a clown doing his gig in one of Frankfurt's illegal cabarets has not one, but two, secret identities. At first we are told that he is a clown moonlighting as a Nazi agent. But at one crucial moment, he is revealed to be an American counter-agent masquerading as the clown, a.k.a. a Nazi spy, to infiltrate the Nazi underground. The *New York Times* commented that the film was divided between "the authentic impact of documentary" and a "nebulous plot."[53]

As they were expressing their doubts about the possibility of capturing German reality through film, Hollywood Europeans were again questioning the virtues of the "people," another pivot of the 1930s paradigm. With the intensification of the domestic Cold War and the anti-communist crusade against Hollywood, Hollywood Europeans often offered a perverse and reversed imitation of Hollywood New Yorkers' optimistic inclusiveness. Just as the New Yorkers made the German people look and sound like good, earnest Americans, the Europeans, once confronted with McCarthyism, discovered ominous similarities between Americans and Nazi Germans. As the New Yorkers extended to the Germans their benign notion of "people," the Europeans extended to Americans their not-too-flattering interpretation of the German *Volk*.

Given their fragile status, Hollywood Europeans were notably prominent in the resistance against HUAC. For example, William Wyler, Fritz Lang, Fred Zinnemann, and Billy Wilder were all among the most outspoken opponents of Cecil B. DeMille's proposal to impose a loyalty oath on all members of the Screen Directors Guild.[54] In December 1947, one month after the first HUAC hearings in Washington, Fritz Lang drew an explicit parallel between Hitler and HUAC.

> An old Latin watchword rings down the centuries as a warning to us today: *Quis custodies ipsos custodes*—who shall watch those who have been sent to watch us? The answer is that we of a later generation have watched them. We have watched them gag Milton; we have watched them while they denounced Copernicus and jailed Galileo; We have watched all the bigots from Savonarola down to Hitler while they defaced and mutilated and made bonfires of the books. The stench of those fires lingers in our nostrils.[55]

For the Hollywood Europeans, McCarthyism resurrected cultural and political memories and fears. The anti-communist witch hunt also confirmed their doubts about the virtues of the ordinary American, which Lang and Dieterle had expressed in *Fury* and *Dr. Socrates*. Hollywood Europeans perceived HUAC as operating with the consent of the American people. It was a variation of "it can happen here," but rather than an indictment of the intentions of the American elites, many exiles turned their cameras to reflect on the weaknesses of the American masses.

Produced, directed, and written by Billy Wilder with the help of Charles Brackett, *A Foreign Affair* at first seems to come directly out of the old 1930s paradigm. Taking its clue from the much debated issue of the fraternization between American troops and German civilians,[56] the film is set in the real ruins of Berlin (in an interesting twist from Wilder's directorial debut, *Menschen am Sontag*, that instead portrayed the life of the city before the war). The plot centers on a government investigation of the "moral malaria" affecting American troops in Berlin. As an American officer of the Psychological Warfare Division, the director had been dispatched to Germany from May to September 1945.[57] Like Spigelgass, Wilder has not much good news to report concerning the postwar efforts and the moral health of the American troops. Germany is far from denazified, and Wilder shows many examples of the ordinary Germans' connection with the regime. But the American people, as represented by the American servicemen, are not up to the task of reeducating Germans. On the contrary, *Graecia capta, Romam captavit* (captive Greece, captured Rome). Rather than civilizing the Germans, American soldiers imitate their captives' moral debauchery: American soldiers trade cigarettes and chocolates for a date with a German girl, and the all-American hero, Captain Pringle (played by John Lund), is involved with singer Erika von Schlütow (played by Marlene Dietrich), the former mistress of a Nazi big shot. To top it all, Erika calls Pringle *Führer* and salutes him with a mocking "Heil Johnny!" As James Agee put it, by the time the Nazi big shot shows up, "the cast has so conducted itself that the Nazi seems the only possible person in the picture one might possibly have sympathy for."[58] Reviled in the American press as hopelessly cynical,[59] *A Foreign Affair* showed nonetheless a definite continuity with the Hollywood Europeans' experience in America, a celluloid thread that connected this film with *Fury* and *Dr. Socrates*. Silenced from the late 1930s to the end of World War II, Hollywood Europeans were again stating their alternative notion of the Hollywood New Yorkers' idea of a fundamentally benign "people."[60]

Wilder was not the only one to blur the boundaries between Germans and Americans. One of Douglas Sirk's last American films, *A Time to Love and a Time to Die* (1958) is a melodrama set in Germany during the war, drawn from the novel by refugee writer Erich Maria Remarque, who also collaborated on the screenplay and played a small role in the film. It centers on a love story between Ernst Graber (played by John Gavin), a Wehrmacht soldier on furlough in Berlin from the Russian front, and Elisabeth Kruse (played by the Swiss actress Lili Pulver), a young woman whose father has been deported and killed in a concentration camp because of his politics. In this melodrama, Sirk took issue with the argument of the "internal emigration" about the possibility of separating private opposition from public submission.[61] The lovers attempt to cut away a private space for decency and humanity within the faltering regime, but the logic of the war makes such separation impossible. The furlough comes to an end, and with it the illusion of privacy in the midst of horror. The more disgusted with Nazism Ernst becomes, the fewer options he has to negotiate compromises within his own conscience. Upon returning to the front, Ernst's refusal to shoot Russian partisans results in his own death. More subtly, the film also softens the obvious distinctions between ordinary Germans and Americans. Reversing the narrative conventions of wartime cinema, Sirk blurs all the markings (accents, posturings, etc.) distinguishing good from evil or Germans from Americans. The shift is clearer if we confront *A Time to Love* with Lang's 1943 *Hangmen Also Die*. In *Hangmen*, Lang divided the good Czechs from the Germans and their collaborators via the accents of his actors: the members of the resistance spoke American English, while their enemies' voices were marked by heavy German accents. Lang remembers that

> in order to make clear to the American public what it is like to be dominated and oppressed by people speaking a different language, I had given all the Czech roles, even the smallest ones, to American actors, who were able to speak flawless English. As opposed to these [American actors]—and, in the film, as opposed to Czech people—I had given all the German roles to German actors, who when they would speak English (in the film therefore, Czech), would do this with a German accent.[62]

While *Hangmen* was part of a cinema that believed in the existence of differences, and the necessity to express them, in *A Time to Love and a Time to Die* the boundaries were blurred. Nazi Germans have American voices, accents, and even familiar American screen personae. One of the Wehrmacht soldiers was impersonated by Don DeFore, a popular character actor famous for the television series "Ozzie and Harriet" who had also played the role of an "all-American" GI in both *A Guy Named Joe* and *Thirty Seconds over Tokyo*. In an increasingly ominous homogeneous, moral, and phonetic universe, Ernst's Gestapo friend has an American accent, while the anti-Nazi Professor Puhlman (played by Erich Maria Remarque) stands out with his German accent.

Realism in Post–World War II Films

The collapse of the 1930s paradigm notwithstanding, cinematic realism did not disappear, but rather survived in other areas of American film-making. Thom Andersen has correctly identified a "*film gris* tradition," developed by the Hollywood Left from 1947 to 1951 when the blacklist completely wiped out the remainder of the original Hollywood community. Yet the *film gris* is less the inheritor of the 1930s paradigm than a continuation of the "veteran noir" of 1945–47. Like the latter, but differently from the former, "this genre grew out of the body of films that have come retrospectively to be called *film noir*." Likewise, many of these films deal with veterans and rely on flashbacks. Solitude replaces social commitment and connection with the "people." As Andersen notes, these films offer little solution beyond the loneliness and often the death of their protagonists, and are "drab and depressing."[63] The less self-conscious and more optimistic 1930s paradigm is possibly better represented by a film such as *Salt of the Earth* (Independent Productions Corporation, 1953), directed by Herbert Biberman, scripted by Mike Wilson, and produced by Paul Jarrico outside of the Hollywood community and studio system in 1953. Like the 1930s films, *Salt* does not stray from a classical Hollywood narrative. As a testament to what had been their investment in the Hollywood of the previous two decades, even outside of the Hollywood forcefield the blacklisted Hollywood progressives still stuck to a people-driven, but essentially Hollywood-esque, melodrama. No hint of contemporary avant-garde discourse is revealed in this film. Rather than the blur of the subconscious, Hollywood progressives seemed preoccupied with the sharp lines of political consciousness.

Salt was a straightforward people narrative, using no flashbacks, that centered on the strike of the Local 890 of the International Union of Mine, Mill, and Smelter Workers against Empire Zinc in Grant County, New Mexico. The actors were a mix of professionals (Will Geer as the local sheriff, Mexican actress Rosaura Revueltas as Esperanza Quintano) and amateurs, while the photography emphasized realism and newsreelism via reliance on the 50-mm objective. The workers at Empire Zinc go on strike against the owners, suffer an initial defeat, and then bounce back to victory because they understand the meaning of unity across racial and gender lines. Certainly, outside of Hollywood, progressives were able to realize an example of progressive cinema uncluttered by the constraints of the Hollywood forcefield. While *The Grapes of Wrath* had ultimately left unresolved the conflict between private and public, family and people, *Salt* solved the conflict, making the former subservient to the latter. Social justice should regulate gender relations within the family. Only if this is achieved will the cause of the people be won.[64]

Salt was not a Hollywood film; however, its production and distribution history de facto highlight the expulsion of the 1930s paradigm from Hollywood. Indeed, explicit social criticism was not the forte of 1950s American films. In 1946, Carey McWilliams denounced Hollywood for practicing a "gray list on themes." Even an Academy Award-winning director, the unnamed friend of McWilliams, was not allowed to tackle domestic problems: "the studios have rejected almost every idea he had suggested in the last two years with the remark: 'Can't you find a love story?'"[65] Caution was understandable. The intensifying anti-communist crusade at home targeted progressive politics and films. Present-day historians may have doubts about the progressivism of some of the Hollywood films, but conservative watchdogs had few doubts at the time. In 1947, the State Department advised against the export of *The Grapes of Wrath* and *Tobacco Road*.[66] In 1954, former OWI chief of the Film Reviewing and Analysis Section, Dorothy B. Jones, found that the number of "social problems" films decreased from 20.9 percent in 1947 to 8.1 percent in 1953. During the same period, "romantic" movies jumped from 10.2 percent to 15.7 percent, and "military" films, absent in 1947, accounted for 6.8 percent of the 1953 Hollywood productions.[67]

In more than one sense, we may say that a perversely mutated version of democratic modernism migrated in the late 1940s' anti-communist films. This should not be surprising. After all, democratic modernism was the only extant political tradition of Hollywood films, a style that the practitioners of the anti-communist cycle had to take into account. On another level, the continuity between the 1930s paradigm and the anti-communist films of the late 1940s offered to those Hollywood progressives who had been marshaled into anti-communist productions the opportunity to continue to think of themselves in a tradition that was in opposition to the studio system. In fact, this continuity made it possible for them to maintain at the level of esthetics a sense of moral consistency endangered by their political choices. Thomas Doherty has it right when he argues that the anti-communist films of the late 1940s and early 1950s were attempting "to achieve the two different ideological missions simultaneously: to be both 'Hollywood' and 'agit-prop.' In one sense, these are not classical Hollywood movies at all."[68] And yet these movies were not "inventing" such tradition, but simply adapting the late 1930s hybridizationist practices to the new demands of McCarthyist America. Among the anti-communist films that Hollywood studios produced between 1948 and 1954, *The Iron Curtain* (TCF, 1948), *Walk East on Beacon* (Columbia,

1952), *Walk a Crooked Mile* (Columbia, 1952), *I Was a Communist for the FBI* (WB, 1951), and *The Red Menace* (Republic, 1949) bear witness to the hybridization between the Hollywood narrative and the tradition of the political documentary. Often, the personnel of progressive Hollywood films moved from one genre to another, each move reflecting their more or less coerced change in politics.[69]

Milton Krims was both a cosmopolitan Hollywood progressive and a fellow traveler when he wrote *Confessions of a Nazi Spy* in 1939.[70] In a paragraph of the draft for an article for *Screenwriter* that was omitted in the published version, Krims confessed that "while I always knew Fascism was an enemy, I once believed Communism was a friend. It is a trying process to discern friends as well as enemies."[71] When HUAC hit Hollywood, the screenwriter changed his politics and sided with the moderates within the SWG. By the time HUAC was interviewing members of the Motion Picture Alliance for the Preservation of American Ideals (MPAPAI) in May 1947, Krims was already working on his script for the *Iron Curtain*, probably the first of the Hollywood anti-communist films. When on November 17, 1947, the SWG condemned the possibility of a blacklist, Krims wrote that the SWG was unduly functioning as a political front and that HUAC had the "right to investigate," and he declared himself ready to sign a loyalty oath "so long as a majority of the full membership" endorsed it.[72]

Whatever changes Krims's politics underwent, the screenwriter stressed the continuity between his experience in *Confessions* and as the writer of *The Iron Curtain*. The adaptation of a real espionage case involving the Soviets and the Canadian government, the film was reminiscent of the 1930s paradigm. It was, in fact, as the *New York Times* noted, "the 1948 version of *Confessions of a Nazi Spy*," significantly "written by Milton Krims who helped write *Confessions*."[73] Krims himself researched extensively, traveling to Canada to meet the Soviet spy-turned-informer, Igor Gouzenko, and several Canadian officials, including the deputy minister of justice, Robert Forsythe. During the trips, Krims combined pleasure with duty, spending almost as much money ($26) for "lodging" as for "liquor" ($18), though in the official expense budget he submitted he replaced "liquor" with "entertainment."[74] Nonetheless, his "Iron Curtain Memoir" was constructed—like Whittaker Chambers's *Witness* a few years later—on the model of *Pilgrim's Progress*, as an intellectual itinerary from the dusk of doubt to the dawn of righteousness. After claiming that "it was entirely up to me to decide whether or not I would do the story,"

Krims described his initial doubts about the project. Maintaining his identity as a liberal, he claimed that at first he mistrusted Gouzenko's articles, published in the Hearst's ultra-conservative *Cosmopolitan*. Definitely, he confesses, the project "involved many factors beyond the usual, the most important of which was my own conscience."[75]

Translating the 1930s realist paradigm from a denunciation of injustices to an endorsement of witch hunts, Krims found a way to recuperate at the level of esthetics what he was abandoning at the level of politics. As a paradigmatic alternative to Hollywood entertainment fare, cinematic realism allowed Krims to present himself as a committed artist almost in opposition to the studio. Had he hybridized facts and Hollywood narrative, and resisted any "temptation to improve the truth, to create more action, more melodrama," *The Iron Curtain* would be a success and no compromise with his conscience would be necessary. "Is this story true?" was then the only crucial question, and, after speaking to Canadian officials, ordinary citizens, and Gouzenko himself, Krims concluded that "the evidence was irrefutable."[76]

In practice, however, Krims's attempts to adapt the 1930s paradigm to the politics of anti-communism were bound to fail. True to its 1930s' people narrative mold, the initial draft of *The Iron Curtain* has no real hero; Gouzenko and Canadian government officials share the spotlight. This time, however, Krims was working solo rather than as an exponent of a political and esthetic network. The studio put immediate pressure on Krims's people narrative structure, arguing that—as it stood—the screenplay "wanders all over the place. . . . There is no longer a perspective of what we are trying to tell. You keep introducing new characters. . . . I miss completely the picturization of this script. . . . *When do we start telling this story?*"[77] The same day, Sol Siegel also informed Krims that Zanuck, not satisfied with the script, was demanding a "one paragraph description of each one of the individual characters" and hoping that the Canadian investigator would develop into a strong character.[78]

As Dan Leab has documented, Zanuck and other Fox executives remained unsatisfied by Krims's slant on the story and kept thinking up scenes and an alternative ending for the movie in order to add melodramatic bite to the script.[79] The executives were on to something. The semidocumentary tradition that *The Iron Curtain* was inheriting was still in opposition to the Hollywood formula. Its narrative structure was people-driven and molded on the idea that reality has no individual hero. This structure had worked in *Confessions*, which pitted the American people against the German (and German-American) Nazis, but was discordant in anti-communist films in which the people themselves are under investigation. Unlike Nazism, communism was not limited by ethnicity. In *The Iron Curtain*, ordinary Canadians gather to hear John Grubb (played by Berry Kroeger)—a Canadian-born party ideologue—read Karl Marx's *Das Kapital* and are easily duped by the communists. In *Red Menace*, another anti-communist semidocumentary made by Republic in 1949, the party big shots and part of the rank and file are played by nonprofessional or little-known, accentless American actors. Though the deranged, heavily accented foreigner is a staple of the genre, communists were often not from without but from within. The documentary, people-driven tradition of *Confessions* was not adaptable to that of the anti-communist films, as it clashed against the notion that the "people" was no longer cast as a hero, but as a suspect.

Caught between these contrasting necessities, anti-communist films often have no workable narrative. In *Red Menace* (Republic, 1949), the hero is slow-witted. He is easily duped by a communist vixen into the party, and then he is saved by a repentant communist. In other anti-communist films, the hero is technology itself and the solution does not come from the American public sphere—as with the American diner of *Confessions*—but from secluded, increasingly secret rooms of surveillance agencies and congressional committees—as in the anti-communist John Wayne vehicle *Big Jim McLain* (WB, 1952). For the progressives, the documentary technology was the best possible frame for photographing and narrating the people; for the anti-communists, such technology becomes a value in itself. If nothing else, it allowed people like Milton Krims to claim a level of continuity between their past and their present. The wordy prologues of these films (*Red Menace*, *I Was a Communist for the FBI*) cite facts, congressional committees, and FBI agents as they become a sort of technocratic ipse dixit, a scientific legitimation of the political message of the film. You need an expert to identify the spies, fight them, and guide the immature American people toward safety.

The Iron Curtain, like most of the anti-communist films, failed at the box office.[80] Interestingly, the only money-making films of the crop were the ones that more markedly distanced themselves from the tradition of the people narrative: the family-centered *My Son John* (Paramount, 1951) and the John Wayne vehicle, *Big Jim McLain*.[81] Produced by Warner Bros., *Big Jim McLain* snatched the realist tradition from the progressives, and—as *Confessions* and many of the war films had done—pretended to be fact. But the film unmoors its plot from the people narrative and draws on mainstream Hollywood to recast the virtues of the people onto its superhuman protagonist. Wayne's character, the macho government investigator Jim McLain, stands in direct opposition to the American people and to the people narrative. Set in Hawaii, the film depicts ordinary Americans as easily duped by the commies. If rescue is to come, it has to come from the leaders, be they Daniel Webster, whose wisdom the script invokes at the beginning; HUAC members, each of whom the film's prologue regales with an individual snapshot; or Big Jim himself, the swashbuckling hero who singlehandedly foils the Reds' plan.

Conclusion

One Last Hollywood Self-Portrait

B y the middle of the 1950s, signs of the demise of the old Hollywood community were everywhere, and in the public discourse the image of Hollywood as a militant intellectual center was rapidly giving way to that of Hollywood as the unapologetically apolitical capital of "that's entertainment." In turn, American intellectuals changed their mind about Hollywood. In 1960, Robert Gessner, a pioneer of film studies at New York University, complained that in the United States film criticism was far behind that of France or possibly Italy. In the United States " '[m]ovies and scholarship' are words which sound strange when heard in juxtaposition. The two [are] not . . . even accorded the respectable status of a sad but legal *mésalliance*." [1] A few years later, Jerzy Toeplitz commented that if we were to reestablish film criticism in the United States, we must "overcome many prejudices and . . . enter by force the University area. So long as this remains undone, . . . film scholarship will be relegated to the very bottom and will not be treated seriously [remaining] . . . an area of operation for amateurs and pseudoscholars." [2]

It was not so much the avant-garde cinema that had been abandoned by American intellectuals. In New York City, Cinema 16 continued to offer its aficionados a weekly dose of Maya Deren, Stan Brackage, and Alexander Hammid. [3] Jonas Mekas's *Film Culture*—founded in 1955—was actively championing "art over commerce," "the responsible filmmaker," and foreign films.[4] What had been abandoned was Hollywood, by then widely considered a stronghold of bad mass culture. In 1959, director Edward Dmytryk summed up this change when he recalled that American intellectuals had first "painted [Hollywood] as a special community of geniuses . . . then in the last ten years they have gone to the opposite extreme."[5] In the span of five or six years, Hollywood went out of fashion in American intellectual circles.

Cold War liberalism contributed to the creation of an anti-Hollywood consensus. Eager to differentiate themselves from the McCarthyites, Cold War liberals denounced the Hollywood Ten not only as Stalinists but also as producers of bad culture, veritable cultural "sell-outs."[6] As a matter of fact, neither Parnell Thomas nor Joseph McCarthy hated Hollywood nearly as much as they hated the Hollywood communists. By and large, McCarthyites actually meant to restore Hollywood to what they saw as its mission: providing entertainment for the American masses. Instead, Thom Andersen acutely notes, for the Cold War liberals "the film writers of the Hollywood Left had succumbed to a double moral corruption— the commercial corruption of Hollywood and the moral and intellectual corruption of the Party."[7]

For the anti-communist liberals, in fact, one way to remain within the vital center was to attack the embattled Hollywood progressives without relying *entirely* on the language of McCarthyism. Therefore, one has the impression that the slaughter of Hollywood and mass culture served as a rationalization for the liberals' failure of nerve in the face of blatant trampling of Constitutional rights by the McCarthyites. The liberals' attitude toward mass culture, and Hollywood in particular, might have served the purpose of condemning and taking a safe distance from the blacklisted Hollywood progressives, while at the same time using a language at least partially different from that of the McCarthyites.

It is in this new context that the rise of the "anxiety of contamination" between high and low, modernism and mass culture, was fashioned. For Americans for Democratic Action (ADA) stalwart Arthur Schlesinger, Jr., "the Hollywood writer . . . has abandoned his serious work in exchange for large weekly paychecks."[8] For Agee's good friend Dwight Macdonald, one of the Cold War liberals, "the main trouble with [Agee's] criticism is that it often tends to be much too uncritical [of Hollywood]."[9] From the columns of *Politics, Dissent, Esquire,* and *The Partisan Review,* Macdonald proceeded to destroy Agee's rather benign view of the movie industry and mass culture, erecting in its place the famous cosmogony of "low, mid, and high cult[ure]." [10] Loosely building on a spurious interpretation of the theories originating from the Frankfurt School, Cold War liberals read Hollywood uniquely as a commercial enterprise producing commercial goods for a capitalist market and participating in the corruption of American taste.[11] The Jewish magazine *Commentary*, hardly a friend to Senator McCarthy, was by far the most extreme. Reviewing John Cheever's *The Enormous Radio and Other Stories* and Budd Schulberg's *Some Faces in the Crowd*, Morris Freedman decried the "Hollywood sense of economy." In describing the migration to Hollywood under the lamp of Joe McCarthy's America, Freedman summarized its artistic achievement succinctly: "the Jews who journeyed West to make movies might have remained in New York to make dresses." [12]

But what about the Hollywood progressives who remained in Hollywood? What was their attitude toward the mass culture industry? Just a few years earlier, Hollywood's cultural, modernist charms had lured these intellectuals to Southern California. The celebration of the hybridization between high and low had been the central theme of Billy Wilder's and Charles Brackett's script for *Ball of Fire* (Sam Goldwyn, 1941)—a film Howard Hawks directed from a story that Wilder had written in Germany before migrating to the United States. In the film, Sugarpuss O'Shea (played by Barbara Stanwyck), a ballerina on the lam, enters the reclusive lives of Professor Bertram Potts (played by Gary Cooper) and seven other academics who have been working for years to complete an encyclopedia. Breaking into Potts's ivory tower, Sugarpuss brings with her the harsh realities of life, including her fiancé Joe Lilac (played by Dana Andrews), an abusive gangster who wants Sugarpuss out of circulation for a while. Her presence, however, shows the professors that their "high" culture, if it is to be useful, needs hybridization with the "low" culture of the real world. In order to write his section on modern English, Potts decides to go to the "people," setting up regular meetings with a citizen committee comprised of a newspaper boy, a garbage man, a barfly, and the ballerina herself. Hybridization, however, means the fusion of high and low, not the populist abandonment of the former. In one of the final scenes, in fact, the professors use their mastery of high culture to disarm the dangerous, philistine thug Duke Pastrami (played by Dan Duryea).

A product of the Hollywood of the 1930s, *Ball of Fire* continues Wilder's discourse about hybridization begun in *Champagne Waltz*.[13] The film fits Wilder's biography as the quintessential Hollywood European, unconcerned with any anxiety about his double identity as a European modernist intellectual and a Hollywood progressive—fundamentally at peace with himself while producing mass culture and collecting fine art. Yet by the early 1950s, Wilder and his films changed. *Ace in the Hole* (Paramount, 1951) described mass media gone murderous through the character of Charles Tatum (played by Kirk Douglas), the reporter who attempts to jump-start his career by exploiting the tragedy of a man trapped in a collapsed mine shaft. Wilder's preceding film, *Sunset Boulevard* (Paramount, 1950), is even more emblematic of his change from the hybridizationist optimism of *Ball of Fire. Sunset* deals with a hack Hollywood screenwriter, Joe Gillis (played by William Holden), kept by Norma Desmond (played by Gloria Swanson), a formerly glamorous star of the Hollywood silent period who shoots him when he decides to leave her. Like other Hollywood films about mass culture made in the 1950s, *Sunset Boulevard* revealed a new unease about being in the business of producing such culture.[14] Depicting the mass culture of the 1950s as shady and immoral, *Sunset Boulevard* conveyed Wilder's painful consciousness of the changes from earlier decades and sharply lamented the loss of the old Hollywood, whose promises had prompted Wilder's emigration in 1934.

As the Hollywood self-portrait that has dominated the postwar discourse about Hollywood,[15] *Sunset Boulevard* hints at the new situation in which Wilder, and many other Hollywood intellectuals, found themselves. They still loved Hollywood films but felt uncomfortable working within the mass culture industry. Reconciling their identity as artists with their work in the new Hollywood was increasingly difficult. Wilder was still too much of an old-school Hollywood progressive to accept the new "that's entertainment" philosophy. For the same reasons, he was also unable to immerse himself in the new avant-garde scene. Making an anti-Hollywood Hollywood movie was the only way out of this conundrum. Wilder was still using the mass media to communicate a political message to the masses. But, ironically, the message was now that the media were not to be trusted.

Notes

Introduction

1. Leo C. Rosten, *The Movie Colony, the Movie Makers* (New York: Harcourt, Brace and Company, 1941), 3.

2. Richard H. Pells, *Radical Visions and American Dreams: Culture and Social Thought in the Depression Years* (1973; repr. Middletown, Conn.: Wesleyan University Press, 1984); William Stott, *Documentary Expression and Thirties America* (1973; repr. Chicago: University of Chicago Press, 1986); Miles Orvell, *The Real Thing* (Chapel Hill: University of North Carolina Press, 1989), especially pp. 198–286.

3. For a convincing interpretation of the "New Deal Era" as extending beyond the confines of the 1930s, see Alan Brinkley, "The Concept of New Deal Liberalism," in Alan Brinkley, *The End of Reform* (New York: Knopf, 1995), 4–14. See also Brinkley, "World War II and the Crisis of American Liberalism," in Lewis A. Erenberg and Susan E. Hirsch, eds., *The War in American Culture*, (Chicago: University of Chicago Press, 1996), 313–30.

4. For the concept of "middle ground," see Richard White, *The Middle Ground: Indians, Empires, and Republics in the Great Lakes Region, 1650–1815* (Cambridge: Cambridge University Press, 1991).

5. For an example of this scholarly attitude see Pells, *Radical Visions*.

6. Chip Rhodes, *Structure of the Jazz Age: Mass Culture, Progressive Education, and Racial Disclosures in American Modernism* (New York: Verso, 1998), 17.

7. Peter Gay, *Freud Jews and Other Germans* (New York: Oxford University Press, 1978), 23.

8. Ibid., 26.

9. Thomas Bender, *New York Intellect* (Baltimore: Johns Hopkins University Press, 1987), 231.

10. Astradur Eysteinsson, *The Concept of Modernism* (Ithaca: Cornell University Press, 1990), 3.

11. Ibid., 11.

12. On "anxiety of contamination" see Andreas Huyssen, *After the Great Divide: Modernism, Mass Culture, Postmodernism* (Bloomington: Indiana University Press, 1986).

13. Malcolm Cowley, *The Exile's Return* (New York: Norton, 1934), 126.

14. Ibid.

15. Michael Denning, *The Cultural Front* (New York: Verso, 1996), 29.

16. James D. Bloom, *Left Letters: The Culture Wars of Mike Gold and Joseph Freeman* (New York: Columbia University Press, 1992), 35–70.

17. Ibid., 113. See also Stanley Aronowitz, "Cultural Politics of the Popular Front," in Aronowitz, *Roll over Beethoven* (London and Hanover: Wesleyan University Press, 1993), 145–46, and the essay by Alan Wald "The 1930s Left in U.S. Literature Reconsidered," in Bill Mullen and Sherry Lee Linkon, eds., *Radical Revisions* (Urbana and Chicago: University of Illinois Press, 1996), 11–26.

18. On the connection between Hollywood and modernism see Sam B. Girgus, *Hollywood's Renaissance* (New York: Cambridge University Press, 1998), 16–18.

19. Cited in Bloom, *Left Letters*, 72.

20. Mike Gold, "Notes on the Cultural Front," *New Masses*, December 7, 1937, 1–5.

21. Bender, *New York Intellect*, 251.

22. On art and "political intention" see Ben Shahn, *The Shape of Things* (Cambridge: Cambridge University Press, 1957), 43–56.

23. On this concept see Martin Jay, *Forcefields* (New York: Routledge, 1993), 1–8, and Richard Bernstein, *The New Constellation* (Cambridge: MIT Press, 1992), 8–9. See also the pioneering work of Kurt Lewin, *Field Theory in the Social Sciences: Selected Theoretical Papers*, edited by Dorwin Cartwright (New York: Harper, 1951). A similar, though independently conceived, theoretical framework is proposed by Pierre Bourdieu in *The Field of Cultural Productions*, edited by Randal Johnson (New York: Columbia University Press, 1993).

24. Richard Maltby, *Harmless Entertainment* (Metuchen, N.J.: Scarecrow Press, 1983), 10.

25. On Hollywood style see David Bordwell, Janet Staiger, and Kristin Thompson, *The Classical Hollywood Cinema: Film Style and Mode of Production to 1960* (New York: Columbia University Press, 1985), especially David Bordwell, "The Classical Hollywood Style, 1917–60," ibid., 1–84.

26. On the relevance of the concept of network for historians see Thomas Bender, *Community and Social Change in America* (Baltimore: Johns Hopkins University Press, 1982), 121–28.

27. On the role of Lawson as a party enforcer see Herbert Kline, ed., *New Theater and Film: An Anthology*, with a commentary by Herbert Kline (San Diego: Harcourt Brace Jovanovich, 1985), 363–67, and supra, chapter 1, note 100. On the relationship between Lawson and some of the Hollywood communists, see the interviews with Hollywood blacklistees gathered in Paul Buhle and Pat McGilligan, *Tender Comrades* (New York: St. Martin's Press, 1997). See especially those interviews with Leonardo Bercovici (30–42) and Paul Jarrico (327–50).

28. In 1993, cultural critic Stanley Aronowitz credited *The Best Years of Our Lives* to Billy Wilder. See Aronowitz, "Cultural Politics of the Popular Front," 159. To take another example, it is symptomatic that after Joseph O'Connor published the critical edition of the script of *I Am a Fugitive from a Chain Gang* documenting

how the famously bleak ending of the film was already present in the first draft of the script (by Sheridan Gibney), Lawrence Levine still affirmed, in a 1992 article in the *American Historical Review*, that it was "the responses of preview audiences [that] convinced Darryl Zanuck of Warner Brothers to create a more powerful conclusion for the classic early Depression exposé." See Joseph O'Connor, ed., *I Am a Fugitive From a Chain Gang* (Madison: University of Wisconsin Press, 1981). Lawrence Levine, "The Folklore of Industrial Society," *American Historical Review* 97 (December 1992): 1369–99.

29. Peiss, *Cheap Amusements*, 226 n. 53.

30. Larry Ceplair and Steven Englund, *The Inquisition in Hollywood* (Berkeley: University of California Press, 1983), 440.

31. See the discussion of Cohen's approach in Steven Ross, "Struggle for the Screen," *American Historical Review* 96 (April 1991): 335–36.

32. See Martin Dworkin, "National Images and International Culture," preface to Lewis Jacobs, *The Rise of American Cinema* (New York: Teachers' College Press, 1967), xi.

33. See Dwight Macdonald, "Masscult and Midcult," in Dwight Macdonald, *Against the American Grain* (New York: Da Capo, 1983), and David Riesman (in collaboration with Reuel Denney and Nathan Glazer), *The Lonely Crowd* (New Haven: Yale University Press, 1950). Walter Benjamin, "The Work of Art in the Age of Its Mechanical Reproduction," in idem, *Illuminations* (New York: Schocken Books, 1969). On the relationship between David Riesman and Theodore Adorno and on the fortunes of Critical Theory in America, see Martin Jay, "The Frankfurt School in Exile" and "Adorno in America," in Martin Jay, *Permanent Exiles* (New York: Columbia University Press, 1985). On the problematic and far from univocal interpretation of mass culture by many of the representatives of the Weimar culture in exile, see Jay's "Massenkultur und deutsche intellecktuelle Emigration. Der Fall Max Horkeimer und Siegfried Kracauer," in Ilja Srubar, *Exil, Wissenschaft, Identität. Die Emigration deutscher Sozialwissenschaftler 1933–1945* (Frankfurt a.M.: Suhrkamp Verlag, 1988), 227–51.

34. Robert Sklar, *Movie-Made America* (New York: Random House, 1975), 316.

35. Michael Paul Rogin has successfully combined historical analysis with psychoanalytic readings of a few films by D. W. Griffith; Lary May has shrewdly analyzed the remains of Victorian culture in early American films; and Steven J. Ross has attempted to explore the activity of worker-film companies in the silent period. Yet most historians have continued to divorce the analysis of the text from the analysis of the society that went to see it, or that produced it. See Michael Paul Rogin, "'The Sword Became Flashing Vision': D. W. Griffith's *Birth of a Nation*," *Representations* 9 (Winter 1985): 150–95. See Steven J. Ross, "Cinema and Class Conflict: Labor, Capital and the State in American Silent Film," in Sklar and Musser, *Resisting Images*, 68–107; Lary May, *Screening Out the Past* (New York: Oxford University Press, 1980).

36. Richard Maltby, "*Film Noir:* The Politics of the Maladjusted Text," *Journal of American Studies* 18 (April 1984): 49–50. See also Maltby, "Cinema, politica e cultura popolare a Hollywood nel dopoguerra, 1945–1960," in Gian Piero Brunetta, *Storia del cinema mondiale*, Vol. II, *Gli Stati Uniti* (Turin, Italy: Einaudi, 2000), 1397–435.

37. Dana Polan, *Power and Paranoia* (New York: Columbia University Press, 1986), 38.

38. Specifically, Polan, *Power and Paranoia;* Tom Gunning, *D. W. Griffith and the Origins of American Narrative Film* (Urbana: University of Illinois Press, 1991); Miriam Hansen, *Babel and Babylon* (Cambridge: Harvard University Press, 1991); and Lary May, *Screening Out the Past.*

39. Sklar, *Movie-Made America*, 175.

40. Max Ophüls, "Hollywood petite ile," *Cahiers du Cinéma* 54 (December 1955): 6.

Chapter One

1. Kevin Starr, *Inventing the Dream: California through the Progressive Era* (New York: Oxford University Press, 1985), 284–85.

2. Cedric Belfrage, *Promised Land* (London: Victor Gollancz, 1938), 184.

3. W. R. Robinson, "The Southern California Real Estate Boom of the Twenties," *Southern California Quarterly* 24 (1942): 25–30. On Hollywood boosterism see Mae Dena Huettig, *Economic Control of the Motion Picture Industry* (Philadelphia: University of Pennsylvania Press, 1944).

4. Belfrage, *Promised Land*, 201.

5. See Cedric Belfrage, "A Gent in Hollywood," unpublished manuscript, Box 10, Folder 19, Cedric Belfrage Collection, New York University-Tamiment Library (NYU-TL). See also the articles by Belfrage in Box 10, Folder 42, in particular "Teas Feature Social Life of Hollywood," *New York Herald Tribune*, August 7, 1927, no page, and "Their European Souls," *Motion Picture Magazine*, February 1930, no page.

6. *Los Angeles Times*, June 4, 1934, 11. Cited in Carey McWilliams, "The Hollywood Gesture," *Pasadena Panorama*, September 1934, 1.

7. McWilliams, "The Hollywood Gesture," 1, 8.

8. Belfrage, *Promised Land*, 349.

9. Cedric Belfrage, "A Gent in Hollywood," unpublished memoir, typed manuscript of chapter titled "Frank," p. 7, Box 10, Folder 6, Belfrage Collection, NYU-TL.

10. *Fortune*, December 1932, 63.

11. An egregious example of this is Richard Maltby, *Harmless Entertainment: Hollywood and the Ideology of Consensus* (Metuchen, N.J.: Scarecrow Press, 1983), but see also Peter Stead, *Film and the Working Class* (London: BFI, 1989).

12. William MacAdams, *Ben Hecht: The Man behind the Legend* (New York: Scribner's, 1990), 101.

13. MacAdams, *Ben Hecht.*

14. James Morrison, *Passport to Hollywood: Hollywood Films, European Directors* (Albany: SUNY Press, 1998), 72.

15. Illegible name to Kenneth Macgowan, July 25, 1928, Box 83, Folder Miscellanea, Kenneth Macgowan Papers, UCLA-Special Collections (UCLA-SC).

16. Abrahmson to Preston Sturges, August 15, 1933, Box 60, Folder 15, Sturges Collection, UCLA-SC.

17. *Variety*, October 1, 1930, 2.

18. *New York Times*, January 24, 1932, sec. 10, p. 4.

19. *New York Times*, December, 8, 1930, 20.

20. Richard H. Pells, *Radical Visions and American Dreams: Culture and Social Thought in the Depression Years* (1973; repr. Middletown, Conn.: Wesleyan University Press, 1984).

21. Polonsky, interviewed by Paul Buhle and Dave Wagner in Paul Buhle and Patrick McGilligan, *Tender Comrades* (New York: St. Martin's Press, 1997), 492.

22. "Julius J. Epstein: King of Comedy," in Pat McGilligan, ed., *Backstory: Interviews with Screenwriters of Hollywood's Golden Age* (Los Angeles: University of California Press, 1986), 178.

23. Howard Koch, *Oral History*, interviewed by Eric Sherman (Los Angeles: American Film Institute Oral History Project, 1974), 28.

24. Budd Wilson Schulberg, *Writers in America: Four Seasons of Success* (New York: Stein and Day, 1983), 15–41.

25. Koch, *Oral History*, 29.

26. Pells, *Radical Visions and American Dreams*, 158. Of course the canonical reference here is Malcolm Cowley's poignant portrait of the changes occurring in the American intellectual scene from the end of World War I to the onset of the Great Depression. See Cowley, *The Exile's Return* (New York: Norton, 1934).

27. Steven H. Gale, *S. J. Perelman: A Critical Study* (Westport, Conn.: Greenwood Press, 1987), 103.

28. *New York Herald Tribune*, April 2, 1933, no page. Dudley Murphy Clipping File, New York Public Library-Billy Rose Collection (NYPL-BR).

29. Samson Raphelson, "Your Mistress Is Your Best Friend After All," *Screen Guilds' Magazine* 3 (1935): 7.

30. See Thomas Bender, *New York Intellect* (Baltimore: Johns Hopkins University Press, 1987), 249–55.

31. See Gary Carr, *The Left Side of Paradise: The Screenwriting of John Howard Lawson* (Ann Arbor, Mich.: UMI Press, 1985), 25.

32. John Howard Lawson, *Roger Bloomer* (New York: Thomas Seltzer, 1923), 196–221.

33. On modernism and the city see Raymond Williams, "The Metropolis and the Emergence of Modernism," in David Kelly and Edward Timms, eds., *Unreal City: Urban Experience in Modern European Literature and Art* (Manchester, U.K.: Manchester University Press, 1985), 13–16.

34. John Dos Passos, "Foreword," in John Howard Lawson, *Roger Bloomer*, viii.

35. See how Leonardo Bercovici, John Bright, and Paul Jarrico remember Lawson's role in Hollywood in Paul Buhle and Pat McGilligan, eds., *Tender Comrades* (New York: St. Martin's Press, 1997), 37, 145, 334.

36. Box 10, Folder 26, Cedric Belfrage Papers, NYU-TL.

37. John Howard Lawson, *Processional: A Jazz Symphony of American Life in Four Acts* (New York: Thomas Seltzer, 1925).

38. Michael Gold, "Notes of the Month," *New Masses*, September 1930, 1–3. Excerpts of the column are reprinted as "Proletarian Realism" in Mike Gold, *Mike Gold: A Literary Anthology* (New York: International Publishers, 1972), 203–8.

39. John Howard Lawson, *Processional* (New York: Thomas Seltzer, 1925).

40. Agee to Father Flye, November 19, 1930. In James Agee, *Letters of James Agee to Father Flye* (Boston: Houghton Mifflin, 1971), 46.

41. Agee to Macdonald, July 21 1927. In Ross Spears and Jude Cassidy, with a narrative by Robert Coles, *Agee: His Life Remembered* (New York: Holt & Rinehart, 1985), 32.

42. Kenneth Macgowan, July 25, 1928, Box 29, Folder 12, Kenneth Macgowan Papers, UCLA-SC.

43. James Morrison, *Passport to Hollywood*, 29.

44. Robert Herring, "Art in the Cinema: The Work of Robert Florey," *Creative Art* 4 (May 1, 1929): 360. Cited in Brian Taves, "Robert Florey and the Hollywood Avant-Garde," in Jan-Christopher Horak, ed., *Lovers of Cinema: The First American Film Avant-Garde* (Madison: University of Wisconsin Press, 1995), 105.

45. Taves, "Robert Florey and the Hollywood Avant-Garde," 94–117.

46. On the Group's influence in Hollywood see Steve Vineberg, "Emotional Insurgents," *American Film*, June 1991, 40–46. See also Russel Campbell, *Cinema Strikes Back: Radical Filmmaking in the United States, 1930–1942* (Ann Arbor, Mich.: UMI Research Press, 1982), 283. On the Group Theater see Wendy Smith, *Real Life Drama* (New York: Knopf, 1990).

47. Smith, *Real Life Drama*, 159.

48. Harold Clurman, "Plans for a First Studio," 1931. The typescript for the lecture is in Box 3, Folder 14, Roman Bohnen Papers, NYPL-BR.

49. Harold Edgar (a.k.a. Harold Clurman), "The Group Theater," *Daily Worker*, October 3, 1933, 5.

50. Smith, *Real Life Drama*, 147–50.

51. Harold Edgar (a.k.a. Harold Clurman), "The Group Theater," *Daily Worker*, October 3, 1933, 5.

52. Sam Brody, "The Revolutionary Film," *New Theater* 1 (February 1934): 20.

53. Leo Hurwitz, "The Revolutionary Film: Next Step," *New Theater* 1 (May 1934): 15.

54. Stuart Liebman, "Documenting the Left," *October* 23 (Winter 1982): 72. On the crisis of the FPL, see Campbell, *Cinema Strikes Back*.

55. See Bertolt Brecht, "Critique de la Representation de New York," *Bref,* 109 (October 1967): 4–9.

56. See also James K. Lyon, *Bertolt Brecht in America* (Princeton: Princeton University Press, 1980).

57. *New York Times*, November 20, 1935. See also Howard Barnes in *New York Herald-Tribune*, November 20, 1935. Burns Mantle in *The Daily News*, November 20, 1935. Wilella Waldorff, New York *Post*, November 20, 1935. *Mother* Clipping File, NYPL-BR.

58. John Gassner, "Mother," *New Theater* 3 (December 1935), *Mother* Clipping File NYPL-BR.

59. *Daily Worker*, n.d., no page. *Mother* Clipping File, NYPL-BR.

60. Stanley Burnshaw, "New Theater," *New Masses*, December 3, 1935, 27–28.

61. "Author of Theater Union's New Play Tells How He Found Worker Audience," *Daily Worker*, October 31, 1935, 5.

62. Albert Maltz, *The Citizen Writer in Retrospect*, interviewed by Joel Gardner, 2 vols. (Los Angeles: UCLA Oral History Project, 1983), 1: 334–35.

63. Ibid., 340.

64. Jan-Christopher Horak, *Fluchtpunk Hollywood* (Münster: Maks Publikationen, 1986).

65. See also John M. Spalek, "Research on the Intellectual Migration to the United States after 1933: Still in Need of an Assessment," in Frank Trommler and Joseph McVeigh, eds., *America and the Germans*, 2 vols. (Philadelphia: University of Pennsylvania Press, 1985), 2: 297.

66. Horak, *Fluchtpunkt Hollywood*, 2.

67. Ernst Karl Winter, "The Common Foe" *Aufbau*, May 15, 1939, 1.

68. Cited in Lewis Jacobs, *The Rise of the American Film* (New York: Harcourt & Brace, 1939), 307.

69. John Baxter, *The Hollywood Exiles* (Taplinger: New York, 1976), 48–53.

70. On the first wave of immigrants from Europe, see Graham Petrie, *Hollywood Destinies: European Directors in America 1922–1931* (London: Routledge & Kegan, 1985).

71. Herbert Ihering, *Von Reinhardt bis Brecht* (Reinbeck: Rohwolt, 1967), 388. My translation.

72. Mary Nolan, *Visions of Modernity* (New York: Oxford University Press, 1994).

73. See Miriam Hansen, "America, Paris, and the Alps," in Leo Charney and Vanessa Schwartz, eds., *Cinema and the Invention of Modern Life* (Berkeley: University of California Press, 1995), 363–402.

74. Nolan points out that while a variety of social and political subjects embraced Fordism, its meaning remained far from universal. If Social Democrats stressed consumption through high wages, German industrialists largely concentrated on Fordism's call for efficiency on the shop floor and increased worker productivity. See Nolan, *Visions of Modernity*.

75. Thomas Saunders, *Hollywood in Berlin* (Berkeley: University of California Press, 1994).

76. Bertolt Brecht, *Gesammelte Werke*, 20 vols. (Frankfurt a.M.: Suhrkamp Verlag, 1967), 20: 10. See also Anton Kaes, "Mass Culture and Modernity: Notes toward a Social History of Early American and German Cinema," in Trommler and McVeigh, eds., *America and the Germans*, 1: 324.

77. Kaes, "Mass Culture and Modernity"; Martin Jay, "Massenkultur und deutsche intellecktuelle Emigration. Der Fall Max Horkeimer und Siegfried Kracauer," in Ilja Srubar, *Exil, Wissenschaft, Identität. Die Emigration deutscher Sozialwissenschaftler 1933–1945* (Frankfurt a.M.: Suhrkamp Verlag, 1988), 227–51.

78. On Kracauer, see Hansen, "America, Paris, and the Alps," 373.

79. See Fritz Lang, "Neuyork-Los Angeles," *Film-Kurier* 292 (December 11, 1924); "Manuskript und Regie," *Film-Kurier* 294 (December 13, 1924); "Von Schauspielern und Menschendarstellern," *Film-Kurier* 297 (December 17, 1924); see also "Zwischen Bohrturmen und Palmen. Ein kalifornischer Reisebericht," *Filmland* (Berlin) January 3, 1925; also "Was lieben und hassen wir am amerikanischen Film," in *Deutsche Filmwoche* (Berlin) October 10, 1925, repr. in Alfred Eibel,

Fritz Lang, choix de textes établi par Alfred Eibel (Paris: Flammarion, 1964), 5–61. Eric Pommer, "Die Siebente und achte Grossmacht," *Film-Kurier* 135 (May 23, 1925).

80. Owen Gorin "Das sensationelle Kalifornien," *Filmland*, March 1925, 17. My translation.

81. Ernst Lubitsch, "Wie ich Hollywood sehe," *Lichtbildbühne*, July 21, 1927, 2. My translation.

82. Ernst Lubitsch, "American Cinematographers," *American Cinematographer*, December 1923, 4, 18–19. The same article was reprinted in *Filmteknik und Filmindustrie*, February 20, 1926, 4. Lubitsch repeats his admiration for American technology in "Concerning Cinematography: A Few Words from Ernst Lubitsch on Cinematic Conditions, as Told to William Stull," *American Cinematographer*, November 1929, 5, 21.

83. James Morrison, *Passport to Hollywood: Hollywood Films, European Directors* (Albany: SUNY Press, 1998), 17.

84. Ibid., 33.

85. Hermann Treuner, *Filmkunstler wir über uns selbst* (Berlin: Sybilla Verlag, 1928), 212. My translation.

86. Neil Sinyard and Adrian Turner, *Journey Down Sunset Boulevard: The Films of Billy Wilder* (Ryde Isle of White: BCW Publications, 1979), 212. My translation.

87. Billy Wilder interviewed by Max Wilk, February 22, 1973. Tape in NYPL-Jewish Collection.

88. Kurt Weill and Lotte Lenya, *Speak Low (When You Speak of Love): The Letters of Kurt Weill and Lotte Lenya*, edited and translated by Lys Simonette and Kim H. Kowalke (Berkeley: University of California Press, 1996).

89. See Hellmuth Karasek, *Billy Wilder* (Hamburg: Hoffman und Campe, 1992), 109–11. On the harshness of American visa policy, see David Wyman, *Paper Walls: America and the Refugee Crisis 1938–1941* (New York: Pantheon, 1968).

90. *Variety*, February 12, 1936, 3.

91. See Gene D. Philips, *Exiles in Hollywood* (Bethlehem: Leigh University Press, 1998), 103. John Russel Taylor, *Strangers in Paradise* (New York: Holt, Rinehart, and Winston, 1983).

92. Namely Max Glass, Hermann Millakowsky, Seymour Nebenzahl, Arnold Pressburger, Gregor Rabinovitch, Eugene Tuscherer, and Erich Pommer. On this, see Jan-Christopher Horak, *Anti-Nazi Filme der deutschsprachige Emigration von Hollywood 1933–1945* (Münster: Maks Publikationen, 1985), 16–18.

93. Maurice Zolotow, *Billy Wilder in Hollywood* (New York: Putnam's, 1977), 47–55.

94. Egbert Krispyn, *Anti-Nazi Writers in Exile* (Athens: University of Georgia Press, 1978), 110.

95. Ludwig Marcuse, *Mein Zwanzigstes Jahrhundert. Auf dem Weg zu einer Autobiographie* (Zurich: Diogenes Verlag, 1975), 223.

96. Donald P. Kent, *The Intellectual Refugee* (New York: Columbia University Press, 1953), 217.

97. Pat McGilligan in his recent, and quite hostile, biography of Fritz Lang (appropriately subtitled, *The Nature of the Beast*) argues that Fritz Lang falsely

spread the rumor that Goebbels had offered him the directorship of the German film industry. According to McGilligan, Lang would have left Germany because of "hurt male pride," as his marriage with Thea von Harbou was collapsing, and because, as the son of a Jewish woman, he was afraid of racial persecution. Pat McGilligan, *Fritz Lang: The Nature of the Beast* (New York: St. Martin's Press, 1997), 180–84. Lang probably exaggerated or adroitly invented Goebbels's offer in order to embellish his anti-fascist past. McGilligan's radical depoliticization of Lang, however, is only halfway convincing, especially given Lang's concern with leftist causes in the United States, something that his personal correspondence amply substantiates. Furthermore, as McGilligan himself recognizes, the director's latest German film, *Das Testament von Dr. Mabuse*, had been banned by Nazi authorities because of the obvious parallel between Hitler and Mabuse.

98. Henry Koster, *Henry Koster*, interviewed by Irene Kahn Atkins (Metuchen, N.J.: Scarecrow Press, 1987), 41.

99. See Saunders, *Hollywood in Berlin*, 162–68.

100. Ibid., 163.

101. Stanley Corkin, *Realism and the Birth of the Modern United States* (Athens: University of Georgia Press, 1996), 163.

102. Bender, *New York Intellect*, 251.

103. On the connection between cinema and modernity, see Leo Charney and Vanessa Schwartz, eds., *Cinema and the Invention of Modern Life* (Berkeley: University of California Press, 1995). The quote is from Charney's and Schwartz's "Introduction," 1.

104. Cited in "Agee and the Movies," in Dwight Macdonald, *Dwight Macdonald on Movies* (Inglewood, N.J.: Prentice Hall, 1969), 4.

105. Ibid. The letter is reported in its entirety in Ross Spears and Jude Cassidy with a narrative by Robert Coles, *Agee: His Life Remembered* (New York: Holt & Rinehart, 1985), 32.

106. *New Theater* 1 (September–October 1933): 7.

107. Michael Denning has noted that the term "cultural front" was "a common metaphor of the times" and was used as early as 1932 by the Baltimore *John Reed Club Magazine*. Mike Gold also called one of his columns "Notes from the Cultural Front." Michael Denning, *The Cultural Front* (New York: Verso, 1996), xix. According to Herbert Kline, Victor J. Jerome asked John Howard Lawson to force Kline out of the magazine at the end of 1936 because *New Theater* was becoming "a vaguely leftist magazine." Herbert Kline, ed., *New Theater and Film: An Anthology*, with a commentary by Herbert Kline (San Diego: Harcourt Brace Jovanovich, 1985), 363–67.

108. *New Theater* 1 (September–October 1933): 3.

109. Pells, *Radical Visions*, 254.

110. Robert Gessner, "Massacre in Hollywood," *New Theater* 1 (March 1934): 17. Cited in Pells, *Radical Visions*, 264.

111. Robert Gessner, "Movies About Us," *New Theater* 2 (June 1935): 12.

112. Luis Norden, "Two Scoundrels Die Hard," *New Theater* 2 (June 1935): 12.

113. Peter Gay, *Freud, Jews, and Other Germans* (New York: Oxford University Press, 1978), 23.

114. Barry Salt, "From Caligari to Who?," *Sight and Sound* 48 (Spring 1979), 119–24.

115. See, for instance, Ulrich Gregor, "Film in Berlin," in Eberhard Roters, ed., *Berlin 1910–1933* (New York: Rizzoli, 1982), 176–78.

116. Walter Schatzberg and Uli Jung, eds., *Filmkultur der Weimarer Republik* (Munich: Saur, 1991).

117. Siegfried Kracauer, *From Caligari to Hitler* (1947; repr. Princeton: Princeton University Press, 1974), 71.

118. Ibid., 232–50.

119. Ibid., 82.

120. Ibid., 242.

121. Ibid., 246–47.

122. On the concept of "middle ground" see Richard White, *The Middle Ground: Indians, Empires, and Republics in the Great Lakes Region, 1650–1815* (Cambridge: Cambridge University Press, 1991), 50–95.

Chapter Two

1. Carey McWilliams, "The Hollywood Gesture," *Panorama*, September 1934, 1, 8.

2. *Los Angeles Times*, cited in ibid.

3. Charles Abrahmson to Bianca Gilchrist, October 17, 1932, Box 60, Folder 9, Sturges Papers, UCLA-SC.

4. Preston Sturges to Charles Abrahmson, September 23, 1932, Box 60, Folder 9, Sturges Papers, UCLA-SC.

5. Charles Abrahmson to Preston Sturges, February 1933, Box 60, Folder 12, Sturges Papers, UCLA-SC.

6. Philip Dunne, *Take Two: A Life in Movies and Politics* (1980; repr. New York: Limelight Editions, 1992), 15.

7. Richard Sheridan Ames, "Footlights on Filmland," *New Theater* 2 (September 1935): 20.

8. See, for instance, Ewald Andre Dupont, "Hollywood," in *Lichtbildbühne*, 1927. Italian translation, Enrico Ghezzi et al., eds., *Vienna Berlino Holllywood* (Venice: Edizioni della Biennale di Venezia, 1981), 46–56.

9. Ernst Lubitsch's home was in a fashionable Bel Air district (268 Bel Air Road) in Beverly Hills, where Peter Lorre also moved once he became a hot property (722 North Linden, Beverly Hills). William Dieterle, employed at the Warner Bros. studio in Burbank, lived in the Hollywood Hills (on 3351 North Knoll Drive). Those who recently arrived and had not yet made a name for themselves lived around the Hollywood district, which, as Jean Renoir noted in 1941, was "apparently not a very choice spot. Fancy people live in Beverly Hills farther West, nearer the ocean." Cited in Célia Bertin, *Jean Renoir: A Life in Pictures* (1986; repr. Baltimore:

Johns Hopkins University Press, 1991), 189. In 1938, Thilde Fontis, a German actress just arrived from Europe, took residence in Hollywood's Lexington Avenue not far from other newly arrived immigrants such as Paul Weigel (5815 Franklin Avenue), Charles Lederer (6715 Hollywood Boulevard), Heinz Herald (8474 Sunset Boulevard), Otto Kruger (210 Woodruff Avenue), and Richard Oswald (6831 Odin Street). Less fashionable than Beverly Hills but relatively affordable, Santa Monica was the district preferred by those Europeans employed in the middle echelons of the studios: Fritz Lang worked at MGM studios in Culver City and lived in Santa Monica (2141 La Mesa Drive), not far from Salka Viertel's home (at 165 Mabery Road) and, after 1941, near Bertolt Brecht.

10. Michael Korda, *Charmed Lives* (New York: Avon Books, 1981), 170.

11. Leo C. Rosten, *The Movie Colony, the Movie Makers* (New York: Harcourt, Brace and Company, 1941), 32–108.

12. Rosten, *The Movie Colony*.

13. Lester P. Cole, *Hollywood Red* (Palo Alto, Calif.: Ramparts Press, 1981), 81.

14. Rosten, *The Movie Colony*, 136. See also James Cagney, *Cagney by Cagney* (1976; repr. New York: Simon & Schuster, 1977), 205. On EPIC campaign in California see Greg Mitchell, *The Campaign of the Century: Upton Sinclair's Race for Governor of California and the Birth of Media Politics* (New York: Random House, 1992).

15. Mitchell, *The Campaign of the Century*, 57.

16. *New Masses*, September 11, 1939, 6. On SPA's and CPUSA's position toward EPIC, see Larry Ceplair, *Under the Shadow of War: Fascism, Antifascism and Marxists* (New York: Columbia University Press, 1987), 191–93. Ceplair also reports that many California "Communists joined EPIC" (Ceplair, *Under the Shadow*, 193).

17. See Mitchell, *The Campaign of the Century*, 499–501.

18. Ibid., 561.

19. Ibid., 360.

20. John Bright, "Naming Names: Sam Ornitz, James Cagney, The Hollywood Reds and Me," *Film Comment* 23 (December 1987): 48.

21. Jan-Christopher Horak, *Fluchtpunkt Hollywood. Eine Dokumentation zur Filmemigration nach 1933* (Münster: Maks Publikationen, 1986), 19.

22. John Russell Taylor, *Strangers in Paradise: The Hollywood Emigres 1938–1950* (New York: Holt, Rinehart, and Winston, 1983); John Baxter, *The Hollywood Exiles* (New York: Taplinger, 1976); Graham Petrie, *Hollywood Destinies: European Directors in America 1922–1931* (London: Routledge & Kegan, 1985).

23. Ludwig Marcuse, *Mein zwanzigstes Jahrhundert* (Zurich: Diogenes Verlag, 1975), 244. My translation.

24. Otto Preminger, *An Autobiography* (Garden City, N.Y.: Doubleday, 1977), 78.

25. See William Ernest Stagen, "Jewish Club of 1933, Los Angeles," Herbert A. Strauss, ed., *Jewish Immigrants of the Nazi Period in the United States* (New York: Saur, 1986), 201–3.

26. "Leider an die falsche addresse geschrieben." Telegram of Rudolph Amendt to Warner Bros., February 16, 1937, *Zola* Production File, USC-WB.

27. "Geld für seine Gruppe zu sammeln Freunde für sie [zu] gewinnen und über seine Tätigkeit berichten." Ferdinand Brüchner to Lang, May 24, 1937, Box 1, Folder B, Lang Papers, American Film Institute in Beverly Hills (AFI-BH).

28. " . . . will ich ihm gern behilflich sein . . . die meisten Menschen Schön bereits mehr als scaronfters für alle möglichen Zwecke angegangen worden sind." Lang to Brüchner, June 15, 1937, Box 1, Folder B, Lang Papers, AFI-BH. My translation.

29. "Ich habe bereits im Februar eine Sammlung hier veranstaltet, und bekam mit der Hilfe von Prf. [Max] Reinhardt, Lubitsch, Joe May, Dupont und uns selbst einen Beitrag von 500$ zusammen, den ich seinerzeit nach drüben schickte. . . . Ich bat Salka Viertel, die sie persönlich kennt, sich mit ihnen in Verbindung zu setzen, bekam aber nil eine Antwort von ihr." Charlotte Dieterle to Lang, August 5, 1935, Lang to Dieterle, September 2, 1935, Box 1, Folder D, Lang Papers, AFI-BH. My translation.

30. "Prospects for the American Theater," *New Theater*, September–October 1933, 4–9.

31. Philip Sterling, "A Channel for Democratic Thought," *Films* 1 (Spring 1940): 7. Emphasis mine.

32. Otis Ferguson, "Life Goes to the Pictures," *Films* 1 (Spring 1940): 24–25.

33. Ralph Steiner and Leo Hurwitz, "A New Approach to Film Making," *New Theater* 2 (September 1935): 22–23.

34. Lincoln Kirstein, "Film Problems of the Quarter," *Films* 1 (Spring 1940): 24–25.

35. Harry Alan Potamkin, "The Year of the Eclipse," *Close Up*, March 1933. Reprinted in Harry Alan Potamkin, *The Compound Cinema: The Film Writings of Harry Alan Potamkin*, edited and introduced by Lewis Jacobs (New York: Teachers' College Press, 1977), 203.

36. *Vanity Fair*, May 1933. Reprinted in Pare Lorentz, *Lorentz on Film* (New York: Hopkinson and Blake, 1975), 110–11.

37. *McCall's*, August 1935. Reprinted in ibid., 128.

38. Cited in Franklin Folsom, *Days of Anger, Days of Hope* (Niwot: University of Colorado Press, 1994), 84.

39. Kenneth Burke, "Revolutionary Symbolism in America," in Henry Hart, ed., *American Writers' Congress* (New York: International Publishers, 1935), 87–94.

40. "I remember, when leaving the hall, I was walking behind two girls. One said to the other, as though discussing a criminal, 'Yet he seemed so honest!' " Daniel Aaron, Malcolm Cowley, Grenville Hicks, and William Philips, eds., "Thirty Years Later: Memories of the First American Writers' Congress," *The American Scholar* 35 (Summer 1966): 506. Building on Arthur Casciato, James D. Bloom has disputed the fact that Burke's address was treated with much hostility at the congress. See James D. Bloom, *Left Letters: The Culture Wars of Mike Gold and Joseph Freeman* (New York: Columbia University Press, 1992), 80.

41. On the League of Professional Groups and its manifesto, see Michael Denning, *The Cultural Front* (New York: Verso, 1996), 98.

42. See Clifford Odets, "Waiting for Lefty," in Odets, *Waiting for Lefty and Other Plays* (New York: Grove Press, 1979), 5–31.

43. Denning, *The Cultural Front*, 102. From a different point of view, Warren Susman also argues that "the most persistent symbol to emerge from the bulk of

the literature of the period . . . was the 'people.'" Warren Susman, "The Culture of the Thirties," in Susman, *Culture as History* (New York: Pantheon, 1984), 178.

44. Denning, *The Cultural Front*, 129–33.

45. *Ballad for the Americans*, text by John Latouche, music by Earl Robinson (New York: Robbins Music Corporation, 1940).

46. I borrowed the notion of "relaxed inclusiveness" from Michael Kazin, *The Populist Persuasion* (New York: Basic Books, 1995), 137.

47. On the evolution of the representation of public spheres see Michele Warner, "The Mass Public and the Mass Subject," Bruce Robbins, ed., *The Phantom Public Sphere* (Minneapolis: University of Minnesota Press, 1993), 234–57.

48. Gary Gerstle, "The Protean Form of American Liberalism," *American Historical Review* 99 (October 1994): 1068. On gender and the Cultural Front see Paula Rabinowitz, *Labor and Desire: Women's Revolutionary Fiction in Depression America* (Chapel Hill: University of North Carolina Press, 1991). On the limitations of the Cultural Front's racial and gender politics see Robert J. Corber, *Homosexuality in Cold War America* (Durham, N.C.: Duke University Press, 1997), 86–100. Also Barbara Melosh, *Engendering Culture: Manhood and Womanhood in New Deal Public Art and Theater* (Washington, D.C.: Smithsonian Institution Press, 1991).

49. On the code and the way it affected Hollywood film at the beginning of the 1930s see Richard Maltby, "The Genesis of the Production Code" and "A Short and Dangerous Life: The Gangster Film, 1930–32" in Giuliana Muscio, ed., *Prima dei codici* (Venezia: Edizioni La Biennale, 1991), 39–81 and 159–74. Gregory Black, "Hollywood Censored: The Production Code Administration and the Hollywood Film Industry, 1930–1940," in *Film History* 3 (1989): 167–89. See also Lea Jacobs, *Wages of Sin* (Madison: University of Wisconsin Press, 1991), and Thomas Doherty, *Pre-Code Hollywood: Sex, Immorality, and Insurrection in American Cinema, 1930–34* (New York: Columbia University Press, 1999).

50. See Douglas Gomery, *The Hollywood Studio System* (New York: St. Martin's Press, 1986).

51. *New Republic*, February 5, 1930, 297.

52. *New York Times*, July 23, 1928, 16.

53. Robert Sklar, *City Boys* (Princeton: Princeton University Press, 1992).

54. Lincoln Kirstein, "James Cagney and the American Hero," in *Hound and Horn*, April–June 1932, 465–67. Reprinted in *Hound and Horn: Essays on Cinema* (New York: Arno Press, 1972).

55. See Robert Sklar, *Movie-Made America* (New York: Random House, 1975), 175.

56. Robert Forsythe, "20 Cooler Inside," *New Theater* 2 (September 1934): 9.

57. Robert Gessner. "Massacre in Hollywood," *New Theater* 1 (March 1934): 17. Cited in Richard T. Pells, *Radical Visions*, 264.

58. Robert Gessner, "Movies About Us," *New Theater* 2 (June 1935): 12.

59. Luis Norden, "Two Scoundrels Die Hard" *New Theater* 2 (June 1935): 12.

60. Harry Alan Potamkin, "The Racketeer Paramount," *New Masses*, November 1930. Reprinted in Potamkin, *The Compound Cinema*, 477–79.

61. On Kirstein, see Sklar, *City Boys*, 50. Harry Alan Potamkin, *Close Up*, March 1933. Reprinted in Potamkin, *The Compound Cinema*, 203.

62. Sklar, *City Boys*, 31–34.

63. Robert Warshow, "The Gangster as a Tragic Hero," *The Immediate Experience* (New York: Doubleday, 1962), 127–33.

64. Jacob Wilk to Roy Obringer, November 1, 1934, *Black Fury* Production File, USC-WB.

65. On Musmanno, see Colin Shindler, *Hollywood in Crisis* (New York: Routledge, 1996), 177. A. Musmanno, *Black Fury* (New York: Fountainhead Publishers, 1966).

66. Joe Breen to Warner, September 12, 1934, *Black Fury* Story File, USC-WB.

67. Hal Wallis to Robert Lord, September 13, 1934, *Black Fury* Story File, USC-WB.

68. Joe Breen to Hal Wallis, October 9, 1934, *Black Fury* Story File, USC-WB. *New Masses*, July 23, 1935, 29.

69. Jim Tully was a protégé of H. L. Mencken. He was the author of several essays condemning the prison system, and the chain gang in particular. See for instance *Shadows of Men* (Garden City, N.Y.: Doubleday, 1930) and *Laughter in Hell* (Garden City, N.Y.: Doubleday, 1932). As a screenwriter, Tully also worked on *The Raven*, directed by Louis Friedlander (Universal, 1935).

70. Walter Wilson, "Chain Gang and Profits," *Harper's Magazine* 166 (April 1933): 537.

71. See John L. Spivak, *On the Chain Gang* (New York: International Pamphlet, series no. 32, 1932); Isaac Herman Schwartz, "Welcome to Our Chain Gang," *New Republic*, April 8, 1931, 200–2; Walter Wilson, "Chain Gang and Profits," *New Republic*, November 9, 1932, 339.

72. Richard Maltby, " 'Baby Face' or How Joe Breen Made Barbara Stanwyck Atone for Causing the Wall Street Crash," in Janet Staiger, ed., *The Studio System* (New Brunswick, N.J.: Rutgers University Press, 1995), 260.

73. On *Way Down South* see Thomas Cripps, *Making Movies Black* (New York: Oxford University Press, 1993), 24–26. German refugee Edgar G. Ulmer maintained that he was never so free to experiment both politically and esthetically as he was while working in the New York Yiddish productions, and, later, for the Hollywood-based Producer Releasing Corporation (PRC). Peter Bogdanovich, "Interview with Edgar G. Ulmer," *Film Culture* no. 58–60 (1974), 189–238. Reprinted in Todd McCarthy and Charles Flynn, *Kings of the Bs: Working within the Hollywood System* (New York: E. P. Dutton, 1975), 337–409.

74. Reinhardt Wulf, "Begegnung mit Douglas Sirk," *Filmkritik*, December 1, 1973, 515. My translation.

75. *Variety*, September 27, 1932, 21.

76. *Vanity Fair*, March 1932. Reprinted in Potamkin, *Compound Cinema*, 118.

77. On Tasker, see Clipping File, NYPL-BR.

78. The ending was possibly shot by John Cromwell, whom *Film Daily* credits with having completed the film. *Film Daily*, July 27, 1932, 7.

79. *Variety*, September 27, 1932, 21.

234 Notes to Chapter Two

80. See for instance *Road Gang* (WB, 1936) directed by Louis King and scripted by Dalton Trumbo.

81. *Variety*, September 27, 1932, 21.

82. Jerome Lawrence, *The Life and Times of Paul Muni* (New York: Putnam's, 1974), 173–75.

83. Evaluation by F. Stephani dated February 19, 1932; in *I Am a Fugitive from a Chain Gang* Story File, USC-WB.

84. Jason Joy to Darryl Zanuck, February 26, 1932. *I Am a Fugitive from a Chain Gang*, Production Code Authority File, Margaret Herrick Library, Academy of Motion Pictures Art and Sciences (AMPAS).

85. On Warner and its theaters see Peter Stead, *Film and the Working Class* (London: Routledge, 1989), 54.

86. Del Ruth to Hal Wallis, undated, *I Am a Fugitive from a Chain Gang* Story File, USC-WB.

87. Brown Holmes, Clipping File, NYPL-BR, and Clipping File, Margaret Herrick Library, AMPAS.

88. Sheridan Gibney, affidavit in the case *Georgia vs. Warner Bros.*, May 23, 1938, *I Am a Fugitive from a Chain Gang*, Legal File, USC-WB.

89. Sheridan Gibney, Clipping File, NYPL-BR.

90. On Gibney and the SWG see *New York Herald Tribune*, March 12, 1939, no page. Sheridan Gibney, Clipping File, NYPL-BR.

91. Joseph O'Connor, who ignores the contemporary political debate about film esthetics, notes that "by stressing the economic and social forces opposing Allen, the Holmes-Gibney screenplay failed to tell enough about Allen himself." O'Connor, "Introduction" to Joseph O'Connor, ed., *I Am a Fugitive from a Chain Gang* (Madison: University of Wisconsin Press, 1981).

92. Brown Holmes and Sheridan Gibney, "Temporary Script," *I Am a Fugitive from a Chain Gang*, Script File, USC-WB.

93. Howard J. Green, Clipping File, NYPL-BR.

94. *New York Times*, November 11, 1932, 17. *I Am a Fugitive from a Chain Gang*, Publicity File, USC-WB. *I Am a Fugitive from a Chain Gang*, Clipping File, NYPL-BR.

95. *Variety*, November 15, 1932, 19.

96. *Vanity Fair*, December 1932, reprinted in Lorentz, *Lorentz on Film*.

97. Potamkin, "The Year of the Eclipse," 207.

98. *The Nation*, November 23, 1932, 514.

99. *New Republic*, December 28, 1932, 173.

100. Guido Fink, "Il crollo delle case di cartapesta," *Cinema e Cinema* (Roma) 6 (January–June 1979): 59. My translation.

101. Potamkin, "Die Dreigroschenoper," *Creative Art*, July 1931. Reprinted in *The Compound Cinema*, 490–2. And again in "Pabst and the Social Film," in *Hound and Horn*, January 1933. Reprinted in *The Compound Cinema*, 413.

102. Joe Breen to the American Association of Motion Pictures Producers, October 31, 1935, *The Merry Widow* PCA File, Margaret Herrick Library, AMPAS.

103. On the tradition of operetta see Ernesto G. Oppicelli, *Operetta* (Genoa: Sagep, 1985).

104. On the history of the waltz see the study by refugee musicologist Eduard Reeser, *The History of the Waltz* (Stockholm: Continental Book Company, 1937), 26.

105. *Champagne Waltz*, "Data for Bulletin for Screen Achievement Records," September 22, 1936. *Champagne Waltz* File, Margaret Herrick Library, AMPAS.

106. Maurice Zolotow, *Billy Wilder in Hollywood* (New York: G. P. Putnam's, 1977), 29–30.

107. Manfred George [?], "Ein Warnungsruf," *Aufbau*, June 7, 1935, 1.

108. See Siegfried Kracauer, *Schriften*, ed. Karsten Witte (Frankfurt a.M.: Suhrkamp Verlag, 1971), vol. 1, *Die Angestellten: aus dem neuestern Deutschland*. See also Sabine Hake, "Siegfried Kracauer" in *The Cinema's Third Machine: Writing on Film in Germany, 1907–1933* (Lincoln: University of Nebraska Press, 1993), 247–71, and Martin Jay, "The Extraterritorial Life of Siegfried Kracauer," in Martin Jay, *Permanent Exiles: Essays on the Intellectual Migration from Germany to America* (New York: Columbia University Press, 1986), 152–97, in particular 157–60.

109. Giuseppe Antonio Borgese, "The Intellectual Origins of Fascism," *Social Research* 1 (November 1934): 475–76. See also his *Goliath: The March of Fascism* (New York: Viking, 1937), which reiterates the thesis.

110. Karl Mannheim, *Man and Society in an Age of Reconstruction* (1935; repr. London: Kegan, Paul, Trench, Trubner, 1940).

111. Ibid., 88–92.

112. Franz Neumann, *Behemoth: The Structure and Practice of National Socialism*, rev. ed. (Oxford: Oxford University Press, 1944), 99. But see also "The Racial People: The Source of Charisma," ibid., 98–129.

113. Daniel Aaron, et al., eds., "Thirty Years Later: Memories of the First American Writers' Congress," 506.

114. See Jan-Christopher Horak, *Anti-Nazi Filme*, 9, and Wolfang Becker, *Film und Herrschaft. Organizationsprinzipien und Organizationsstrukturen der Nazionalsozialistischen Filmpropaganda* (Berlin: Volker Spiess, 1973), 60.

115. Henry Koster, *Oral History*, interviewed by Irene Kahn Atkins (Metuchen, N.J.: Scarecrow Press, 1987), 33.

116. Gaetano Salvemini, *Under the Ax of Fascism* (New York: Viking, 1936).

117. Lang's secretary to Van Riemsdyck, Book Service New York, November 7, 1935, Box 2, Folder S, Lang Papers, AFI-BH.

118. See Alfred H. Barr, "Nationalism in German Films," *Hound and Horn* January–March 1933, 278. Bernard Rosenberg and Harry Silverstein, eds., *The Real Tinsel* (New York: MacMillan, 1970), 333–50. On Lang's decision to leave Germany see Pat McGilligan, *Fritz Lang: The Nature of the Beast* (New York: St. Martin's Press, 1997), 180–84.

119. About Fritz Lang's departure see his autobiographical essay in Rosenberg and Silverstein, eds., *The Real Tinsel*, 333–50, esp. 336. Mann is cited in Anthony Heilbut, *Exiled in Paradise* (Boston: Beacon Press, 1983), 237.

120. See Chapter 3 of this volume.

121. Selznick to Katherine Corbaley, August 27, 1934, Box 1, Folder C, Lang Papers, AFI-BH.

122. Lang to Katherine Corbaley, May 14, 1935, Box 1, Folder C, Lang Papers, AFI-BH.

123. P. J. Wolfson to David Selznick and Fritz Lang, June 30, 1934, Box 1, Folder W, Lang Papers, AFI-BH.

124. See Chapter 3 of this volume. See also Lang correspondence with Irving Lerner, Box 3, Folder Lerner, Lang Papers, AFI-BH.

125. Walter White to MGM, May 28, 1936, Box 1, Folder F, Lang Papers, AFI-BH.

126. Humphrey Cobb to Fritz Lang, July 9, 1936, Box 1, Folder C, Lang Papers, AFI-BH.

127. *New Masses*, July 1936, 11. In the 1960s, the director told Peter Bogdanovich that when it came to the anti-racist message of his films he was ready to fight "as a Trojan" to address the racial dimension of American lynching, but was frustrated by the studio's adamant policies concerning the representation of race. For instance, Lang had shot a scene in which African Americans listen approvingly to the district attorney condemning the practice of lynching. Lang said, "This scene was cut out. I don't know why they let me *shoot* it—that's the peculiar thing." See Peter Bogdanovich, *Fritz Lang in America* (New York: Praeger, 1969), 32. Yet Lang had in fact been more willing to compromise than his later statements would lead one to believe. The original shooting script for the film, signed by Norman Krasna, Bartlett Cormack, and Fritz Lang, already marks the scene as "if possible." See *Mob Rule*, script by Norman Krasna, Bartlett Cormack, and Fritz Lang. Script approved by Joseph L. Mankiewicz, dated February 10, 1936, with additions. Script Collection, AMPAS.

128. Script for *Mob Rule*, Script Collection, AMPAS.

129. The original ending in fact has Katherine simply moving toward Joe and the camera. Lang was not happy with the change. "Frankly I agree with you that *if this holds up before an audience*, it is to be preferred as an ending," Joseph Mankiewicz wrote the director, yet the scene had to be re-shot "for our protection." See *Mob Rule*, Script Collection, AMPAS. See also Mankiewicz to Lang, April 25, 1936, Box 1, Folder M, Lang Papers, AFI-BH.

130. For instance, to express his contempt for the gossipy women who spread the news of Joe's capture, Lang relied on visual symbols rather than dialogue, by cutting from the women to a group of geese. See Bogdanovich, *Fritz Lang in America*, 52.

131. Transcript of Evening Herald & Express Radio interview with Fritz Lang by Jimmie Vandiveer, "Roving Reporter," June 16, 1936. Emphasis is mine. Box 1, Folder F, Lang Papers, AFI-BH.

132. *Variety*, October 9, 1935, 14. See W. R. Burnett, "Dr. Socrates," *Collier's*, March 16–April 20, 1935.

133. Wallis to Lord, June 11, 1935, *Dr. Socrates* Production File, USC-WB.

134. Screenplay by Carl Erikson and Abem Finkel. Temporary Revised, May 22, 1935, *Dr. Socrates* Script File, USC-WB.

135. McCall to Wallis, June 12, 1935, *Dr. Socrates* Production File, USC-WB.

136. Hal Wallis to Robert Lord, June 22, 1935. *Dr. Socrates* Production File, USC-WB.

137. Sam Ornitz to Rose Pastor Stokes, December 12, 1932, Box 2, Folder 59, Rose Pastor Stokes Collection, Microfilm edition, NYU-TL.

138. Victor J. Jerome to Ornitz, May 6, 1934, Box 5, Folder 151, Rose Pastor Stokes Collection, NYU-TL.

139. Earl Browder to Ornitz, July 30, 1934. Ornitz to Browder, August 6, 1934, Box 5, Folder 151, Rose Pastor Stokes Collection, NYU-TL.

140. Richard Sheridan Ames, "Footlights on Filmland," *New Theater* 2 (September 1935): 20.

Chapter Three

1. Manfred George to Katia Mann, April 10, 1939, George Nachlass, Schiller National Museum, Deutsches Literaturarchiv, Marbach am Neckar.

2. Manfred George to Maurice Feldman, October 15, 1953, George Nachlass, Schiller National Museum, Deutsches Literaturarchiv, Marbach am Neckar.

3. Erika and Klaus Mann, *Escape to Life* (Boston: Houghton Mifflin, 1939), 277.

4. Nancy Schwartz, *The Hollywood Writers' War* (New York: Knopf, 1982), 14–15.

5. On the history of the SWG see Schwartz, *The Hollywood Writers' War*, and Larry Ceplair and Steven Englund, *The Inquisition in Hollywood: Politics in the Film Community 1930–1960* (1979; repr. Berkeley: University of California Press, 1983), 16–46.

6. Rupert Hughes, Clipping File, Library of the Academy of Motion Picture Arts and Science (AMPAS).

7. Ralph Block had written for both the New York *Herald Tribune* and the *New Republic* before working his way up the hierarchy of the New York offices of the studios, first as director of advertising and publicity for Goldwyn Pictures, then in 1926 working for the Paramount offices. See his obituary in *Variety*, January 16, 1974, 95.

8. See Schwartz, *Hollywood Writers' War*, 70–75; Ceplair and Englund, *The Inquisition in Hollywood*, 37–39.

9. Zanuck's testimony before the National Labor Relations Board, 1939, cited in Schwartz, *The Hollywood Writers' War*, 60.

10. Budd Schulberg, *What Makes Sammy Run* (1941; repr. London: Allison and Busby, 1992), 132–33.

11. See Behrman, Clipping File, AMPAS. Behrman, Clipping File, New York Public Library, Bill Rose Collection (NYPL-BR). See also Kenneth T. Reed, *S. N. Behrman* (Boston: Twayne, 1975).

12. S. N. Behrman, *Biography* (New York: Farrar and Rinehart, 1933), 14.

13. *New Yorker*, January 20, 1934, 30–35.

14. *Post*, November 27, 1939, Buchman Clipping File, NYPL-BR.

15. *New York World Telegram*, October 23, 1937, Raine Clipping File, NYPL-BR.

16. Dorothy Parker, "To Richard with Love," *Screen Guilds' Magazine* 3 (May 1936): 8.

17. See Leo C. Rosten, *The Movie Colony, the Movie Makers* (New York: Harcourt, Brace and Company, 1941), 384.

18. SDG's negotiating committee (Howard Hawks, John Ford and Edward Sutherland) to Darryl Zanuck, August 24, 1937, Box 4, Folder SDG, Lang Papers, AFI-BH.

19. *New York World Telegram*, October 23, 1937, Raine Clipping File, NYPL-BR.

20. James Morrison, *Passport to Hollywood: Hollywood Films, European Directors* (Albany: SUNY Press, 1998), 12.

21. Anthony Heilbut, *Strangers in Paradise* (New York: Beacon Press, 1983), 228–60. John Baxter, *The Hollywood Exiles* (New York: Taplinger, 1976); John Russel Taylor, *Strangers in Paradise* (New York: Holt, Rinehart, and Winston, 1983). For a recent revision of Ophüls's Hollywood career see Lutzt Bacher, *Max Ophuls in the Hollywood Studios* (New Brunswick, N.J.: Rutgers University Press, 1996).

22. Wolfgang Gersch, "Antifaschistisches Engagement in Hollywood," in Eike Middel, ed., *Exil in den U.S.A.* (Frankfurt a.M.: Röderberg Verlag, 1980), 419.

23. Lubitsch to Wallis, February 24, 1937, Personal Files, Correspondence 1936–37, Wallis Papers, AMPAS.

24. "Verzeihe bitte diese Belästigung, aber ich darf nichts unversucht lassen, wenn es so schwer ist, Arbeit zu finden." Paul Weigel to Henry Blanke, n.d., *Zola* Production Files, University of Southern California, Warner Brothers Archives (USC-WB).

25. Lang to Blanke, September 13, 1936, Box 1, Folder B, Lang Papers, AFI-BH.

26. "Man betrachtet Schünzel hier allgemein als einen Nazi." Kohner cited in Helmut G. Asper, "Herzasthma des Exils" in *Film-Dienst* 52 (22 June 1999): 43–45. On Kohner see Frederik Kohner, *The Magician of Sunset Boulevard* (San Francisco: Morgan Press, 1977).

27. Lang to Katz, January 14, 1937, Box 3, Folder K, Lang Papers, AFI-BH.

28. "Vermeiden wollten, mit anderen emigranten wieder Deutsch zu sprechen." Cornelius Schnauber, *Fritz Lang in Hollywood* (Wien: Europaverlag, 1986), 52.

29. Lang to Brüchner, June 15, 1937, Box 3, Folder B; Toller to Lang, June 30, 1937, Box 3, Folder T, Lang Papers, AFI-BH.

30. Teddy LeBeu (Lang's personal secretary) to Van Riemsdyck Book Service, New York, November 7, 1935, Box 2, Folder R, Lang Papers, AFI-BH.

31. Braun to Lang, September 12, 1937, Box 3, Folder B, Lang Papers, AFI-BH.

32. Lang to Pem (Paul Markus), June 13, 1936, Box 2, Folder P, Lang Papers, AFI-BH.

33. See Lang Papers, AFI-BH. Especially Boxes 1 and 2.

34. Ibid.

35. Mildred Leibner (executive secretary of the American Committee for Anti-Nazi Literature) to Lang, April 6, 1937; Harry Ward (American League against

War and Fascism) to Lang, September 4, 1937; Lang's subscription to *Volksfront* is dated April 9, 1937; Edward K. Kern (Associated Film Audience) to Lang, May 18, 1937, Box 3, Folder A, Lang Papers, AFI-BH.

36. Lang to Kraft, January 3, 1937, Box 3, Folder Kraft, Lang Papers, AFI-BH.

37. Lerner to Lang, March 1937, Box 3, Folder Lerner, Lang Papers, AFI-BH.

38. Lerner to Lang, April 9, 1937; Lang to Lerner, April 19, 1937, Box 3, Folder Lerner, Lang Papers, AFI-BH.

39. Lerner to Lang, April 26, 1937, Box 3, Folder Lerner, Lang Papers, AFI-BH.

40. Lerner to Lang, August 1937, Box 3, Folder Lerner, Lang Papers, AFI-BH.

41. Lang to Lerner, August 19, 1937, Box 3, Folder Lerner, Lang Papers, AFI-BH. It was no excuse. In his contract, signed May 12, 1937, Lang had "agree[d] to devote his entire time and attention and best talents and abilities to the service of the corporation." Box 9, Folder 12, Lang Papers, USC-WB.

42. Lerner to Lang, n.d., Lang to Lerner, December 22, 1937, Box 3, Folder Lerner, Lang Papers, AFI-BH.

43. Lerner to Leyda, February 1, 1938, Alphabetical Correspondence, Folder Lerner, Leyda Papers, NYU-TL.

44. Lerner to Lang, May 17, 1937. Most likely, the film was *People of the Cumberland* (Frontier Films in cooperation with Highlander Folk School, 1938).

45. In April 1937, Lang wrote to Howard Eastbrook that his picture, *White Bondage*, had "nothing to do with my idea for a picture based on sharecroppers and the South." Lang to Eastbrook, April 9, 1937, Box 3, Folder E, Lang Papers, AFI-BH.

46. Charles Katz to Lang, January 22, 1937, Box 3, Folder K, Lang Papers, AFI-BH. Green, a professor of English at a North Carolina university, was the author of *The House of Connelly* (produced by the Group in 1931) and of an adaptation of *The Good Soldier Schweik*, which the Group had staged as *Johnny Johnson* in 1935.

47. Lang to Agee, June 1, 1937, Box 3, Folder A, Lang Papers, AFI-BH.

48. Lang to Lerner, April 19, 1937, Box 3, Folder Lerner, Lang Papers, AFI-BH. Upon learning the news from Lerner, Agee wrote Lang that he "was very sorry you will not be doing a picture on the subject, and hope it is only for the present: certainly one or even several of the world's better pictures could come out of that set up, and country." Agee to Lang, May 18, 1937, Box 3, Folder A, Lang Papers, AFI-BH.

49. Lang to Book-of-the-Month, September 24, 1937, Box 3, Folder M, Lang Papers, AFI-BH.

50. Behrman to Viertel, November 24, 1965, Salka and Berthold Viertel Nachlass, Schiller National Museum, Deutsches Literaturarchiv, Marbach am Neckar. S. N. Behrman, *People in a Diary* (Boston: Little Brown, 1972), 149.

51. Donald Ogden Stewart, *By a Stroke of Luck* (London: Paddington Press, 1975), 228.

52. *Aufbau*, October 25, 1940, 9.

53. Leo Hurwitz, "One Man's Voyage: Ideas and Films in the 1930s," *Cinema Journal* 15 (Fall 1975): 11.

54. *New Theatre* 3 (April 1935).

55. Larry Ceplair, *Under the Shadow of War: Fascism, Antifascism and Marxists* (New York: Columbia University Press, 1987), 7.

56. *New Theatre* 4 (May 1936): 6–8.

57. Report of the Los Angeles Bureau of the FBI to Washington (unnamed recipient), February 18, 1943, page 117. In *Communist Activity in the Entertainment Industry: FBI Surveillance Files on Hollywood, 1942–58*, edited by Daniel J. Leab (Bethesda, Md.: University Publications of America, 1991), Reel 1, microform edition.

58. Bernard F. Dick, *Hellman in Hollywood* (London: Farleigh Dickinson University Press, 1982), 86.

59. On Merker and the debate within the German Communist Party about the "Jewish issue" see Jeffrey Herf, "From the Periphery to the Center: German Communists and the Jewish Question, Mexico City, 1942–45," in Herf, *Divided Memory* (Cambridge: Harvard University Press, 1997), 40–68.

60. Hubertus zu Löwenstein, *Abenteurer der Freiheit* (Berlin: Ullstein, 1983), 164. My translation.

61. Ibid., 165.

62. Lang to Paul Kohner, May 4, 1936, Box 1, Folder K, Lang Papers, AFI-BH.

63. Donald Ogden Stewart to Lang, April 19, 1937, Box 3, Folder H, Lang Papers, AFI-BH.

64. Thilde Forster to Lang, October 26, 1936, Box 3, Folder F, Lang Papers, AFI-BH.

65. *News of the World* (hereafter *NOW*), August 7, 1937, 1.

66. See "Woman's Committee to Aid Refugees," *Anti-Nazi News*, November 20, 1936, 3. "Decline of Letters: Best Writers of Germany Banned Today," *NOW*, April 10, 1937, 5. "One Affidavit Will Rescue Family of Four," *NOW*, September 2, 1938, 2. "Works of German Craftsmen Greeted Here—Kurt Weill, Composer—Kathe Kollwitz, Artist," *NOW*, May 30, 1937, 3. HANL also published some of John Heartfield's photomontages. See *NOW*, December 20, 1936, 3.

67. "NOW Gets Orchids from German Editor Who's Not a Nazi," *NOW*, August 7, 1937, 7.

68. Salka Viertel, *The Kindness of Strangers* (New York: Holt, Rinehart, and Winston, 1969), 211.

69. *NOW*, August 7, 1937, 1, 3.

70. Lang to Beatrice Buchman, August 3, 1937, Box 3, Folder B, Lang Papers, AFI-BH.

71. Stewart to Lang, September 7, 1937, Box 3, Folder H, Lang Papers, AFI-BH.

72. "Program of the Hollywood Anti-Nazi League for the Defense of American Democracy," (1938?), Box 99, Folder HANL, Extremist Literature Collection, UCLA-SC.

73. Ibid.

74. See Isobel Steele, *I Was a Captive of Nazi Germany* (Malvina Pictures Production, 1937); Shepard Traube, *Hitler, Beast of Berlin* (Producers Releasing Corporation, 1934).

75. *NOW*, May 30, 1937, 8.

76. MacLeish cited in Charles Wolfe, "The Poetics and Politics of Nonfiction: Documentary Film," in Tino Balio, *Grand Design* (New York: Scribner's, 1993), 355.

77. Cited in Ceplair and Englund, *The Inquisition in Hollywood*, 105.

78. *Anti-Nazi News* (later renamed *News of the World*), November 20, 1936, 3.

79. See the code in John Belton, ed., *Movies and Mass Culture* (New Brunswick, N.J.: Rutgers University Press, 1996), 135–40.

80. For example, in 1936 Fox tried to convince the Nazi *Filmkammer* that the star of its *Country Doctor*, Jean Herscholt, was of pure Aryan descent and "dug into the records in an attempt to convince the Nazis that Jean Herscholt is not Jewish or has no Jewish relatives for at least three generations." *Variety*, November 25, 1936, 13.

81. *NOW*, June 25, 1938, 2; June 11, 1938, 3; May 30, 1937, 7; May 28, 1938, 2. As for *Three Comrades*, *NOW* argued that "it is not any kind of version of Remarque's book. In fact, you can't, unless you've read the book, tell which are the Nazis and which are their opponents."

82. *NOW*, June 25, 1938, 2.

83. *NOW*, June 11, 1938, 3.

84. *NOW*, May 28, 1938, 2.

85. Besides Dieterle, nine refugees are credited for *The Life of Émile Zola:* producer Henry Blanke; screenwriters Heinz Herald and Geza Herczeg; costumist Ali Hubert; editor Rudi Fehr; and actors Vladimir Sokoloff, Walter O. Stahl, Egon Brecher, and Iphigenie Castiglioni. *Blockade* (United Artist, 1938): composer Werner Janssen, costumist Ali Huber, actor Valdimir Sokoloff, and cinematographer Rudolf Maté. *Juarez* (WB, 1939): producers Henry Blanke and Wolfang Reinhardt; composer Erich Korngold; writer Franz Werfel; editor Rudy Fehr; and actors Walter Fenner, Walter O. Stahl, Vladimir Sokoloff, and Claude Rains. *The Hunchback of Notre Dame* (RKO, 1939): writer Bruno Frank, choreographers Ernst and Maria Matray, and actors Curt Bois and Gretl Dupont. *Dr. Ehrlich's Magic Bullet* (WB, 1940): producer Wolfang Reinhardt, writer Heinz Herald, and actors Albert Bassermann, Hermine Sterler, Sig Arno, Paul Andor, and Ernst Hansmann. *A Dispatch from Reuters* (WB, 1940): writer Wolfgang Wilhelm, producer Henry Blanke, and actors Albert Bassermann, Walter O. Stahl, Wolfang Zilzer, Frederick Mellinger, Paul Andor, and Ernst Hansmann.

86. Marta Mierendorff, *William Dieterle. Der Plutarch von Hollywood* (Berlin: Henschel Verlag, 1993), 90–100. Thomas Elsaesser, "Film History as Social History: The Dieterle Warner Brothers Bio-Pic," *Wide Angle* 8 (1985): 15–32.

87. Elsaesser, "Film History as Social History," 27. Bertolt Brecht, "Wilhelm Dieterles Galerie grosser bürgerlichen Figuren," in *Retrospektive William Dieterle* (Berlin: Internationale Filmfestspiele, 1973).

88. Manfred George to William Dieterle, March 13, 1939, George Nachlass, Schiller National Museum, Deutsches Literaturarchiv, Marbach am Neckar.

89. "Thomas More" by Max Horkheimer, March 30, 1948, Box 9, AFI-BH.

90. Wallis to Robinson, December 22, 1939, Box 36, Folder 9, Edward G. Robinson Papers, USC-WB. For the meaning that the Hollywood leftists attributed

to these films, see also Joe Freeman, "Biographical Films," *Theater Arts*, December 1941, 900–6; and Howard Koch, "The Historical Film: Fact and Fantasy," *Screenwriter* 1 (January 1946): 1–10.

91. Report of the Los Angeles Bureau of the FBI to Washington (unnamed recipient), February 18, 1943, p. 72. In FBI Confidential Files, *Communist Activity in the Entertainment Industry: FBI Surveillance Files on Hollywood, 1942–58*, edited by Daniel J. Leab (Bethesda, Md.: University Publications of America, 1991) microform edition, Reel 1.

92. Charlotte Dieterle to Hal Wallis, October 1, 1935, *Pasteur*, Production File, USC-WB.

93. Al Allenborn to Tenny Wright, *Juarez*, Daily Production and Progress Report, November 11, 1938. Tenny Wright to Jack L. Warner and Hal Wallis, December 6, 1938, *Juarez* Production File, USC-WB.

94. For the meaning of these biopics in the context of the Cultural Front see Joe Freeman, "Biographical Films," *Theater Arts*, December 1941, 900–6.

95. Joseph R. Morrow, M.D., to Edward G. Robinson, March 4, 1940, Box 38, Folder 14, Robinson Papers, USC-WB.

96. "You have turned the film that was entertainment unadulterated into something more than that, to entertainment that has elements of real art in it," wrote German writer Heinz Herald about Dieterle. Heinz Herald, "William Dieterle—50 Years," *Aufbau*, July 9, 1943, 13.

97. See Leo Lowenthal's notion of "idol of consumption" and "idols of production" in his "Biographies in Popular Magazines," in Paul Lazarsfeld and Frank Stanton, eds., *Radio Research 1942–43* (New York: Duell, Sloan and Pearce, 1944), 507–48.

98. Marta Mierendorff, *William Dieterle. Der Plutarch von Hollywood* (Berlin: Henschel Verlag, 1993), 82–90.

99. *Dr. Socrates* was on schedule between June 14 and July 15, 1934. *Pasteur* was shot between August 12, 1935, and October 2, 1935 (one day behind schedule). Daily Progress and Production Report Files for both films in USC-WB.

100. Blanke to McEwen, July 5, 1935. Final script by Sheridan Gibney and Pierre Collings, still titled "The Death Fighter," July 22, 1935, *Pasteur* Script File, USC-WB.

101. Curtiz to Wallis, January 30, 1935; Curtiz to Chodorov, January 30, 1935. Florey is cited in Elsaesser, "Film History as Social History," 18.

102. *New Masses*, February 25, 1936, 30; *The Nation*, March 4, 1936, 293;

103. Mierendorff, *William Dieterle*, 98.

104. Memo of Henry Blanke to Dorothy Hagemann, February 9, 1937, *Zola* Story File, USC-WB.

105. Elia Kazan, *A Life* (New York: Knopf, 1988), 264.

106. Heinrich Mann, "Zola," *Die weissen Blätter* 11 (1919), 1312–82. See also Egbert Krispyn, *Anti-Nazi Writers in Exile* (Athens: University of Georgia Press, 1978), 48.

107. Heinz Herald to Lou Espinoza, August 31, 1936, *Zola* Story File, USC-WB.

108. In particular the writers examined *L'Affaire Dreyfus* by Hans J. Rehfisch

and Wilhelm Herzog, adapted in French by Jacques Richepin, represented at the Theatre du Nouvel-Ambigu in Paris from February 10 to March 29, 1931, and *Dreyfus* by Richard Oswald (Süd Film A.G., 1930). See *Zola*, Story File, USC-WB.

109. *New Masses*, August 17, 1937, 27; *New Republic*, August 18, 1937, 188–89.

110. On Jewish studio moguls and assimilation see Neal Gabler, *An Empire of Their Own* (New York: Pantheon, 1986).

111. Hal Wallis to Walter McEwen, February 11, 1937, *Zola* Story File, USC-WB.

112. Norman Reilly Raine, Heinz Herald, and Geza Herczeg, *The Life of Émile Zola*, final script (March 16, 1937), 51, Script Collection, AMPAS.

113. Joe Breen of the Hays office advised Jack Warner that the film cited the risque novel too many times. Warner agreed and penciled a "no" next to the item. Breen to Warner, February 12, 1937.

114. *NOW*, October 2, 1937, 2.

115. Paul J. Vanderwood, "Introduction," in *Juarez*, Paul J. Vanderwood, ed. (Madison: University of Wisconsin Press, 1983).

116. Wolfgang Reinhardt to Blanke, November 24, 1937, *Juarez* Picture File, USC-WB. On the film, see also John Huston, *An Open Book* (New York: Knopf, 1980), 74. My translation.

117. Wolfgang Reinhardt to Heinz Blanke, November 2, 1938, *Juarez*, Picture File, USC-WB. My translation.

118. "Jedes Kind muss erkennen, dass Napoleon mit seiner mexicanischen Intervention niemand anders ist als Mussolini plus Hitler mit ihrem Abentuer in Spanien." Wolfgang Reinhardt to Blanke, November 24, 1937, *Juarez* Picture File, USC-WB.

119. Al Allenborn to Lee Anthony, September 24, 1938. *Juarez*, Picture File, USC-WB.

120. Henry Blanke to Hal Wallis, August 17, 1938; Francis Lederer to Wallis, July 1, 1938; Blanke to Wallis, July 20, 1938; Trilling to Hal Wallis, September 19, 1938, *Juarez* Picture File, USC-WB.

121. November 11, 1938, *Juarez*, Daily Progress Report File, USC-WB.

122. Vanderwood, "Introduction," 18. Mierendorff, *Dieterle*, 343.

123. *Juarez*, Publicity File, USC-WB.

124. *New Masses*, May 9, 1939; *The Nation*, May 6, 1939.

125. On West see Tom Dardis, *Some Time in the Sun* (New York: Scribner, 1976), 176. On Lionel Stander see Paul Jarrico, *Oral History*, interviewed by Larry Ceplair (Los Angeles: UCLA Oral History Program, 1991), 29.

126. On the notion of "intended reader" see June Schlueter, "The Private and Public Lives of a Dramatic Text," in Matthew C. Roudanné, ed., *Public Issues, Private Tensions* (New York: AMS, 1993), 281–93.

127. *NOW*, January 26, 1938, 1.

128. *Newsweek*, July 9, 1938, 9.

129. On topical films see Giuliana Muscio, "Print the Legend. I 'Newspaper films,' la Depressione, e il Codice Hays," *Cinema e Cinema* (January–April, 1985): 55–61.

130. Edward G. Robinson to Hal Wallis, October 20, 1938, Box 36, Folder 20, Edward G. Robinson Papers, USC-WB. See also Leon G. Turrou, *The Nazi Conspiracy in America* (1939; repr. Freeport, N.Y.: Books for Libraries Press, 1972).

131. Robinson to Wallis, October 20, 1938, Box 36, Folder 20, Edward G. Robinson Papers, USC-WB.

132. Wallis, *Starmaker*, 71.

133. Ed Sullivan, "Hollywood," n.d. See also *New York Herald Tribune*, Paris edition, February 15, 1939, no page. *Confessions of a Nazi Spy* (hereafter *Confessions*) Clippings File, USC-WB.

134. *Los Angeles Times*, April 28, 1941. Scrapbook 5, Hedda Hopper Collection, AMPAS.

135. Draft of letter from Steven Trilling to American Consul General, Berlin, Germany, March 8, 1939, *Confessions* Picture File, USC-WB. About U.S. immigration policies concerning the refugees see David Wyman, *Paper Walls: America and the Refugee Crisis, 1938–1941* (1968; repr. New York: Pantheon, 1982).

136. Memo from Trilling to Wallis, January 30, 1939, *Confessions* Picture File, USC-WB. In the credits, Reicher was ultimately given the pseudonym of Celia Sibelius.

137. *California Jewish Voice*, March 31, 1939, 7.

138. Among them William von Brinchen, Rudolf Amendt, Sig Rumann, Paul Lukas, Wolfgang Zilzer, Hans von Morhart, Hans von Twardowski, Willie Kaufman, Martin Kosleck, Hedwiga Reicher, Henry Victor, and Frederick Vogeding.

139. This had been achieved through lengthy negotiation with the Hollywood trade unions and met the complete approval of the cast, including Edward G. Robinson. See Wallis to Taplinger, Obringer, Selzer, and McEwen, March 20, 1939. *Confessions* Picture File, USC-WB.

140. Robert Taplinger to Wallis, February 28, 1939. *Confessions* Picture File, USC-WB.

141. *Variety*, May 3, 1938, 16. Emphasis mine. See also Archer Winsten's review in the *Post*, April 29, 1939, 11, and Louella Parson's review in *Examiner*, May 5, 1939, Box 1, Folder 1, *Confessions* Clipping File, USC-WB.

142. See Turrou, *The Nazi Conspiracy in America*.

143. On the G-man story and its success see Richard Gid Powers, *G-Men: Hoover's FBI in American Popular Culture* (Carbondale: Southern Illinois University Press, 1983), 78, 95–111. Among the G-men pictures see *Public Enemy's Wife, Public Enemy Number One, Whipshaw, Mary Burns, Fugitive, Let 'em Have It, Show Them No Mercy!* and *Border G-Men*.

144. Powers, *G-Men*, xv.

145. *New York Times*, April 2, 1939, no page. *Confessions* Clippings File, NYPL-BR.

146. *Variety*, May 3, 1939, 16. See also Louella Parson's review in *The Examiner*, May 5, 1939.

147. See Morris Watson, "The Living Newspaper," *New Theatre* 3 (June 1936): 6–9, 33.

148. "starkste Antinazi propaganda . . . Amerikas erster Antinazi-Film." *Aufbau*, May 1, 1939, 16.

149. *Confessions* File, Production Code Authority Collection, AMPAS. On PCA and *Confessions* see Gregory D. Black and Clayton R. Koppes, *Hollywood Goes to War: How Politics, Profits, and Propaganda Shaped World War Two Movies* (New York: The Free Press, 1987), 27–30.

150. Memo from Hal Wallis to Litvak, February 14, 1939. *Confessions* Picture File, USC-WB.

151. *Confessions* Picture File, USC-WB.

152. *New York Times*, January 22, 1939, no page. Edward G. Robinson Clippings File, NYPL-BR.

153. *Film News*, March 1939, 1.

154. *New Masses*, May 9, 1939, 27–28; *The Nation*, May 20, 1939, 595; *NOW*, May 5, 1939, 1. In 1955, Cold War liberal critic Robert Warshow argued that *Confessions* was as much an epitome of the culture of the 1930s (and of what was wrong with it) as the novel *The Grapes of Wrath* and the song *Ballad for Americans*. See Warshow, "The Culture of the Thirties" in Warshow, *The Immediate Experience* (1962; repr. New York: Atheneum, 1970), 34.

155. Donald Ogden Stewart, *Oral History*, interviewed by Max Wilk (Beverly Hills: American Film Institute Oral History Project, 1971), 90.

156. *Dead End*, April 29, 1937, Script Collection, AMPAS.

157. Peter Roffman and Jim Purdy, *The Hollywood Social Problem Film: Madness, Despair and Politics from the Depression to the Fifties* (Bloomington: Indiana University Press, 1981), 136–37.

158. On Albert Bein see Gary Gerstle, *Working Class Americanism* (New York: Cambridge University Press, 1989), 162 note 23. Wolfson was a sponsoring member of the progressive Associated Film Audiences. *Film News*, August 1939, 3.

159. On *Pins and Needles*, see *New York Times*, December 11, 1938, sec. 10, p. 4.

160. B. R. Crisler, "Bulletins and comments," *New York Times*, September 17, 1940, sec. 9, p. 3.

161. William Stull, "Camera Work Fails True Mission When It Sinks Realism For Beauty," *American Cinematographer*, February 1938, 56, 59.

162. Bette Davis, "Where Did You Get That Hat?," *Screen Guilds' Magazine* 4 (1936): 14.

163. *Variety*, March 29, 1939, 3.

164. Cited in Richard Maltby, "The Genesis of the Production Code," 70. In Giuliana Muscio, ed., *Prima dei codici* (Venice: Edizioni La Biennale, 1991), 39–81. Interestingly, Elsaesser notes a continuity between "the gritty realism" of Warner social pictures and the "authenticity of the biopic." Elsaesser, "Film History as Social History," 23. Though historical, Dieterle's biopics still embraced a variation of the realistic esthetic and swapped the realism of the New York streets for the authenticity of reconstruction. Lengthy descriptions of scientific processes abound in *Pasteur* and *Dr. Ehrlich*. The research departments of Warner Bros. assembled enormous "bibles" for *Ehrlich, Juarez, Zola*, and *Pasteur*. For *Juarez*, the studio rented "an entire library of books on the Mexico of Maximilian, consisting of

several hundred volumes and thousands of pictures," and built an extra room close to the set to house the material. Memo of Herman Lissauer to McEwen, August 11, 1938. Research File, USC-WB. By 1938, Dieterle was asking the WB research department head, Dr. Herman Lissauer, details such as "How did Maximilian's mother begin and end a letter to him?" Lissauer answered dutifully: "She called him Max or 'my Max'." General Research Record, *Juarez*, Research File, USC-WB.

165. See for example Richard Maltby, *Harmless Entertainment* (Metuchen, N.J.: Scarecrow Press, 1983), 10. For a more recent restatement of the "harmless entertainment thesis" see Thomas Cripps, *Hollywood High Noon* (Baltimore: Johns Hopkins University Press, 1997), 1–7. For the agency and the politics of the actual filmmakers there is hardly leeway. Others turn the story upside down. They accept that the relations of power were in favor of the "system," but they discover the creativity—the genius—of the system itself. Producers knew their trade; if they were the real authors of the Hollywood style, so be it. See Thomas Schatz, *The Genius of the System: Hollywood Film-making in the Studio Era* (New York: Simon & Schuster, 1989).

166. Peter Bogdanovich, *Fritz Lang in America* (New York: Praeger, 1969), 38.

167. Lang to Lerner, June 27, 1937, Box 3, Folder Lerner, Lang Papers, AFI-BH.

168. Zukor to Le Baron, August 17, 1937, Box 3, Folder Le Baron, Lang Papers, AFI-BH.

169. *New Masses*, June 12, 1938, 30.

170. See Neal Gabler, *An Empire of Their Own* (New York: Random House, 1989), 338–47. See also Patricia Erens, *The Jews in American Cinema* (Bloomington: Indiana University Press, 1984).

171. *Variety*, May 3, 1938, 16.

172. "To All People of Good Will," *Equality* 1 (May 1939): 3.

173. Mary Nolan, "Antifascism under Fascism: German Visions and Voices," *New German Critique* 23 (Winter 1996): 51. On the Frankfurt Institute see Martin Jay, "The Jews and the Frankfurt School: Critical Theory's Analysis of Anti-Semitism," *New German Critique* 19 (Winter 1980): 137–49. According to Jay, anti-Semitism was not discussed in the Institute's 1935 collective volume *Studien über Autorität und Familie* (*Studies on Authority and Family*). Jews are mentioned neither in Herbert Marcuse's 1934 essay "Der Kampf gegen den Liberalismus in der Totalitären Staatsauffassung" ("The Struggle against Liberalism in the Totalitarian Concept of the State") nor in Leo Lowenthal's 1937 "Kurt Hamsun. Zur Vorgeschichte der autoritären Ideologie" ("Kurt Hamsun: On the Prehistory of Authoritarian Ideology"). In 1939 Horkheimer did write an essay on "Die Juden und Europa" ("The Jews and Europe") but even there the philosopher "continued to subsume anti-Semitism under the more general rubric of the crisis of capitalism" (p. 138).

174. "Faschismus und Antisemitismus sind nicht notwendig Synnonym." "Ein Warnungsruf," *Aufbau*, June 7, 1935, 1.

175. Robert H. Jackson, "How to Save America from Anti-Semitism," *Aufbau,* July 1, 1939, 1.

176. Wexley was the author of the "blue pages"—dated February 10, 1939— containing the scene in Griebl's office between the Nazi and Renard. Wexley to Walter McEwen, February 21, 1939, and McEwen to Wexley, February 22, 1939, *Confessions* Picture File, USC-WB. See also the final shooting script in *Confessions* Script File, USC-WB.

177. Shooting Script, 150. Blue pages dated March 3, 1939, *Confessions* Script File, USC-WB.

178. René Cenower to Edward G. Robinson, October 30, 1938, Box 38, Folder 21, Robinson Papers, USC-WB. My translation.

179. See "Liberalism in Hollywood," *Ken,* April 27, 1939, 9–11. See Helen Gahagan Douglas, *A Full Life* (Garden City, N.Y.: Doubleday, 1982), 136.

180. See also *Variety,* December 14, 1939, 5.

181. Illegible to Robinson, December 13, 1938, Box 30, Folder 14b, Robinson Papers, USC-WB.

182. *New York Times,* January 22, 1939, no page, Edward G. Robinson Clippings File, NYPL-BR.

183. Robinson to Wallis, October 20, 1938, Box 36, Folder 20, Robinson Papers, USC-WB. Emphasis in original.

184. Bosley Crowther, "Realistic Stepchild of the Movies," *New York Times Magazine,* August 25, 1940, 12–13. Manfred George, "Was geht in Hollywood an," *Aufbau,* May 1, 1939, 6. My translation.

185. See Miriam Hansen, "*Schindler's List* is not *Shoah:* The Second Commandment, Popular Modernism, and Public Memory," *Critical Inquiry* 22 (Winter 1996): 306.

186. On Murphy see William Moritz, "Americans in Paris," in Jan-Christopher Horak, *Lovers of Cinema: The First American Film Avant-Garde* (Madison: University of Wisconsin Press, 1995), 118–36.

Chapter Four

1. Leo C. Rosten, *The Movie Colony, the Movie Makers* (New York: Harcourt, Brace and Company, 1941), 133–34.

2. Richard Sheridan Ames, "Footlights on Filmland," *New Theatre* 2 (September 1935): 20.

3. Located at 2905 Sunset Boulevard, in its three years of existence, Contemporary Theater had showcased the talent of New York radicals, producing *Peace on Earth, Sailors of Cattaro,* and in 1936 Irwin Shaw's *Bury the Dead* under the direction of German refugee Egon Brecher. See the program for "Bury The Dead," a Contemporary Theater Production, Belasco Theater, June 1, 1936. Los Angeles Public Library, Main Branch, Theater Collection.

4. Edward Gering to Lang, n.d. (1937?), Box 4, Folder G, Lang Papers, American Film Institute, AFI-BH.

5. *Variety*, April 5, 1939, 1.

6. Edda Fuhrich-Leisler und Gisela Prossnitz, *Max Reinhardt in Amerika* (Salzburg, Germany: Otto Müller Verlag, 1976), 274–327.

7. Ibid., 283–84.

8. Henry Meyer, *Oral History* (New York: Columbia University Oral History Project, 1959), 110. On the Theater Alliance see also Paul Buhle and Pat McGilligan, *Tender Comrades* (New York: St. Martin's Press, 1997), 240–41.

9. Walter Wicclair, *Von Kreutzberg bis Hollywood* (Berlin: Henschel Verlag, 1976), 146. The actor remembers that he used the "wonderful theater" of the Alliance to stage his *Arm wie ein Kirchenmaus*.

10. Seventy-five percent of those who have underwritten the Alliance are "professional theater people," while 25 percent are "Los Angeles teachers, doctors, trade unionists and churchmen." *Meet the People*, playbill for the Mansfield Theater. *Meet the People* File, New York Public Library, Billy Rose Collection, NYPL-BR.

11. Program for *Meet the People* at Hollywood Playhouse, n.d. (between February and July 1940). *Meet the People* File, NYPL-BR.

12. See reviews of *Meet the People*, in *Meet the People* Clipping File, NYPL-BR.

13. *Hollywood Citizen News*, March 14, 1940; *Meet the People* File, Los Angeles Public Library, Theater Division.

14. *Hollywood Citizen News*, February 12, 1940; *Meet the People* File, Los Angeles Public Library, Theater Division.

15. *Hollywood Citizen News*, July 20, 1940; *Meet the People* File, Los Angeles Public Library, Theater Division.

16. *Hollywood Citizen News*, June 27, 1940; *Meet the People* File, Los Angeles Public Library, Theater Division.

17. *Hollywood Citizen News*, August 20, 1940; *Meet the People* File, Los Angeles Public Library, Theater Division.

18. *Hollywood Citizen News*, March 14, 1940; *Meet the People* File, Los Angeles Public Library, Theater Division.

19. See the Mansfield Program, *Meet the People* File, NYPL-BR.

20. Program for the version of the play produced by the Edwin Piscator Dramatic Workshop at the New School for Social Research, n.d. *Meet the People* File, NYPL-BR.

21. *Variety*, January 31, 1940, no page. *Meet the People* File, NYPL-BR.

22. *Hollywood Reporter*, August 24, 1938, 1–2.

23. Rosten, *The Movie Colony*, 145.

24. *New York Times*, August 15, 1940, 1, 22.

25. Laura Fermi, *Illustrious Immigrants: The Intellectual Migration from Europe* (Chicago: University of Chicago Press, 1968), 27.

26. U.S. House of Representatives, 75th Congress, Special Committee on Un-American Activities, *Hearings* (Washington, D.C.: U.S. Government Printing Office, 1938), 543.

27. Ibid., 618–21, 700–1. About the alien threat see also the hearings of Harper I. Knowles and Ray E. Nimmo (ibid., 2001–20).

28. Martin Dies, "The Reds in Hollywood," in *Liberty*, February 17, 1940, 48.

29. *Public Opinion Quarterly* 2 (October 1939): 595.

30. FDR prohibited Ickes from delivering his speech "Playing with Loaded Dies." The "sordid practices" remark referred to the 1939 Committee's raid on the archives of the Chicago branch of the American League for Peace and Democracy. See Kenneth O'Reilly, "The Roosevelt Administration and Legislative-Executive Conflict: The F.B.I. vs the Dies Committee," *Congress and the Presidency* 10 (1983): 79–93.

31. *Variety*, August 21, 1940, 22.

32. *Variety*, August 28, 1940, 1. The best account of the Dies Committee in Hollywood is in Larry Ceplair and Steven Englund, *The Inquisition in Hollywood* (1978; repr. Berkeley: University of California Press, 1983).

33. George Allison Phelps, *An American's History of the Movies* (Los Angeles: Zenith, 1941). The Neely Bill was meant to outlaw the practice of compulsory block booking, through which Hollywood studios would rent movies in "blocks" comprising blockbusters and features of B and C quality. On the bill see Muscio, *La Casa Bianca e le sette Majors* (Padua, Italy: Il Poligrafo, 1990), 122–30, and her *Hollywood's New Deal* (Philadelphia: Temple University Press, 1996).

34. Gerald P. Nye, "War Propaganda: Our Madness Increases as Our Emergency Shrinks," in *Vital Speeches of the Day* 7 (September 15, 1941): 720–23.

35. U.S. Senate, 77th Congress, Senate Subcommittee of the Committee on Interstate Commerce, Investigation on Propaganda in Motion Pictures on Senate Resolution 152, *Hearings* (Washington, D.C.: U.S. Government Printing Office, 1942), 11.

36. On the refugee filmmakers in Europe see Jan-Christopher Horak, *Anti-Nazi Filme* (Münster: Maks Publikationen, 1986), 8–18.

37. *New York Times*, March 2, 1941, sec. 9, p. 5.

38. See Jan-Christopher Horak, *Fluchtpunkt Hollywood. Eine Dokumentation zur Filmemigration nach 1933* (Münster: Maks Publikationen, 1986). I extrapolated the figures from Horak's bio-dictionary.

39. *Variety*, April 5, 1939, 1.

40. *Chicago Tribune*, October 29, 1939, no page, Scrapbook 3, Hedda Hopper Scrapbook Collection, AMPAS.

41. *Aufbau*, October 19, 1940, 8. *New York Times*, September 22, 1940, sec. 9, p. 3.

42. *Variety*, October 9, 1940, 4.

43. *New York Times*, October 13, 1940, sec. 9, p. 5.

44. *New York Times*, March 2, 1941, sec. 9, p. 5.

45. The name of the director is followed by the arrival year and the date and title of his first film: Steve Sekely (1938, *A Miracle on Main Street*, 1940); William Lee Wilder (1938, *The Ghost Music*, "treatment" sold but not realized, 1939); Alexander Hammid (1939, *Lights Out in Europe*, documentary 1939 and *The Forgotten Village* 1941); Leslie Kardos (1939, *The Streets of Cairo*, 1940); Andrew Marton (1939, *A Little Bit of Heaven*, 1940); Alexander Norris (1940, *Overture to Glory*, 1940); Richard Oswald (1939, *The Captain of Koepenik*, 1941); Gerd Oswald (1939, first assistant to Richard Oswald's *The Captain of Koepenik*, 1941); Curtis Bernhardt (1940, *My Love*

Came Back, 1940); Zoltan Korda (1940, *The Jungle Book*, 1942); Robert Siodmak (1940, *West Point Widow*, 1941); Alexander Korda (1941, *That Hamilton Woman*, 1941); Lothar Mendes (1941, *International Squadron*, 1941).

46. Franz L. Bunfel, "Berufschancen der Immigration in Los Angeles," *Aufbau*, September 5, 1941, 14. My translation.

47. "Die Grösse Prüfung," *Aufbau*, November 1, 1938, 1.

48. The life of Norman Burnstine is still one of those obscure areas of Hollywood history. The AFI-BH's *Catalog of Feature Films* lists him as the author of the script for *Sins of the Fathers* in 1928, and of two low-budget Republic features of the late 1930s, *Invisible Enemy* and *Arson Squad*, both dated 1938. After those films his only credit was *Dr. Ehrlich's Magic Bullet* (WB, 1940). Patricia King Hanson, ed., *The American Film Institute Catalog. Feature Films: 1931–1940* (Berkeley: University of California Press, 1993).

49. Norman Burnstine to Henry Blanke, July 27, 1938, *Ehrlich* Story File, University of Southern California-Warner Brothers Archives (USC-WB).

50. Norman Burnstine, "Treatment" untitled, October 8, 1938, *Ehrlich* Script File, USC-WB.

51. Final script, October 13, 1939, *Ehrlich* Script File, USC-WB.

52. Burnstine to Hal Wallis, August 21, 1939. *Ehrlich* Story File, USC-WB.

53. Wolfgang Reinhardt to SWG arbitration committee, December 8, 1939. *Ehrlich* Story File, USC-WB.

54. David Commons, "A Talk with Dieterle," *Film Survey* 2 (December 1939): 7.

55. Buhle and McGilligan, *Tender Comrades*, 613.

56. Charles Glenn, "*What Makes Sammy Run?*: Story of a Hollywood Heel," *Daily Worker*, April 7, 1941, 7. Charles Glenn, "Hollywood Can Be Won to the Side of the American People," *Daily Worker*, April 23, 1941, 7.

57. The most egregious example of the melodramatic version is in K. Lloyd Billingsley, *Hollywood Party* (Rocklin, Calif.: Prima, 1998), 48–49. But see a revealing summary of Buddy Schulberg's testimony in Victor Navasky, *Naming Names* (New York: Viking, 1980), 239–46. See also Elia Kazan, *A Life* (New York: Doubleday, 1988), 399–400.

58. Samuel Sillen, "Sammy Glick and Johnny Dobrejcak," *New Masses*, April 29, 1941, 22–23.

59. W. L. Rivers, "Conniving and Copulating Ghosts," *The Clipper*, June 1941, 20–22. Paul Jarrico believes that the Jewish issue was the cause for the polemics over the novel. See Patrick McGilligan, "A True Blue Red in Hollywood: An Interview with Paul Jarrico," *Cineaste* 22 (1998): 38.

60. On Gold's novel see James D. Bloom, *Left Letters* (New York: Columbia University Press, 1992), 31.

61. Budd Schulberg, *What Makes Sammy Run?* (1941; repr. London: Allison & Busby, 1992), 209.

62. Ibid., 122.

63. On the crisis of HANL see Nancy Lynn Schwartz, *The Hollywood Writers' War* (New York: Knopf, 1982), 140–47. Bonnie Claire Smith's citation is from page 147.

64. *Hollywood Now*, April 16, 1940, 1.

65. "finanzielle Hilfsstelle für ins Unglück geratene Europäer, inbesondere Refugees und zum Teil Künstler, Schauspieler, Musiker und so weiter." Marta Mierendorff, *William Dieterle. Der Plutarch von Hollywood* (Berlin: Henschel Verlag, 1993), 111–17. See also E. Bond Johnson, "Der European Film Fund in Hollywood," in John M. Spalek and Joseph Strelka, eds., *Deutsche Exilliteratur seit 1933* 2 vols., (Bern, Switzerland: Francke AG Verlag, 1976), 1: 135–46.

66. See Johnson, "Der European Film Fund in Hollywood," 137.

67. Frederick Kohner, *The Magician of Sunset Boulevard* (Palos Verdes, Calif.: Morgan Press, 1974), 105–12.

68. Ibid., 110. Jack Warner gave four, Louis B. Mayer gave six, and Harry Cohn gave ten.

69. Buhle and McGilligan, *Tender Comrades*, 673.

70. Paul Jarrico, *Oral History*, interviewed by Larry Ceplair (Los Angeles: UCLA Oral History Program, 1991), 111.

71. Buhle and McGilligan, *Tender Comrades*, 689.

72. Ibid., 494.

73. Cited in Schwartz, *The Hollywood Writers' War*, 154.

74. Ibid., 151.

75. Donald Ogden Stewart, *By a Stroke of Luck* (London: Paddington Press, 1975), 247–49.

76. *Variety* (January 31, 1940, no page) refers to the mockery of Stalin and the pro-Roosevelt skit. *Meet the People* Clipping File, NYPL-BR. D. W. Churchill, "Autumnal Leavings in Hollywood," *New York Times*, October 22, 1939, sec. 9, p. 5.

77. On the alliance and the debates within it, see the testimony of Danny Dare in HUAC, *Investigations of Communists Activities in the Los Angeles Area*, 83rd Congress (Washington, D.C.: U.S. Government Printing Office, 1953): 268–92, esp. 282–83. See also " '41 Revue Director Links Skits to Reds" in *New York Times*, March 23, 1953, no page. In *Meet the People* Clipping File, NYPL-BR.

78. *Meet the People*, playbill for the Mansfield Theater, 18. *Meet the People* Program File, NYPL-BR.

79. See the list in *The Clipper*, 2 (June 1941): 3.

80. *Arise My Love* (October 17, 1940) scripted by Billy Wilder and Charles Brackett and directed by Mitchell Leisen. *The Mortal Storm* (June 21, 1940) directed by Frank Borzage, scripted by Georg Froeschel, Claudine West, and Andersen Ellis. *Three Faces West* (August 19, 1940), directed by the British communist director Bernard Vorhaus and scripted by Sam Ornitz, Joseph Moncure March, and Hugh Herbert. *Four Sons* (June 16, 1940) directed by Archie Mayo and scripted by John Howard Lawson. *The Man I Married* (August 7, 1940) directed by Irving Pichel and scripted by Oliver H. P. Garrett. *Underground* (June 28, 1941) directed by People's Education Center instructor Vincent Sherman. *Escape to Glory* (November 10, 1940) directed by John Brahm and scripted by P. J. Wolfson. *Foreign Correspondent* (August 29, 1940) directed by Alfred Hitchcock and scripted by Charles Bennett, Joan Harrison, James Hilton, and Robert Benchley. *The Great Dictator* (October 15, 1940) written, directed, and produced by Charles Chaplin. *Escape* (November 12,

1940) directed by Mervyn Le Roy and scripted by Arch Oboler. See Alice Goetz, ed., *Hollywood und die Nazis* (Hamburg: Arbeitsgemeinschaft Kino, 1977), reprinted in La Biennale di Venezia, *Vienna Berlino Hollywood. Il cinema della grande emigrazione* (Venezia: Edizioni La Biennale, 1981), 177–79.

81. See the list of the signers of the call in "Fourth American Writers' Congress," *The Clipper* 2 (June 1941): 3.

82. Fritz Lang to Nichols, January 30, 1941, Box 8, Folder N, Lang Papers, AFI-BH.

83. The play premiered at the Martin Beck Theater in New York, April 1, 1941. *Watch on the Rhine* is in Lillian Hellman, *Four Plays* (New York: Modern Library, 1942).

84. Wolfe Kaufman, "War, Propaganda, and Hollywood," *The Clipper* 1 (August 1940): 27–30. *New York Times*, June 8, 1940, is quoted in Gary Carr, *The Left Side of Paradise* (Ann Arbor, Mich.: UMI Research Press, 1984), 81.

85. Alvah Bessie, "Watch on the Rhine," *New Masses*, April 15, 1941, 27. See also the mixed review by Ralph Warner in *Daily Worker*, April 4, 1941, 7, which argues that a "fabric of omissions" hangs over the play.

86. Donald Ogden Stewart, *Fighting Words* (New York: Harcourt & Brace, 1940), 166–67.

87. *Aufbau*, May 1, 1939, 16. My translation.

88. *News of the World*, May 5, 1939, 1. On classical Hollywood narrative as protagonist-driven, see David Bordwell and Kristin Thompson, *Film Art: An Introduction* (Reading, Mass.: Addison-Wesley, 1979), 58.

89. David Wolff, "Fact into Film in *Confessions of a Nazi Spy*," *Films* 1 (1939): 81–84.

90. H. N. Swanson to Matson and Dugan, April 6, 1939, Box 90, Folder Turrou, Leonard G., H. N. Swanson Collection, AMPAS.

91. *Variety*, August 16, 1939, 22.

92. See Hal Wallis, *Starmaker* (New York: MacMillan, 1980), 72. The film was banned in Yugoslavia, Austria, Italy, Denmark, Norway, Sweden, Cuba, and Costa Rica. On British censorship of *Confessions*, see Dereck B. Mayne to Albert Doane, June 30, 1939, *Confessions* File, Production Code Administration Archives, AMPAS.

93. *Variety*, May 17, 1939, 1.

94. Cited in Bernard F. Dick, *The Star-Spangled Screen: The American World War II Film* (Lexington: University Press of Kentucky, 1985), 87.

95. Charles K. Feldman to Grace Dobish, June 24, 1939; Ned Martin to Feldman, June 26, 1939; Martin to Feldman, June 29, 1939; Charles K. Feldman Papers, Folder 878, AFI-BH.

96. Leon Askin to Leo Lania, September 11, 1940, Lania Collection, Box 1, Folder 1, State Historical Society of Wisconsin, Madison, Wisconsin. My translation.

97. *Liberty*, June 6, 1940, 25.

98. Wilhelm Dieterle, "P.S. to Movie Symposium," *Decision*, April 1941, 85.

99. On the political meaning of *The Sea Hawk* (WB, 1940) see Sidney Rosenzweig, *Casablanca and Other Major Films of Michael Curtiz* (Ann Arbor, Mich.:

Umiversity of Michigan Press, 1992), 48.

100. *New York Times*, November 25, 1939, sec. 10, p. 4.

101. The film was later cited for warmongering during the hearing of the Nye Committee. See Karol Kulik, *Alexander Korda* (London: W. H. Allen, 1975), 245–52. On historical film as political metaphor see Leger Grindon, *Shadows on the Past* (Philadelphia: Temple University Press, 1994), 1–26.

102. On the film see Robert Sklar, *City Boys* (Princeton: Princeton University Press, 1992), 120.

103. See Edward G. Robinson, *All My Yesterdays*, with Leonard Spigelgass (New York: McGraw Hill, 1985), 165.

104. Klaus Mann, "What's Wrong with Anti-Nazi Films?," *Decision*, August 1941, 31.

105. Ibid.

106. Ibid., 34.

107. Manfred George, "Hollywood's Politische Probe," *Aufbau*, July 1, 1939, 4. My translation.

108. See, for example, Peter Stead, *Film and the Working Class* (London: BFI, 1989), 88–91. But the most egregious example of this reductive interpretation of the film is to be found in Colin Shindler, *Hollywood in Crisis* (New York: Routledge, 1996), 77–78.

109. Guthrie's column—"Woody sez"—on the film is cited in Ellen Graff, *Stepping Left* (Durham, N.C.: Duke University Press, 1997), 140.

110. Steinbeck to Otis, December 15, 1939. John Steinbeck, *A Life in Letters*, edited by Elaine Steinbeck and Richard Wallesten (New York: Viking, 1975), 195.

111. Frank S. Nugent, "A Too Familiar Family," *New York Times*, February 18, 1940, sec. 9, p. 5.

112. Edwin Locke, "Adaptation of Reality: *The Grapes of Wrath*," *Films* 1 (Spring 1940): 54–55.

113. Agee to the editors of *Films* (1939), Box 1, Folder Agee, Jay Leyda Papers, NYU-TL.

114. Mordecai Gorelik, *New Theaters for Old* (New York: Samuel French, 1940), 27.

115. Ibid., 166.

116. On *Juarez* see ibid., 238–40. On the other films see ibid., 334.

117. Ibid., 437. On Gorelik see also Pells, *Radical Visions*, 255–57.

118. Jones to Gorelik, April 16, 1940, "Mordecai Gorelik—Robert Edmund Jones: Correspondence about *New Theater for Old*," *Educational Theater Journal* 20 (March 1968): 39.

119. Jones to Gorelik, April 19, 1940. Ibid., 43.

120. See the authors' interview with John Weber in Buhle and McGilligan, *Tender Comrades*, 689.

121. John Howard Lawson, "New Theaters for Old," *New Masses*, March 18, 1941, 23–26.

122. *New Masses*, April 22, 1941, 22.

123. See William Stott, *Documentary Expression and Thirties America* (1973; repr.

Chicago: University of Chicago Press, 1986), esp. 238–57.

124. See, for example, B. R. Crisler, "Bulletins and Comments," *New York Times*, September 17, 1940, sec. 9, p. 3.

125. See Pells, *Radical Visions*, 287–91.

126. Kael cited in Michael Denning, *The Cultural Front* (New York: Verso, 1996), 363.

127. Cedric Belfrage, "Orson Welles's *Citizen Kane*," *The Clipper* 2 (May 1941): 12–14. Emphasis in original. See also the positive review ("magnificent if unfinished portrait") by Joy Davidman, "Citizen Kane," *New Masses*, May 13, 1941, 28–29. Also, Emil Pritt, "Orson Welles and *Citizen Kane*," *New Masses*, February 4, 1941, 27.

128. See Denning, *The Cultural Front*, 363–64.

129. In particular, Hearst was the polemical target of a play Michael Gold had been working on throughout the 1930s. See James D. Bloom, *Left Letters: The Culture Wars of Mike Gold and Joseph Freeman* (New York: Columbia University Press, 1992), 38.

130. In his brilliant discussion of *Kane*'s deep-focus photography, David Bordwell does not grasp the political dimension of Welles's and Toland's choices. See Bordwell, "Deep Focus Photography," in David Bordwell, Kristin Thompson, and Janet Staiger, *The Classical Hollywood Cinema* (New York: Columbia University Press, 1984), 347–48.

131. Cited in Bordwell, "Deep Focus," 348.

132. Peter Bogdanovich and Orson Welles, *This Is Orson Welles*, edited by Jonathan Rosenbaum (New York: Harper Collins, 1992), 61.

133. James Agee, *Agee on Film* (New York: Grosset & Dunlap, 1967), 83. Agee puts "originality" in quotation marks. On the relationship between Orson Welles and the Cultural Front, see Michael Denning, "The Politics of Magic: Orson Welles's Allegories of Anti-Fascism," Denning, *Cultural Front*, 362–402.

134. *The Daily Worker*, October 16, 1940, 7. Otis Ferguson, "Less Time for Comedy," *New Republic*, November 4, 1940, reprinted in Otis Ferguson, *The Criticism of Otis Ferguson* (Philadelphia: Temple University Press, 1971), 316. Rudolph Arnheim, "Anti-Fascist Satire," in *Films* 1 (Winter 1940): 30–34. Interestingly, in his Weimar years Arnheim had championed Chaplin and what Thomas Saunders calls the "slapstick synthesis." See Thomas Saunders, *Hollywood in Berlin* (Berkeley: University of California Press, 1994), 220–22.

135. Already in 1932, Sturges was planning to turn *A Cup Of Coffee* into a movie. See Sturges to Charles Abrahmson, September 23, 1932, Sturges Collection, Box 60, Folder 10, UCLA-SC. On Sturges and *Christmas in July*, see Diane Jacobs, *Christmas in July* (Berkeley: University of California Press, 1992), 220–22. On his friendship with Chaplin and Lubitsch see the correspondence between Sturges and the two directors in Box 64, Folder 23, and Box 75, Folder 42, in Preston Sturges Papers, UCLA-SC. Max Ophuls and Robert Siodmak expressed their gratitude for what Sturges did for the German refugees in their autobiographies. See Max Ophüls, *Spiel und Dasein* (Stuttgart: Henry Groverts, 1961), 224, and Robert Siodmak, *Zwischen Berlin und Hollywood* (Munich: Harbig, 1980), 97.

136. Preston Sturges to Crowther January 19, 1942, Sturges Papers, Box 65,

Folder 31, UCLA-SC.

137. In the final version, a bunch of convicts watch a Disney short. Originally Sturges wanted to cite Chaplin as an example, though he ultimately settled for Disney. See Jacobs, *Christmas in July*, 257.

138. *Daily Worker*, January 30, 1942, 7. Ferguson, *Criticism*, 410–11.

139. Ernst Lubitsch, "Mr. Lubitsch Takes the Floor for Rebuttal," *New York Times*, March 29, 1942, sec. 8, p. 3.

140. *Daily Worker*, March 8, 1947, 7. *New York Times*, March 7, 1942, 13. Farber is in *New Republic*, September 7, 1942, 283. Agee is in *Time*, March 16, 1942, 90. On the refugees' reaction see "An Interview with Walter Reisch," in Herman Weinberg, *The Lubitsch Touch* (New York: Dutton, 1968), 215–25. On Rosza and Lubitsch, see also Scott Eyman, *Ernst Lubitsch: Laughter in Paradise* (New York: Simon & Schuster, 1993), 295. At the 1943 UCLA Writers' Congress, Virginia Wright and David Hanna termed the film "the most ridiculous picture dealing with Nazism." See Virginia Wright and David Hanna, "Motion Picture Survey," Box 1, Folder The Nature of the Enemy, Writers' Congress Papers, UCLA-SC.

141. Donald Crafton, "Pie and Chase: Gag, Spectacle and Narrative in Slapstick Comedy," in Henry Jenkins and Kristine Karnick, *The Classical Hollywood Comedy* (New York: Routledge, 1995), 106–19.

Chapter Five

1. Tina Daniel, "Interview with Marguerite Roberts and John Sanford," in Paul Buhle and Patrick McGilligan, *Tender Comrades* (New York: St. Martin's Press, 1997), 571–84. Joseph McBride, *Frank Capra: The Catastrophe of Success* (New York: Simon & Schuster, 1992), 459.

2. Sanford to Capra, May 2, 1942, cited in McBride, *Frank Capra*, 463. Sanford was indeed a communist and was identified as such by Martin Berkeley in 1951. See Tina Daniel, "Interview with Marguerite Roberts and John Sanford," and McBride, *Frank Capra*, 561.

3. William E. Leuchtenburg, "The New Deal and the Analogue of War," *The FDR Years* (New York: Columbia University Press, 1996), 35–74. On the United States's unpreparedness see William O'Neil, *A Democracy at War* (New York: The Free Press, 1995), 75–103.

4. O'Neil, *A Democracy at War*, 75–103.

5. Among them, of course, Pare Lorentz's *The Plow That Broke the Plains* (1936) and *The River* (1938) had been the most successful in endorsing, respectively, Rexford Tugwell's Relocation Authority and the Tennessee Valley Authority. On Hollywood and the Roosevelt administration, the best account is the recent Giuliana Muscio, *Hollywood's New Deal* (Philadelphia: Temple University Press, 1996). For a comparative approach to Lorentz, see also Peter C. Rollins, "Ideology and Film Rhetoric: Three Documentaries of the New Deal Era (1936–1941)," in Peter C. Rollins, *Hollywood as Historian* (Lexington: University Press of Kentucky, 1983), 32–48.

6. Richard W. Steele, *Propaganda in an Open Society* (Westport, Conn.: Greenwood Press, 1985).

7. Gregory D. Black and Clayton R. Koppes, *Hollywood Goes to War: How Politics, Profits, and Propaganda Shaped World War Two Movies* (New York: The Free Press, 1987), 48–81.

8. Ibid.

9. O'Neil, *A Democracy at War*, 250.

10. Customarily, prior to the war overseas distribution made up one third of the profit of a film. After the war started, Hollywood still relied on the Latin American and British markets to contribute a sizable share of a film's net profits after the booming domestic market had covered production and distribution costs. See John Izod, *Hollywood and the Box Office, 1895–1986* (New York: Columbia University Press, 1988), 111–31. On the role of Bell see Black and Koppes, *Hollywood Goes to War*.

11. War Activities Committee 1945 report, *Movies at War: Report of the WAC of the Motion Picture Industry* (Washington, D.C.: War Activities Committee, 1945), 28. Cited in Doherty, *Projections of War* (New York: Columbia University Press, 1993), 60.

12. See the "Government Information Manual for the Motion Picture Industry," dated June 2, 1942. Emphasis in original. Reprinted in *Historical Journal of Film, Radio, and Television* 3 (1983): 171–80.

13. Walter Wanger to Gardner Cowles, Jr., July 30, 1942, Box 3, Folder Motion Pictures, Series E. 6B, OWI Papers, Records of the Office of the Director, National Archives Records Administration, Suitland, Maryland.

14. Black and Koppes, *Hollywood Goes to War*, 65–81.

15. Association of Motion Pictures Producers, Inc., and Motion Pictures Producers and Distributors of America, "The Production Code," reprinted in John Belton, ed., *Movies and Mass Culture* (New Brunswick, N.J.: Rutgers University Press, 1996), 138.

16. Roy Hoopes, *When the Stars Went to War* (New York: Random House, 1994), 169–92.

17. Lang to Leo Weaver, May 12, 1942, Box 8, Folder W, Lang Papers, AFI-BH.

18. Célia Bertin, *Jean Renoir: A Life in Pictures* (1986; repr. Baltimore: Johns Hopkins University Press, 1991), 190.

19. See Michael Korda, *Charmed Lives* (New York: Avon Books, 1981).

20. *Aufbau*, October 2, 1942, 17.

21. *Aufbau*, February 20, 1942, 15.

22. 77th Congress, *Congressional Record. Senate*, 87 (Washington, D.C.: Government Printing Office, 1942): 9758–59. See also Geoffrey Perrett, *Days of Sadness, Years of Triumph: The American People, 1939–1945* (New York: Coward, McCann and Geoghegan, 1972), 218.

23. *Aufbau*, April 17, 1942, 17.

24. "Dieses Schicksaal Tausenden von Hitlerhassern, jüdischen und christlichen Antifaschisten, seit dem letzten Freitag im Staat Kalifornien zu Teil geworden ist!" Ralph Nunberg, "Wir klagen nicht an," *Aufbau*, April 3, 1942, 17.

25. In commenting on the deportations organized by the War Relocation Authority, the magazine showed the pervasiveness of the essentialist and racist notion of "Japanese people." "Most of us come from a mixture of European blood," the magazine argued, "and we can understand how a man of European descent thinks and feels—even though we do not agree with him. But the Japanese has an instinctive feeling for his Fathers, his family, and his living relatives, and this we cannot understand." ("man Die meisten von uns bestehen aus einer Mischung von europäischen Blut, und wir können verstehen, wie ein Mann europäischer Abstammung denkt und fühlt—selbst wenn wir nicht mit ihm übereinstimmen. Aber der Japaner hat eines instinktives Gefühl für seine Vorfahren, seine Familien und seine lebenden Verwandten, und die können wir nicht verstehen"). *Aufbau*, February 6, 1942, 15.

26. Lang to Willy [?], February 2, 1942, Box 8, Folder Miscellanea, Lang Papers, AFI-BH.

27. Captain Gordon S. Mitchell to Fritz Lang, June 5, 1942, Box 6, Folder A, Lang Papers, AFI-BH.

28. Robert Sklar, *Movie-Made America: A Cultural History of the American Movies* (New York: Random House, 1975), 249.

29. Robert Siodmak, *Zwischen Berlin und Hollywood* (Munich: Harbig, 1980), 150–51.

30. Salka Viertel, *The Kindness of Strangers* (New York: Holt, Rinehart, and Winston, 1969), 265.

31. John Francis Kreidl, *Nicholas Ray* (Boston: Twayne, 1977), 24.

32. Roy Hoopes, *When the Stars Went to War*, 169.

33. John Bright, *John Bright*, interviewed by Larry Ceplair (Los Angeles: University of California Oral History Project, 1991), 25.

34. Edward Dmytryk, *Odd Man Out* (Carbondale: Southern Illinois University Press, 1996), 4.

35. See Joseph McBride, *Frank Capra: The Catastrophe of Success* (New York: Simon & Schuster, 1992), 457–65.

36. Philip Dunne to T. H. Westerman, 1943 (no month, no day), Box 5, Folder Correspondence 1943–44, Dunne Papers, USC-Cinema and Television Library (USC-CTL).

37. Viertel to Houseman, April 9, 1942, Box 1, Folder 3, Houseman Papers, UCLA-SC.

38. Philip Dunne, *Take Two: A Life in Movies and Politics* (1980; updated ed. New York: Limelight Editions, 1992), 165. For Congressional attacks on OWI see Holly Cowan Shulman, *The Voice of America: Propaganda and Democracy, 1941–45* (Madison: University of Wisconsin Press, 1990), passim.

39. *Aufbau*, May 14, 1943, 11. Donald Hough noted that this was also a problem as American actors were complaining that "the recent influx of foreign players, directors and technicians is taking too much money from American picture people, without superior ability." Donald Hough, "War Is Changing the Movies," *Los Angeles Times*, March 15, 1942.

40. Salka Viertel to Lube [?], n.d., Viertel Nachlass, Schiller National Museum, Deutsches Literaturarchiv, Marbach am Neckar.

41. Dunne to Frank G. Andrews Civil Aeronautic Administration, April 14, 1943, Box 5, Folder Correspondence 1943–44, Dunne Papers, USC-CTL.

42. See McBride, *Frank Capra*, 449.

43. Harold Medford, "Report from a GI Typewriter," *Screenwriter* 1 (June 1945): 15–22. Lester Koenig, "Back from the War," *Screenwriter* 1 (August 1945): 23–28. Robert R. Presnell, "The Great Parenthesis," *Screen Writer* 1 (September 1945): 12–16. Donal Trumbo, "Notes on a Summer Vacation," *Screenwriter* 1 (September 1945): 17–41. Sidney Buchman, "A Writer in VIP Clothing," *Screenwriter* 1 (October 1945): 17–31. Thomas Spencer Jones, "Can They Still Look Back?" *Screenwriter* 1 (December 1945): 31–35.

44. John Huston, *An Open Book* (New York: Knopf, 1980), 90–91.

45. Between his film crew and the crew of the Canadian Corvette hunting U-boats in the Atlantic, Ivens told an anonymous interviewer in 1944, "there was a kind of comraderie with jokes about how the movie people were not fast enough." Ivens, "Interview," 1944, untitled and undated, Folder 4, Joris Ivens–Herman Shumlin Collection, AMPAS.

46. John Howard Lawson, "The Obligatory Scene," *New Theater* 3 (March 1936): 18–19.

47. On William Clothier see *American Cinematographer*, August 1946, 21a–22a; Win Sharples, Jr., "A Conversation with William Clothier," *Filmmakers Newsletter*, August 1973, 27–31.

48. *New Masses*, May 2, 1944, 28. James Agee, *The Nation*, April 15, 1944. Repr. in James Agee, *James Agee on Film: Comments and Reviews* (New York: Beacon Press, 1964), 88.

49. Joris Ivens, script for *Action Stations!*, undated. Folder 4, Ivens-Shumlin Collection, AMPAS.

50. See Midge Mackenzie, *John Huston War Stories*, Barnsbury Productions, 1998. See also Huston, *An Open Book*, 125–26.

51. See Midge Mackenzie, *John Huston War Stories*.

52. Edgerton's other claim—that they were also "conservative in ideology"—seems to me hardly justifiable within the historical context of these films and their times. See Gary Edgerton, "Revisiting the Recordings of War Past: Remembering the Documentary Trilogy of John Huston," in Gaylyn Studlar and David Desser, eds., *Reflections in a Male Eye* (Washington, D.C.: Smithsonian Institution, 1993), 33–61.

53. Joris Ivens, "Notes on Documentary Film," June 11, 1943, Folder 14, Joris Ivens-Herman Shumlin Papers, AMPAS.

54. Hermine Rich Isaacs, "War Front and Film Fronts," *Theater Arts*, June 1944, 345.

55. McBride, *Frank Capra*, 460–63.

56. On the film see McBride, *Frank Capra*, 497–98. John W. Dower has stressed how the film "was a potpourri of most of the English-speaking world dominant cliches about the Japanese enemy." See John W. Dower, *War without Mercy* (New York: Pantheon, 1986), 19–23.

57. The most penetrating analysis of Capra's documentaries is contained in Thomas Doherty, *Projections of War* (New York: Columbia University Press, 1993), 16–35.

58. As late as the fall of 1940 Roosevelt stated off the record that the United States would not declare war on Germany even if Germany declared war on the United States. If they did, historian Gerhard L. Weinberg reports, "the Americans would defend themselves only if others attacked." See Gerhard L. Weinberg, "From Confrontation to Cooperation: Germany and the United States, 1933–1949," in Frank Trommler and Joseph McVeigh, eds., *America and the Germans*, 2 vols. (Philadelphia: University of Pennsylvania Press, 1985), 2:50.

59. *New Masses*, September 21, 1943, 30.

60. The script that Lillian Hellman had originally prepared for William Wyler was the story of a chance meeting between a black soldier, John, and a young, dissatisfied black youth, Chris, on the eighteenth anniversary of the Emancipation Proclamation. In the course of the evening, which included Joe Louis's fight over the radio, the recounting of a lynching, and a concert of Paul Robeson at the Lincoln Memorial, John succeeds in convincing Chris that the America of Lincoln is worth fighting for even though the lynchers are present both inside and outside the United States. Fraught with Cultural Front myths and icons— from Paul Robeson singing Earl Robinson's *Ballad for Americans* to the Lincoln Memorial—Hellman's script nonetheless made African Americans' experience in America a blemish in the nation's ideal of social justice by explicitly referring to John's experiences of lynching, Jim Crow segregation, and black poverty. If the film affirmed the necessity for African Americans to fight for the United States, it also stressed that at stake was a better future rather than an uncertain present, and a shameful past. Capra rejected the script, and when William Wyler balked, Capra assigned the project to director Stuart Heisler, a moderate and, overall, untalented filmmaker. He also commissioned African-American playwright Carlton Moss to write a new story, whose "black rebelliousness," he says in his autobiography, he also toned down. Part of the problem was also the director Capra chose, who seemed to have had little enthusiasm for the project. "The film," Heisler himself told a reporter a few months after its release, "only sharpened existing prejudice . . . [and] was well received only in areas where the intelligence level has prevented the growth of racial prejudice." Lillian Hellman's script is in Box 10, Folder 1, Stuart Heisler Collection, UCLA-SC. Heisler's quote is from "Advance for AMS," July 1, 1944, Box 10, Folder 3, Stuart Heisler Collection, UCLA-SC. On the film see also Frank Capra, *The Name above the Title* (New York: MacMillan, 1971), 358–62.

61. Michael Paul Rogin, "Ronald Reagan, the Movie," in Rogin, *Ronald Reagan, the Movie* (Los Angeles: University of California Press, 1987), 1–43.

62. Paul Virilio, *War and Cinema* (1984; Eng. trans. New York: Verso, 1989), 58.

63. James Agee, *The Nation*, October 30, 1943. Repr. in Agee, *James Agee on Film*, 56.

64. Ibid.

65. *World*, March 27, 1898, 15.

66. See *Roosevelt's Rough Riders* (1898); *Skirmish of Rough Riders* (1898); *Advance of Kansas Volunteers at Callocan* (1898). On these films see my "Did Private Nolan Get His Glory? Movies Press and Audiences during the Spanish American War," *Columbia Journal of American Studies* 3(1) (1998): 141–58.

67. Jeanine Basinger, *The WWII American Combat Film* (New York: Columbia University Press, 1986), 37.

68. See Koppes and Black, *Hollywood Goes to War*, 256.

69. Paul Schiller, "Ausländer-boom in Hollywood?," *Aufbau*, February 19, 1943, 9. This did not fail to worry Hedda Hopper who attacked the refugees for being overpaid. See *Aufbau*, March 17, 1943, 20; *Aufbau*, April 4, 1943, 11; and *Aufbau*, November 11, 1943, 15. Hopper had already attacked the refugees before Pearl Harbor. See her syndicated column for October 29, 1941, Hopper Scrapbook Collection, AMPAS.

70. Cited in James K. Lyon, *Bertolt Brecht in America* (Princeton: Princeton University Press, 1980), 46.

71. Hans Kafka reports the news in his columns in "Hollywood Calling," in *Aufbau* February 19, 1943, 15. Berlin actor Roland Varno stepped in, in place of Lederer. When Lang was doing the casting for *Hangmen*, Thomas Mitchell refused to be cast as a quisling. "Tell Lang—no—wouldn't play a Quisling for all the tea in China," wrote Mitchell to Johnnie Maccio. T. W. Baumfeld to Lang, September 3, 1942, *Hangmen Also Die* File, Lang papers, USC-CTL.

72. Frederik Kohner, *The Magician of Sunset Boulevard*, (1974; repr. San Francisco: Morgan Press, 1977), 121.

73. OWI's review of the feature film, April 5, 1943, no author, Folder *Mr. Lucky*, Group Record NND 785067, NARA, Suitland, Maryland. On the film see also Black and Koppes, *Hollywood Goes to War*, 106–7.

74. And yet, the legacy of the gangster—an efficient, but scarcely disciplined or morally motivated combatant—was ambiguous enough to serve more than one purpose and could not be entirely discarded. The gangster was evil, and yet all-American; violent, and yet perfectly equipped for a war. In speeches delivered by Edward G. Robinson during the conflict, the actor constructed a complicated and fascinating dialogue between himself and his screen persona, one in which the legacy of the gangster was both called upon and exorcised. In a speech delivered at a meeting of civilians to collect war bonds, the gangster was used as a counterpart of Hitler, a threat to society. See speech titled "Little Caesar," 1944, Box 30, Folder 4, Edward G. Robinson Papers, USC-Cinema and Television Library. In other instances, however, Little Caesar, the tough immigrant from the Chicago slums, allowed Robinson to relate to the violence of the soldiers' experience, and, in part at least, to their social class. Through Little Caesar, Robinson—the wealthy, refined art collector who had not been able to enlist because of his age—metamorphosed into a working-class American trained in the business of kill or be killed, and whose physical courage was not redoubtable. In one speech he delivered on an army base, Robinson took a submachine gun out of a violin case and shouted, "Pipe down, you mugs, or I'll let you have it. . . . This it the Kid himself talking—Little

Caesar, remember?" Robinson then proceeded to tell the story of Little Caesar. The gangster wanted to enlist but was given a 4F by the draft board. "As far as we are concerned," the doctors tell him, "you'll never be Edward G.I. [*sic*] Robinson." But, contrary to the board's recommendations, Little Caesar goes to war anyway. Robinson switched back to himself at the end of the speech, telling the soldiers that this is the "most privileged moment of my life, . . . [because] I have seen the men who are defeating Hitler." Edward G. Robinson, Speech dated June 16, 1944, Box 30, Folder 2, Robinson Papers, USC-CTL.

75. *New Republic*, September 7, 1942, 283.

76. *New York Times*, November 18, 1943, 29.

77. *New Masses*, December 7, 1943, 27.

78. Jack Warner to General H. H. Arnold, April 7, 1943, *Air Force* Production File, USC-WB.

79. The anti-Japanese racism was also denounced by several observers, among them R. M. MacIver from Columbia University's Department of Sociology and Lawrence Jaffa of the YMCA. MacIver to Warner, April 30 1943; Yaffa to Warner, May 3, 1943, *Air Force* Production Files, USC-WB.

80. Poynter to Warner, February 4, 1943, and Bell to Warner, February 6, 1943, *Air Force* Production File, USC-WB.

81. *Daily Mirror*, February 4, 1943, 31.

82. Alex Evelove to Hurt Blumenstock, October 29, 1942, *Air Force* Production File, USC-WB. On the film's credits see also Robert Sklar, *City Boys* (Princeton: Princeton University Press, 1991), 143.

83. Dudley Nichols, Treatment for *Air Force*, *Air Force* Script File, USC-WB.

84. *Air Force* Production Sheet, no author, no date, *Air Force* Production File, USC-WB.

85. *The Nation*, February 20, 1943. Repr. in Agee, *James Agee on Film*, 38–39.

86. *Daily Worker*, February 10, 1943, 7. *Air Force* Clipping File, USC-WB.

87. *The People's World*, March 27, 1943, 4. *Air Force* Clipping File, USC-WB. For OWI's dismay before anti-Japanese films such as *Little Tokyo, USA*, see Koppes and Black, *Hollywood Goes to War*, 72–78.

88. Ioris Ivens, Lecture, March 24, 1943, Folder 14, Ivens-Shumlin Papers, AMPAS.

89. W. M. Wright to Jack Warner, May 22, 1942, *Air Force* Production Files, USC-WB.

90. Donald Hough, "War Is Changing the Movies," *Los Angeles Times*, March 15, 1942.

91. Obringer to Earl Davis, June 23, 1942; Herman Lissauer to Jack Sullivan, May 11, 1942, *Air Force* Production Files, USC-WB.

92. *Air Force* Production Notes, no date, *Air Force* Production Files, USC-WB.

93. Joseph McBride, *Hawks on Hawks* (Los Angeles: University of California Press, 1982), 90.

94. *Air Force* Production Notes, no date, *Air Force* Production Files, USC-WB.

95. Todd Rainsberger, *James Wong Howe, Cinematographer* (New York: A. S. Barnes, 1981), 22–23.

96. James Wong Howe, "Documentary Films and Hollywood Techniques," Box 3, Folder The Documentary Film, Writers' Congress Papers, UCLA-SC. Nor was Howe an isolated example. For the diffusion of 16 mm technique in Hollywood during the conflict, see Patricia R. Zimmermann, "Fighting with Film: 16 mm Amateur Film, World War II, and Participatory Realism," in Patricia R. Zimmermann, *Reel Families: A Social History of Amateur Film* (Bloomington: Indiana University, 1995), 90–111.

97. Lion Feuchtwanger, "On the character of the Germans and the Nazis," Box 1, Folder Writers in Exile, Writers Congress Collection, UCLA-SC.

98. Thomas Mann, "The Exiled Writer's Relation to His Homeland," Box 1, Folder Writers in Exile, Writers Congress Collection, UCLA-SC.

99. Thomas Mann, "Germany and the Germans," Mann, *Germany and the Germans* (Washington, D.C.: Library of Congress, 1945), 1–19. On the issue see Anthony Heilbut, *Exiled in Paradise* (Boston: Beacon Press, 1983), 325–49. Erhard Bahr, "Die Kontroverse um *Das andere Deutschland*," in John M. Spalek and Joseph Strelka, eds., *Deutschse Exilliteratur seit 1933*, 2 vols. (Bern, Switzerland: Francke Verlag, 1989). Herbert Lehnert, "Thomas Mann and Bertolt Brecht," in John M. Spalek and Robert Bell, *Exile: The Writers' Experience* (Chapel Hill: University of North Carolina Press, 1982), 187–201. On conservative American publicists and Germany see Hans W. Gatske, *Germany and the United States* (Cambridge: Harvard University Press, 1980), 136–40. Mann's position had been expressed in much less sophisticated and poignant terms by refugee Emil Ludwig, whose *How to Treat the Germans* (New York: Willard Publishing, 1943), endorsed the view that it was the German people's arrested development and natural disposition toward intellectual servility, rather than unemployment, that produced Nazism and Hitler. Ludwig advocated Germany's dismemberment, air bombing ("the vertical second front"), the public burning of all Nazi literature, and even a twenty-year ban of Richard Wagner's "Ring."

100. See "Germany without Illusions," *New Republic*, October 30, 1944, 553–56. Max Lerner, "A Plan for Germany," *The Nation*, October 7, 1944, 395–97. J. Jerome, "If Hitler Died Tomorrow," *New Masses*, April 27, 1943, 14–16. Hans Berger, "What About Germany?," *New Masses*, August 8, 1944, 3–6. If some of them—like Max Lerner—were opposed to the famous Morgenthau's plan for the total deindustrialization of Germany, it was because they interpreted the plan as a punishment for the German industrialists. See Lerner, "A Plan for Germany." On the Morgenthau plan see Carl C. Hodge and Cathal J. Nolan, " 'As Powerful as We Are': From the Morgenthau Plan to Marshall Aid," in Carl C. Hodge and Cathal J. Nolan, eds., *Shepherd of Democracy? America and Germany in the Nineteenth Century* (London: Greenwood Press, 1992), 56–72.

101. Edward G. Robinson, Untitled Speech, n.d. (1945?), Box 29, Folder 30, Robinson Papers, USC-CTL.

102. "Government Information Manual for the Motion Picture Industry," *Historical Journal of Film, Radio, and Television* 3 (1983): 176.

103. Wright and Hanna, "Motion Picture Survey," Folder The Nature of the Enemy, Writers' Congress Papers, UCLA-SC. Howard Eastbrook, "The Writer in

War and Peace," Folder The American Scene, Writers' Congress Papers, UCLA-SC.

104. Hans Kafka, "Hollywood Calling," *Aufbau*, January 15, 1943, 11.

105. *Aufbau*, March 5, 1943, 9.

106. See entry of August 1, 1943, Bertolt Brecht, *Journals, 1934–1945*, edited by John Willett, translated by Ralph Manheim (New York: Routledge, 1993), 288. See also Bertolt Brecht's lecture, "Das andere Deutschland," in Brecht, *Gesammelte Werke*, vol. xx (Frankfurt a.M.: Suhrkamp Verlag, 1967), 285–86.

107. See John Willett's editorial note, Brecht, *Journals 1934–1945*, 500.

108. On the original, Lang writes an initialized note "No answer" for his personal secretary. Brecht to Lang, n.d., Box 1, Folder 13, Lang Papers, USC-CTL.

109. Brecht to Tillich, April 1944, in Bertolt Brecht, *Letters* (London: Methuen, 1990), 378.

110. See John M. Spalek, "Research on the Intellectual Migration to the United States after 1933: Still in Need of an Assessment," in Trommler and McVeigh, eds., *America and the Germans*, 293.

111. Emmet Lavery to Lester Cowan, September 14, 1944, Box 3, Folder Correspondence, Writers' Congress Papers, UCLA-SC.

112. Ring Lardner, Jr., "Tomorrow a New Germany?," *Screenwriter* 1 (July 1945): 15–18.

113. Lubitsch had planned to narrate the last hundred years of German history through the character of a fictional German, Joseph Schmidt, demonstrating a continuity between Bismarck's Germany and Hitler's Reich. On the film's production, see Scott Eyman, *Ernst Lubitsch: Laughing in Paradise* (New York: Simon & Schuster, 1993), 310. Capra's film followed this lead, recounting how from Sedan onward, Germany feigned peacefulness and compunction after each war. Germany is, however, according to the film, like "Dr Jekyll and Mr Hyde." The problem, the commentary of the film asserts over the images of a crowd of Germans, is that "Germans are all the same."

114. Fritz Lang, "Über die Zusammenarbeit mit Brecht an *Hangmen also Die*," in Jurgen Schebera, *Hangmen also Die. Drehbuch und Materialen zum Film* (Berlin: Henschel Verlag, 1985), 163–70.

115. Edward G. Robinson, "Interview notes," undated, Box 30, Folder 4, Robinson Papers, USC-CTL.

Chapter Six

1. See Thomas Schatz, *Boom and Bust: The American Cinema in the 1940s* (New York: Scribner's, 1997), 285–328. On the federal government and the Paramount case see Giuliana Muscio, *Hollywood's New Deal* (Philadelphia: Temple University Press, 1996).

2. Indeed, by July 1942 Sturges's restaurant was such a well-known place of anti-fascist activities that it had become the target of anti-Semitic attacks. In July, a manager of the restaurant informed Sturges that a Mr. Reeve from Santa Monica had called to ask whether Charlie Chaplin was at the restaurant and warned the

restaurant that "at ten o'clock a bomb was to go off, or someone would start a fight to completely wreck the place, or something would happen. . . . He said he did not care what I did or if we believed him, but he knew for a fact that an attack of some kind was to be made because of the Jews we have here. . . . Just before hanging up he said it might be at ten or at eleven, but when the time was ripe and there were enough Jewish people here it would happen." Unsigned memo of Players' employee, possibly to Preston Sturges, July 12, 1942, Box 55, Folder 5, Sturges Collection, UCLA-SC.

3. Preston Sturges, *Hail the Conquering Hero*, temporary script, June 13, 1943, Box 8, Folder 11, Preston Sturges Papers, UCLA-SC.

4. Sturges to Mrs. George Kaufman, May 15, 1944, Box 54, Folder 3, Sturges Papers, UCLA-SC.

5. In *Miracle on Morgan Creek*, Sturges told the story of the simple-minded and militarily unfit Norval Jones (played by Eddie Bracken), who marries Trudy Kockenlocker (played by Betty Hutton), who has been seduced and abandoned by a marine.

6. Sturges to Mrs. George Kaufman, May 15, 1944, Box 54, Folder 3, Sturges Collection, UCLA-SC.

7. Box 3, Folder Appendix, Writers' Congress Papers, UCLA-SC.

8. "Writers Congress 1943, Program," Box 3, Folder Ephemera, Writers' Congress Papers, UCLA-SC.

9. *Los Angeles Times*, October 2, 1943, no page. Writers' Congress, Clipping File, UCLA University Archives.

10. James Wong Howe, "Documentary Films and Hollywood Techniques," Box 1, Folder The Documentary Film, Writers' Congress Papers, UCLA-SC.

11. "Notes on the Discussion," Box 1, Folder The American Scene, Writers' Congress Papers, UCLA-SC.

12. Virginia Wright and David Hanna, "Motion Picture Survey," Box 1, Folder The Nature of the Enemy, Writers' Congress Papers, UCLA-SC.

13. Joris Ivens, "Notes on Documentary Film," June 11, 1943, Folder 13, Ivens-Shumlin Papers, AMPAS; and "The Documentary Film and Morale," Box 1, Folder The Documentary Film, Writers' Congress Papers, UCLA-SC.

14. See Thomas Doherty, *Projections of War* (New York: Columbia University Press, 1994), 181–204.

15. For instance, Mayer had been instrumental in getting Pare Lorentz's *The Plough that Broke the Plains* distributed in commercial theaters. See Robert Snyder, *Pare Lorentz and the Documentary Film* (Norman: University of Oklahoma Press, 1968), 32–48.

16. Arthur L. Mayer, "Documentary Film and Box Office," Box 1, Folder The Documentary Film, Writers' Congress Papers, UCLA-SC.

17. *New Masses*, May 9, 1939, 28.

18. Paul Lazarsfeld, "An Episode in the History of Social Research," in Donald Fleming and Bernard Bailyn, eds., *The Intellectual Migration* (Cambridge: Harvard University Press, 1969): 270–337.

19. Ibid.

20. Paul Lazarsfeld and Robert K. Merton, "Studies in Radio and Film Propaganda," *Transactions of the New York Academy of Science*, 6(2) (December 1943): 58–

75.

21. Kenneth Macgowan, "Festival Valuable to the Screen," *Mohawk Drama*, 1939, no page, Box 51, Folder 2, Macgowan Papers, UCLA-SC.

22. Macgowan to Mildred Raskin (executive secretary of the People's Educational Center), May 31, 1946, Box 69, Folder 16, Macgowan Papers, UCLA-SC.

23. William F. Ogburn to Macgowan, November 2, 1945, Box 69, Folder 16, Macgowan Papers, UCLA-SC.

24. Macgowan Papers, Box 60, Folder 10, UCLA-SC.

25. Los Angeles *Daily News*, June 8, 1946.

26. Undated UCLA press release related to Macgowan's appointment. Kenneth Macgowan File, UCLA-University Archives.

27. Kenneth Macgowan, draft of "Hollywood Learning and Reaching," possibly published in *National Theater Council Bulletin* in 1945, Box 59, Folder 12, Macgowan Papers, UCLA-SC.

28. Hans Kafka, "Hollywood Calling," *Aufbau*, November 9, 1945, 19. See also the partially dated clipping in Folder Actors Lab, Series III, Roman Bohnen Collection, NYPL-BR.

29. Bohnen to Cheryl Crawford, October 21, 1945, Box 3, Folder Crawford, Series II, Roman Bohnen Collection, NYPL-BR.

30. Roger Morris, *Richard Milhous Nixon: The Rise of an American Politician* (New York: Henry Holt, 1990), 540–46, and Helen Gahagan Douglas, *A Full Life* (Garden City, N.Y.: Doubleday, 1982), 240–44. See also Greg Mitchell, *Tricky Dick and the Pink Lady* (New York: Random House, 1998).

31. Among them: Humphrey Bogart, Jean Arthur, John Cromwell, John Garfield, Irvin Pichel, Edward G. Robinson, Emmet Lavery, Lena Horne, and Ring Lardner, Jr., to Herman Shumlin, Charles Boyer, Paulette Goddard, William Wyler, and Lewis Milestone. See the stationery for the Scully campaign in Box 1, Folder Miscellanea, Hollywood Studio Strike Collection, UCLA-SC.

32. Emmet Lavery, "You Never Can Tell," *Screenwriter* 2 (August 1946): 29–35.

33. Undated memo of Samuele T. Farquhar to Clarence Dykstra, Series 335, Box 77, Folder 12, UCLA-University Archives.

34. Verbatim transcription of the memorial service for Kenneth Macgowan, May 3, 1963, Box 83, Folder Miscellanea, Macgowan Papers, UCLA-SC.

35. Houseman to State Department functionary (name illegible), May 17, 1955, Box 5, Folder M, Houseman Papers, UCLA-SC.

36. Jim Windolf, "From *Best Years* to Our Years," *New York Observer*, March 24, 1997, 21. *Best Years* won the Oscar for Best Picture, Best Screenplay (Robert Sherwood), Best Director (Wyler), Best Music (Hugo Friedhofer), Best Actor (Frederic March), Best Editing (Daniel Mandell), and Best Supporting Actor (Harold Russell).

37. Hermine Rich Isaacs, "The Picture of Our Lives," *Theater Arts* 31 (January 1947): 39–43.

38. See William Wyler, "No Magic Wand," *Screenwriter* 1 (February 1946): 1–14.

39. K.H., "Hollywood nach dem Krieg. Ein Interview mit Billy Wilder," *Aufbau*, May 7, 1943, 10.

40. Albert Maltz, "War Film Quality," *New York Times*, August 19, 1945, sec. 2, p. 3.

41. H. R. Isaacs, "A Picture of Our Lives," *Theater Arts* 31 (January 1947): 39.

42. Dalton Trumbo, "Minorities and the Screen," Box 1, Folder Minority Groups, Writers' Congress Papers, UCLA-SC. See also The Writers' Congress, "A Declaration of Principles to the American Entertainment Industry," Box 1, Folder Resolutions, Writers' Congress Papers, UCLA-SC.

43. Harry Hoijier, "Statement of the Problem," Box 1, Folder Minority Groups, Writers' Congress Papers, UCLA-SC.

44. Congressional Record, vol. 90, pt. 8, 1143–44. See also Larry Ceplair and Steven Englund, *The Inquisition in Hollywood* (1979; rev. ed. Berkeley: University of California Press, 1983), 212.

45. Congressional Record, vol. 91, pt. 6, July 18, 1945, 7737. Incidentally, Rankin quoted Max Ophuls (whose name he misspelled as "Max Opels") as "the refugee French Communist who is now one of the new motion pictures directors" although Ophuls would not realize a movie in Hollywood until *The Exile* in 1947.

46. Sid, "Time to Name Names," *Variety*, March 15, 1944, 3.

47. Carey McWilliams, "Hollywood Gray List," *The Nation*, November 19, 1949, 491–92. On the strike, see also Schwartz, *The Hollywood Writers' War*, 220–32, and Schatz, *Boom and Bust*, 156–58, and 305–7.

48. Ceplair and Englund, *The Inquisition in Hollywood.*

49. The English translation of Duclos's article "On the Dissolution of the American Communist Party" is in *Political Affairs* 24 (July 1945): 656–72. See also Maurice Isserman, *Which Side Were You On?* (New York: Oxford University Press, 1984), 217–20. On Browder see James G. Ryan, *Earl Browder: The Failure of American Communism* (Tuscaloosa: University of Alabama Press, 1997), 243–73.

50. Paul Buhle and Patrick McGilligan, *Tender Comrades* (New York: St. Martin's Press, 1997), 37.

51. Cited in Nancy Schwartz, *The Hollywood Writers' War* (New York: Knopf, 1982), 225.

52. *New York Times*, August 20, 1952, Schoenfeld Clipping File, NYPL-BR.

53. Victor Navaski, *Naming Names* (New York: Penguin Books, 1981), 264.

54. For the reference to the "proletarian pioneers" see Mike Gold. "Notes on the Cultural Front," *New Masses*, December 7, 1937, 1–5. *Daily Worker*, February 12, 1946, 6.

55. See Mike Gold, "Notes on the Cultural Front," *New Masses*, December 7, 1937, 1–6. Kenneth Macgowan, "Some Gleams of Hope in Hollywood," *New York Times*, August 11, 1946, sec 6, pp. 20, 38–39. Mike Gold to Macgowan, September 1, 1946, Box 68, Folder 9, Macgowan Papers, UCLA-SC.

56. Jerome had expressed doubts about the timid appreciation of Hollywood films contained in Lawson's *Theory and Techniques of Playwriting and Screenwriting* (New York: Putnam's, 1949), in Victor J. Jerome, *The Negro in Hollywood Films* (New York: Mass and Mainstream, 1950). See John Howard Lawson, *The Film in the Battle of the Ideas* (New York: Mass and Mainstream, 1953), 21.

57. Summarizing Greenberg's thought, Diana Crane correctly writes that for Greenberg "avant-garde aesthetic tradition and popular culture were totally dissimilar and that any contact between them would endanger the former." Diana Crane, *The Transformation of the Avant-Garde: The New York Art World, 1940–85* (Chicago: University of Chicago Press, 1987), 64.

58. Clement Greenberg, "Avant-Garde and Kitsch," in Clement Greenberg, *Art and Culture: Critical Essays* (Boston: Beacon Press, 1961), 3–21.

59. Lionel Trilling, "The Situation in American Writing: A Symposium," *Partisan Review* 6 (Fall 1939): 111. On the relationship between Trilling and the middle-class audience, see Thomas Bender, "Lionel Trilling and American Culture," *American Quarterly* 42 (1990): 324–47. Repr. in Thomas Bender, *Intellect and Public Life* (Baltimore: Johns Hopkins University Press, 1993), 106–24.

60. Lionel Trilling, "The Function of the Little Magazine," introductory essay to William Phillips and Philip Rohv, eds., *The Partisan Reader: Ten Years of Partisan Review, 1933–1944* (New York: Dial Press, 1946). Repr. in Lionel Trilling, *The Liberal Imagination* (New York: Doubleday, 1957), 97–98.

61. Clement Greenberg, "The Later Thirties in New York," in Greenberg, *Art and Culture*, 231.

62. Albert Maltz, "What Shall We Ask of Writers," *New Masses*, February 12, 1946, 19–23. Maltz was a graduate of Columbia College and the Yale Drama School, a former member of the Theater Union, and the recipient of the 1938 O'Henry Memorial Award. In 1935, his play *Black Pit* won the 1935 *New Theatre*'s Award for the best play against war and fascism. Maltz had won an Academy Award for the anti-racist short *The House I Live In* and had written the critical and popular successes *Destination Tokyo* (with Delmer Daves) and *Pride of the Marines.*

63. Samuel Sillen, "Which Way Left Wing Literature?" published in six installments. *Daily Worker*, February 11, 1946, 6; *Daily Worker*, February 12, 1946, 6 and 8; *Daily Worker*, February 13, 1946, 6 and 8; *Daily Worker*, February 14, 1946, 6 and 9; *Daily Worker*, February 15, 1946, 6; *Daily Worker*, February 16, 1946, 6. See also Howard Fast, "Art and Politics," *New Masses*, February 26, 1946, 6–8; Joseph North, "No Retreat for the Writers," *New Masses*, February 26, 1946, 9–10; Alvah Bessie, "What Is Freedom for Writers?" *New Masses*, March 12, 1946, 8–10; John Howard Lawson, "Art Is a Weapon," *New Masses*, March 19, 1946, 18–20; William Z. Foster, "People's Cultural Policy," *New Masses*, April 23, 1946, 6–10. By that time Maltz had made a public self-criticism ("Moving Forward," *New Masses*, April 9, 1946, 8–10, 21–22) where he had admitted his "mistakes" and agreed with Sillen.

64. See Ronald Radosh, "The Blacklist as History," *The New Criterion*, December 1997, 12–17. Even an excellent account such as that by Daniel Aaron, for example, does not cite the contributions in favor of Maltz's position that *New Masses* published. See Aaron, *Writers on the Left*, 386–89. See, for instance, Sanora Babb, "Another Viewpoint," *New Masses*, March 12, 1946, 10.

65. Babb, "Another Viewpoint," 10.

66. S. L. and Eugene Feldman in "Readers' Forum," *New Masses*, March 12, 1946, 11. B. G. and Edna Richter in "Readers' Forum," *New Masses*, March 19,

1946, 21.

67. Joseph North, "The Artist's Dilemma," *New Masses*, February 26, 1946, 10.

68. See Sillen, "Art as a Weapon," *Daily Worker*, February 13, 1946, 4; Sillen, "Ideology and Art," *Daily Worker*, February 14, 1946, 9. Trilling, "The Function of the Little Magazine," *The Partisan Reader*, 88–99. Regardless of the party's reaction to Maltz, many Hollywoodians appear to have been responsive to Maltz's concerns. Interestingly, when Hollywood finally produced *Studs Lonigan* (1960) from the novel by James T. Farrell, himself one of the principal victims of the party's cultural blunders, several former members of the Cultural Front showed up in the film's credits. The film was directed by Irving Lerner, independently produced by Philip Yordan, and written by Arnaud D'Usseau and Bernard Gordon (though Yordan also contributed to the script writing). On the film see Pat McGilligan, *Backstory 2: Interviews with Screenwriters of the 1940s and the 1950s* (Berkeley: University of California Press, 1991), 342.

69. Robert K. Merton, *Mass Persuasion: The Social Psychology of a War Bond Drive* (New York: Harper, 1946), 12.

70. Paul F. Lazarsfeld, *The People Look at the Radio* (Chapel Hill: University of North Carolina Press, 1946), 12.

71. Ibid., 48–49.

72. Ibid., 70.

73. Dwight Macdonald, "Masscult & Midcult," in Macdonald, *Against the American Grain* (1962; repr. New York: Da Capo, 1983), 73. Originally published in *Partisan Review* 26 (Spring 1960). Before being revised and published in this form, the essay was first published as "A Theory of Popular Culture" in *Politics* (February 1944), then revised as "A Theory of Mass Culture" in *Diogenes* (Summer 1953).

74. Kenneth Macgowan, "Some Gleams of Hope in Hollywood," *New York Times*, August 11, 1946, sec. 16, pp. 20, 38–39.

75. Alexander Hammid, "New Fields—New Techniques," *Screenwriter* 1 (May 1946): 21–27.

76. Ivens to Leyda, February 5, 1941, Alphabetical Correspondence, Folder Ivens, Leyda Papers, NYU-TL.

77. Charles K. Feldman to Joris Ivens, February 1, 1943, Folder 875, Feldman Collection, American Film Institute.

78. *PM*, November 27, 1945, 20. See also Joris Ivens, *The Camera and I* (1969; repr. New York: The International Publishers, 1974), 242–45.

79. *Screenwriter* 9 (September 1946): 10–11.

80. Lewis Jacobs, *The Rise of American Cinema* (New York: Harcourt & Brace, 1939), 468. Curtis Harrington, "The Dangerous Compromise," *Hollywood Quarterly* 3 (1947–48): 405.

81. Lewis Jacobs, "Experimental Cinema in America," *Hollywood Quarterly* 3 (1947–48): 111–24 and 278–93.

82. See Scot MacDonald, "Cinema 16: Documents toward a History of the Film Society," *Wide Angle* 19 (1997): 8.

83. Siegfried Kracauer, "Filming the Subconscious," *Theater Arts* 32 (February

1948): 37–38.

84. See "An Interview with Amos Vogel," in *Wide Angle* 19 (1997): 70. See also Lauren Rabinovitz, "Experimental and Avant-Garde Cinema in the 1940s," in Thomas Schatz, *Boom and Bust: The American Cinema in the 1940s* (New York: Scribner's, 1997), 447–50.

85. Cited in Scot MacDonald, "Cinema 16," 9.

86. Ibid., 61.

87. See Hans Richter, *The Struggle for the Film* (1976; repr. New York: St. Martin's Press, 1986), a very Brechtian theory of filmmaking that Richter wrote in the 1930s, though he failed to get it published. It is interesting to note that in 1941, Richter had asked Fox producer Kenneth Macgowan for employment in the Hollywood studio. See Lang to Macgowan, November 26, 1941, Box 7, Folder Mc, Lang Collection, AFI-BH.

88. The citation is from the film. The six episodes are ordered as follows: (1) Max Ernst, (2) Fernad Leger, (3) Man Ray, (4) Marcel Duchamp, (5) Alexander Calder, (6) Hans Richter.

89. "I cannot feel that there is anything really original about them—that they do anything important, for instance, which was not done, and done to an ill-deserved death, by some of the European avant-gardists . . . of the 1920s." *The Nation*, March 2, 1946, 269.

90. Ibid. Marking the slow but definite declension of the paradigm, Deren's was generally well received by the New York mainstream critics. See Maria Pramaggiore, "Performance and Persona in the United States Avant-Garde: The Case of Maya Deren," *Cinema Journal* 36 (1997): 17–40.

91. Clancy Sigal, *Going Away: A Report, A Memoir* (1961; repr. New York: Dell, 1970).

92. Budd Schulberg, *The Disenchanted* (1951; repr. London: Allison and Busby, 1983), 9.

93. Clifford Odets, "On Coming Home," *New York Times*, July 25, 1948, sec. 2, p. 1.

94. Ibid., 58–59.

95. Clifford Odets, "On Coming Home," *New York Times*, July 25, 1948, sec. 2, p. 1. Notably, the Hollywood dream was still alive in some quarters. A progressive exhibitor from Cliffside Park, New Jersey, reminded Odets of "audiences (consisting, in general, mainly of working people and others of too moderate means to afford Broadway or New York) enjoy Miss Grable's legs but this does not prevent them from attending in comparable numbers pictures like *Crossfire, None but the Lonely Heart*. . . ." *New York Times*, August 1, 1948, sec. 2, p. 1.

96. Macgowan to Martin Agronski (ABC anchorman), June 13, 1949. Edward R. Murrow to Macgowan, April 26, 1950. Howard K. Smith to Macgowan, April 19, 1950, Box 4, Folder 66, Series 393, UCLA-University Archives.

97. On the oath controversy at UCLA see Ellen W. Schrecker, *No Ivory Tower: McCarthyism and the Universities* (New York: Oxford University Press, 1986), 118–25.

98. William M. Wadman to Richard H. Hill, August 4, 1953, Folder *Hollywood*

Quarterly, Alphabetical Files, UCLA-University Archives.

99. Dykstra to Warner, August 15, 1947, Series 359, Box 228, Folder 163, UCLA-University Archives.

100. "Minutes of the Theater Arts Department," September 13, 1947, Series 1634, Box 1, Folder 2, UCLA-University Archives. See also Kenneth Macgowan, "Film in the University," Draft, Box 59, Folder 12, Macgowan Papers, UCLA-SC.

101. Ibid.

102. Kenneth Macgowan, draft of "Film in the University," Box 59, Folder 12, Macgowan Papers, UCLA-SC.

103. Norman G. Dyhrenfurth to Macgowan, February 12, 1952, Box 59, Folder 7, Macgowan Papers, UCLA-SC.

104. Donald P. Kent, *The Refugee Intellectual: The Americanization of the Immigrants, 1933–1941* (New York: Columbia University Press, 1953), 186.

105. Curt Goetz and Valerie von Martens, *Wir wandern, wir wandern* (Stuttgart: Deutsche Verlagsanstalt, 1963), 307.

106. See Jan-Christopher Horak, *Fluchtpunk Hollywood* (Münster: Maks Publikationen, 1986). See also my "Fritz Lang, i 'moguls' e altri 'recent citizens.' Hollywood come straniero interno tra il 1933 e il 1953," in Mario Pozzi, ed., *Lo Straniero interno* (Florence, Italy: Ponte alle Grazie, 1993), 180.

107. William Dieterle to Ludwig Berger, October 1948, Ludwig Berger Papers, Deutsche Akademie der Künste, Berlin. My translation.

108. Viertel to Weigel, July 26, 1957, Correspondence File, Helen Weigel Paper, Bertolt Brecht and Helen Weigel Archive, Berlin. My translation.

109. Salka Viertel to Houseman, December 1, 1953, Box 6, Folder V, Houseman Papers, UCLA-SC.

Chapter Seven

1. Siegfried Kracauer, "Those Movies with a Message," *Harper's Magazine*, June 1948, 568.

2. Dana Polan, *Power and Paranoia* (New York: Columbia University Press, 1986), 12.

3. *Hollywood Quarterly* 1 (June 1945): 47.

4. In the 1980s, Paxton still wondered why HUAC had spared him. See *Dictionary of Literary Biography*, vol. 24, *American Screenwriters*, 2d series (Detroit: Gale, 1986), 277–83.

5. *Crack Up* was not the only film of the period that attacked highbrow attitudes to life as expression of a murderous personality. See, for instance, the character of the snobbish Waldo Lydecker (played by Clifton Webb) in *Laura* (TCF, 1944), directed by Otto Preminger from the bestseller by Cultural Fronter Vera Caspary. Webb will play almost the same role in Henry Hathaway's *The Dark Corner* (TCF, 1946), written by Cultural Fronter Bernard Schoenfeld.

6. *New York Times*, September 7, 1946, 11.

7. On the veterans see James T. Patterson, *Grand Expectations: The United States, 1945–74* (New York: Oxford University Press, 1996), 12–15.

8. See, for example, Irving Pichel, "Areas of Silences," 53.

9. Cited in Patterson, *Grand Expectations*, 13.

10. Leonard Spigelgass, "Kiska Journal," *Screenwriter* 1 (June 1946): 1–11.

11. Franklin Fearing, "Warriors Return: Normal or Neurotic?," *Hollywood Quarterly* 1 (June 1945): 97–110.

12. See Nicholas Christopher, *Somewhere in the Night: Film Noir and the American City* (New York: Free Press, 1997), 75.

13. Interview with director Edward Dmytryk in *Crossfire*, Turner Classic Movies Video Edition, TCM, 1996.

14. Scott cited in Robert J. Corber, *Homosexuality in Cold War America* (Durham, N.C.: Duke University Press, 1997), 86.

15. *Till the End of Time* is the story of a young soldier coming home to Los Angeles from the front. The film makes clear that coming home is a societal trauma— one that the institution of the family is not able to soften. It is only government institutions such as the Veterans Administration along with the solidarity between former servicemen across social and racial lines (the former soldiers find a new cause in the struggle against a group of racist, native "superpatriots") that can ensure a better world.

16. Interview with director Edward Dmytryk in *Crossfire*, Turner Classic Movies Video Edition, TCM, 1996.

17. Ibid. The film received Oscar nominations for best picture, best screenplay, best director, best supporting actor (Ryan), and best supporting actress (Gloria Grahame).

18. See John Houseman, "War and Film," *Hollywood Quarterly* 2 (November 1946): 31–36.

19. Adrian Scott "You Can't Do That," *Screenwriter* 3 (August 1947): 4–7.

20. Adrian Scott, "Some of My Worst Friends," *Screenwriter* 3 (October 1947): 1–6.

21. Kracauer, "Those Movies with a Message," 568–69.

22. Interview with director Edward Dmytryk in *Crossfire*, Turner Classic Movies Video Edition, TCM, 1996.

23. John Belton, ed., *Movies and Mass Culture* (New Brunswick, N.J.: Rutgers University Press, 1996), 189.

24. Bolsley Crowther, "The Movies Forget Something," *New York Times*, June 16, 1946, sec. 2, p. 1.

25. Kracauer, "Those Movies with a Message," 568–70. See also Corber, *Homosexuality in Cold War America*, 13.

26. On cinema and war see Paul Virilio, *War and Cinema*, translated by Patrick Camiller (1984; Eng. trans. New York: Verso, 1989).

27. Another future member of the Hollywood Ten, Alvah Bessie, is supposed to have worked on the synopsis of the film. See Robert Sklar, *City Boys* (Princeton: Princeton University Press, 1992), 162–65.

28. Huston's documentary, however, was deemed by the military to be too radical for exhibition. In 1947–48, Huston's own involvement in progressive politics and the Progressive Party's campaign did not improve the film's chances of getting

distributed. In 1970, when the Government Archives of American Film asked permission to show publicly its copy of *Let There Be Light*, the War Department still refused. See John Huston, *An Open Book* (New York: Knopf, 1980), 125–26. Only in January 1981, thirty-five years after *Let There Be Light* was made, did the military lift its veto so that the film could receive limited distribution.

29. Robert Corber, *In the Name of National Security* (Durham, N.C.: Duke University Press, 1993), 12.

30. It is also important to note that mental health *was* a real problem after WWII when psychiatrists Karl and William Menninger reported that one thousand men were released daily from the military because of mental disorders. See Emily S. Rosenberg, " 'Foreign Affairs' after WWII," *Diplomatic History* 18 (Winter 1994): 59–70, but in particular, 66–67. See also Jeanne L. Brand, "The National Mental Health Act of 1946: A Retrospect," *Bulletin of the History of Medicine* 39 (May–June 1965): 231–45.

31. See Fredric Jameson, *The Political Unconscious: Narrative as a Socially Symbolic Act* (Ithaca: Cornell University Press, 1981).

32. John Hertz, ed., *From Dictatorship to Democracy* (Westport, Conn.: Greenwood Press, 1982), 15.

33. Enzo Collotti, *Storia delle due Germanie 1945–1968* (Turin, Italy: Einaudi, 1968), 252. See also John H. Hertz, "Denazification and Related Policies," in Hertz, ed., *From Dictatorship to Democracy*, 15–38.

34. Richard T. Pells, *Not Like Us* (New York: Basic Books, 1996), 43.

35. Crowther on *New York Times* remarked about the "strange disregard for the sensibilities of those who suffered and bled during the cause of defeating German aggression in WWII." *New York Times*, October 18, 1951, 32. *Aufbau* did not review the film.

36. *The Nation*, September 8, 1945, 238.

37. Reinhold Niebuhr, "A Lecture to Liberals," *The Nation*, November 11, 1945, 491–92.

38. Orson Welles played the role of the German Nazi hiding in America in his *The Stranger*. Edward Dmytryk's film *Cornered*, from a script by communist John Wexley and another progressive Hollywood New Yorker, John Paxton, tells the story of Dick Powell as a Canadian soldier trying to unearth the truth about his French wife's death during the war. The wife has been killed by a French fascist who is now hiding in Latin America plotting the resurrection of the Axis in the next twenty years.

39. *The Asphalt Jungle*, temporary script dated July 15, 1949, Folder The Asphalt Jungle Script Material, John Huston Collection, AMPAS.

40. See John Mariani, "Let's Not Be Beastly to the Nazis," *Film Comment* 15 (January 1979): 49–53.

41. Dmytryk maintains that he is still a socialist; see Edward Dmytryk, *Odd Man Out* (Carbondale: Southern Illinois University Press, 1995), 3.

42. *New York Times*, April 3, 1958, 23.

43. *Aufbau*, September 21, 1945, 14.

44. "die Notwendigkeit für Hundertausende von Nazis die Todestrafe oder langer Kerkerstrafen zu verhängen. . . . die einfache Gerechtigkeit verlangt dass Milionen von Nazis bestraft werden." *Aufbau*, October 26, 1945, 5.

45. Maurice Zolotow, *Billy Wilder in Hollywood* (New York: G. P. Putnam's Sons, 1977), 137.

46. Peter Bogdanovich, *Fritz Lang in America* (New York: Praeger, 1969), 113.

47. Douglas Sirk, *Sirk on Sirk*, interviewed by Jon Halliday (London: Secker and Warburg, 1971), 79.

48. *Aufbau*, June 25, 1948, 13.

49. Sirk, *Sirk on Sirk*, 79.

50. Salka Viertel, *The Kindness of Strangers*, 306.

51. Ernst Lubitsch was consistent with his anti-realist esthetic and shot *That Lady in Ermine* as his last film before his untimely death. After the Americana of *Swamp Water* and *The Southerner*, Jean Renoir's cinema went back to the a-geographical nineteenth-century France of the *Diary of a Chambermaid* (1946), written by Burgess Meredith from Octave Mirabeau's novel. After the patriotic *Margin for Error* (1943) and *In the Meantime, Darling* (1944), Otto Preminger directed the noirs *Laura* (1945) and *Fallen Angel* (1947), and went all the way back to the *papier mâché* with *A Royal Scandal* (1946, Czarist Russia), *Centennial Summer* (1946, Philadelphia 1876), *Forever Amber* (1947, England of Charles II), and, in collaboration with Lubitsch, with *That Lady in Ermine* (1948). After *The Lost Weekend*, and immediately before *A Foreign Affair*, Wilder shot *The Emperor's Waltz* (Paramount, 1948), a fairy tale with Bing Crosby and Joan Fontaine set in 1901 Vienna. Ophuls directed his American masterpiece, *Letter from an Unknown Woman*, from the script of Howard Koch from the great novel by Stefan Zweig set in nineteenth-century Vienna.

52. "Scandal in Vienna," Treatment by Fritz Lang, June 28 1951, Box 8, Folder Scandal in Vienna, Fritz Lang Collection, USC-CTL.

53. *New York Times*, May 21, 1948, 19.

54. On Zinnemann see Brian Neve, "A Past Master of His Craft: An Interview with Brian Neve," *Cineaste* 23 (1997): 17. On Lang, see Elia Kazan, *A Life* (London: Pan Books, 1989), 417–18. On Wyler, see Paul Henreid, *Ladies Man: An Autobiography*, with Julius Fast (New York: St. Martin's Press, 1984), 181–88. See also John Huston, *An Open Book* (1981; repr. London: Columbus Books, 1988), 132.

55. Fritz Lang, "Freedom of the Screen," in *Theatre Arts*, December 1947, 52–55; reprinted in Richard Koszarski, *Hollywood Directors, 1941–1976* (New York: Oxford University Press, 1977), 134–42.

56. See, for instance, Victor H. Bernsterin, "Americans in Berlin," *PM*, November 14, 1945, 4; "The GI Legacy in Germany," in *Newsweek*, June 16, 1947, 48–51. These problems had even found a place in a comic strip featured by the magazine of the U.S. Army, *Stars and Stripes*. In the strip, a German matron, Veronika Dankenschon, equipped with a Swastika-decorated miniskirt, was out to lure innocent American soldiers into her bed. "Occupation in Germany," *Life*, February 10, 1947, 85–95.

57. "Billy Wilder privat," *Aufbau*, June 25, 1948, 13.

58. *Time*, July 26, 1948, 38–39.

59. The movie was attacked on the floor of the Senate, where congressmen argued that it had placed American GIs on the same level as Nazis. Evaluating Wilder's career in 1953, *Hollywood Quarterly* (now *The Quarterly of Film, Radio, and Television*) wrote that the Austrian director "depicts only the weakness and shortcomings of the American people, ridicules their habits, but never senses the strikingly salubrious strength of this vibrantly young republic." The Defense Department issued a press statement refuting the film as a faithful portrayal of American troops in Berlin and forbidding its distribution in the German area under its control. S. Schulberg, "A letter about Billy Wilder," *The Quarterly of Film, Radio, and Television* 7 (Summer 1953): 65. Even Charles Brackett, the faithful collaborator in all of Wilder's movies, refused to have a part in it. See Maurice Zolotow, *Billy Wilder*, 153–55.

60. After *A Foreign Affair*, Wilder went back to Germany in 1961 to shoot *One, Two, Three*. James Cagney, as the Coca-Cola executive in West Berlin, does not fare much better than Pringle. Cagney runs an office replete with former Nazis, and his gangster persona highlights the explicit comparison between the industrialist and the gangster (including the famous "Mother of God" line from *Little Caesar*), while his wife still calls him "Mein Führer."

61. The film did not meet any critical or popular success in West Germany. On German reactions see Elisabeth Läufer, *Skeptiker des Lichts. Douglas Sirk und seine Filme* (Frankfurt a.M.: Fischer Verlag, 1987), 167.

62. Fritz Lang, "Über die Zusammenarbeit mit Brecht an *Hangmen also Die*," in Jurgen Schebera, *Hangmen also Die. Drehbuch und Materialen zum Film* (Berlin: Henschel Verlag, 1985), 163–70. My translation.

63. Thom Andersen, "Red Hollywood," in Suzanne Ferguson and Barbara Groseclose, eds., *Literature and Visual Arts in Contemporary America* (Columbus: Ohio State University Press, 1985), 183. As *film gris* he identifies the following thirteen films: Robert Rossen's *Body and Soul* (1947), Abraham Polonsky's *Force of Evil* (1948), Jules Dassin's *Night and the City* (1950) and *Thieves' Highways* (1949), Nicholas Ray's *They Live by Night* (1949) and *Knock on Any Door* (1949), John Huston's *We Were Strangers* (1949) and *Asphalt Jungle* (1950), Michael Curtiz's *The Breaking Point* (1950), Joseph Losey's *The Lawless* (1950) and *The Prowler* (1951), Cyril Endfield's *Try and Get Me* (1951), and John Berry's *He Ran All the Way* (1951). Interestingly, Andersen dates Nick Ray's gloomy *They Live by Night* according to its distribution date, 1949, rather than the year when it was written and shot, 1946.

64. On the film, see Tom Miller, "Class Reunion: *Salt of the Earth* Revisited," *Cineaste* 13 (1984): 31–36. The United States was experiencing racial struggle, and émigrés were depicting some sectors of American society as a hotbed of anti-Semitism. See especially Nathan W. Ackerman and Marie Jahoda, *Anti-Semitism and Emotional Disorder: A Psychoanalytic Interpretation* (New York: Norton, 1950), and Leo Lowenthal and Norbert Guterman, *Prophets of Deceit* (New York: Harper, 1949).

65. Most contemporary Hollywood observers agreed that there was only one possible exception. As McWilliams noted, "racial tolerance is apparently the one

controversial theme that may be presented from the liberal or progressive point of view." The legacy of the Left was still visible in the anti-prejudice and anti-racist message films released in Hollywood from 1947 to 1951. All of them were written by Hollywood progressives, including *Crossfire*, *Gentleman's Agreement* (directed by Kazan from a script by Moss Hart, from the book by Laura Hobson), *Lost Boundaries*, *Intruder in the Dust* (written by Ben Maddow), *Home of the Brave* (written by Carl Foreman and Arthur Laurentz), *Pinky* (directed by Elia Kazan from a script by Dudley Nichols and Philip Dunne), and *No Way out* (written by Joseph Mankiewicz and Lesser Samuels). Carey McWilliams, "Hollywood Gray List," *The Nation*, November 19 1949, 491–92. But the optimistic, integrationist, and inclusive solution offered by these films was in tune with both the legacy of the 1930s and conservative intentions to tranquilize Americans. In sync with the paradigm, these films repeated the lesson of *Confessions of a Nazi Spy* and a 1930s notion of American people that was inclusive and yet unable to tackle the reality of historical differences. Already in reviewing *Gentleman's Agreement*, Hermine Rich Isaac remarked that the film was naive insofar as it "den[ied] the differences among races, religions, or spiritual traditions . . . instead of knowing them for what they are: as variation in kind, not in quality." Hermine Rich Isaac, "Love and the Beast," *Theater Arts* 32 (1948): 31–34. On these films see also Thomas Cripps, *Making Movies Black* (New York: Oxford University Press, 1993), 215–49.

66. *Los Angeles Times*, July 18, 1947, 1.

67. Dorothy B. Jones, "Communism and the Movies: A Study of Film Content," in John Cogley, ed., *Report on Blacklisting* (Washington, D.C.: The Fund for the Republic, 1956), Vol. 1, 283–84.

68. Thomas Doherty, "Hollywood Agit-Prop: The Anti-Communist Cycle, 1948–54," *Journal of Film and Video* 40 (Fall 1988): 16.

69. Milton Krims in *The Iron Curtain*, Leo Rosten in *Walk East on Beacon*, the famous *March of Time* producer Louis de Rochemont in the same film, Irwin Shaw and Mark Robson in *I Want You* (1952).

70. He had studied at the University of Oregon, at the Sorbonne, and in Rome, Italy, and he was fluent in Italian, French, and German. During the war, the screenwriter had joined the army and had been a regular contributor to the *Air Force Magazine*. Biographical Sketch, Milton Krims Papers, Box 5, Folder 31, AMPAS. Writing in his journal, Krims vented the usual feelings of the average Hollywood progressive in uniform. "I love America," reads the draft of one poem scribbled in his wartime notebook. "Home of the free. . . . / we are all Americans / Kansas to Maine, / we are all the same / Kansas to Maine, / we are all the same / Virginia, Oregon, / Black and White, / Brooklyn and Boston, / Polak and Jew, Irish and Catholic, / Rhode Island too." Milton Krims Papers, Box 6, Folder Journal WWII, AMPAS.

71. Undated draft for "*The Iron Curtain* Diary," Box 5, Folder 5, Milton Krims Papers, AMPAS.

72. Krims, "A Statement," undated (November 1947?), Box 3, Folder 14, Milton Krims Papers, AMPAS.

73. Scrapbook 5, Box 4, Folder 19, Milton Krims Papers, AMPAS.

74. Box 5, Folder 9, Milton Krims Papers, AMPAS.

75. Undated draft for "*The Iron Curtain* Diary," Box 5, Folder 5, Milton Krims Papers, AMPAS.

76. "*The Iron Curtain* Diary," *Screenwriter*, September 1948, 14. The draft is in Box 5, Folder 9, Milton Krims Paper, AMPAS.

77. Sol Siegel to Krims, July 14, 1947, Box 5, Folder 10, Milton Krims Papers, AMPAS.

78. Sol Siegel to Krims, July 14, 1947, Box 5, Folder 10, Milton Krims Papers, AMPAS. Eventually, in the final version of the script, dated October 1947, the main character will be Igor Gouzenko.

79. Eventually, Fox rewrote the last part of Krims's script. In the released film, contrary to fact, the Canadian government does not help Gouzenko, who finally confronts the Soviet thugs by himself and is saved by the police at the very last moment. See Dan J. Leab, "*The Iron Curtain* (1948): Hollywood's First Cold War Movie," *Historical Journal of Film, Radio, and Television* 8 (1988): 153–89.

80. Ibid., 175.

81. Thomas Doherty, "Hollywood Agit-Prop: The Anti-Communist Cycle, 1948–54," *Journal of Film and Video* 40 (Fall 1988): 22.

Conclusion

1. Cited in Ramona Curry, "25 Years of SCS: A Sociopolitical History," *Journal of Film and Video* 38(2) (Spring 1986): 46.

2. Jerzy Toeplitz, "Film Scholarship: Present and Prospective," *Film Quarterly*, 16(3) (Spring 1963): 31.

3. On Cinema 16 see Scot MacDonald, "Cinema 16: Documents Toward a History of the Film Society," *Wide Angle* 19 (1997).

4. On Mekas see Greg Taylor, *Artists in the Audience* (Princeton: Princeton University Press, 1999), 85, and David E. James, *To Free the Cinema: Jonas Mekas and the New York Underground* (Princeton: Princeton University Press, 1992).

5. Edward Dmytryk, *Oral History* (New York: Columbia University Press, 1959), 32.

6. See Arthur Schlesinger, Jr., "The Highbrow in American Politics," *Partisan Review*, 19 (March—April 1953): 157–65. Harvey Swados, "Popular Taste and 'The Caine Mutiny,' " *Partisan Review*, 19 (March—April 1953): 248–56. See also Arthur Schlesinger, Jr., *The Vital Center: The Politics of Freedom* (Boston: Houghton Mifflin, 1949), 125–26.

7. See Thom Andersen, "Red Hollywood," in Suzanne Ferguson and Barbara Groseclose, eds., *Literature and Visual Arts in Contemporary America* (Columbus: Ohio State University Press, 1985), 144. See also ibid., 183.

8. Arthur Schlesinger, Jr., *The Vital Center*, 125–26.

9. Ross Spears and Jude Cassidy, with a narrative by Robert Coles, *Agee: His Life Remembered* (New York: Holt & Rinehart, 1985), 140.

10. See Dwight Macdonald, "Masscult and Midcult," *Partisan Review* (Spring

1960), in Macdonald, *Against the American Grain* (1962; repr. New York: Da Capo, 1983): 3–75.

11. Martin Jay persuasively writes that Critical Theory did not gather much popularity during the Frankfurt School's stay in the United States from 1934, when Horkheimer arrived at Columbia University from Geneva, to 1950 when he moved the Frankfurt School back to Bonn. "There was however an area in which Critical Theory did have an influence in the fifties, the debate over mass culture, which reached its crescendo in the middle of the decade." Martin Jay, "The Frankfurt School in Exile" in Martin Jay, *Permanent Exiles* (New York: Columbia University Press, 1986), 46. By the late 1980s, historian Steven J. Ross noted, the legacy of the Frankfurt School was still dictating the terms of the debates about mass culture in disparate fields such as sociology, communication studies, and history. Steven J. Ross, "Struggles for the Screen," *American Historical Review* 96 (April 1991), 334–35.

12. On *Commentary* and McCarthy see James Rorty, "The Anti-Communism of Senator McCarthy," *Commentary* 16 (August 1953): 112–19. Morris Freedman, "New England and Hollywood," *Commentary* 16 (October 1953): 392. Also cited in Andersen, "Red Hollywood," 179.

13. Cameron Crowe, *Conversations with Wilder* (New York: Knopf, 1999), 191–95.

14. See for instance Robert Rossen's portrait of mass politics in *All the King's Men* (Columbia, 1949), Fritz Lang's contempt for realist and commercial art in *Scarlet Street* (Universal, Walter Wanger producer, 1945) and for mass marketed music in *Blue Daliah* (Paramount, 1946). See also the Hollywood self-portrait by Vincent Minnelli, *The Bad and the Beautiful* (MGM, 1952), or the remake by George Cukor, from the same piece by Moss Hart, of the 1937 film *A Star is Born* (WB, 1954).

15. *Sunset Boulevard* was the only Hollywood self-portrait to be listed by the National Film Preservation Board in the National Film Registry since the registry's inception in 1989.

Index